The Antebellum Period

The Antebellum Period

JAMES M. VOLO
AND DOROTHY DENNEEN VOLO

American Popular Culture Through History
Ray B. Browne, Series Editor

GREENWOOD PRESS
Westport, Connecticut • London

Library of Congress Cataloging-in-Publication Data

Volo, James M., 1947–
    The Antebellum Period / James M. Volo and Dorothy Denneen Volo.
        p. cm. — (American popular culture through history)
    Includes bibliographical references (p.) and index.
    ISBN 0–313–32518–9 (alk. paper)
        1. United States—Civilization—1783–1865.   2. United States—History—1815–1861.
    3. Southern States—Civilization—1771–1865.   4. Popular culture—United States—
    History—19th century.   5. Popular culture—Southern States—History—19th century.
    I. Volo, Dorothy Denneen, 1949– II. Title. III. Series.
    E166.V65   2004
    973.6—dc22   2004043892

British Library Cataloguing in Publication Data is available.

Library of Congress Catalog Card Number: 2004043892
ISBN: 0–313–32518–9

First published in 2004

Greenwood Press, 88 Post Road West, Westport, CT 06881
An imprint of Greenwood Publishing Group, Inc.
www.greenwood.com

Printed in the United States of America

The paper used in this book complies with the
Permanent Paper Standard issued by the National
Information Standards Organization (Z39.48–1984).

10 9 8 7 6 5 4 3 2 1

Contents

Contents

Series Foreword

Popular culture is the system of attitudes, behaviors, beliefs, customs, and tastes that define the people of any society. It is the entertainments, diversions, icons, rituals, and actions that shape the everyday world. It is what we do while we are awake and what we dream about while we are asleep. It is the way of life we inherit, practice, change, and then pass on to our descendants.

Popular culture is an extension of folk culture, the culture of the people. With the rise of electronic media and the increase in communication in American culture, folk culture expanded into popular culture—the daily way of life as shaped by the *popular majority* of society. Especially in a democracy like the United States, popular culture has become both the voice of the people and the force that shapes the nation. In 1782, the French commentator Hector St. Jean de Crèvecoeur asked in his *Letters from an American Farmer*, "What is an American?" He answered that such a person is the creation of America and is in turn the creator of the country's culture. Indeed, notions of the American Dream have been long grounded in the dream of democracy—that is, government by the people, or popular rule. Thus, popular culture is tied fundamentally to America and the dreams of its people.

Historically, culture analysts have tried to fine-tune culture into two categories: "elite"—the elements of culture (fine art, literature, classical music, gourmet food, etc.) that supposedly define the best of society—and "popular"—the elements of culture (comic strips, bestsellers, pop music, fast food, etc.) that appeal to society's lowest common denominator. The so-called educated person approved of elite culture and scoffed at popular culture. This schism first began to develop in Western Europe in the fifteenth century when the privileged classes tried to discover and develop differences in societies based on class, money, privilege, and life styles. Like many aspects of European society, the debate between elite and popular cultures came to the United States. The upper class in America, for example, supported museums and galleries that would exhibit "the finer things in life" that would "elevate" people. As the twenty-first century emerges, however, the distinctions between popular culture and elitist culture have blurred. The blues songs (once denigrated as "race music") of Robert Johnson are now revered by musicologists; architectural students study buildings in Las Vegas as examples of what Robert Venturi called the "kitsch of high capitalism"; sportswriter Gay Talese and heavyweight boxing champ Floyd Patterson were copanelists at a 1992 SUNY New Paltz symposium on Literature and Sport. The examples go on and on, but the one commonality that emerges is the role of popular culture as a model for the American Dream, the dream to pursue happiness and a better, more interesting life.

To trace the numerous ways in which popular culture has evolved throughout American history, we have divided the volumes in this series into chronological periods—historical eras until the twentieth century, decades between 1900 and 2000. In each volume, the author explores the specific details of popular culture that reflect and inform the general undercurrents of the time. Our purpose, then, is to present historical and analytical panoramas that reach both backward into America's past and forward to her collective future. In viewing these panoramas, we can trace a very fundamental part of American society. The "American Popular Culture Through History" series presents the multifaceted parts of a popular culture in a nation that is both grown and still growing.

Ray B. Browne
Secretary-Treasurer
Popular Culture Association
American Culture Association

Introduction

The antebellum period, particularly in the American South, conjures images of oversized verandas, lazy rivers churned by the paddle wheels of luxurious steamboats, exaggerated hoop skirts, and trees hung with Spanish moss. At first glance, the slower pace of the Civil War antebellum period, 1820–1860, seems to have rendered it an era untouched by time. The South seemed to cling to an idyllic, if mechanically inefficient, simplicity while remaining suspended in the past like a character in a romance novel. Meanwhile, the North was developing its industrial strength and a modern sophistication concerning business, ethics, and morality. In order to meet the needs of an expanding nation, canals, railroads, fabric mills, and vast cities filled to overflowing with immigrants all seemed to spring from the very soil of the North. This simple dichotomy between North and South is the stuff of history textbooks and grammar school recitations, but the antebellum period was actually exceedingly complex and replete with contradictions.

American society and culture was at once chivalrous and crude; hospitable and harsh; and bold and backward. It is difficult today to conceive of a society that could elevate civility, personal behavior, and honor to such high standards; and yet perpetuate an institution that denied basic human status to a large portion of its population. Individual Southern plantations were virtually self-sufficient "city-states" lacking little in the way of food or the means to provide for their daily needs; yet the region was almost totally dependent upon remote markets, manipulative agents, and manufactures located in the North. The plantation aristocracy ruled the South like feudal lords, but they were critically starved for cash, virtually steeped in perpetual debt, and constantly fearful lest their slaves should kill them in their beds.

Moreover, the entire cultural life of the nation seemed to radiate from the great cities and universities above the Mason-Dixon line. Notwithstanding its cultural accomplishments during the period, the North with its great urban centers was no American Zion. Northerner city dwellers, while reveling in their vast catalog of reform movements regarding abolition, public education, temperance, prison reform, and women's rights, seemed incapable of separating the unfortunate victims in society from a personal responsibility for their plight. Reformers and idealists emphasized cultural integrity, social rehabilitation, and personal reformation among the poor of the teeming and increasingly industrialized cities of the North, but the Northern elite remained intolerant of immigrants, Catholics, the poor, or free African Americans living in their midst. Consequently, the poor stayed in their crime-ridden environment; women and children were continually abused by derelict husbands and fathers; alcohol flowed freely until the 20th century; and the freed slaves remained on the bottom rung of social and economic life.

It is commonly taught in history class in school that a handful of states, formed into a weak republic after the American Revolution, were welded into a nation in the crucible of civil war. Yet the antebellum period was a time when America gained much of the morality, ethical strength, and integrity that characterized the nation during that conflict. The antebellum period was a bridge from the innocence of the early years of isolation on the Atlantic coast of North America to that of a mature nation willing to take its place in the wider world and stand astride the continent like a colossus. The period saw the establishment of free public schools and esteemed institutions of higher learning; advances in art and artistry; and unforeseen developments in technology and productivity. Historians and writers have, all too frequently, treated the antebellum decades as a necessary but unimaginative prelude to the "real" history found in the study of the Civil War. However, the period had its own culture, leaders, achievements, stars, and superstars; and it deserves to be viewed as a distinct entity.

This study of the popular culture of the antebellum period conveys certain key concepts in an attempt to bind together the people, places, movements, and attitudes of the period. Among these are important cultural developments in art, music, literature, performance, religion, and education. Moreover, this study aims to enlighten the reader to a number of crucial changes made during the period in the areas of architecture, fashion, food, invention, travel, and family structure. Many of these features have not only come to characterize the period, but they also served as themes that permeated the attitudes, beliefs, and actions of many antebellum Americans.

The work is dedicated to the history of the antebellum period and of the American lifestyle as it was in the decades before the Civil War. It looks at certain events outside this period to provide continuity and closure. For instance, it travels as far back as 1794 to a time when Eli Whitney saw the need to mechanize the time-consuming removal of cottonseeds from raw cotton, and it assumes a knowledge of the events of the Civil War immediately following secession. Nonetheless, the vast majority of the text deals with the period from 1820 to 1860, the cultural life of the country, and the perceptions of society, politics, and family in the years before the outbreak of the war.

An attempt has been made to include the findings of recent research and the informed speculation of modern historians in this regard. However, certain older historical volumes and eminent authors remain definitive authorities in given areas, especially where more recent studies are lacking as in the area of performance arts. These have been used extensively not only as sources of information but also as mirrors to the contemporary antebellum world. Because prime sources can provide profound insight, a number of contemporary materials have been included. Extensive use has been made of period newspapers, diaries and journals, and instructional texts, as well as a large number of tables and charts found in period reference books and directories. A large number of photo-illustrations representing the period have been created by the authors. The historic sites and museums that serve as the background for these were selected for their devotion to authenticity and structural veracity. In addition to the visual information provided, these illustrations are meant to help the reader view events, places, and people as antebellum contemporaries may have seen them. The selection process in this regard was also affected by the judgment of a number of knowledgeable colleagues of the authors and by the editors of this work.

The personalities profiled in this study of cultural life include well-known writers, historians, inventors, scientists, artists, entertainers, musicians, and educators—particularly those who were prominent during their lifetimes. Little has been included concerning famed politicians, political campaigns, or the turbulence surrounding the major political disputes of the 1820s and 1830s, such as questions concerning the Nation Bank, Nullification, or the spread of slavery into the territories. These are well considered by other works that are not focused on popular culture. Nonetheless, because an interest in politics was epidemic during the period, it is treated as a popular activity bordering on a fad. Additionally, it is hoped that other parts of the work concerning slaves, bankers, gamblers, prostitutes, laborers, and farmers give voice to the nameless individuals who often go unnoticed in standard histories but who, nonetheless, make up the vast majority of the people who lived in the antebellum period.

Timeline of the Antebellum Period

1788

The national capital at Washington, D.C., is created from land carved from the states of Maryland and Virginia.

1791

The states ratify the Bill of Rights.

1793

Congress passes the first Fugitive Slave Law, making it illegal to aid or prevent the arrest of runaway Negro slaves.

1796

Congress authorizes the construction of Zane's Trace, a road from western Virginia to Kentucky.

1799

Alexander Hamilton publishes Report on the Subject of Manufactures describing the state of American industry.

1800

Washington, D.C., becomes the national capital.

Congress divides the Northwest Territory into Ohio and Indiana.

Spain cedes the Louisiana Territory to France.

Second Great Awakening begins near the Gaspar River Church in Kentucky.

1802

Congress establishes the U.S. Military Academy at West Point.

1803

Ohio becomes the 17th state.

United States makes the Louisiana Purchase from France.

Meriwether Lewis and William Clark begin their explorations.

Supreme Court establishes the Principle of Judicial Review by declaring an act of Congress unconstitutional in *Marbury v. Madison*.

1804

Black slaves declare independence in Haiti after defeating a large French army in a bloody revolt.

Eli Whitney signs a contract with the Federal government for the manufacture of 10,000 muskets in just two years.

1805

Congress forms Michigan Territory.

Ice is successfully shipped from New England to the West Indies.

The Free School Society of New York City is founded; it is renamed the Public School Society of New York in 1826.

1808

U.S. Congress prohibits the importation of African slaves.

James Madison is elected as the fourth president.

1809

Congress forms Illinois Territory.

1810

United States annexes West Florida.

1811

First boat to steam down the Mississippi River reaches New Orleans.

1812

Congress declares war on Britain—War of 1812.

First faculty appointed at West Point.

U.S. frigate *Constitution* defeats British frigates *Guerriere* and *Java* in separate ship-to-ship contests.

U.S. frigate *United States* captures British frigate *Macedonian*.

Louisiana becomes the 18th state.

The remnant of the Louisiana Purchase becomes the Missouri Territory.

1814

U.S. fleet defeats the British fleet on Lake Champlain, NY.

British bombard Fort McHenry in Baltimore.

British capture Washington, D.C., and burn the Capitol and White House.

Antiwar Federalists at the Hartford, CT, convention threaten to have New England states secede.

1815

General Andrew Jackson defeats the British at the Battle of New Orleans.

Treaty of Ghent ends the War of 1812.

First class graduates at West Point.

1816

Indiana becomes the 19th state.

1817

Mississippi Territory is divided into Alabama Territory and the 20th state of Mississippi.

Seminole Indians attack white settlers in Florida and Georgia.

1818

Connecticut abolishes property qualifications for voting.

United States and Britain establish the U.S.-Canadian border to the Rocky Mountains at the 49th parallel but not for Oregon.

General Andrew Jackson invades Florida to punish the Seminole and executes two British citizens.

The first American sewing machine is invented by John A. Doge and John Knowles.

1819

Spain, told to control the Indians or give up the remainder of Florida, cedes the region to the United States and sets the western boundary of the Louisiana Purchase in the Adams-Onis Treaty.

Supreme Court upholds the right of Congress to establish a National Bank and establishes the Doctrine of Implied Powers in *McCulloch v. Maryland,* a blow to strict construction of the Constitution.

Virginia's General Assembly passes a law prohibiting the teaching of reading to Negroes.

Depression of 1819. Banks foreclose on more than 50,000 acres of farmland in Kentucky and Ohio.

Alabama becomes the 22nd state.

1820

Congress agrees to the Missouri Compromise. Maine is admitted as a free state (23rd); Missouri is admitted as a slave state (24th).

James Monroe reelected as president.

Boston opens a school solely for black children.

Government offers as little as 80 acres of land to settlers for $1.25 an acre.

The General Land Office expressly prohibits the sectioning of land smaller than 160 acres.

1821

Stephen Austin establishes the first American settlement in Texas with the approval of the Mexican government.

New York and Massachusetts abolish property qualifications for voting.

1822

Florida is organized as a territory.

Denmark Vesey's slave rebellion uncovered in Charleston, SC. Vesey and 34 others are executed.

South Carolina adopts the Negro Seaman Law, which places all free Negro seamen under arrest until their ships leave port.

1823

Monroe Doctrine warns Europe to stay out of the affairs of the Western Hemisphere.

Cotton mills in Massachusetts begin producing cloth with water-powered machinery.

The Mormon religion founded by Joseph Smith.

1824

United States agrees to 54° 40' for the lower limit of Russian possessions in North America.

1825

With the electoral support of Henry Clay, John Quincy Adams is selected by the House of Representatives as president over Jackson, who had initially received the most votes.

Democratic Party is formed with Andrew Jackson at its head.

Congress adopts the Indian removal policy.

The Erie Canal opens an important route connecting New York State with the Ohio and Mississippi Valleys.

The University of Virginia is founded.

Preserving foods in tinned iron cans is first patented in America by Ezra Daggett.

1826

Both Thomas Jefferson and John Adams die on July 4th.

The Free School Society of New York City is renamed the Public School Society of New York.

1827

United States and Britain agree to joint occupation of Oregon.

Congress gives the president the right to call out the militia.

The first black newspaper, *Freedom's Journal*, is published in New York.

The term "technology" is first used.

1828

Andrew Jackson is elected president.

South Carolina declares the national tariff unconstitutional nullification.

1830

Robert Y. Hayne debates Daniel Webster over states' rights and the nature of the Union.

Congress adopts the Indian Removal Act, sending Indians to Oklahoma Territory.

The first functional sewing machine is produced in France by Barthelemy Thimonnier.

Godey's Lady's Book is published.

1831

Nat Turner leads a slave revolt in Virginia.

The Anti-Masonic Party is formed.

Prudence Crandall, a Pennsylvania Quaker, opens a school for black girls in Connecticut.

Supreme Court upholds the removal of the Cherokee nation from Georgia.

1832

Black Hawk War with the Sauk Indians of Illinois commences.

Andrew Jackson reelected as president.

South Carolina Nullification Convention nullifies the 1828 and 1832 Tariffs.

Cholera epidemics sweep American cities.

Brigham Young converts to Mormonism.

1833

Oberlin College is established as an abolitionist center.

American Anti-Slavery Society is formed.

Slavery is abolished in the British Empire.

1834

Whig Party is formed.

Senate censures Jackson for killing the National Bank.

First Methodist mission and farming settlement is founded in Oregon.

Cyrus McCormick patents the mechanical reaper.

Walter Hunt, an American, produces a hand-cranked sewing machine.

Jacob Perkins patents an early system for refrigeration.

Maria Monk's *Awful Discourses of the Hotel Dieu Nunnery of Montreal* is first published.

The Ursuline Convent in Charlestown near Boston is burned.

Anti-Abolition Riots break out in Northern cities.

1835

Texas revolts against Mexican rule.

An unsuccessful attempt to assassinate Jackson is made.

The Seminole Indian War begins with the massacre of U.S. troops.

Samuel Colt invents the revolving pistol.

1836

Mexican General Antonio Santa Anna massacres Texans at the Alamo.

Samuel Houston defeats Santa Anna at the Battle of San Jacinto and Texas becomes an independent republic.

Arkansas becomes the 25th state.

Congress forms Wisconsin Territory.

William H. McGuffey publishes the first of his standard elementary school readers.

Virginia Military Institute is founded.

Martin Van Buren is elected president.

1837

A general economic depression becomes the Panic of 1837.

Supreme Court membership is increased from seven to nine justices.

Mount Holyoke Seminary for women opens in Massachusetts.

Victoria becomes the Queen of England.

1838

U.S. troops forcibly remove the Cherokee from Georgia (Trail of Tears).

Congress adopts the "Gag" rule limiting discussion of antislavery.

Congress creates a new patent law to deal with competing claims to inventions.

Some Northern states pass Personal Liberty Laws to obstruct the capture of fugitive slaves.

The Underground Railroad is developed.

Samuel F.B. Morse introduces the Morse code.

First *McGuffey's Eclectic Reader* is released.

Congress forms Iowa Territory.

1839

The *Amistad* slave ship is found off Long Island, NY.

Louis Daguerre invents the daguerreotype, the first successful form of photography.

1840

Congress passes the Subtreasury Bill in an effort to stem the effects of the ongoing Panic of 1837.

William Henry Harrison is elected president.

1841

John Tyler becomes president when Harrison unexpectedly dies of pneumonia.

The *Amistad* Africans are freed by the Supreme Court.

Immigration to the United States from Ireland and Britain approaches 300,000 in the previous 10 years.

1842

Rhode Island liberalizes voting requirements.

The New York City Public School Department is formed.

Seminoles are defeated and removed to Oklahoma.

The right of workers to strike established by the Massachusetts State Court.

Dr. Crawford Long uses anesthetic gas in his surgery.

1843

The great migration on the Oregon Trail begins.

Congress finances a telegraph line between Baltimore and Washington, D.C.

Charles Dickens publishes *A Christmas Carol*.

1844

Samuel F.B. Morse sends first telegraph message: "What God hath Wrought!"

Uriah Boyden invents a more efficient turbine waterwheel.

Composer Stephen C. Foster gains recognition.

In Philadelphia, two Catholic churches and 30 Irish homes are burned.

Dominicans successfully revolt against the Haitian government by forming the Dominican Republic.

Joseph Smith assassinated at the hands of a mob in Carthage, IL.

James K. Polk is elected president.

1845

Florida becomes the 27th state.

Texas accepts annexation to become the 28th state.

The potato crop in Ireland fails producing the Great Famine.

An economic depression causes many European Jews of German descent to immigrate to America.

Mexico begins military operations to stop the annexation of Texas.

U.S. Naval Academy opens at Annapolis, MD.

1846

The Mexican War begins.

General Zachary Taylor defeats the Mexicans at Palo Alto, Resaca de la Palma, and Monterey (Mexico).

U.S. naval forces occupy Monterey, CA, and San Francisco, CA.

Oregon boundary is set at the 49th parallel.

Congress exempts lands acquired from Mexico from the Wilmot Proviso.

Congress establishes Smithsonian Institution.

Elias Howe patents the lockstitch sewing machine mechanism.

Dr. William Morton discovers the properties of sulfuric ether as an anesthetic. It is used by Dr. J.C. Warren during the removal of a tumor from the face of a patient.

Iowa becomes the 29th state.

1847

Irish immigration reaches 100,000 in a single year.

Liberia (Africa) becomes a free and independent republic for former slaves with the aid of the American Colonization Society.

Brigham Young assumes the leadership of the Mormon Church.

General Zachary Taylor defeats Santa Anna at Buena Vista.

General Winfield Scott captures Veracruz; defeats the Mexicans at Cerro Gordo, Churubusco, Molino del Ray, and Chapultepec; and enters Mexico City.

California comes under U.S. control.

John Pitkin Norton starts the School of Applied Chemistry at Yale.

1848

Treaty of Guadalupe Hidalgo ends the Mexican War.

Wisconsin becomes the 30th state.

Zachary Taylor is elected president.

Women's Rights Convention held in Seneca Falls, NY.

Cast iron is used for the first time to build multistoried buildings.

Gold is discovered in California.

1849

Congress establishes Minnesota Territory.

California requests admission as a free state.

California Gold Rush begins.

Cholera epidemic sweeps the South.

George Corliss patents a more efficient four-valve steam engine.

1850

Millard Fillmore becomes president upon the death of Taylor.

Senator Henry Foote of Mississippi threatens Senator Thomas Hart Benton of Missouri with a pistol in the Senate chamber

Compromise of 1850 allows California into the Union as a free state.

New Mexico and Utah are formed as territories.

Fugitive Slave Law is strengthened and the slave trade is abolished in the District of Columbia.

The population of New York City reaches 500,000 persons.

Cholera epidemic sweeps the Midwest.

1851

Maine enacts a prohibition on alcoholic beverages.

Isaac Singer patents the continuous stitch sewing machine.

1852

Franklin Pierce is elected president.

Harriet Beecher Stowe publishes *Uncle Tom's Cabin*.

Horse-drawn steam fire engines are invented.

Safety matches are invented.

1853

Washington Territory is formed by Congress.

Gadsden Purchase from Mexico fills out U.S. continental borders.

Yellow fever epidemic sweeps through New Orleans leaving thousands dead.

Baltimore and Ohio Railroad is completed to the Ohio River, and the New York Central Railroad is formed.

Elisha Otis invents the safety elevator for passengers.

1854

Congress passes the Kansas-Nebraska Act.

The modern Republican Party is formed.

Massachusetts Emigrant Aid Society sends antislavery settlers to Kansas.

George Fitzhugh publishes *Sociology for the South, or the Failure of Free Society,* defending slavery.

Thirteen thousand Chinese immigrate to the West Coast of the United States.

Nativist, or Know-Nothing, Party wins local offices in New York, Massachusetts, and Delaware.

Horace Smith and Daniel Wesson invent the first practical brass cartridge revolver.

1855

Stephen Douglas's "popular sovereignty" makes Kansas such a battleground of opposing forces that it is called "Bleeding Kansas."

The first public high school for girls is opened in Boston.

Elmira College for women opens.

Christian Sharps produces an efficient breech-loading rifle.

U.S. government adopts the conical minié ball as a standard bullet for its firearms.

Frank Leslie publishes his first *Illustrated Newspaper.*

1856

Proslavery "border ruffians" attack and burn Lawrence, KS.

Radical abolitionist John Brown kills five proslavery men in Kansas.

Senator Charles Sumner is caned by Representative Preston Brooks in the Senate chamber.

James Buchanan is elected president.

Hiram Sibley founds Western Union.

1857

Supreme Court decides against Dred Scott, declaring the Missouri Compromise unconstitutional and declaring that Congress has no right to limit slavery in the territories.

George Fitzhugh publishes *Cannibals All! or Slaves without Masters,* which contends that slavery is a positive good.

Economic depression sweeps the country.

North Carolina removes the property qualifications for voting.

Frederick Law Olmsted designs Central Park in New York City.

Federal troops try to restore peace in Kansas Territory.

1858

Minnesota becomes the 32nd state.

Abraham Lincoln and Stephen Douglas debate during a run for the Senate.

Kansas becomes a free territory.

A religious revival sweeps the nation accompanied by prayer meetings in the cities and camp meetings on the trail.

U.S. troops suppress the Mormon militia and restore order to Utah Territory.

Lyman Blake patents a leather sewing machine that attaches the soles to the uppers mechanically, greatly facilitating the shoemaking process.

Christian Sharps produces an efficient breech-loading rifle.

Cryrus W. Field lays a continuous transatlantic telegraphic cable from Newfoundland to Ireland.

1859

Oregon becomes the 33rd state.

Cotton production in the United States reaches 2 billion pounds per year.

John Brown seizes the U.S. Arsenal at Harper's Ferry hoping to start a slave rebellion in Virginia.

John Brown is hanged for murder, treason, and conspiracy.

1860

Abraham Lincoln is elected president.

South Carolina secedes from the Union.

South Carolina seizes the U.S. arsenal at Charleston.

1861

Mississippi, Florida, Alabama, Georgia, Louisiana, and Texas secede and join South Carolina in forming a confederate government at Montgomery, AL.

Jefferson Davis and Alexander H. Stephens are elected president and vice president of the Confederacy.

Confederate forces fire on Fort Sumter in Charleston Harbor in South Carolina forcing Federal troops to surrender.

Virginia, Arkansas, North Carolina, and Tennessee secede.

Confederate capital moves to Richmond, VA.

Lincoln proclaims a blockade of Southern ports.

Congress abolishes flogging in the U.S. Army.

Robert E. Lee resigns from the U.S. Army and joins his state, Virginia, after turning down the command of Federal forces.

General Winfield Scott is given command of the Federal Army.

Telegraph wires connect New York and California.

Kansas becomes the 34th state.

Matthew Brady begins a photographic record of the Civil War.

Confederate forces rout the Federals at the first major battle of the Civil War Battle at Bull Run (Manassas, VA).

1862–1865

The Civil War is fought, producing more than 600,000 deaths.

General Robert E. Lee surrenders at Appomattox, VA, in April 1865.

John Wilkes Booth assassinates Lincoln in April 1865.

General Stand Watie (a Native American) is the last Confederate commander to surrender to Federal forces in June 1865.

PART I

Everyday Life: The World of Youth

The Antebellum Period

1

Everyday America

Remembering the "Good Olde Days"
—First used in 1844 by Phillip Hone, Mayor of New York

SOCIETY

Modernization

As the antebellum period began, America was approaching its golden anniversary as an independent political state, but it was not yet a nation. There was considerable disagreement among the residents of its many geographical sections concerning the exact limits of the relationship between the Federal government, the older states, and the individual citizen. In this regard, many factions invoked concepts of state sovereignty, centralized banking, nullification, popular sovereignty, secession, all-Americanism, or manifest destiny. However, the majority deemed republicanism, social pluralism, and constitutionalism the primary characteristics of antebellum America. Slavery, abolition, and the possibility of future disunion were considered secondary issues.

Cultural and social changes were sweeping the cities of America during the period. Industry and urbanization had moved the North toward a more modern society with an unprecedented set of novel cultural values, while the South had essentially lagged behind in the traditions of the 18th century. The mixing of traditional folkways with a more modern vision of America had caused social influence, political authority, and traditional concepts of family to become uncertain, unstable, and somewhat ambiguous. Historians have noted that the differences between the "folk culture" of the South and the "modern culture" of the North fueled the broad-based reform movements of mid-century and may have ignited the turmoil over state sovereignty and slavery in a form of "culture war." The debate surrounding these questions, driven by an intensely partisan press, "not only aroused feelings of jealousy, honor, and regional pride, but raised fundamental questions about the future direction of the American society."[1]

The most obvious modern element in Northern society was the rapid growth of its urban centers as more and more people flocked to the cities to find work in the factories. Although the class structure was still dominated by the old social elite, a new middle class was striving to become socially acceptable; and it was becoming increasingly difficult for the community to distinguish between the two. Unfortunately, the distinctions between these and the urban lower classes continued to be characterized by sharp contrasts in wealth, ethnic origin, and religion. The lower classes of the North were exceedingly poor and composed, in large part, of immigrants. Between 1820 and 1860, the top three major countries of origin respectively were Ireland, Germany, and Great Britain. These three supplied 85 percent of all immigrants to the United States in the antebellum period.[2]

In 1800, the entire United States had been an essentially rural country. Fewer than 6 percent of it population of 5 million lived in towns with populations larger than 2,500. Only Philadelphia and New York had populations greater than 25,000. The settlement of the Mississippi Valley and the Northwest Territories during the first half of the 19th century had contributed to a vast internal migration. Ironically, as the number of family farms increased so did the population of the major cities. By 1850, the population of the country had risen to 23 million, and more than 30 percent had settled into towns larger than 2,500 persons. Although three-quarters of the population was still involved in agriculture, the expansion of commerce and industry had drawn almost 2 million factory workers into towns that were both old and new. The urban population thereby became the fastest-growing segment of the population.

The number of towns having more than 10,000 persons increased from 6 to more than 60 in less than half a century. Cities as distinct as Providence and Chicago were experiencing similar rates of growth. A number of small coastal towns became booming cities by mid-century in response to America's rise to maritime greatness in the clipper ship era. Boston, Salem, Portland, and New Haven, for example, were all active coastal trading cities in 1850. Salem was among the top five seaports in the nation with respect to the value of the trade that passed through it annually. Other towns grew due to their proximity to railroads. Boston alone was the terminus for no fewer than seven railroads. Westward expansion along the growing system of canals and the successful navigation of the western rivers by steamboats made a number of inland ports equally important. These included Buffalo, Syracuse, Cleveland, Pittsburgh, Cincinnati, Louisville, Memphis, Natchez, and St. Louis.

The cities that had been the largest at the turn of the century remained so and experienced the greatest rates of population growth. By 1850, New York City boasted a population of more than 500,000 people. Philadelphia, Boston, Newport, Baltimore, New Orleans, and Charleston had grown to hold hundreds of thousands of persons. Nonetheless, Southern cities had attracted fewer than 10 percent of the population of the region. The physical size of American cities also increased from less than a one-mile radius to that of four or five miles. Northern cities were characterized by a well-defined and established business district and the beginnings of the suburbs. Unfortunately, there was also an enormous growth in slums, tenements, and ethnically segregated residential areas filled with the poor and uneducated.

Many of the poorest immigrants were Irish Catholics. The Irish were the first truly urban group in America, living in crowded slums rife with crime and disease and experiencing severe religious prejudice at the hands of the Protestant majority. "Help Wanted" advertisements were often followed by signs stating, "Irish Need Not Apply." One of the ironic characteristics of the new modernism in Northern society was the simultaneous existence of antislavery sentiment and severe ethnic prejudice among upper-class Protestants. This is especially surprising in view of the prominence of social reform movements in the North.

The South was a structured hierarchical society tied to tradition and continuity rather than progress and change. Southerners strove to maintain a romanticized version of the old aristocratic order as it was before the American Revolution. They were remarkably intolerant of social reform and disdainful of activism; yet they thought of themselves as well mannered, chivalrous to women and children, religious, and protective of all that was still fundamentally good in America. They lionized the stratified, but benevolent, social order portrayed in the 19th-century romance novel and often acted the parts of popular fictional characters in their response to real-life situations in a way that seems preposterous to us. The "miserable artisan and his daughter," too much honored by the slightest notice of the son of the plantation master, retained the "insolence" to tell him that his notice was unwelcome.[3]

Family

The vast majority of Southern citizens were small farmers and planned their lives around rural activities and seasonal chores such as barn raising, quilting bees, planting, haying, and harvesting. Family members usually cooperated in completing chores. This togetherness was thought to foster feelings of kinship and traditional family values. Their concept of time was based on general divisions of the day (e.g., sunrise and noon) and the year (e.g., spring and summer), and they set their appointments or ended the workday by this standard. Free white laborers and artisans were paid by the completion of a task, and rarely by the clock or calendar. The system provided continuity in the work relationship between employer and employee, and it was not unusual for one family to be employed by another in the same capacity for several generations.

While many Northerners were still farmers, a growing segment of the population was becoming tied to the cities and factories. Middle-class men who had grown up in the first half of the century could remember a childhood spent living in a family working environment, either on the farm, in a cottage at the mill, or in a room behind the family shop. But as the century progressed, men's work increasingly took place in the special atmosphere of a business premises like the factory or office. Fathers commonly left the home to work for 10 to 14 hours, and their children rarely saw them during daylight hours. A father's work and workplace became foreign to his children. This tendency to "go to work," rather than to "work at home," led to the virtual removal of men from the home environment, leaving it the sole province of the female. With the general availability of the pocket watch, these men increasingly lived their lives by the clock. Factory workers were expected to work in shifts dictated by the public clocks that came to be prominently displayed on towers, in the streets, and on the factory walls. The idea of being "on time" represented a significant change in the lifestyle of most city dwellers; and since the North was the most urbanized section of the country, being "on time" became characteristic of Northern life.[4]

Conversely, Southerners, who had no need to work by the clock, were often viewed as shiftless and lazy. Southern laborers feared the development of the unprecedented "work for wage" economy of the cities, and they saw Northern wage earners as degraded and enslaved persons. The city worker sold himself into economic bondage for a wage, and Southerners dreaded the expansion of a similar "work for wage" system almost as much as abolitionists dreaded the expansion of slavery. Southern whites were clearly anxious to maintain their status as freemen, even if this required that they be very poor freemen. Many in the laboring class believed that the North was determined to enslave them to the factory system or counting house. The modern egalitarian society of the North was viewed with disdain and seen as degenerate and immoral. Rising crime rates in the cities, flagrant and open prostitution, and the squalid conditions of the urban lower classes were proffered as proof of Northern inferiority.

The South was led by a privileged planter class whose elite lifestyle was maintained at the expense of the rest of society. This planter aristocracy

Although the household became more female dominated as the period continued, a man's place became more authoritarian. This illustration shows a father, book in hand, surrounded by his loved ones in the privacy of the family parlor having a beverage (coffee, tea, or chocolate).

relied on its kinship network and social status as a means to personal success. Outsiders saw Southern culture and institutions as backward, inefficient, and harmful to the American nation as a whole. Nonetheless, the Southern elite voluntarily assumed the role of benefactor and knight errant to all other levels of their society. This obligation was extended to their slaves in an ambiguous, but serious, way. Many Southerners were genuinely concerned for the physical and moral welfare of their slaves but only in terms of continued racial separation and subjugation. Failing to acknowledge the good in Southern society because it was tied to slavery caused increasingly acrimonious, alienating, and violent rhetoric to become the norm of political and social debate as the war approached.

Planter Aristocracy

Wealthy antebellum planters saw themselves and their class as the natural leaders of their communities and as a social elite whose wants were rightly supplied by the labor of the rest of society. Historically, the South had been neither democratic nor purely aristocratic. Instead, Southern politics had reached a balance much closer to the classical Roman concept of the republic, a public order in which the power rested with an elite group of people who ruled for the good of all. The planters saw an outward display of benevolence toward black slaves, always tempered by the limits of the institution, as a tool that elevated the character of their class-making them independent, generous, affectionate, brave, and eloquent. Many planters were genuinely concerned for the physical and moral welfare of their slaves but only in terms of continued racial separation and subjugation. Slaves and servants not only made their master's wealth evident, but they also helped to sustain it with their labor and their obedience.

Few in the Southern planter class actually had aristocratic roots. This greatly intensified the need of the social structure and the hierarchy to define itself in historically acceptable terms. The planters invented a social mythology in which the blood of their class was deemed noble or at least tinted blue. Most upper-class Southerners incorrectly traced their ancestry to the royalty of Europe—a royalty that still ruled due to its blood ties to past kings. Planters with an English heritage might claim their descent from the Cavaliers of the English civil wars of the 1640s. No mere followers of the Stuart Kings, planter ancestry might be derived from dukes, earls, knights, and loyal squires who had ridden at Nasby. Those with Scotch-Irish blood, who could not trace their ancestors back to the Bruce or Brian Boru, easily found ancestors among the Celtic chieftains of their clan. There were enough Southern families who had legitimate family trees of this sort—the Lees, the Fairfaxes, and the Randolphs, for instance—to maintain the "truth" of the fiction.

Although half of the white population of the South had come to the colonies as indentured servants, generations of close and sometimes carefully planned intermarriage spread the royal connections so thin that all families of position and power in the South could claim rule by some form of "divine right." Marriage into an influential family was also a distinct advantage in politics. Thomas Jefferson's father had substantially improved his social standing by marrying a daughter of the well-placed

Randolph family, and John Marshall's marriage into the powerful Ambler family brought him influential connections that ultimately led him to a seat on the Supreme Court. Whether through birth, marriage, or myth, support of the Southern gentry was indispensable for the man who would rise in politics.

The upshot of all this ancestral mythology was that the planters themselves came to believe it. They behaved in a haughty manner reminiscent of the old nobility of Europe; taught their sons an aristocratic code of social behavior; married their daughters as if sealing treaties between feudal estates; and demanded positions of authority and command in their communities. "Civilization would cease but for the universal desire of white men to become aristocrats," wrote George Fitzhugh in *Cannibals All, or Slaves without Masters* (1857). Strangely, this proved a self-fulfilling delusion, as the planter aristocracy generally responded to the deference of the white underclasses and to the submission of their black slaves with benevolence and a sense of chivalric obligation. The Southern elite voluntarily assumed the role of benefactor and knight errant to all other levels of their society. Like knights on a quest, Southern men felt obliged to counsel and defend, not only their own families, but also all females and minor children placed under their protection.[5]

As the early decades of the antebellum period wore on toward the war, the Northern opposition to slavery came to criticize the aristocratic pretensions of the South, and Southerners found some necessity to explain themselves. Fitzhugh recorded a defense of the Southern way of life that would be used over and over during the antebellum years. "Pride of pedigree . . . ancestral position . . . [and] respectable connexion [*sic*] . . . will, ere long, cease to be under the ban of public opinion. Every man in America desires to be an aristocrat, for every man desires wealth, and wealth confers power and distinction, and makes its owner an unmistakable aristocrat. What vile hypocrisy, what malicious envy and jealousy, to censure and vilify in others, that which every man of us is trying with might and main to attain . . . [the] desire to found a family and make aristocrats of their posterity."[6]

The planter aristocracy successfully dominated Southern society for almost two centuries by applying their wealth and political influence to the wheels of government. Their numbers were so small that no more than 50,000 persons—men, women, and children—in a population of several million qualified as part of this class. As long as the planters could support themselves with the products of their own plantations, they were relatively insulated from economic depression and spiraling consumer prices. This economic security, once the hallmark of the great plantations, which stood like isolated agricultural city-states across the South, gradually became less certain as the war approached.

Kinship

Family was the most conservative and inviolable of upper-class institutions. Many of the best American families had resided in the same section of the country for hundreds of years. By the time of the Civil War,
there was hardly a family of note that did not occupy at least the same
social position that it had at the time of the founding of the colonies. Periodically, the family would gather, and cousins, aunts, and grandparents
would trace the family tree from long before the Revolution. In order to
maintain their high social position and authority, it was important for
socially elite families to have a strong sense of obligation to their blood
relatives.

In this regard, maternal uncles and aunts played an essential role of
great trust. "A mother's trust that her brothers and sisters would take care
of the children in case of her death gave special significance to the role of
the uncle and aunt." While uncles and aunts could be relied upon for
monetary assistance, guidance, or support, nieces and nephews need not
be orphaned to call upon them. Extenuating circumstances of many kinds
could and did bring the influence of these relatives into play in terms of
a tightly knit kinship network.[7] A number of words and expressions have
endured expressing this obligation, including "kinfolk," "blood kin,"
"blood ties," and "kissing cousins."

Intermarriage between second and third cousins was common in the
South because it perpetuated the family name, fortune, and bloodline.
However, it was almost unheard of in Northern families. In a historical
study of Southern and Northern families numbering 100 each, 12 percent
of Southern marriages were between cousins whereas not a single case
was found in the Northern sample. Although such findings could be laid
at the door of Southern clannishness, it should be remembered that
Northern young people living in cities and towns had many more opportunities to meet prospective mates, unrelated to them by blood, than
Southerners who were largely isolated on plantations.[8]

With kinship came advantage and obligation. Birth into one of
America's leading families was essential to making a political career almost everywhere. Social prominence, business and political influence, and
the presumption of ability—whether it was present or not in an individual—were inherited from one's father or uncle in much the same way
that businesses, land, or slaves were inherited. Fathers expected their first-
born male heirs to follow in their footsteps; they also were protective of
their daughters, providing their sons-in-law with influence if not money.
Daughters who remained unmarried into their adult years were often
given the position of companion to their fathers. Granddaughters in similar circumstances were treated in much the same way, especially in the
absence of a living father. Men were similarly solicitous of their nieces,

daughters-in-law, and all their children. So pervasive was the assumption that kinship ruled that men were given positions as sheriffs, justices of the peace, militia captains, or county lieutenants by influential relatives without the slightest charge of favoritism being made by anyone in the system.

Siblings were treated in a hierarchical manner with all the male offspring being given a superior position over their sisters. The inferior position of females, often supported by state law, implied an obligation that was placed upon men to defend the honor of their female relations. A brother could intervene in the affairs of his sisters and their circle of friends with or without their permission. At times these brothers could take on a very combative stance when dealing with a sister's reputation. Female cousins came under the same type of protection. As women were not permitted to correspond with men who were not relations, many young women had no knowledge of men who were not their blood relatives until after their marriage. Even then their social relationships with males were limited to the friends and acquaintances of their husbands.

Courtship and Marriage

The continuation of the family name and fortune through marriage was the most conservative of social institutions, and the rules, customs, and traditions that surrounded courtship and marriage were well established. There were multiple purposes for marriage in this period. The obvious ones were to provide for childrearing and to assure the continuity of the family fortune through the instrument of inheritance. The unspoken purpose was to provide a socially acceptable outlet for sexual relations.

While young men were free to remain single, all young, respectable women were expected to begin seeking out a marriage partner appropriate to their social position as soon as they left adolescence. Nonetheless, a widower with young children was expected to remarry for the sake of his motherless offspring if no appropriate female relation, such as an unmarried sister or aunt, were available to care for them. Before a man could hope to prosecute a courtship successfully, he had to establish himself in a profession or come into his inheritance. Courtships could be protracted if the suitor's financial expectations took some period to come to fruition. This fact tended to drive up the age of eligible suitors or increase the disparity in years between a well-established husband and a young wife still in her childbearing years. In the North, the difference in age between husband and wife during the antebellum period averaged a mere two years, while Southern couples were separated by an average of six.

Women who remained unmarried often lived with other relatives and looked to them during financial emergencies. Many young women looked to their maternal aunts and uncles in this regard for support, guidance, and companionship. In the absence of a father or uncle, a young woman might depend on her own brother for a roof over her head. Few men could shirk their responsibilities to a female relative without a loss of reputation and community standing. This was especially true in the South where the role of benefactor was an essential characteristic of plantation life. Nonetheless, an unmarried adult woman was often awkwardly placed in the kinship scheme. Many of these women made their contribution by helping with routine household tasks and could make a few dollars by spinning flax and wool for others. It is from this practice that the term "spinster" has come to refer to an older unmarried woman.

As the 19th century proceeded, a major cultural change took place as women gradually gained a modicum of control over themselves and the property that they brought to a marriage. This generally paralleled a similar movement in Victorian Britain. In many Northern homes, the focus increasingly came to rest on the wife and children. In response, there evolved a growing formalism and rigid authoritarianism that antebellum husbands demanded of their families and households when they were present. On Southern plantations, an older, more traditional male-dominated formalism—highly characteristic of the 18th century—continued to hold sway. Although these factors were most strongly entrenched among the Southern planters, they established a trend in marital custom throughout the South. For daughters of the planter class, wealth was the primary factor in arranging a marriage or choosing a husband. Furthermore, in order to maintain their social position, intermarriage between cousins far enough removed to dispel charges of consanguinity was common among the planter aristocracy. Finally, women in the South married at a younger age—almost four years younger on average—than their Northern counterparts.

A particularly attractive or well-heeled woman might have groups of suitors vying for her attentions. Typically, parents encouraged such groups to call together upon their daughter at home because they believed the practice discouraged gossip. Under such circumstances, young men had little opportunity of measuring the women's attitude toward their individual suit. Most gentlemen resorted, therefore, to a go-between in the early stages of any serious courting in order to gauge whether or not their more formal attentions would be rebuffed. The woman's brothers or male cousins often served in this capacity. All but the most eligible men met with a series of mild rebuffs as young women were discouraged by their parents from taking too many prospective fiancés into their social circle before selecting one from a small group of two or three as a husband.

Unmarried couples—even those who were formally engaged—might easily offend the community if their behavior was perceived to be sexual in any context. The betrothed might never have touched and certainly should never have shared a romantic kiss. As women were not permitted to correspond with men who were not relations, many young women had no knowledge of men who were not their blood kin. For this reason, they favored cousin marriages, wherein they were at least familiar with their prospective partner. Courting couples were never left alone, and chaperones (sometimes in the form of an elderly and trusted slave) were always present. Nonetheless, anxious parents frequently married off their daughters at 15 or 16, fearing that they might become involved in some sexual impropriety that would cause them to be shunned by prospective suitors. Overt sexuality at any stage in a woman's life before marriage would certainly meet with social ostracism and might actually result in criminal indictment for fornication in some jurisdictions.

Upon their marriage, young women passed from the domination of their fathers to the equally powerful authority of their husbands. Women had little or no legal standing in the courts, could not sign enforceable contracts, and held no tangible assets in their own names in most states. A husband and wife were considered one person in law, and the very existence of the wife was often incorporated and consolidated into that of the husband. Until late in the period, the property brought to a marriage by the wife legally became that of her husband. Many widows disdained remarriage having in their bereavement finally found relief from the overbearing power of even the best of husbands and fathers. Nonetheless, in some states a widow might lose her property rights to her adult sons, if not otherwise provided for by the will of the spouse. Only for a brief period—usually between puberty and marriage—did women have any real control over their fate. Yet this control was very limited, residing solely in their ability to choose a husband from among a set of suitors acceptable to her family.

MANNERS AND MORES
Hospitality

The North had developed towns and villages as it expanded, spawning numerous public houses and inns every few miles that could provide needed quarters to the traveler. The South, however, grew as counties with travel accommodations appearing with great infrequency and mainly along only the major commercial routes. One diarist noted that during a six-month journey through the South he came upon public houses less than once a week. Born of necessity, in a region where sweeping plantations produced few travelers and left the countryside bereft of small villages, Southern hospitality developed as a general custom wherein a traveler might ask for lodging at any private home happened upon as nightfall approached.

There was a considerable gap in expectations, however, between some Northern travelers and the hospitable Southern homeowner. Period writings of Northern travelers document that they confronted a grudging hospitality in the South characterized by rude behavior, wretched fare, and poor accommodations. Southern readers deeply resented these stories and some vowed to show any Yankee seeking hospitality just how paltry such situations could be. Part of this problem may have arisen from the fact that many Northerners were viewing the relationship with a dictionary definition of hospitality in mind. To them, hospitality meant receiving and entertaining visitors without remuneration. Some Southerners saw hospitality as the kindness of permitting a complete stranger to take shelter with them, and they had no problem declaring the exact price expected in return upon being approached by an unknown traveler. In 1860, a traveler in Mississippi recorded that he was usually received free of charge, if the house belonged to people of means, or paid the customary charge of one dollar for which he was furnished with supper, lodging, breakfast, and food for his horse. Southerner travelers, especially those of "quality," may have been treated differently in homes below the Mason-Dixon line for they commonly describe warm receptions that always found "room for one more" in even the humblest abodes and gracious hostesses who seemed able to repeat the miracle of the loaves and fishes.

Certainly, what elevated the phrase "Southern hospitality" to its current connotation would be the lavish presentations and courtesies extended to invited guests or to visitors who presented themselves with letters of introduction to prominent plantation owners. Guests could anticipate the assistance of servants in preparing their dress, luxuriant presentations of abundant food and drink, and free use of the plantation's amenities such as horseback riding, libraries, and gardens. Period letters and journals often describe parties of multicourse meals, which one senses are taking place with uncommon regularity and are probably reserved for holidays or special occasions. One breakfast description included cornbread, buckwheat cakes, boiled chicken, bacon, eggs, hominy, fish, and beefsteak all being served at a single sitting. A "hunt" breakfast provided as a brunch after a morning of riding with the hounds might also include a variety of beverages including light wines and sweet liquors. Dinner offerings were likely to be equally as impressive. An 1833 letter detailed a dinner that began with very rich soup and continued with a saddle of mutton, ham, beef, turkey, duck, eggs with greens, potatoes, beets, and hominy. After the circulation of champagne, came dessert, which offered plum pudding and tarts followed by ice cream and preserves and peaches preserved in brandy. Lastly, came figs, raisins, almonds, and wines that included port, Madeira, and a sweet wine for the ladies.

Duty and Honor

Although the two were not mutually exclusive, there is some truth in viewing the South as a society with a profound sense of honor; while the

North as a whole seemed driven more by duty, a communal conscience analogous to a compact made with God. Americans of the early 19th century were strongly influenced by such sentiments. The consciousness of duty resonated particularly well with the parallel development of social reform in the North. To shirk duty was to violate the collective conscience and offend morality by omission. Devotion to one's duty was viewed as a personal responsibility rather than as a collective obligation. "We all of us have a duty to perform in this life," wrote one journalist. It was not enough to support the norms of society from a distance. Duty required that a man place his life on the line. Many Southerners also cited obligations to duty in their writings and speeches, but they were much more likely to speak of honor.[9]

Honor was primarily a masculine concept that dealt with one's public image and reputation. There is ample evidence of a link between the romantic themes of adventure, glory, and honor, which appeared in the popular literature of the period and the letters and diaries of the Southerners. Nonetheless, Southerners also viewed honor in a contemporary light, and the continued popularity of dueling attests to the vitality of the sentiment in the Southern psyche. They often wrote of being dishonored in the eyes of their "revolutionary ancestors" should they fail to defend their families or the Southern cause and lifestyle. Nonetheless, the appeals to duty and honor were most often found among the letters and journals of the more literate upper classes.[10]

Dueling (Duelists)

The golden age of dueling lasted from 1830 to 1860. However, affairs of honor, where men resorted to the use of arms to settle personal grievances, were part of American culture dating form colonial times. The dancing masters of the 18th century, who had taught the finer points of swordsmanship to the gentry along with the latest dance steps from Europe, largely abandoned the teaching of dance in the antebellum period to open fencing schools and academies of dueling dedicated to teaching the requisite skills of both sword and pistol. Well-known duelists occupied much the same position in antebellum society as sports figures do in modern times. They were followed through the streets, fawned upon by waiters in restaurants, and had their mannerisms and dueling styles copied by the young men. Although formal in its procedures and socially acceptable at the highest levels of society, dueling quickly lost favor in the North and came to be seen as characteristically "Southern." This view has been reinforced in modern times by numerous films and romantic novels.

Quarrels among citizens of the upper class never ended in simple fisticuffs, and it was social suicide to strike a blow in anger. The possibility of being involved in a duel was a social reality for all those who considered themselves gentlemen or who dealt in politics. At all levels of society, individual liberty, manliness, and respect for social position were held in such high esteem that one put his life and personal honor on the line to protect them. Even in the midst of polite conversation, gentlemen were always on guard to protect their integrity. Nowhere in America, and possibly in the Western world, was dueling so universally practiced as in the antebellum South, and it was in New Orleans that the practice of dueling reached its zenith. As Southern society also favored a relaxed cordiality among social equals, the two notions of rigid honor and social familiarity often required a delicate touch. Defending one's honor reached such heights of absurdity that a moment of awkwardness might result in a challenge that could not, with honor, be ignored.

Ironclad rules and traditions governed every stage of the duel from the moment of the "insult" up to the hours immediately after the combatants had met on the field of honor. In some circles, the *Code Duello*, supported by an incredibly strict adherence to a sense of honor, was regarded with the same reverence as a religion. In the decades before the Civil War, the specter of dueling shadowed every fashionable social function, the theater, the opera, anywhere, in fact, where there might be the least breach of etiquette, the slightest lapse in politeness, or the smallest hint that a business dealing was unethical, even if it was. Truth might be an admirable defense against libel or slander in a court of law, but it had no standing in affairs of honor. A word and a challenge were the purest form of the dueling code. The purpose of a duel was to resolve a point of honor, not simply to kill an enemy. Opponents who lost sight of this might be looked upon as murderers by purists, who saw the entire process as an exercise in character.[11]

Initially, only swords were used in dueling and, consequently, there were few fatalities. However, with the advent of the more lethal percussion cap pistol and its reliable ignition system, fatalities increased. No attempt has been made to determine the absolute number of duels that were fought in the South, as the task is both daunting and the records of duels were somewhat concealed by the need to evade the laws that tried unsuccessfully to prevent them. Certainly, the number of duels fought in this period figures in the thousands and the fatalities in the hundreds. In the decades before the Civil War, there was hardly a man in public life in Louisiana who had not faced a duel, and many had fought several. Ten duels were fought on a single day at the Oaks, a favorite field of honor. Many of these affairs grew out of political party wrangling, which was, unfortunately, lacking in restraint and sophistication in this period. Duels sometimes ran through a political party or social grouping in a series involving one individual after another, one encounter producing the next. Dueling began losing favor in the South mostly because it degenerated either into contests with shot guns, axes, and clubs or brawls between groups of lower-class men using fighting knives and repeating pistols.

Only the violence of the Civil War was able to overshadow this apparent lust for individual combat.

Prostitution

The openness of prostitution in the 19th century scandalized the social and religious elite everywhere. Proper ladies universally frowned upon any man who was too open in his lustfulness; but in a male-dominated society they could do little to enforce their displeasure on the male population at large. Upper-class unmarried men involved in a relationship with prostitutes, black or white, seem to have received a special dispensation from society, especially in the South and West.

The nightly trade in amorous economics was available in most large towns and cities in America. Most prostitutes were poor white women who worked their clientele in cheap saloons, hotels, or dance houses. These women were of the lowest class, commonly having taken up prostitution in their teens. They moved in and out of the dance houses and bordellos and could be brought in from the street for as little as a dollar. They were described as "degraded beings [and] habitual drunkards" who were "remarkable for bestial habits and ferocious manners."[12]

The manifestation in which prostitution appeared in Southern cities was somewhat dictated by the class and means of the clientele. White prostitutes of varying quality were available almost everywhere, but some Southern men of wealth seemingly relied on the common practice of supplying themselves with a quadroon (mixed race) mistress for short-term affairs. Others, too far displaced from cities to conveniently satisfy their lustful desires with a professional harlot, simply considered every slave cabin a bordello. Comely slave girls brought exaggerated prices on the auction block with mixed race, "light-skinned girls" bringing a premium.

Although ordinances were passed that prohibited the renting of rooms to prostitutes in most cities, local politicians or the police often protected bordello owners. A madam might run a bordello by openly obtaining an annual license at a small cost. These licenses prohibited soliciting on the streets or from the doors and windows of the bordello. Indictments for prostitution, charging the keeping of a "disorderly house," usually targeted madams who engaged in interracial social activity. Within these bounds, the authorities made little attempt to halt the expansion of the trade into the residential areas of the city, forcing the more virtuous residents to abandon their homes in pure frustration. The so-called high-class places were operated with considerably more circumspection. These bordellos were housed in brick or brownstone buildings filled with mahogany woodwork, brass fixtures, and marble fireplaces—and furnished with fine carpets, pianos, furniture, art, and statuary—making them some of the most pretentious and luxurious residences in the country. Only the finest wines and champagnes were served; the ladies wore evening gowns while being entertained by musicians, dancers, and singers in the public rooms; and the ladies changed to the finest lingerie in their boudoirs. As many as 30 women might work in a single house, each paying a fee to the madam, and receiving between 5 and 20 dollars for a amorous experience.

Any romantic notions involving these practices, without regard to the fine trappings that surrounded them, should best be avoided as sentiment rather than as an unbiased assessment of the situation. Any other conclusion, even from a historic perspective, would be lacking in sensitivity with regard to the effects of the sexual exploitation experienced by the young women who practiced this trade. Poor kinless women received little protection from a patriarchal society in which "gentlemen" considered them a proving ground for their sexual prowess. For these women there was no return route to social acceptability once their female purity and innocence had been violated.

Miscegenation

One of the unique features of slavery in this period was the pervasiveness of miscegenation, or interracial sexual activity. Many free black women turned to prostitution in the absence of any hope of economic security. The desire of white men to have sexual contact with black females was not unheard of in the North and West, but it was seemingly so common in the South that there was no social stigma attached to it. An antebellum abolitionist confidently reported that half the slave population of the South was mixed with white blood. However, statistical analysis suggests that fewer than 10 percent of the slaves in the South were of mixed ancestry; and only a small percentage of the children born to slaves in a given year were fathered by white men.[13]

The extent of miscegenation is somewhat obscured by the superfluous methods used by 19th-century investigators to quantify the mixed race population of the South as mulattos (half black), quadroons (one quarter black), and octoroons (one eighth black) by the criteria of the outward appearance of the skin and the absence or presence of certain "defining" racial features. A large population of mixed race persons "passing for white" may also have obscured any meaningful estimates at the time.

Evidence suggests that female slaves were often bribed, cajoled, or simply seduced by their masters, but any romantic notions involving the practices of miscegenation are best avoided by historians. Notwithstanding this reservation, some white Southerners demonstrated a long commitment to their black mistresses; recognized their mixed race offspring; and attempted to provide for their upkeep and well-being. Often this took the form of a public admission after death, and many interracial alliances were recognized in a planter's will. The white children of such men often went to great lengths to undo those parts of their father's will favorable to their biracial siblings. The courts rarely upheld a will favorable to mixed race children in the face of a concerted effort by their white relations, especially if the whites were the elder sons.

The question of how common sexual affairs between slaves and masters actually were, as opposed to how often they appear as titillating tidbits of gossip in journals and letters, is undecided. Southerners went to great lengths to structure laws and cultural norms that would prohibit such interaction. Many slaveholding states passed antimiscegenation measures providing severe social penalties for white men who openly bedded black women and massive physical retaliation for any sexual activity upon any black men who had relations with white women.

The concept of white women willingly sleeping with black men was a proposition too explosive for the delicate egos of white males. White women were expected to respond to blacks as they would to any animate property, like pets, ignoring the indelicacy of even naked adult males. Young Southern women were expected to steel themselves into viewing the naked slave as a dehumanized object, no more indelicate than live-stock in the barnyard. Documented cases of the daughters of wealthy plantation owners bearing mixed race children are rare, and, when found, they are accompanied by tales of social rebuff, revulsion, or personal disaster.

RELIGION

Religious Revival

The United States has been a predominantly religious country from its inception, and the antebellum period was one of great religious revival fueled largely by a Protestant crusade in the East, camp revivals in the settlements and on the frontiers, and a political backlash brought about by an immense influx of Irish Catholics into the cities of America. The religious character of the country was essentially rooted in the Protestant-ism of England, Scotland, and Wales, but many new sects had joined the list of traditional Christian religions popular before the Revolution. Europe was swept by great religious wars and moral awakenings during the colonial period, which resulted in waves of religious zealots and exiles crossing the Atlantic. Spanish and French Catholics, Protestant Walloons and Huguenots, Dutch Calvinists; English Puritans, Quakers, Scotch-Irish Presbyterians, German Lutherans; Baptists, Anabaptists, and Moravians were all moved by much the same religious spirit. Yet religious bigotry influenced many largely well-meaning clergymen, both Catholic and Prot-estant, and encouraged intolerance among those who chose to do God's work.[14]

The First Great Awakening, a complex movement among a number of interrelated religious groups, swept through colonial America in the 18th century. Begun in the 1720s by the Reverend Theodore J. Frelinghuysen, a Dutch Reform minister from New Jersey, this movement spread into New England and reached its peak in the 1740s under men like Jonathan Edwards. In the South, it continued through the American Revolution in several distinct phases led respectively by Presbyterians, Baptists, and Methodists. Everywhere, the First Great Awakening stressed personal religion and multiplied the number and variety of churches and congregations. There was an estimated 3,100 religious congregations in the English colonies at the close of the colonial period. While this number was almost equally divided among the three regions of New England, the Middle states, and the Carolinas, there was an unequal distribution among the different denominations giving each region a distinct religious character.[15]

The Protestantism of the framers of the Constitution from New England had been essentially related to the Puritanism of the Congregational Churches, whereas those from the South were generally Church of England (Anglican). Quakers, considered dissenters since colonial times, congregated mainly in Pennsylvania, and pockets of Catholicism could still be found in Maryland. The country was also characterized by a wide variety of newcomers: Germans, Scandinavians, Swiss, Welsh, French Huguenots, and Jews. The Scotch-Irish immigrants added an element of Presbyterianism to American religious life, and later the Baptist Church became popular among the Welsh and Germans. The frontier digested a wide variety of these immigrants, but most of them were within the same religious compass of essential Protestantism. Both the Presbyterians and the Baptists played a major role on the frontier. Lutherans—largely Germans and Scandinavians—were the first to introduce a new element to the religious mix. Nonetheless, their churches were essentially Protestant, and they were assimilated with little fuss into the American social fabric.

Yet not all of the religious sects of antebellum America were considered legitimate by society in general because many sects espoused doctrines that were obviously on the fringe of traditional Christian beliefs. Some Christian evangelical revivals, particularly those headed by incendiaries such as the Reverend Charles G. Finney of western New York and the Reverend Lyman Beecher of Boston, provoked less-thoughtful followers of mainstream American Protestantism to take up the rhetoric of the anti-immigrant and anti-Catholic. They created and published salacious rumors and anecdotes that distorted the beliefs and activities of many of these minority religions. A number of these minority religions can be considered pietist in nature because they generally abandoned a strict church structure and hierarchy. Shakers, Quakers, Moravians, Fourierists, Mennonites, Anabaptists, and other pietist sects generally emphasized inner spiritual life and a personal path to salvation and denied the need for a more formal ecclesiastical organization.

Although Quakerism had been a major component of American religious life since colonial times, it was essentially a pietist religion and many Americans viewed its adherents with suspicion. Moreover, the English-speaking Quakers, Shakers, and Fourierists were largely distinct from the Mennonites, Amish Anabaptists, and Moravians who originated in Germany, Switzerland, and other parts of central Europe. The Germans penetrated into the far northwestern portion of New Jersey and west into the region of Reading and Harrisburg, Pennsylvania. They tended to separate themselves from other groups, a process aided by their lack of the English language. Joshua Gilpin, traveling through this region, noted, "I never knew before the total want of a language for in this respect we might as well have been in the middle of Germany." Isolated in this manner, the Germans achieved a far greater social solidarity than any other group on the frontier.[16]

A Second Awakening

It was the Christian revival at the beginning of the 19th century—generally viewed as the Second Great Awakening—that most affected the religious life of American society before the Civil War. This religious revival drew its vitality from the Southern and western frontiers rather than from New England. Beginning near the Gaspar River Church in Kentucky in July 1800, the spark of faith was ignited at camp meetings in the Midwest and was proclaimed throughout the nascent frontier settlements by an army of traveling evangelists and self-ordained preachers. Some ministers, having been brought up on "rigid Calvinism" and having been taught to preach "the doctrine of particular election and reprobation" in earlier years, revolted and, having no correct books on the new theology, "plunged into the opposite extreme, namely, universal redemption." This sort of evangelism, with its strong emotional appeal, spirit of optimism, and promise of unconditional salvation to all of mankind was particularly influential among 19th-century Americans.[17]

Peter Cartwright, a contemporary observer of the process, noted, "Ministers of different denominations came in, and preached through the country: but Methodist preachers were the pioneer messengers of salvation in these ends of the earth. . . . A Methodist preacher in those days, when he felt that God had called him to preach, instead of hunting up a college or Biblical institute, hunted up a hardy pony, or a horse, and some traveling apparatus, and with his library always at hand, namely the Bible, Hymn Book, and Discipline, he started, and with a text that never wore out or grew stale, he cried, 'Behold the Lamb of God, that taketh away the sin of the world!' In this way he went through storms of wind, hail, snow and rain; climbed hills and mountains; traversed valleys; plunged through swamps; swam swollen streams; lay out all night, or tied to a limb slept with his saddle blanket for a bed, his saddle or saddle bags for his pillow, and his old big coat or blanket, if he had any, for covering."[18]

During the day nothing appeared unusual in the sprawling and smoke-filled revival camps with their scattering of white tents, knots of canvas-covered wagons, and bands of scurrying children and barking dogs. The occupants followed the same slow-paced routines of cooking, cleaning, and caring for the livestock found in other camps on the immigrant trails. However, nighttime drew the faithful together and transformed them into an army of God. With campfires blazing, a thunderous din of singing, and preachers beseeching the gathering to repent so that they might be saved from the fires of hell, the crowds reached a peak of religious frenzy. A circuit riding preacher, Lorenzo Dow, described a camp meeting in his journal: "About three thousand people appeared on the ground, and the rejoicing of old saints, the shouts of the young converts, and the cries of the distressed for mercy, caused the meeting to continue all night." Many shook, jerked, and rolled on the ground until they fell away in a faint.[19]

Methodists and Baptists reaped a rich harvest of souls at this time. By the 1830s, Methodism had become one of the two largest religions in the country, and the Baptists, in particular, had made great inroads into the black population, both free and slave. Under the influence of an evangelical spirit, most American Protestants came to believe that the path to salvation lay in placing themselves in a position to receive God's grace if they were worthy. This belief was to have a profound effect on Civil War soldiers who strove to be worthy of God's protection by exhibiting courage and steadiness under fire.

The Second Great Awakening spread new religious sects like a wildfire. Campbellites, Shakers, Rappites, Fourierists, and other minor religions popular in the North espoused theories of associative communism and utopian socialism by making provisions for the correction of inequalities of temporal possessions among their members. Many members gave up all their wealth or placed it at the disposal of the congregation. Unitarians (the followers of which were largely devoted abolitionists), Universalists, and Disciples of Christ splintered away from established Churches, while Mormons and Adventists sprang from the soil of America itself. Nonrevivalist churches, especially in the more traditional South, trailed behind. Of 891 Unitarian and Universalist churches known to exist in 1850, only 23 existed below the Mason-Dixon line.[20]

Quakers

George Fox and Margaret Fell founded Quakerism, or the Society of Friends, in 17th-century England. The first adherents to the new sect—

many of whom were of Welsh ancestry—were drawn largely from farmers who lived on the fringe of the cultural, economic, and social mainstream. Quakerism was a radical religion that attracted these generally independent people by preaching the virtues of the family as the basic disciplining and spiritualizing authority in society as opposed to that of magistrates and church prelates. Due in part to their devotion to the decentralization of authority, many Quakers devoted themselves to their religious duties by creating nearly autonomous personal households.[21] Every one and every thing in the Quaker household—wives, children, and business—were subjected to a familial order rooted in morality. The burden of producing, sustaining, and incorporating morality, and civic and economic virtues, into the household was taken on by the entire family and supported by the community at large. Outside authorities such as an intolerant established priesthood, an authoritarian upper class, or even a pedantic university system were considered "not only unnecessary but even pernicious."[22]

Although sparsely settled throughout much of the country, Quakers maintained a political influence in Pennsylvania that well outweighed their number. Their neat, well-tended farms and social solidarity were among the characteristics that made the state one of the most prosperous in America. Yet the unique form of the Quaker community and its pacifist sentiments left the Society of Friends distrusted by the wider community in general. In applying their principles, Quakers relied heavily upon a religious and spiritual form of human relations. They radically reorganized their Church from one that required the performance of a series of external disciplines and the reception of a well-prepared sermon, as among the Puritans, into one in which the silent meeting and a personal conversion took precedence.[23]

The Quaker community also gave unprecedented moral authority within the household and within the congregation to the women of their sect. They thereby radically changed the structure of the traditional household, especially in the areas of authority over childrearing, courtship, and marriage. Women were encouraged to discuss and legislate on "women's matters" in specially designed women's meetings set up for the primary purpose of controlling courtship and marriage within the community.[24]

The basic unit of Quaker settlement was the family farm of about 250 to 300 acres—an initial size to which much was added with time. Family holdings were often widely dispersed, and Quaker farmers were accustomed to moving about on horseback or in wagons over the undulating and often flat countryside of southeastern Pennsylvania. Quaker fathers devoted a great deal of their energy to the accumulation of land that would be devolved onto their sons or would otherwise benefit their daughters when they married. The overwhelming majority of Quaker children in America married other Quakers locally and tended to stay within the meetinghouse discipline. They thereby quickly found themselves related to one another in their local communities, not only by religion, but also by shared genetics. This web of kinship was partly responsible for the strong ties exhibited by a community of people who were otherwise defiantly anti-institutional.[25]

Moravians

The Moravians were among the least fanatical of the sects that came to America. With roots in the teachings of John Huss and John Wycliffe, the Moravians (Fratres Unitas) had become one of the most important Protestant groups in central Europe at the beginning of the 17th century. Nonetheless, they suffered decades of persecution in the Thirty Years' War (1618–1648) during which they were hounded from their homes until only a few faithful families were left in the sect by the end of the century. Most of these took refuge in Saxony. From there, they began to spread their faith to the West Indies, Africa, Asia, and America—particularly to the native populations of southeastern Pennsylvania, Delaware, and the back country of the colonial South. They dealt fairly with the Indians in terms of buying land and scrupulously adhered to their agreements. Moravian preachers and settlers thereby provided an important positive link between the early immigrants to America and the native population on the frontier.

The Moravians professed a common unity among all Christians, a goal that proved too high-minded for most Americans who were dedicated to a narrower field of Protestant doctrine. Although Moravian influences were more important in colonial times than in the antebellum period, their religious beliefs strongly influenced John Wesley, a leader in the evangelical movement and the founder of Methodism. Nonetheless, because Moravians refused to take oaths or to bear arms in times of war, the majority of other Protestants viewed them with a good deal of suspicion. Only their very small numbers and general isolation from other communities kept them from being the targets of prejudice and repression.[26]

Shakers

Founded in 1758 by Ann Lee, who styled herself as the spiritual mother of the community, Shakerism was a celibate religious movement rooted in Protestantism. The religion is most noted for being founded by a woman, and there was a strand of early feminism that punctuated its doctrine and organization. Actually named the United Society of Believers in Christ's Second Coming, the religion took on the name of Shakerism because of the dancing and shaking that characterized some of its rituals. Shakerism was brought to America by Mother Ann Lee in 1774 and was most successful in New England. In the antebellum period, it made great gains in membership in Ohio and Kentucky. Like many other groups that followed a sort of social Christian doctrine, the Shakers believed in communal living, productive labor, and a closed, self-sustaining economy. "Without Money, Without Price" was one of their mottos. Shakers came to be known for a distinctive craftsmanship and folk art characterized by simplicity, and they printed, published, and distributed their own writings.

The religious doctrines of the community included a belief in the direct communication of some of its members, known as seekers, with other celestial realms inhabited by Most High God, Holy Mother Wisdom, Lord Jesus Christ, Mother Ann, and a cast of angels, patriarchs, prophets, apostles, and saints drawn from the Bible. Shakers practiced absolute celibacy and suffered from the need to attract new adherents to their communities, as there was no natural increase due to birth. By the 1850s, this aspect of the religion caused a good deal of concern as the number of young men entering the fold diminished to the point that many communities had to hire nonadherent workers to perform heavy tasks such as plowing.

Fourierists

The followers of social architect Charles Fourier would be relatively unimportant except that they included a group of literary giants from New England known as transcendentalists, who practiced a form of Christian humanitarianism at Brook Farm in Massachusetts. These included Ralph Waldo Emerson who wrote of the group's adherents, "in obediance to [their] most private being, [they] find [themselves], though against all sensuous probability, acting in strict concert with all others who follow their private life." As can be seen, Fourier's views were somewhat convoluted and difficult to grasp. The basic tenet of Fourierism was a crusade for social harmony. Fourier believed that the basic force that ruled all the aspects of social order, including passion, was attraction. Only by balancing all the possible attractions could social harmony be attained.

The religious aspects of Fourierism were essentially organized around the shared Protestant beliefs of its adherents, whereas the social aspects of the movement were dedicated to balancing individualism and ego with group membership and shared responsibility. Communal production was segregated into specific working groups with more than 40 discrete craft specializations that were ultimately assembled into larger series. The final products were meant to sustain a small, self-contained community. The New England group at Brooks Farm sought to propagate the movement by buying a weekly column in Horace Greeley's *Daily Tribune* and by publishing their own work in *The Dial*. Nonetheless, the movement was largely unsuccessful in sustaining itself, falling heavily into debt because of the lack of expertise exhibited by its adherents, who were much better at crafting essays and poems than furniture and textiles.[27]

Mormons

The Mormonism (Church of Jesus Christ of the Latter-day Saints) may have been the most vigorously persecuted religious sect in the antebellum period. As possibly the most important fringe religion of the period, Mormonism was the great catchall of the evangelical movements. Patriarchs, angels, and demons seemed to punctuate the semi-Biblical rituals of Mormon metaphysics. At one time or another, every Protestant heresy in America was championed by one or the other of the spokesmen for the Latter-day Saints. Yet Mormons were generally courageous, dedicated, and hard-working people unfairly targeted by the more established religions.

Joseph Smith, who saw himself as a present-day biblical prophet, founded the Mormon religion in 1823. Nonetheless, Brigham Young is more closely associated with the Church leadership in the antebellum period. Smith based the religion on the Book of Mormon, a new scripture translated from golden plates originally written by a person named Mormon, who had made his way to the North American continent with others from Jerusalem. Here, Mormon organized certain records that he and his fellows had brought with them from Israel and inscribed them on the plates before his death. The Latter-day Saints believed that Mormon's son, Moroni, hid the plates in the hill of Cumorah near Palmyra, Missouri, hundreds of years before the discovery of America. The Lord purportedly spoke directly to Smith revealing their contents. The resulting *Book of Mormon* restored all the ancient orders of the Bible—elders, teachers, apostles, enforcers, and deacons—and all the ancient rights including baptism by immersion and the sacraments. Other doctrines were added from modern-day revelation; but a return to polygamy (taking more than one wife at the same time) was the cause for which the Mormons were most often persecuted.

Brigham Young was a convert to Mormonism in 1832. Within months of his conversion, his first wife died leaving him with two small daughters, and he quickly remarried for the sake of the children (he ultimately took 17 wives). Originally from New York State, Young traveled the country trying to make converts, and he turned much of his energy to the work of his new religion. He moved to Kirtland, Ohio, at the urging of Smith, who advised that all the "Saints" do so. Brigham brought a little knot of converts with him from New York and found that dozens of such groups were pouring into Kirtland. Here, in a form of religious socialism, a good part of the possessions of each newcomer was turned over to the Church treasury for its support.

In 1834, Young was selected as one of the Twelve Apostles who stood next to the three-man presidency of the Church headed by Smith. This group decided to move the Church to Missouri in order to support their brethren who were suffering from burnings and beatings at the hands of the general population. Once in Missouri, Smith and some of his companions were arrested by the territorial governor, and the growing hoard of Mormons were officially warned to leave the state or face the ire of both the population and the territorial militia. Young, who had quite accidentally missed being apprehended, suddenly found himself the only major leader of the group with freedom of movement; but he was now solely responsible for almost 12,000 homeless and frightened people. He made arrangements to purchase land on the banks of the Mississippi River in Illinois in the name of the Church, and he moved his charges there.

Meanwhile, Joseph Smith and his companions managed to escape jail in December 1839. Shortly thereafter, they joined the Saints in Illinois. Here Smith unfolded his plan for Nauvoo, the "beautiful" city of the Saints, and began an impressive building project. However, many of the non-Mormon residents in Illinois became fearful of the large, well-equipped military force that the Mormons maintained for their own protection. They began to view Smith as a danger both economically and politically. In 1844, the Mormons decided to run Smith for the U.S. presidency. This decision led almost immediately to Smith's assassination at the hands of a mob in Carthage, Illinois; the abandonment of Nauvoo; and the removal of the Saints to Iowa. Young, braving the storm of internal Church politics, reassumed the leadership of the Twelve Apostles and became Church president in 1847. This series of events put practical control of the Mormon religion in his hands for the next three decades.

In 1848, having decided to leave the United States to escape further persecution, Young turned west to the great American desert. Having been persecuted in Ohio, Missouri, and Illinois, advanced parties of Mormons hurried into the Great Salt Lake Valley of Utah leaving more than 13,000 refugees waiting in Iowa and Nebraska for the signal to move west. By 1849 Young's vision of a Mormon empire in the West had taken root. Exactly two years after they had entered the valley, the Mormons had built a city with an irrigation system, had established themselves across the Great Basin, and had entered into treaties of peace with the local native population. Young successfully helped the Mormons to maintain their influence in the West until his death in 1877.

Slaves and Religion

The Africans, who were first brought to the Americas as slaves, came from diverse cultural and religious backgrounds. Upon arrival at a plantation, they found themselves intermingled with other blacks who held a wide range of beliefs and practiced a multiplicity of religious rites. The desire to hold true to ancestral customs was a strong one, and some slaves would periodically steal away to neighboring farms to join with others from the same ethnic group. This diversity, however, produced an openness that transcended cultural differences with a common mystical relationship to the divine and the supernatural. African religious practices were marked by a communication with the natural world and a joyful expression of overt sexuality that shocked the generally prudish Protestant plantation owners. Lacking an understanding of the African culture and having no desire to cultivate one, slaveholders did their best to strip slaves of their native religious cultures. Effectively, however, these practices were merely driven underground to be practiced in secret.

By the close of the 18th century and as an outgrowth of the Second Great Awakening, many whites felt it was their duty to bring Christianity to the slaves. Protestantism leveled all men as sinners before God, regardless of wealth or color, and an intense commitment by evangelists and revivalists to black conversion was focused largely on the slave communities. The success of the undertaking was facilitated by a number of factors. Generally, the slave community was open to this religious movement. Second-, third-, and even fourth-generation slaves had fewer cultural and linguistic barriers to Christian instruction than their forebears. The emotionalism, congregational response, and plain doctrine of revivalist preaching proved favorable to well-disposed African Americans, and it resonated somewhat with their religious heritage. Remnants of African dance and song found a home in the spirituals of evangelical Protestantism. Finally, black freemen generally abandoned their former religious practices in favor of Christianity in order to be less conspicuous within the white community.

The egalitarian perspective of this religious movement opened the way for black converts to participate actively in churches as preachers and even as founders of their own congregations. Slaves had the freedom to attend church with their owners (although discretely seated in the rear or among the rafters), but in some instances they were allowed to worship at independent black churches. Even so, the majority of slaves who had the opportunity to become church members in the first decades of the 19th century were household servants, artisans, and urban residents rather than field hands.

By the 1830s, evangelical churchmen had become increasingly committed to the idea of an aggressive program of plantation missions in order to bring Christianity to rural slaves. Planters were generally amenable to the concept of slave conversion in a theological sense, although two slave revolts led by black preachers Denmark Vesey and Nat Turner found validation for their cause in scripture. These uprisings produced huge setbacks in any latitude afforded slaves regarding their religion. Planters were expected to join missionary societies and to support local churches with money for the plantation missionaries. Proponents of the cause adopted the techniques of northern Bible and temperance societies to raise Southern consciousness by printing sermons and essays, adopting resolutions, and devoting entire conferences to the topic. However, the distance between plantations made ordinary pastoral care almost impossible.

Southern slaveholders began to see that scripture could be used to sanction a kind of Christian social order based on mutual duty of slave to master and master to slave as found in Ephesians 6:5–9. The ideal of a Christian master-slave relationship fed the Southern myth of the benevolent planter-patriarch who oversaw the simple, helpless black. As the decades advanced, growing uneasiness toward Northern abolitionists created ambivalence in Southerners regarding the instruction of slaves in Christianity. However, the criticism of Northern churchmen made Southerners more sensitive to their duty, and the supporters of plantation missions continued to remind slaveholders of their religious duties toward their blacks. Plantation mistresses in particular were urged to take an active role in slave instruction by reading sermons to them, including them in family prayers, and conducting Sabbath schools. The mistress led some household slaves in prayer each morning.

By the eve of the Civil War, it was not unusual for slaves to outnumber whites at racially mixed churches. This manifestation of the plantation missionaries' success was misleading, however, because it represented only one component of the slaves' religious experience. In the secrecy of their cabins and amid brush or "hush arbors," slaves met free from their owner's gaze and practiced a religion that addressed many issues other than a slave's biblical subservience to his master. Absolute freedom was often the subject of their prayer. Through prayer, song, and "feeling the spirit," slaves gained renewed strength and hope. These informal prayer meetings were filled with spirituals that perpetuated continuity with African music and performance. The drums, which had once been a vital part of African spiritual expression, were replaced by rhythmic hand clapping and foot stomping known as "shouting." Rather than truly adopting Christianity, the slaves had adapted it to themselves.

Generally, slaves faced severe punishment if they were found attending nonsanctioned prayer meetings. Gathering in deep woods, gullies, and other secluded places, they created makeshift rooms of quilts and blankets that had been wetted down to inhibit the transmission of voices. A common practice was to place an iron pot or kettle turned upside down in the middle of the floor to catch the sound. The roots or symbolism of this belief have been lost. On occasion, rags would be stuffed into the mouth of an overzealous worshiper. Slave narratives repeatedly speak to the uplifting nature of these meetings.

An underground culture of voodoo, magic, and conjuring were practiced in areas where there were large numbers of slaves from the islands of the Caribbean or where African snake cults—which handled serpents as part of their ritual—had been imported and adapted. It would be a mistake to believe that the majority of slaves followed voodoo. That was more characteristic of those from Haiti and other West Indian islands. However, many slaves exhibited a respectful attitude toward occult practices in general. Newly imported slaves from Africa brought with them a periodic infusion of non-Christian religious practices and mystical beliefs that kept the echoes of older naturalistic religions alive. Nonetheless, the power of the voodoo priests and other conjurers never reached the level it had enjoyed in the islands or in Africa.

The Quaker religion openly welcomed black and Native American worshipers. While the Catholics had minority representation in their churches in the North, they were able to maintain their position in the South only by making concessions to the etiquette of white supremacy. Separate black congregations also grew in number among many Protestant sects because the white congregations of their several denominations did not welcome them. A growing army of black ministers was thereby able to found parishes among the freemen and slaves of the South. The African Methodist Episcopal (AME) Churches had some of the most prominent black ministers of the period.

Judaism

Jews made up only a small proportion of the American population before the late 19th century. However, Sephardic Jews, those whose ancestry lay in the Iberian Peninsula, had significant communities in both New York and Louisiana. The practice of Judaism in New York was almost as old as the colony itself, and at least one Jewish congregation was active in New Amsterdam under Dutch rule during the 17th century. In 1845, an economic depression caused many European Jews, especially those of German descent, to immigrate to America. They brought an early form of Reform Judaism with them. In their synagogues, they innovated the ritual; used German, English, and Hebrew in their services; and allowed men and women to be seated together. Nonetheless, most still observed the traditional laws in their homes and read and spoke the Torah in Hebrew only. The lack of intermarriage between the German-speaking newcomers to America and the more established Sephardic Jews tended to keep the communities apart. Apparently, Jews experienced little overt anti-Semitism in the antebellum period, and a significant number of individuals played important roles in the coming war as commanders and in government.

Catholics

Added to the confusion caused by a myriad of immigrants entering America's cities was the fact that many of the poorest and least educated were Catholic. In the 1830s, the Roman Catholic Church was possibly the only religion in America not divided over doctrine. The Roman Church was intolerant of criticism, unapologetically authoritarian, resolute, and unalterable in its structure. It was the oldest and best-organized religion in the Western world, and it demanded the unquestioned obedience of its members to the will of the Pope. A "Protestant Crusade" to stem the growing influence of the Catholics began in the 1820s and increased in proportion to Catholic immigration, which grew most precipitously in the 1840s and 1850s with the flood of Irish immigration. The Nativist movement, truly reactionary and discriminatory in its nature, was rooted in a traditional abhorrence of authoritarian Roman papism, and it focused largely on the mass of Irish Catholic immigrants who were filling the Northern cities.

Among the texts circulating through the bookstores and publishing houses of America were a number of anti-Catholic works, including "escaped nun" publications. The ostensible theme of this genre was the immorality of the Catholic Church and its institutions. While in the guise of being uplifting and informative, these stories actually served as a sort of pornographic literature. The most successful of the "escaped nun" stories was Maria Monk's *Awful Discourses of the Hotel Dieu Nunnery of Montreal*, which was first published in 1834. Therein, Maria detailed her stay in the Ursuline Convent and charged that she saw holy sisters killed for failing to surrender their bodies to the lusts of the priests. Having been ravished in this manner herself, she claimed to be pregnant. Maria also detailed the hiding places of the bodies of the babies born to the inmates of the convent and killed to keep the awful secret of Catholic lust and degeneration. The book, conveniently interspersed with the intimate details of this sexual activity, claimed that the Roman Church actively promoted the "prostitution of female virtue and liberty under the garb of holy religion."[28]

Maria's tale was as false as the author herself. She was almost immediately unmasked as a prostitute of long standing who had never seen the inside of a convent. Unscrupulous publicists and radical crusaders continued to use the work with reckless abandon, however. A mob of about 50 workmen, incensed in part by the book, took it upon themselves to burn the Ursuline Convent in Charlestown near Boston in 1834. Irish Catholic homes were burned, and a number of Irishmen were attacked in the streets. In 1844, a similar incident took place in Philadelphia, where two Catholic churches and 30 homes were burned. Protestant crusaders clashed with Irish Catholic bands, leaving more than a dozen dead and scores injured. Maria's book, more popular than most slave narratives and antislavery tracts, sold more than 300,000 copies before the Civil War, a volume of sales rivaled at the time only by Harriet Beecher Stowe's *Uncle Tom's Cabin*. Anti-Catholic forces trotted it out again in 1928 when Alfred E. Smith, a Catholic, ran for president of the United States.[29]

The Catholic archbishop of New York, John Hughes, took an unquestionably militant stand in defense of his Church. He rallied the largely Irish Catholic population of the city in defense of Catholic institutions, and surrounded churches, convents, and schools with armed guards. Hughes also fought to have anti-Catholic books and the King James version of the Bible banned from the public schools. Catholic radicals burned a great number of protestant Bibles that came into their possession. Hughes undertook a series of lectures in which he predicted the inevitable victory of Catholicism over the Protestant heresy. The final result of the New York controversy was the elimination of all Bibles and Bible reading from the tax-supported schools. Ironically, this very early separation of Church and State crusade, led by a priest, clearly sharpened the dispute and helped to swell the ranks of the Nativist, or Know Nothing, political party in the 1840s and 1850s, which used anti-Catholicism and the evils of popery as foundation stones of their all-American rhetoric.

Death and Dying

Amid the romanticism and sentimentalism of the 19th century, death was viewed from a different perspective than in earlier times, or even than it is today. High infant mortality and the tragic loss of loved ones to disease or accident in the prime of life made coping with death a part of daily living. Accidents were common in a society that had few safety regulations in industry and public transportation. Charles Baldwin of Catskill, New York, kept a diary that contained a special section headed, "Accidents, Catastrophes, Etc." Some of his entries involving fatalities included:

> Explosion of Powder Mills at High Falls; Wesley Sitser severely injured by machinery at Broom Corn Factory; explosion of the boiler on the "Isaac Newton." Honora Barrigan horribly crushed in machinery in Woolen Mills at Leeds; explosion of locomotive at Catskill Station, fireman died; fall at a span of the old bridge; a drowning in a bleach-vat at the paper mill; an explosion of the soda water generator at Smith's Drug Store.[30]

Death simply was not the taboo topic of today's modern society. Children's stories and poems contained references to death. Battlefield deaths provided inspiration for songwriters. There are numerous examples of popular piano sheet music that detailed and sentimentalized the final moments of dying heroes. "Comrades, I Am Dying" contains the following lines:

Comrades, comrades, I am dying! I see my mother now:
See her coming down from heaven with a wreath upon her brow.
God has sent her to the soldier, she will teach him how to die;
And when He has called my spirit, she will bear it to the sky.[31]

It is difficult to imagine a family wanting to gather around the piano in the parlor to sing about a soldier's final moments, but to the 19th-century mind this was not the morbid activity it would be labeled today. Rather, death was the final scene of life's drama as written by the finger of God.

Following the Second Great Awakening of the late 18th century, religious belief allowed people to anticipate the salvation of their souls in a manner unknown to former times. In the short story "The Star Vision," a dying boy describes a dream foretelling his death and his afterlife. He says, "Then I wished to be a star, Mother."[32] Death was, in a certain way, a joyous occasion, an opportunity to be joined once again to family who had already passed on to their reward. Following the untimely death of her brother, Hal, in a duel, 19-year-old Sarah Morgan recorded these thoughts:

> [T]here is no disappointment in the tomb . . . better to be laying in your grave, Hal, with all your noble longings unsatisfied, than to have your heart filled with bitterness as it would have been. . . . Those glorious eyes, with God's truth sparkling in them, are now dimmed forever, Hal. Yet, *not* forever; I shall see them at the Last Day; bury me where I may see them again. O please God, let me die as calmly as he. And let Hal be the first to welcome me, and lead me before Thee.[33]

Attitudes toward graveyards, once thought to be places of evil, had also shifted from previous times. The grave was now profoundly symbolic in a romantic sense. The term "cemetery," from the Greek for "sleeping chamber," replaced the earlier phrase "burying ground." Family monuments were a physical manifestation of the philosophical shift in attitudes toward death from the 18th to the 19th century. The tombstone skeletons and death heads of previous times, meant to instill fear in the living, were replaced with angels and cherubs who would accompany the departed on their journey to heaven. Following the death of Mary Barnwell in the 1850s, Mary Chesnut wrote the following in her diary, "Not in anger—not in wrath—came the angel of death that day. He came to set her free from a world grown too hard to bear."[34] It was not uncommon for antebellum tombstones to bear more reassuring epitaphs such as:

Harriet Miles
Fell asleep in Jesus
January 16, 1857
Aged 15, years
Her last word was HAPPY[35]

Earlier grave markers contained elaborate epitaphs and flat carvings. Mid-century monuments were three-dimensional works carved in the style of European sculptures, creating a virtual museum of memorials. Overall, the new monuments heralded symbols of hope, immortality, and the renewal of life. Ivy was used to symbolize memory, an important component of mid-19th-century mourning. The poppy represented peaceful sleep, and the anchor symbolized hope. Oak denoted immortality, and the acorn was the renewal of life. Equally frequent were the trappings of home and family. Books, hats, chairs, the representation of a favorite pet, or even the façade of the family home were carved on monuments in loving memory of the departed. This symbolic language became so complex that manuals were written to interpret their meanings. Edward Fitzgerald wrote a book on rural cemeteries that included an "Appendix on Emblems" detailing the significance of 26 common symbols. "The world outside was changing, and seemed to be turning upside down. But at least in the permanence of the graveyard, traditions could be maintained—indeed maintained, exaggerated, and sentimentalized—if not for those still living, at least for posterity, and for posterity's remembrance of the dead."[36]

Children's graves received unprecedented attention for the first time in America. In former centuries, children were mourned but they were buried in a solemn simplicity that seemingly represented the dread of death and an ultimate fate predestined by an angry God. Early death in the antebellum period brought pain and sorrow to parents and loved ones just as surely as it does today. However, the period was alight with an evangelical spirit that replaced limited salvation for the chosen few with universal salvation for the just. Amid the pain, loss, and sorrow of early death was the assurance of a young child's salvation, the infant being "free from the sin and stain of this low earth."[37] Upon the passing of her infant girl, Cornelia Peake McDonald recalled a friend's words of reassurance: "You may live to thank Him [God] for taking your precious little babe from the sorrow and evil to come."[38] Months later McDonald recorded, "I would not bring her back if I could to resume the burden her Savior removed that day when she fled from my arms as the sun was setting."[39]

Such statements represent an attitude toward the fragility of young life that is difficult for the 21st-century mind to accept, but it must have been a great consolation to parents who lost a child during the birthing process or later to sickness or accident. Even some of the popular literature of the antebellum period, such as Stowe's *Uncle Tom's Cabin,* seemingly celebrated the passing of young innocents because it was thought that their brief existence protected them from the corrupting influences of an unreformed world.

Rural cemeteries provided separate sections for children making it easier for a young family, unable to afford a family plot, to bury their child in a more comforting setting. These young or stillborn children could later be reinterred when the family was more established and secured a family plot or mausoleum. Families who could afford it often created gravestone markers steeped in sentiment and imagery. The most common image was that of the sleeping child. Sleep, as a tie between life and death, was a recurring theme of the period. The image makes a connection back to the home where the youth once slept. It brought to mind the comforting picture of a child safely tucked away in his or her bed. Other items appearing on memorials included rattles, dolls, or favorite playthings. The use of toys in such a permanent form reflects the period's recognition of the naturalness of play and a lasting reminder of the separate worlds of children and adults. Sculptural portrayals of children and their belongings ensured that they would remain forever one with the goodness of the home. They would be undisturbed and constant, forever innocent in the world. The child with a lamb is another recurring image that reinforced the belief in the closeness of children with nature.

Empty furniture was also depicted on many memorials. An unfilled chair or empty cradle was commonly used to symbolize the child's unfulfilled life. A song popular among families of the antebellum period, "The Vacant Chair," reinforces this graveyard imagery, as does another, "Sleep today, O early fallen, In thy green and narrow bed."[40] Judith McGuire, a Virginian at mid-century reflecting on the effects of the looming war with the North, wrote, "In all the broad South there will scarcely be a fold without its missing lamb, a fireside without its vacant chair."[41] In Charles Dickens's *A Christmas Carol* (1843), the author also used the imagery of the small chair, empty beside the fireplace, to fix in his readers' minds the potential tragedy to the Cratchit family of the loss of Tiny Tim to chronic illness. This was a fate all too common for children in a period with only the rudiments of proper medical knowledge to care for them.

Yet the fear that death held during this period focused less on of the ending of life and more on never having been loved nor lamented. In *A Christmas Carol*, Dickens portrays the spirits and ghosts of Christmas as remarkably worldly in their appearance and temporal in their outlook. The awakening of a social conscience in the character of Scrooge is uppermost in their endeavors. Nonetheless, it is the specter of his own unlamented death, a topic of great concern to persons of the 19th century, that brings Scrooge around. Yet even a morally awakened Scrooge refused to devote his life to social reform. Instead, he acts out his reformation on a very personal level assuring the survival of Tiny Tim as best he can.[42]

Mourners of the period went to great lengths to demonstrate their love and devotion to the deceased. Writing elegies for departed friends was popular. Sometimes these black-bordered tributes were attached to the coffin or to the hearse. Other times, they were decorated with designs abundant with death imagery and distributed as souvenirs to the mourners. It was not uncommon for them to be printed in local newspapers. When asked by a surviving friend to see to the proper care of a dead companion whom she had never known, Cornelia Peake McDonald wrote, "Betty and I wept over him tears of sincere sorrow, the more so as we thought that perhaps ours . . . would be all that would fall on his lonely bier."[43]

The loss of family members and the personal trauma of death became the focus a mourning ritual that became an extended, almost institutionalized process. Widows were expected to remain in mourning for two and a half years. This time was divided into three segments. During heavy mourning the widow wore only black with collars and cuffs of folded black, untrimmed crepe with no other trim. She might wear a simple bonnet but never a hat. Her face would be covered entirely in a long, heavy, black crepe veil whenever she left home. Silk fabrics could be used for dresses, bonnets, or capes, but these had to have matte finishes. Not even ribbons were allowed to have a gloss. Kid gloves were not permitted. Gloves had to be made from cotton or silk, or crocheted or knit from thread. Handkerchiefs were made of the sheerest white linen with a broad, deep black boarder. Jewelry was restricted to jet black—usually unpolished—and even that would not be worn during the initial months of bereavement. Dark furs were permitted in cold weather. Throughout the entire mourning period a widow's hair had to be worn in a simple style.

The initial period of deep mourning was followed by full mourning, which still required the wearing of black but permitted black lace collars and cuffs. Veils were permitted to be shortened and could be made of net or tulle. Lighter veils were also allowed. Handkerchiefs needed only to have a narrow black band border. Polished jet jewelry was allowed as well as some gold or glass beads. Half mourning was the final stage. During this period, print and solid colored dresses of gray or lavender were permitted. A bonnet might be trimmed with lace and have white or violet flowers adorning it. Common reading materials reinforced these customs. *Godey's Lady's Book* carried a story about a young woman preparing to attend her first party after the death of her father. The young woman declined to wear simple bracelet pearls, fearing she would be too conspicuous, thus illustrating the strong effect mourning ritual had on fashion propriety.[44]

Some women, of course, chose to remain in mourning for longer periods, even the rest of their lives. It was not unusual even in a small community to have scores of women, of various ages, attired totally in black for the remainder of their lives after the death of beloved husbands. However, widowhood could provide a number of social and economic benefits especially with regard to the control of money and property, a privilege denied to most married females. Moreover, a properly behaved widow could fall back upon her bereavement to ward off the pressure from her relatives to remarry. Nonetheless, for women who wanted to remarry in a period of less than two and a half years, accommodations were made. She was permitted to be married without great ceremony in a conservative gray dress, but she was also expected to complete the period of mourning following the new union out of respect for the first husband. If a woman married a widower, she was expected to dress in half mourning for the remainder of her husband's mourning period.

Not surprisingly, men were not so nearly restricted in their attire or activities during mourning as women, possibly because they needed to continue to earn a living. Their period of public bereavement lasted from as little as three months to a full year depending on their relationship to the deceased. Fashion required them to wear a plain white shirt with black clothes, shoes, gloves, and hat. This differed little from what the properly dressed businessman would wear in any case. Some men followed this with a period of gray. The only distinguishing additions would be a black crepe band on their arm, on their hat, or sewn to the border of their cuffs. Widowers were encouraged to remarry following a respectable period, particularly if they had young children. Mourning attire was suspended for the wedding day, but reestablished immediately thereafter.

Children were not sheltered from death and mourning. Mrs. Lydia Child, in her *Mother's Book*, advises that children not be allowed to be frightened by death. She encourages mothers to share the beautiful imagery of returning to heaven, to be with the angels, with even very young children. Older children were to take part in the mourning ritual wearing black and crepe upon the death of a parent for six months, followed by three months each of full and half mourning with lessening degrees of black. Children in mourning under the age of 12 wore white in the summer and gray in the winter. Suits were trimmed with black buttons, belts, or ribbons. Even infant robes were trimmed in black. Often, out of practicality, children's regular clothing was dyed for mourning rather than purchased new.

A woman mourning the death of her father, mother, or child wore black for a period of one year. For grandparents, siblings, or someone having left the mourner an inheritance, the proper period was six months. The obligation for an aunt, uncle, niece, or nephew extended for only three months and white trim was allowed throughout this time. Families in mourning often restricted their contacts with the outside world. Following the death of her mother-in-law, Mary Chesnut made the following diary entry: "Mr. Chesnut being in such deep mourning for his mother, we see no company."[45]

Martine's Hand-Book of Etiquette, and Guide to True Politeness details the proper protocol for condolence visitation:

Visits of condolence should be paid within a week after the event which occasions them; but if the acquaintance be slight, immediately after the family appear at public worship. A card should be sent up; and if your friends are able to receive you, let your manners and conversation be in harmony with the character of your visit. It is courteous to send up a mourning card; and for ladies to make their call in black silk or plain-colored apparel. It denotes that they sympathize with the afflictions of the family; and such attentions are always pleasing.[46]

Mourning dress was one of the first areas where mass-produced clothing gained acceptance. The need for the proper attire to conform to the rigid rules regarding dress often came unexpectedly. There were many people who felt that it was unlucky to keep black crepe in the home between deaths. Surviving items from previous losses were often discarded after they were no longer required. Providing mourning attire and accessories became a worthwhile commercial endeavor. Some retailers, such as J.S. Chase and Company of Boston, dealt exclusively in mourning goods. There was a great demand for black crepe for veils, collars, cuffs, skirt trim, and armbands. Other needed items included black hat pins, straight pins, and buttons. Millinery and jewelry, which met the expectations of society, were equally in demand. Mourning caps were such common items, with virtually no design differences for age or demand for customization, that milliners commonly made these when they had nothing else to do. Those in mourning also required stationery and calling cards that were bordered in black. Many companies made fortunes in mourning clothing and related ancillary materials.

Perhaps the most favored of these goods was mourning jewelry. Sentimental melancholy for its own sake was a hallmark of gentility and refinement. The simple wearing of mourning jewelry transferred virtue to the wearer. Mourning pins and rings were given to mourners as keepsakes. Frequently, in the interest of economy, the gifts were of two price levels. The more expensive gifts were given to close friends and family, whereas less-expensive items could be more widely distributed.

Jet, onyx, and black glass or "French jet" were extensively used, but it was jet that reached an unprecedented popularity. Whereas "French jet" is black glass, true jet is fossilized driftwood formed, like coal, by decaying vegetation over hundreds of thousands of years. Jet is found in stagnant water—often seawater, and the greater the depth of the water, the harder it is. Jet was made into carved beads for necklaces, brooches, bracelets, and earrings. Its inherent lightness allowed for the creation of pieces that would have been impractical had they been made from another material. Additionally, jet was relatively inexpensive, yet it was attractive and properly somber.

Another jewelry trend that came into full flower in this period was "hair work." This was not a new fashion. To some degree, hair jewelry had been popular from the beginning of the century, but during the war it reached new heights. Rings, lockets, brooches, bracelets, watch chains, almost any kind of jewelry was likely to include human hair in one way or another. Sometimes the hair was that of a living person, but more often it was from a departed loved one. The period song, "Bear Gently, So Gently, Roughly Made Bier," subtitled "Burial at Camp," contains the following line: "From the damp clotted hair sever one precious tress."[47] Judith McGuire concluded her record of a burial with: "We cut a lock of his hair, as the only thing we could do for his mother."[48]

Godey's Lady's Book championed the use of hair jewelry quoting an English writer, Leigh Hun, who said, "Hair is at once the most delicate and lasting of our materials, and survives us, like love. It is so light, so gentle, so escaping from the idea of death, that with a lock of hair belonging to a child or friend, we may almost look up to heaven and compare notes with the angelic nature—may almost say: 'I have a piece of thee here, not unworthy of thy being now.'"[49]

The simplest method to prepare such a relic was to encase a lock of hair under a crystal that would be mounted in a ring, brooch, or locket. More elaborate pieces contained miniature allegories of grief. Often, parts of designs, or their entirety, were made of human hair. Sometimes, the miniatures were portraits of the deceased mounted on a background of their hair. Another variation of this form was "hair painting." This "lost art" appears to have used finely chopped hair mixed into the pigments of the paint, but no description of the exact process seems to have survived. Finally, hair was sometimes plaited in many strands and was then formed into watch chains, fobs, brooches, rings, necklaces, earrings, and bracelets. These might have been made for oneself from the hair of a loved one or made as a gift out of the giver's hair.

Pattern books like Campbell's *Self-Instructor* contained numerous patterns for incredibly intricate hair jewelry designs. *Godey's Lady's Book* offered designs, instructions, and even finished pieces. If a woman had not the talent to create a piece herself, she could furnish the hair to a jeweler who would then create the desired item based on hundreds of designs that were offered.

The rising popularity of photography during the period also extended into the mourning ritual, and some photographers specialized in posthumous pictures. Period advertisements carried the names of many photographers who offered this specialty. The photographer normally came to the home, but it was not unusual for the deceased to be taken to the studio. Infants were the most common subjects of this type of photograph. Perhaps this was because there had been little opportunity to capture the child's likeness in life; or perhaps it provided a concrete reminder of a life that had passed too quickly. The deceased child might be posed cradled in a parent's arms or might be shown resting on a pillow as if in sleep.

Future President James Garfield, serving as a soldier in the Civil War, hurried home to have a picture taken with his dead infant in his arms. Photographers sometimes borrowed from the imagery of portrait painters and included a cut rose in the picture symbolizing a bloom cut early—the death of a child. The family of Maria Jane Hurd created a memorial card for the deceased 12-year-old, which contained her portrait, copied from a daguerreotype taken at age six. Beneath this, they enumerated her "Resolutions for the New Year," which were "found in her little portfolio after her death."[50]

A woman in mourning often occupied herself with stitchery, paperwork, or other memorial projects. Memorial work abounded with symbolism. A butterfly symbolized the passing from this world to the next. A sheaf of wheat denoted the passing of an elderly person. Pansies, in the language of flowers, meant "think of me." The most persistent symbol, by far, was the weeping willow. The very shape of the willow brought to mind the image of a mourner bent over with grief. Mourners in funerals often carried willow branches as symbols of resurrection. Personalized items such as pets, ships, churches, and distant towns were also memorialized.

Memorial pictures worked in silk embroidery were most common. A typical scene contained black-clad mourners beside an urn-topped gravestone beneath the hanging boughs of a weeping willow tree. Some memorial pictures were painted, frequently by young girls still in school. These could be for a relative long deceased or could be kept and then completed by inscribing the name of that person on the waiting tomb at a later date. Occasionally, they were used for the painter herself. During the late 1830s, memorial pictures published by Nathaniel Currier could be purchased as lithographs. A mourning card could then be pasted on to complete the scene. Another form of memorial, although less popular, was cut paperwork. The cut paperwork contained similar imagery, and the contrast of white against black was stark and visually effective. These could either be done by the mourner or purchased and personalized by inserting a memorial card identifying the deceased.

Theorem paintings, oils, and pen-and-ink sketches were also created as memorials but with less frequency. Watercolors were also used to construct memorials. These tended to be gayer than some other kinds of works due to the colors. Watercolors were even used in conjunction with other forms of artwork. Some embroidered pictures contained watercolor skies or had watercolor faces pasted or sewn on to the needlework. As many as four different media could be used in the creation of a single work.

Immortals were fairly large, ornate floral arrangements made from wax, cloth, beads, or hair and were covered by tall glass cases. The complex designs contained flowers that were often made from hair of the deceased, which had been woven or braided over wire. Wreaths might also include yarn, seeds, berries, feathers, or dried flowers. These were later framed in shadowboxes to be displayed in parlors. Sheaves of wheat used to decorate the casket were often preserved in a similar fashion.

Death rituals among slaves and free blacks, especially in the South, often retained their African meanings. In dying, one "went home." To a slave, this was a reason to celebrate, for it meant freedom. Graves were decorated, as they were in Africa, with the last items that the deceased had used. The most common articles were pottery or glass containers, but medicine bottles, toys, dolls, and quilts were also used. It was essential that the items be broken in order to break the tie to the living. Failure to do so was believed to invite a similar fate to the surviving family. Some slave owners gave a portion of the day for the funeral of a departed slave and even allotted food for the following celebration. Others required that the funeral be held at night. Mourning clothing restrictions were not likely a part of slave mourning traditions; however, evidence suggests that some slaves had mourning clothing. It is very likely that these items were initially purchased for them following the death of "the master" and could later be used to mourn losses in their own family or community.

Although the process of embalming had long been known, the effort to preserve physical remains had not been practiced beyond the needs of medical research. During the Civil War, however, a new market opened. Itinerant embalmers, mostly doctors, traveled to battlefields and used arterial embalming to preserve bodies for shipment home. In some instances, these embalmers contracted their services to soldiers prior to battle in the event of their demise. This process created a professionalism not found in "undertaking" before the war. It was no longer enough to provide a coffin, a horse, and a special carriage. Undertakers now required a special skill that set them apart from the carpenters and casket makers who preceded them.

THE ECONOMY

A Nation of Mechanics

Early America was deemed a nation of mechanics by the more theoretically focused scientists of Europe. The 19th-century sense of the term "mechanics" included artisans, craftsmen, and other persons who worked with their hands. Today we would classify them as technicians rather than research scientists. America was certainly a nation of mechanics during the antebellum period, and it continued to be so throughout the remainder of the century.

American inventors made the United States a warehouse of wonders for the world. While European scientists delved into the nature of matter, heat, light, or electricity, Americans were producing practical applications of these scientific principles in the form of inventions that generally helped to improve life. These inventors showed great ingenuity in the antebellum period, and important advances were made in many fields, including the development of a practical telegraph, the evolution of the mechanical reaper, the use of ether as anesthesia, and the harnessing of steam power for waterborne commerce. Other the other hand, the invention of safety matches, the development of a lace-making machine, and the patenting of the attached rubber pencil eraser seemed frivolous. Yet all of these advances affected the daily lives of those in the antebellum period.

Inventions

During the antebellum period it was not unusual for a person to choose a career as an inventor. Inventiveness seemed to be an American trait, and it was widely believed that any mechanical problem could be solved if one applied enough hard work and creativity to it. As early as 1820, German political economist Georg Friedrich List wrote, "There is no clinging to old ways; the moment an America hears the word invention he pricks up his ears."[51]

Unfortunately, as more inventors worked on a particular problem, their solutions tended to converge around the naturally correct one. This is a repetitive characteristic of the practice of engineering known as "convergent technology." In 1838, Congress created a new patent law to deal with competing claims to inventions. Up to that time, anyone who claimed a

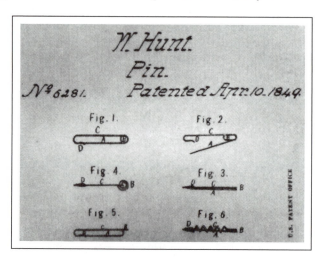

The patent drawings for a newly developed
safety pin submitted to the U.S. Patent Office
in 1849 are deceptively simple.

patent received one, even if competing claims for the same invention were made. The new law established, for the first time, the principles of formal research, requiring the patent office to withhold a patent until all other prior patents had been scrutinized for the inclusion of important original ideas. Ironically, the pace of invention accelerated under the new law. Before 1838, no more than 500 patents had been granted. In the next decade alone, more than 10, 000 were issued. Unscrupulous advertisers used this circumstance to advance themselves in the newspapers as agents of the Patent Office, who for a fee, would act as "preparers of Caveats, Specificiations, Assignments, and all the necessary Papers and Drawings" so that inventors might be "saved the time and cost of a journey to Washington, and the delay there, as well as [being saved] all the personal trouble in obtaining their patents."[52]

Labor

The greatest changes in employment and manufacturing prior to the Civil War were in the transition from hand labor to increased mechanization in almost every task. Household manufacturing, which was still widespread in the 1820s, declined in importance during the next four decades. Many of the items consumers once made for themselves, including basic things such as tools, textiles, and clothing, now came from factories. The craftsman, who previously made goods to the specifications of individual customers who they knew, now enlarged his shop or took a place in a factory to turn out ready-made products for the general public. The financial capital needed for increasing mechanization caused certain geographic areas blessed with inexpensive waterpower or access to raw materials to become centers for the manufacture of specific items. Danbury, Connecticut, with its hat factories; Lowell, Massachusetts, with its textile mills; and Pittsburgh, Pennsylvania, with its iron foundries are examples.

Domestic manufacture remained strong in many rural areas of the country and in many industries where it was not immediately possible to apply power and machine technology to the required task. Shoemaking can serve as an example in this regard. At a time when power machinery had not yet been developed for making shoes, the process was one ruled by trained specialists who made hand-cut and hand-sewn shoes. The invention of a machine to produce small wooden pegs to attach the leather soles to the upper part of the shoe changed the way shoemakers assembled their wares. The quiet stitching of sole to upper was replaced by the dull sound of the cobbler's hammer. At the same time, sewing machine technology was successfully applied to the stitching of leather, resulting in the establishment of factories in which women sewed the uppers together and the men attached them to the lower structure of the shoe and fitted the finished product with soles and heels by hand. As a result of mechanization, there were more people involved in shoemaking than in any other industry in the nation save agriculture. By 1858, Lyman Blake had patented a sewing machine that attached the soles to the uppers mechanically, greatly facilitating the shoemaking process. This made the price of shoes, especially work shoes, much more affordable. Sizes and widths were first introduced to shoe production at this time. The general public could now buy shoes in sizes, and slave owners could provide cheaply made shoes to slaves by the barrel. Although harness and saddle making remained male-dominated crafts, the extension of power stitching to the entire shoemaking process left the traditional shoemaker with little beyond specialty work and a small repair business.

The conversion to machine operations brought many more women in to the manufacturing trades and wrought changes in the relationship between labor and management that reverberate even today. The right to strike was first established by the Massachusetts State Court in 1842 when a group of mill girls in Lowell, Massachusetts, refused to return to work at their looms because of long working hours. In 1860, 800 female workers from the shoemaking factory in Lynn, Massachusetts, went

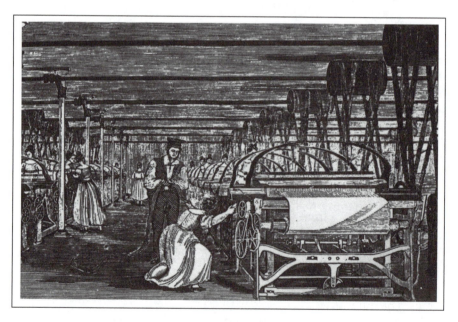

Labor in the factory mills of New England was difficult for the women who generally manned the machines. The foreman—always male—took little pity on hardworking "mill girls," who often put in 16 hours a day at the machines for very limited wages.

on strike for higher wages. They took to the streets dressed in their best hoopskirts and carrying parasols in a March snowstorm. The strike lasted more than two weeks, and the results were somewhat ambiguous with the shop manager being thrown into a pond. Nonetheless, as the Civil War began, many Northern women were hired to make pistol holsters, riding boots, infantry shoes, cartridge boxes, and other leather items, and other women wove the cloth and sewed the uniforms for hundreds of thousands of Federal soldiers on water-powered mechanical looms and sewing machines. These ladies generally filled the civilian positions of men drafted away from their trades and into the Federal armies.

Clothing Production

During the previous century, machines had been adapted to producing not only cloth, but also knitted stockings and socks in wool and cotton. The immediate effect of this mechanization was to place an entire category of traditional stocking makers out of work. This had resulted in local uprisings in England and France by workers in this area of clothing production. Stocking looms, machinery, and the slotted wooden cards that controlled the complex operation were attacked. French workers wedged a wooden shoe, or sabot, into the mechanisms to disrupt production thereby giving rise to the related term "saboteur."

The development of a practical sewing machine contributed not only to the domestic production of clothing but also to the growth of the ready-made clothing industry. John A. Doge and John Knowles invented the first American sewing machine in 1818, but their machine failed to join any useful amount of fabric before malfunctioning. Barthelemy Thimonnier produced the first functional sewing machine in 1830 in France. This hand-cranked model sewed well, but produced only a chain stitch, like that used in embroidery. If the loose ends of the thread were pulled, the entire stitch might unravel. In 1834, Walter Hunt, an American, produced a hand-cranked machine that could sew in a straight line with remarkable speed, but it was Elias Howe who patented the lockstitch mechanism in 1846. This used thread from two different sources, one following the needle and the other on a reciprocating shuttle, that locked each stitch in place by passing one thread through a loop created in the other.

Howe's lockstitch method was effective, and other inventors in this area adopted it. Principle among these was Isaac Singer, who put his machines into mass production around 1850. Singer's machine had several improvements over that of Howe's. The needle moved up and down rather than side to side, allowing the operator to more readily make turns and curves when joining fabric. Moreover, many of his models were powered by a foot treadle, leaving both hands free to guide the fabric. Singer also incorporated into his mechanism Allen Wilson's invention of a rotary

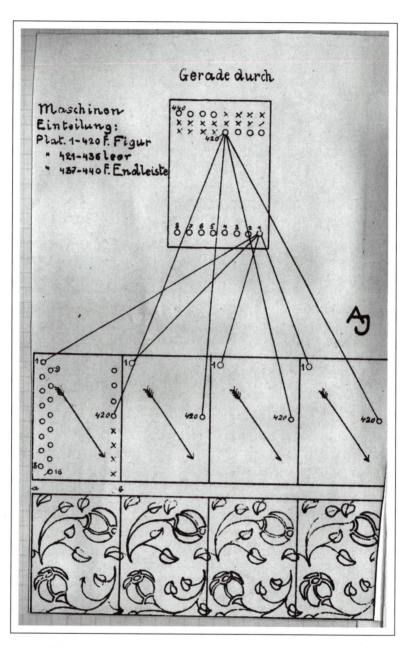

This fabric guide for setting up a power loom is in German. A wooden card set up in this fashion would cause the loom to weave the pattern at the bottom. This new technology was almost like programming a computer.

shuttle hook. In 1854, Howe sued Singer for infringement of the lockstitch patent and won patent royalties from him. Howe realized more than 2 million dollars from these royalties during the next 10 years. During the Civil War, he donated a large portion of this money to the Union Army, equipping an entire infantry regiment at his own expense.

By 1860, the continuous stitch sewing machine, first used with cloth, had quickly been modified to make lacework. An English patent for a lacework machine had been granted to John Fisher in 1844 but the patent had been lost in the Royal Patent Office, opening this area of manufacture to a wide variety of imitators. However, intricate handmade lacework remained more fashionable with consumers than the machine-made product throughout the period.

Farming

Agriculture was also the beneficiary of new processes, simplified methods, and the genuine mechanical insight that characterized this period of invention. In 1834, Cyrus McCormick patented a mechanical reaper that increased agricultural efficiency and volume of food production enormously. Almost 1,000 of the 6,600 patents issued in 1857 and 1858 were for agricultural and farm machinery—many of which were variations on McCormick's patent. Theories abound that laborsaving farm machines would have eradicated race-based slavery within the century, but such inventions tended to benefit Northern farmworkers more than slaves on Southern plantations where free manual labor remained more economical than costly machines.

Notwithstanding the economy of slave labor, as early as 1794 Eli Whitney saw the need to mechanize the time-consuming removal of cottonseeds from the desirable long staple raw cotton. His invention of the cotton gin made cotton fiber a more thoroughly marketable material and stimulated the growth of cotton agriculture in the South. The widespread adoption of the cotton gin during the antebellum period allowed a slave, who could process 100 pounds of cotton per day without the machine, to produce 1,000 pounds of fiber in the same amount of time. Unfortunately, it also breathed new life into the institution of slavery by making cotton production more profitable and providing a financial bulwark for the retention of slavery in the Deep South. By mid-century, cotton accounted for two-thirds of the exports of the United States. The profitability of cotton increased both the number and the value of slaves as plantation owners put more and more acreage under cultivation and attempted to spread the practice of slavery to new territories. Estimates show that by 1860 there were more than 3.6 million black slaves in the states that were to form the Confederacy. Without the cotton gin, the archaic plantation system might well have faded into obscurity.

Mass Production

One of the outgrowths of industrialization was the development of the concept of mass production. Among other innovations, Eli Whitney's application of the concept of interchangeable parts in the mass production of all types of mechanical items stands out among his accomplishments. This was particularly true with regard to the manufacture of firearms. Formerly, a musket or rifle was built by a single craftsman or small group of gunsmiths who fitted the weapon together piece by interconnecting pieces—lock, stock, and barrel. Every screw and fastener was handmade and hand-fitted. The lock, a complicated mechanism that began the firing sequence, might contain a dozen tiny parts, each fitted precisely to its neighbors by hand. However, the parts from one lock might not fit with the parts from another, even if the same gunsmith made them. Because each weapon produced in this manner was different, the process slowed the manufacture of large quantities of weapons and made even simple repairs difficult and time consuming. In a two-year period, using traditional methods, the national armories of the United States produced a total of only 1,000 muskets. Many weapons designed for the civilian market came with their own bullet molds and fired a unique caliber of bullet. The standardization and distribution of military ammunition was also time consuming and difficult.

By utilizing precision machine tools, Whitney hoped to standardize the precision with which parts were manufactured and ensure that those from one weapon could be interchanged with those of another with little fuss. Moreover, ammunition could be distributed and shared among the troops of the same army, and spare parts could be kept on hand for quick repairs in the field. In a demonstration before President Thomas Jefferson in late 1801, Whitney assembled a number of complete, operable muskets from piles of parts picked at random by generally skeptical government officials. In 1804, Whitney signed a contract with the Federal government for the manufacture of 10,000 muskets in just two years; however, he constantly had to plead for extra time to complete the contract as he ran into unforeseen obstacles. Nonetheless, by 1818, he had installed an advanced machine-milling tool at the Federal arsenal at Springfield, Massachusetts. Thereafter, the ideas of mass production and interchangeable parts that Whitney pioneered remained the basis for the machine manufacture of all types of precision devices. Whitney died in 1825, but his son, Eli Whitney Jr., continued to operate his father's arms manufactory in Hamden, Connecticut.[53]

In 1835, Samuel Colt invented the first practical revolving pistol. Colt's firearm, with its many imitators, became the standard for all cap-and-ball revolvers of the Civil War. Colt sold millions of his revolvers in both the military and civilian markets. Exhausted cylinders from one Colt pistol could be quickly interchanged for a new one in a few seconds. In 1854, Horace Smith and Daniel Wesson invented the first practical brass cartridge revolver that could be quickly loaded with a self-contained load of powder and bullet. Smith and Wesson revolvers were generally of too small a caliber to be adopted by the military, but soldiers brought thousands to war as "lifesavers." Only with the precision of machines could the cartridges be turned out in vast number. In 1858, Christian Sharps produced an efficient breech-loading rifle for military use based on his own 1848 patent that eliminated the need to ram home a charge from the muzzle end of the weapon. The Sharps carbine saw a great deal of action in the bloody conflict between the proslavery and abolitionist forces in Missouri, and it was one of the weapons supplied to antislavery zealots by supporters of John Brown. Nonetheless, the armies generally issued breechloaders only to cavalry or other specialty troops, and muzzle-loading long arms remained the premier weapon of most Civil War infantry.

In 1855, the Federal government adopted the highly efficient conical minié ball as a standard bullet for its infantry firearms. This lethal bullet of approximately .58 caliber, developed by Captain Claude Minié, could be loaded into rifles more easily than round balls of the same weight. When fired, the soft lead at the base of the minié ball expanded to grip the spiral rifling in the barrel thereby increasing, in a single invention, both the accuracy and the rate of fire of a military musket. The adoption of the minié ball by both sides in the Civil War, and by many foreign powers, is a leading factor in explaining the increased casualty rates among soldiers in battle as compared to prior conflicts. Although only a few weapons were fitted with the new telescopic sight, most military muskets of the period had open sights that could be adjusted to hit targets at 800 yards or more. It has been estimated that more than 3 million minié balls and other small-arms rounds were fired during the three days of battle at Gettysburg (1863) alone.

Metallurgy

By 1840, wood charcoal had been replaced as a fuel and reducing agent in blast furnaces producing pig iron by a more efficient byproduct of coal called "coke." The consequent decrease in the price of ferric materials spurred a spate of technological advancement in the areas of architecture, engineering, power, and transportation. In 1840, the first pianofortes were produced using a cast-iron frame that would not be crushed under the tremendous tension of the dozens of wire piano strings. This led to a major revolution in concert music. In 1848, cast iron was used for the first time to build multistoried buildings, and the height of these tall structures, some reaching more than five floors, moved Elisha Otis to invent the safety elevator for passengers in 1853. Higher quality iron and steel, taken together with a theoretical revolution in steam technology, allowed George Corliss to patent a more efficient four-valve steam engine in 1849, which, in turn, spurred the introduction of horse-drawn steam fire engines. The U.S. Patent Office issued more than 350 patents for improved steam engines, boilers, and railroad or steamboat equipment in the decade of the 1850s alone.

Telegraphy

A fundamental revolution in communications was begun in 1844 when Samuel F.B. Morse sent the first telegraph message from Baltimore to Washington. The essential technological advance that allowed Morse to create telegraphy was the ability to draw out copper wire at an economical price, which was developed by the British metallurgical industry a decade earlier. Up to that point, electric communication over long distances was simply not feasible, even if the technological challenges of telegraphy had been surmounted earlier. Morse's ability to send a message by electric current over wires many miles apart was the result of over a decade of research and was built upon the development of the wet cell battery by Italian Alessandro Volta in 1800 and the electromagnetic studies of the American scientist Joseph Henry at Princeton University in 1836.

Volta had used the natural characteristics of two different metals and an acid to build a "voltaic cell" or battery. It was unlike the Leyden jars of Benjamin Franklin, which could be charged with static electricity that discharged almost instantaneously when a conducting loop was inserted between the poles. The battery, composed of zinc and copper discs placed alternately on top of one another and interleaved with cardboard moistened with a dilute acid, produced a steady electric current as long as there was metal left to be consumed. While no two pieces of metal produced a large voltage, by placing each cell in series (positive to negative) with the next, the individual voltages were added. By the time of the Civil War, a practical battery made from two different compounds of lead and sulfuric acid was available. A series of these batteries allowed the U.S. Military Telegraph, a branch of the Federal Army, to send a message over 10 miles of wire from a single wagon fitted with telegraphic equipment.

Joseph Henry—working part time and without the splendid facilities of his scientific rival Michael Faraday at the Royal Society of London—had increased the size and power of the battery and had invented the first electromagnet, the first electric motor, and the first electromagnetic telegraph, with which he sent a faint signal through a mile of wire arrayed around his laboratory. While neither his motor nor his telegraph were more than laboratory toys, Henry had also devised a system of relays by which a current, made faint by traveling through a long length of wire, might be increased and exactly repeated. This was a pivotal discovery shared by Henry during his meetings with Morse in 1835 and utilized by Morse to make long-distance transmission possible. Henry also suggested in 1843 that Morse's wire could be insulated by stringing it high above the ground from glass knobs fixed to wooden poles. In the same year Morse ran an underwater wire, insulated in a natural material similar to rubber known as gutta-percha, 13 miles from Martha's Vinyard to Nantucket.

The telegraph key used to send the sets of dots and dashes was designed by a partner of Morse named Alfred Vail. It was a simple strip of spring steel that could be pressed against a metal contact to send letters and numerals via a predetermined code. Later models of the transmitting key and the signal receiver were developed about a pivoting lever action that allowed the gap to be more easily adjusted. Also significant were Morse's consultations with another partner, Leonard Gale, a professor of chemistry at New York University, regarding electrochemistry. Armed with the discoveries of Volta, Henry, Vail, and Gale, and his own innovations, Morse produced a telegraph that was an immediate success. The 1844 patent application for the telegraph also included a method for recording the dots and dashes on paper. This and the code itself were the only parts of the invention solely attributable to Morse.

Within 10 years of the first telegraphic message, more than 23,000 miles of telegraph wire crisscrossed the country. Newspapers quickly began using the "wires" to collect news, and the Associated Press and other news agencies set up their own wire services. By 1848, even small communities were reading dispatches from the Mexican War. However, there was no traffic control system for the various independent telegraph companies or even for individual operators within the same company. Several operators might obliterate any meaning among the hundreds of dots and dashes by trying to use the same line at the same time. In 1856, Hiram Sibley founded Western Union, which eventually bought up all the patents for competing telegraphy systems and combined the best features of each into one dependable system.

In 1858, after two attempts, Cryrus W. Field was able to lay a continuous transatlantic telegraphic cable from Newfoundland to Ireland. It worked for some time, and the public reacted with jubilation. However, mishandling of the insulation during the cable's deployment caused the underwater line to fail. Nonetheless, the cause of fault was known and could be addressed, but not before the war intervened.

On the eve of the Civil War, telegraph wires connected most Eastern cities, a transcontinental telegraph connected New York to California, and a transatlantic telegraphic cable—although then silent—stretched from Canada to Europe. The telegraph profoundly affected Americans. It helped develop the American West, made railroad travel safer, allowed businesses to communicate more efficiently, and spread political speeches and ideas across the country in a single day. The Confederate Army utilized the existing civilian telegraphic system of the South to issue orders between commanders and to communicate with the government in Richmond, and Abraham Lincoln was known to spend long hours contemplating the war reports in the Western Union office in Washington, D.C. However, telegraphy also brought the horrors of battle and long lists of casualties from the front lines of the war almost instantaneously to the parlors of America.

Morse was plagued by lawsuits regarding his telegraphic patents. This was a common circumstance among inventors during the period as they sought to claim sole credit for complex inventions. Although Henry consistently backed Morse and frequently appeared in his defense in court, Morse became embittered toward him. This may have been due to the scientific community's recognition of Henry as the first builder of an electromagnetic telegraph. They understood, better than Morse, the complexity and difficulty of his accomplishment, especially the role played by Henry's relay. In 1855, Morse attacked Henry in the press. He wrote, "I shall show that I am not indebted to him for any discoveries in science bearing upon the telegraph." Henry refused to take up the argument himself. Instead, he applied to the Board of Regents of the Smithsonian Institution to look into the matter. In 1857, they found Morse's arguments "a disingenuous piece of sophisticated argument [that] perverted the truth." This generally ended the controversy, and Henry went forward to help found the National Academy of Sciences and the American Association for the Advancement of Science. During the Civil War, Henry served as a science advisor to President Lincoln.[54]

Photography

In 1839 when Louis Daguerre invented the daguerreotype, the first successful form of photography, he had little idea that it would be an American, Matthew Brady, who would become the best-known photographer of the antebellum period. Brady established studios in New York and Washington before the war and gained lasting fame for his visual record of the Civil War. His photographic galleries were very popular and admission was expensive, yet people flocked to his studios to have photographic portraits taken in their best clothes. *Cartes de Visite*, photographs a little larger than modern business cards mounted on thick cardboard stock, were possibly the most popular form of civilian photograph in the early period. Thousands of such photos exist. "Cabinet photos," of a size on the order of five inches by eight inches, were much more rare. Lacking the ability to make enlargements from negatives, the photographs of this period were largely contact prints. These were the same size as the glass plate negative. Photographers used ingenious methods for producing duplicates, including having four to eight lenses mounted on their cameras simultaneously thereby producing the same number of identical pictures on a single glass plate in a sitting.

Food Preservation

The technology of preserving foods in tinned iron cans had been developed by the French in the first decade of the century, and was first patented in America by Ezra Daggett in 1825. The heat used in preparing the contents destroyed the bacteria, and the sealed container prevented new contamination. By 1849, a machine was developed that limited the amount of hand labor needed to produce tin cans, further stimulating the processing of food as a commercial endeavor. Lobster and salmon were the first foods to be commercially canned. The canning of corn, tomatoes, peas, peaches, and additional varieties of fish rapidly followed. The patenting by Gail Borden of a process for making canned condensed milk in 1856 was a major step forward in this area. By 1860, 5 million tinned cans were being produced annually. Although the process was decades old, many American men saw their very first canned foods during the war. Less momentous advances in the area of food preservation included the invention of the icebox by Thomas Moore in 1803; the successfully shipping of ice from New England to the West Indies in insulated containers in 1805; and the patenting of an early system for refrigeration in 1834 by Jacob Perkins.

Science

In Europe during the 1820s and 1830s, an entire generation of science students was being exposed to research laboratories, observatories, medical schools, hospitals, and scientific institutes. Many Americans went to England, Germany, France, Italy, Switzerland, and Sweden to learn the theoretical principles of science, and they returned to America to try to share the practical aspects of the science they had learned. However, they were faced with an American public who did not see the need for theoretical science of this sort and could not imagine how the marriage of science and technology could be of any use in developing the economy or settling the political questions that faced the nation. Inventions seemed to spew forth from ingenious and creative sources rather than from formally trained researchers. Only after the economic and industrial development in America had a foothold did the need for formal technical education become apparent.

The 1840s was the first period in American history to have an extensive group of professional scientists and researchers on hand, but Americans did not seem to know what to do with them as they valued novel gadgets and innovative machines over high-sounding theories. Nonetheless, in the physical sciences, Joseph Henry in Albany was keeping pace with the electrical discoveries of Michael Faraday. Charles Goodyear was vulcanizing rubber for which he received a French patent in 1844. George Henry Corliss was busy improving the steam engine in Providence, Rhode Island.

In the field of earth science, Matthew F. Maury was charting the prevailing winds and ocean currents of the sea-lanes of the world by consulting the logs of the whaling vessels, taking anecdotal evidence, and compiling the results. He shared his findings with the skippers of the clipper ships, which set speed records around Cape Horn by using them. In 1842, James P. Epsy was appointed the country's first national meteorologist, and Charles Wilkes was leading an expedition of discovery along the Arctic coast. In 1854, Benjamin Silliman, Jr., was analyzing crude oil samples from the Titusville, Pennsylvania, oil field of Colonel Edwin Drake—an important development in petroleum exploration in America.

In the field of biological sciences, Asa Gray was on his way to becoming America's leading botanist. At the same time, a 31-year-old dentist named Dr. Horace Wells had discovered the numbing effect of nitrous oxide gas. He convinced Dr. Crawford Long to use the gas in his surgery in 1842 while removing a tumor. The operation was performed with no evidence of suffering on the part of the patient. Another dentist, Dr. William Morton, discovered the properties of sulfuric ether as an anesthetic. In 1846, as he applied the ether, Dr. J.C. Warren, a renowned surgeon at Massachusetts General Hospital, performed the removal of a tumor from the face of a patient. At the conclusion of the surgery, Warren exclaimed to all present, "Gentlemen, this is no humbug!" The first use of ether as an anesthetic created a great sensation in the medical world and a good deal of controversy over the patenting of the method. Oliver Wendell Holmes, the doctor-poet of the antebellum period, wrote, "Everybody wants to have a hand in [this] great discovery."[55]

Jeffries Wyman, a professor of anatomy at the Lawrence Scientific School (at Harvard) accumulated a vast stock of anatomical data on apes and gorillas that contributed to Charles Darwin's theory of evolution. His careful investigations of the anatomy of the "Negro" and "Caucasian" races in 1850 had great technical merit, but his findings were used in an unfortunate manner by slave masters to uphold the concept of a natural order of society based on racial slavery. Many of the thousands of patented inventions and technical breakthroughs made during the antebellum period can be demonstrated to have led directly to the modern form of today's American society.

Strangely, the Civil War would produce an entire cadre of surgeons whose skills were honed in the many battlefield surgical tents that characterized the war. Surgeons were pushed to the limits of their skills by battlefield wounds and were forced by circumstances to experiment with new procedures and protocols. This experience accelerated the science of medicine in the decades after the war.

Industry

It is commonly thought that the economy of the American South—those states that would become the Confederacy—was deficient when compared to that of the North in many critical areas of industry, including manufacturing, transportation, and communications. Certainly the North, treated as a separate nation, was one of the giants of industrial production on the world stage prior to the Civil War, ranking just behind Great Britain in the value of its manufacturing output. However, the Southern Confederacy, taken as an independent nation, would have ranked as the fourth richest among all the economies of the world in 1860, having more wealth than many industrial countries such as France, Germany, or Denmark. Admittedly, Southern economic strengths lay largely in its agricultural production, but its manufacturing base was better developed than many other nations that were considered to have entered the industrial age at the time.

Much of the South's fortune and capital continued to be tied up in land and in slaves leaving little for investment. With increasing wealth built upon shipbuilding, whaling, shop keeping, and textile production, there was no similar lack of uncommitted capital in the North. The growth of the factory-owning middle class in the North during the first decades of the antebellum period was rapid and remarkable. New factories and machinery had absorbed more than $50 million of Northern investment capital in the decades of the 1820s and 1830s. Some Northern money went to fund canals and other long-term projects, but only a small portion of Northern wealth found its way into Southern industrial development.

Although agriculture remained the main occupation of most people, many small-business New England farmers and agricultural workers, existing on the margins of poverty, abandoned the farm fields and livestock pens to take unskilled jobs in the factories. Additionally, thousands of impoverished and unskilled Irish immigrants were herded into the mills of New England to work up to 16 hours a day. Cotton mills in Massachusetts began producing cloth with water-powered machinery as early as 1823. Uriah Boyden invented a more efficient turbine waterwheel in 1844, and company-owned mill towns like Holyoke, Massachusetts, located at the falls in the Connecticut River and founded to support the textile industry there, grew to house thousands of residents. By 1851, there were many commercial looms operating under steam power. As workers streamed to urban areas to take manufacturing jobs, the number of cities with more than 8,000 residents swelled from only 6 in 1790 to 141 in 1860.

Canals and railroads created whole new cities or turned sleepy farming villages into industrial centers. Cleveland and Pittsburgh, for example, newly connected to the coalfields of Ohio and iron mines of the Great Lakes by the Ohio Canal prospered, and Cincinnati and Chicago grew in response to the consolidation of the rail lines connecting them to the markets of the East.

Nonetheless, much of the industrial expansion in the North, and the capital that it represented, was swept away by the economic panic of 1837. Nine-tenths of the factories in the Northeast closed, and at least 33,000 commercial and industrial failures were reported. By 1839, the surplus of cash in state coffers had disappeared. Many states had counted on these funds to complete projects creating new roads and canals. Northern factory workers lost their jobs as manufacturers closed their businesses for lack of credit. Tens of thousands of factory workers were suddenly unemployed. This was an unfamiliar circumstance in a rural America that had formerly relied on individual business concerns and small shops to employ the small percentage of nonagricultural workers in the labor force. Angry crowds of unemployed factory workers, unable or unwilling to return to farming, mobbed the streets of major cities demanding lower prices for food, rent, and fuel, while factory owners appealed to the Federal government for financial help and to the state government for a protecting force of militia. Many canal projects were put on hold for the duration of the crisis, and new investment in this form of transportation was largely redirected to the railroad building mania of the 1840s. The whaling industry declined in this period and virtually collapsed in the 1850s. The glory of the American wooden clipper ship was over, and Great Britain's steamships took up much of the global oceanic trade. Slowly the nation recovered, regaining much of its prosperity in the1840s and expanding in the 1850s under the influence of the giant gold strike in California. However, overall American shipping went into a decline before the war, which lasted into the 1890s.

The Northern industrial economy was again threatened on the eve of the Civil War by the depressions of 1854 and 1858. The financial panic of August 1857, brought on by the failure of the Ohio Life Insurance Company (a major investor in the Ohio and Mississippi Railroad), caused a weeklong stock market crash with issues loosing 8 percent to 10 percent a day as a whole series of overextended companies failed. Runs on the banks and outright bank failures were the order of the day. Many of these were involved in railroad construction. The *New York Herald* (October 9, 1857) was revolted by the number of business suspensions, failures, and bankruptcies.

During such panics, the South suffered from the resulting crash in demand for cotton as mills and factories, especially those in England, were unable to collect on American debts and themselves went into bankruptcy. Many Southern slaves found that they faced the auction block for the first time as even the most humane slave owners were forced to raise cash in order to pay the bills they had accumulated in expectation of the sale of their crops. Nonetheless, the agricultural abundance of the South made it one of the more resilient sectors of the national economy, providing for itself in the short term. Corn was the major crop grown in the South. It was used locally as food for man and feed for livestock and poultry. Rice, tobacco, sugar, leather, lumber, turpentine, and cotton accounted for three-fourths of the national export trade in 1860.

In terms of dollars, however, the antebellum period witnessed cotton becoming "king." In 1790, annual cotton production amounted to only 3,000 bales, but it rose to 178,000 bales in just 20 years. This increase is generally attributed to the introduction of the cotton gin in 1793. The Sea Islands of South Carolina and Georgia were noted for the production of luxury cotton with its long, delicate, and silky fibers that could not be grown profitably anywhere else in the world. Even so, continuous experimentation to improve the quality of luxury cotton produced a superfine fiber that the world eagerly sought for making laces and fine fabrics. Even in the face of widely fluctuating prices, this cotton provided the Southern gentry with a relatively stable market and a virtually inexhaustible wealth. By mid-century the introduction of a superior cotton boll from Mexico, which could be more easily picked, increased production again. Expanded agricultural investment in the new western lands of the South, coupled with the widespread utilization of the cotton gin, boosted cotton production to almost 4 million bales per annum by the Civil War.

Oddly, reliable statistics concerning Southern industry and manufacturing are rare and difficult to assess from the distance of more than a century. Civil War historian Harold S. Wilson has noted that the generally accepted view of the industrial capacity of the South in the antebellum period may need revision, and some limits may need to be put to the present generalizations made by the economic historians of the past. According to Wilson, by the act of secession, the industrial capability of the Southern states "was brought to a pinnacle of development and then to a great extent perished in the holocaust of the war." The demands of a wartime economy may have blurred a true measure of the extent of the South's industrial system, and immediate postwar analyses by Northern observers may have been prejudiced against any positive findings.[56]

Southern apologists and other contemporary spokespersons had pointed out the strength of the Southern economy before the war intervened. Although some of their positive comments concerning Southern industrial capacity were propaganda, much of the statistical material they cited was certainly accurate. Senator Andrew Johnson of Tennessee, later vice president and president of the United States, noted in 1860 that the copper mines of his state kept seven smelting furnaces in constant operation annually and that the number of Tennesseeans engaged in manufacturing was virtually the same as that in some New England states. Moreover, Tennessee produced more woolen textile, more corn, more wheat, and 150 times more pig iron than New Hampshire and was building 1,100 miles of railway while New Hampshire was laying down 200 miles annually.

Representative Alexander Stephens of Georgia, later vice president of the Confederacy, made similar statistical comparisons between his state and Ohio, then the most prosperous state in the Union. Stephens noted that with half the population, Georgia produced more agricultural products than Ohio—even if cotton were excluded—more beef and pork, and more wool. Georgia had 38 cotton and woolen mills, 1,000 more miles of railroad, and twice the annual capital investment in new manufacturing ventures as Ohio. Some of Stephens's remarks were disingenuous and did not take into account the fact that much of the investment in Ohio predated that in Georgia, leaving Ohio's present annual rate lower although the absolute dollar amount of investment was higher.

Thomas J. Kettell, a contemporary author, economist, and Southern apologist, made a number of interesting comparisons with European nations. He pointed out that the South as a whole in 1860 had approximately 9,000 miles of railway as compared to 6,000 in England and Wales, 4,000 in France, and a little over 2,000 in Prussia. There were 31 major canals, two of the 10-largest ocean harbors in the world (both serving New Orleans), and two major inland ports (Louisville, Kentucky, and St. Louis, Missouri). One-third of all the telegraph lines, 15,000 miles of it, were in the Southern states, more than in all of continental Europe at the time.

Joseph Kennedy, superintendent of the Federal Census in 1860, noted the South's 52 paper mills producing 12 million pounds of paper annually, its 1,300 leather shops and tanneries, its three major ironworks capable of making locomotives and steam engines, its more than 100 smaller iron furnaces, foundries, and rolling mills, and its 115 precision machine shops. Southern shoemakers produced 65,000 pairs of work shoes annually, and its leatherworkers provided the entire nation with most of the hides and most of the bark needed for tanning them. Kennedy also noted the establishment in the South of 250 cotton mills, 153 woolen mills, and almost 500 carding and fulling mills. The textile mills alone represented almost 70 percent of the U.S. total, but they were located largely in the border states and northern Virginia. There were 45 woolen mills and 63 carding mills in Virginia alone that produced over 1 million yards of fabric, enough for 200,000 suits of clothing annually. Moreover, the Southern textile mills, more recently built and based on a superior technology, were four times more efficient than those in the North and eight times better than those in Great Britain. Based on findings like these, modern researchers have begun to reevaluate their judgments about the extent of the technological inferiority of the Southern states before the war and to reshape the picture of Southern industry commonly advanced in history texts.

2

The World of Youth

In colleges and halls in ancient days,
When learning, virtue, and truth
Were precious and inculcated with care,
There dwelt a sage called Discipline.
But Discipline, a faithful servant long,
Declined at length into the vale of years.
                    —*The Journal of American Education*, 1862

God grant that our State may never need their services [but]
should the terrible cry, "To Arms!" be ever heard from her, the
graduates and cadets of her military schools will be the main
element of her defense.
                    —A visitor to the Virginia Military Institute[1]

THE BOUNTIFUL HEARTLAND

The vast majority of Americans lived in the rural regions of America, and
their children worked and learned in the simple surroundings of farm-
steads, agricultural buildings, and plowed fields. Men and women spent
most of their time living and working side by side. A wife was expected
to manage the household and to care for the children, but she was also
expected to help in the economic affairs of her husband, acting as his representative or even his surrogate if the situation warranted it. A husband
was expected to provide for his family and to guide and educate his children. The daily routines and tasks of a husband and a wife might have
been very distinct, but they worked toward a common goal: the well-being
of the family. A husband and wife, and in fact all family members, were

interdependent. Each and every member was expected to contribute to the welfare of the family unit as their gender, age, and ability permitted.

In the American heartland men and women worked beside their children and grandchildren in an idyllic, if not a mechanically efficient, simplicity. Children spent a good deal of their time hauling water and carrying firewood, and they learned their occupations firsthand by doing simple chores, sewing, spinning, cooking, and tending the crops and animals. Many of these tasks were assigned by the gender of the child: girls performed household chores and tasks in the garden plot with their mother; boys worked in the farmyard, the woodlot, and the fields with their father. A good deal of a woman's time was spent in seasonally appropriate activities such as gardening, preserving fruits and vegetables, and making such household essentials as candles, soap, and other seasonal necessities. With these tasks young children could be helpful. Men and older boys took on the physically demanding work where strength was their predominant asset. Nonetheless, if any task needed to be accomplished, almost anyone in the family could be asked to complete it.

While Southern planters with their slaves could own thousands of acres, the average American farm family occupied a farmstead of just under 200 acres. A farmstead of this size generally supplied all that was needed for the typical rural family. Forty acres of cleared land supported a home, a barn, and a garden plot filled with vegetables and herbs for the family's use. Another 40 could be used as a woodlot providing fuel, building materials, and rough forage for hogs and chickens. Forty acres of plowed land allowed for a cash crop of corn, cotton, or wheat (little more could be tended by a family in a planting season); and the last 40 acres supported the remaining livestock with grazing and hay. Generally one acre of hay was needed to winter a large animal such as a horse, dairy cow, or steer. Some farmers turned out lumber and wooden shingles to supplement their income. Others cleared additional land for a small cash crop of tobacco or to raise livestock for sale. Only with the help of every member of the family could a typical farmer attempt such labor-intensive measures. Although these strategies rarely resulted in a large cash surplus, hunger was generally absent from the typical family farmstead.

The standard family farm of 160 acres was no mere mathematical accident. Many farms established in the colonial period in Pennsylvania or New York spanned 300 or 400 acres, a manageable size for a family operation with room left over to partition the land among the adult children. However, in the American Midwest, farms of 160 acres were very common because of the way the government divided the territorial lands after the American Revolution. The Federal government recognized the efficiency of the 160-acre formula as early as 1784, when it established the framework of local government in Ohio, and again in 1796 in the Northwest Territories. Public lands that were open to settlement were surveyed and divided into townships that were six miles square (36 square miles). Each of the 36-mile square *sections* in the township contained 640 acres. In well-watered regions with average rainfall, each *quarter section* of 160 acres was considered capable of sustaining a family farmstead. Moreover, one section in each township was reserved for the support of the town government and another for the support of a public elementary school. This support could be realized through the sale of timber, firewood, forage, or minerals or through leasing the land or rights to private parties. A single farmer could own more than one-quarter section—and many did—but in 1820 the General Land Office expressly prohibited the sectioning of land smaller than 160 acres. Only in urban areas could the landed be further divided into building lots. In the period of Reconstruction after the war, it was suggested that freed slave families be given 40 acres and a mule so that they could support themselves. Such an arrangement, seemingly generous from the perspective of more than a century, would actually have sentenced even the hardest-working family to a mere subsistence living with no hope of securing any cash or profit.

MOLDING YOUNG MINDS

When not working, children were made responsible for pursuing their education. The home, of course, was the first place where the foundations of education were laid. Mothers were responsible for the very early education of their children. This included a shaping of their moral character. *The Mother's Book*, by Mrs. Lydia Child, advocated the deliberate and early cultivation of a child's intellect. After describing some simple amusements for very young children, Mrs. Child advised, "But something ought to be mixed with these plays to give the child the habits of thought" that might convert basic daily activities into stimulating intellectual endeavors.[2] She urged that older children be reminded that the more knowledge they gained the more useful they would be as adults. Additionally, it was essential that children be fortified with solid moral foundations. Mrs. Child cautioned against selecting readings for children that merely culminated in a moral. "The morality should be in the book, not tacked upon the end of it." With such home training, children entered school at ages four or five with certain basic moral and cultural understandings upon which would be built a formal education.[3] A lesson concerning the value of education printed in a school reader of the period stated, "The highest objects of a good education are, to reverence and obey God, and to love and serve mankind. Every thing that helps in attaining these objects, is of great value, and every thing that hinders us, is comparatively worthless."[4]

Most young children spent their formative years at home among their siblings. Given the relative isolation of the family farmstead or widely dispersed plantations, children spent almost all of this time surrounded by brothers and sisters. In some families, children of the same gender might pair off according to their approximate age. Although sisters often cultivated enduring and affectionate relationships, brotherly closeness in childhood often evolved into internecine rivalries in adulthood for inherited property or family position. This was especially true in the hierarchal world of the South, but it was not uncommon elsewhere due to the dominant role men where expected to take in the antebellum social order.

Decisions as to who would farm, who would be apprenticed to a trade, and who would be sent for advanced schooling were generally made to benefit the family as a whole. These determinations were not always equitable from the individual's point of view, but this was a secondary consideration to a greater good—the welfare of the family. Those young men who had few family connections or wealth were subject to serving out their lives as farmers or laborers. The constant partitioning and subdividing of land among children and grandchildren often made the size of individual holdings impractical. Young men were often forced to remove to the territories in order to find sufficient land to set up a farmstead of their own and marry. Beyond marriage, young women did not have even the limited choices provided to men. The few occupations open to females produced little income, and they either married or relied on relatives for the remainder of their lives.

Because of the closeness of antebellum families, it was not unusual in large households to farm out an extra child, even an older teenager, to a blood relative. This child was usually a daughter as they were considered a drain on family resources because they posed "little or no hope of return." On the other hand, because boys could work in the fields and strike out on their own when grown, "a son was thought too valuable to part with under any circumstances." Kinship ties were strengthened between families who took in an extra child. The system worked fairly well. Younger children could depend on their relations for financial assistance, a proper upbringing, and a modicum of individual attention; and older children received support and guidance by forming close relationships with members of an extended family.[5]

Fathers were always the final authority in the household, but they clearly understood the demanding nature of childcare with half a dozen children bustling around, each trying to engage a parent's attention at every moment. In a male-dominated society, many men were plagued by the incessant demands of their little ones, and therefore chose to enjoy them from a distance. Although women were equally bothered by the noise of children and their demands for attention, they were more likely to accept the role of parent and domestic supervisor than men. Historian Catherine Clinton has noted, "Because the role of motherhood was elevated and enhanced during the early republican era, women perhaps suffered more keenly [than men] from the duties imposed on them as parents." Besides providing a basic education, a mother also "carried out the unpleasanter task of daily discipline, policing her children's behavior, interceding in quarrels among siblings, and doling out demerits, lectures, and whippings."[6]

The 18th-century practice among financially well-to-do families was to provide a wet nurse or servant to care for the immediate needs of the children. This method of childcare had largely gone out of favor in 19th-century America, and having older children entrusted to slaves or servants ran counter to the advice available in the literature for parents that sprang forth from the publishers of the cheap press. Moreover, it was feared that older children might be negatively influenced by the behavior of slaves and servants, and white children were warned by their parents to be cautious of Negroes and hired help. A contemporary mother wrote to her children in this regard, "[O]n no account familiarize with them—be kind and civil and never converse with them about family affairs of any kind."[7]

Infants suckled for about a year, and the choice to nurse was a very personal one. Many women preferred to have a wet nurse, but they were made fearful of the results of using a surrogate on their child's upbringing by the largely anecdotal musings of supposed child experts. Although regular nursing was a physical strain, wet nurses were usually employed only when a mother's own milk failed or her recovery from childbirth was in question. Upper-class women tended to turn the task over to a white hired woman, and newspapers were filled with advertisements seeking available wet nurses. Southern folklore notwithstanding, the practice of employing black slaves to suckle white infants was generally avoided in the antebellum period.

Prominent among Southern traditions was the stereotypical character of Mammy. Plantation records acknowledge the presence of female slaves who held a position equivalent to that of a head housekeeper or caregiver to the master's children. Yet their appearance in the antebellum record is incidental and outnumbered to a great degree by the employment of white governesses. Not until after the war were there a significant number of black women in such circumstances. The secure place of the Mammy in the mythology of the plantation has been created by a combination of historic revisionism and romantic imagination that seems at first to have been a projection of the slave owners' own delusions about how their household slaves were devoted to them on a personal level—a repeated allusion found in contemporary Southern diaries, especially those of young women.[8] Moreover, the image of the black wet nurse reduced the slave to "an animal-like state of exploitation . . . to be milked, warm bodies to serve white needs."[9] Certainly, female slaves were maintained to help with the supervision of children, but they were generally mistrusted and prohibited from any close contact with white children for fear that it would weaken the slave-master relationship.

About 50 percent of children outside the American South attended school with some regularity. Some areas of the Midwest and New England had enrollments as high as 90 percent. Attendance in rural areas suffered from the fact that many parents "task[ed] their children heavily with farm labor, and [not] until such tasks are finished are they allowed to start school." School might be in session in some communities for only three or four winter months in an entire year. The modern cycle of the school year, with its two-month summer vacation, still mirrors the 19th-century need for the labor of children in agricultural regions during the busy growing season.[10]

In the Northeast and Midwest, where formal schooling existed, common schools were typically open to all the children in the community and paid for by the community either by subscription or taxation. The largely rural nature of the South generally hampered the creation of an effective public school system except in more densely populated areas. With no textbooks being published in the South before the Civil War, Southern teachers depended upon Northern or European sources for their materials. Moreover, financially able Southerners preferred to send their children to private institutions rather than public schools. Private academies, which flourished in this period, offered reasonably good instruction primarily in the classics. Large domestic complexes on Southern plantations sometimes contained separate buildings designed to serve as schoolrooms for the children of well-to-do families who hired tutors.

Conditions in common schools varied tremendously from community to community. Most provided no more than crude benches without backs, slates for writing, and a limited number of shared books. There were few, if any, educational standards at this time. The length of the school day and school year varied as the individual community saw fit. The schools were supervised by a group of designated citizens who oversaw operations. Their duties included, "the levying of tax, the location of school houses, the purchase and sale of school property, the appointment and dismissal of teachers, and the selection of studies and textbooks." The dedication and expertise of these directors was, however, often called into question.[11]

Children of Poverty

Conditions for children in the urban areas of America were quite different from those found in the American heartland. By the 1840s, Northern cities were filled with the poor, uneducated children of immigrants who were packed into shanties, tenements, and ramshackle boarding houses. The streets of the cities were scenes of prostitution, gambling, drunkenness, and other forms of wrongdoing. Street gangs, often led by deceitfully clever adults and composed of grimy-faced and coarse adolescents, ruled whole areas of certain cities and worked in concert with corrupt politicians, neighborhood wardens, and political machines. In a country supposedly blessed with economic abundance, it was difficult to understand the causes and conditions that led to such poverty, illiteracy, and crime among such a large segment of the population. Yet these were the obvious disturbing realities in antebellum America for anyone who chose to see them.

Poverty, ignorance, crime, and intemperance drew forward a number of well-meaning social reformers from among the upper and middle classes. They generally viewed the poor immigrant population as human raw material "to be acted upon, to be improved, manipulated, elevated and reformed."[12] An implicit faith in the perfection of America left many among the socially conscious upper classes with the notion that these social ills were capable of eradication if the systematic roadblocks and characteristic reluctance to change among the old order were removed. Believing that the root cause of ignorance, drunkenness, and crime was poverty, some of the earliest organizations to gain popular support were societies for the prevention of pauperism.

Reform advocates, focusing on the urban environment, railed against towns that licensed grog shops, saloons, and houses of prostitution. They defamed politicians who allowed gambling halls and dens of iniquity to flourish, or who refused to take the temperance pledge. However, compassion quickly changed to disapproval, criticism, and castigation of the poor themselves. In 1827, an investigatory committee of the New York Society for the Prevention of Pauperism unhesitatingly reported that the vice found in large eastern cities was attributable in large part to the actions of the poverty-stricken residents themselves. The report found most of the poor of New York City "depraved and vicious." Of course, few of the reformers on the committee thought to ask the poor what they felt were the primary causes of their condition. The poor may have listed unfair labor practices, ethnic or religious bias, and unscrupulous landlords as causes of their plight; but they were generally quiet on the subject.

As the extent of poverty among the urban immigrant population of the North reached epidemic proportions, complacency and pity quickly gave way to a heightened suspicion of the poor themselves. "Surely the poor were partly to blame for their own misery, having succumbed to the vice of idleness or intemperance . . . victims of the numerous temptations set before them by society."[13] Some Northerners and many in the South, unconvinced of the menace to their communities that was posed by poverty and disease among the lowest level of the social order, were distressed by the radical way social activists approached their task. While there remained a strong belief in individualism, personal strength of character, and the ability of Americans to overcome the handicaps of their environment, by the 1850s such concepts were becoming identified more and more with conservative resistance to social reform. Opposition forces

Prominent Charitable and Reform Organizations Boston: 1859	
American Education Society	Punishment
American Peace Society	Mass., Society for the Relief of Widows
Association for Relief of Aged	and Orphans
Indigent Females	Mass. State Temperance Committee
Asylum and Farm School for Indigent	Needle-Women's Friend Society
Boys	New England Female Moral Reform
Boston Aid Society for Discharged	Society
Convicts	New England Immigrant Aid Society
Boston Charitable Society	New England Non-Resistance Society
Boston Total Abstinence Society	Parent Washington Total Abstinence
Charitable Association of the Boston	Society
Fire Department	Penitent Female Refuge
Children's Friend Society	Sailors' Snug Harbor
Children's Mission to the Children	Scots Charitable Society
of the Destitute	Seaman's Aid Society
Church Home for Orphan and	Society for Prevention of Pauperism
Destitute Children	Society for Relief of Aged and Indigent
Fatherless and Widows' Society	Clergymen
Female Orphan Asylum	Society for Relief of Widows and
German Immigrant Aid Society	Orphans
House of the Angel Guardian	Society Propagating the Gospel Among
Humane Society of Massachusetts	the Indians
Infidel Relief Society	Southern Aid Society
Irish Charitable Society	State Temperance Committee
Mariners' Total Abstinence Society	St. Vincent De Paul's Orphan Asylum
Massachusetts Asylum for the	Temporary Home for the Destitute
Blind	Trustees of Donations for Education
Massachusetts Temperance Society	in Liberia
Mass. School for Idiotic and Feeble-	Widows and Single Women's Society
minded Youth	Young Men's Benevolent Society
Mass. Society for Abolition of Capital	Young Men's Christian Association

Source: Boston Directory (1859).

found many of the reform proposals unrealistic, grandiose, sanctimonious, and antagonistic to traditional American concepts of personal rights and freedoms.

The reform movement of the 19th century was, in fact, characterized as one of activism of the " haves" for the " have-nots" rather than a demand for reform from those who were oppressed. This form of personal protest would not become popular until late in the century. Activists formed a sort of reform elite, which not only had the conceit to decide upon the areas of society that needed reformation but also attempted to differentiate be-

tween the worthy poor, whose lot was due to misfortune, and the corrupted and unworthy idlers.

Wives abandoned by their husbands and widows with small children
were almost universally viewed as among those worthy of public assistance. Women were commonly prohibited from many trades. When they
were permitted employment, they were routinely given the lowliest work,
and if it was a job also given to men, women were paid less for the same
work. Many women, alone and destitute, ended up as prostitutes. A contemporary observer described their plight.

> Of all the human race, these poor creatures are the most pitiable; the ill-usage
> and the degradation they are driven to submit to are indescribable; but from
> habit they become callous, indifferent as to delicacy of speech and behav-
> ior, and so totally lost to all sense of shame that they seem to retain no qual-
> ity which properly belongs to women but the shape and the name.[14]

Charitable organizations existed to serve these people, but their main
strategy was to send these poor wretches back to their homes or parents.
This was not always possible for immigrants whose homes were thousands of miles away. The reformers concluded that eliminating the stain
of poverty from the fabric of American society would require the isolation of the poor, by force if necessary, from their sources of temptation and
the instruction of the destitute in the habits of industry and labor. The
poor, regardless of the individuality of their plight, would receive aid only
while confined within a series of public almshouses and workhouses.
Once inside, they would be taught order, discipline, and responsibility. A
group of New England philanthropists was assured in 1843 that the
almshouse was "a place where the tempted are removed from the means
of their sin, and where the indolent, while he is usefully and industriously
employed . . . is prepared for a better career."[15] This grandiose plan resulted in institutions that were little more than places of unrelenting work
and severe discipline, even for those of eight or ten years of age.

The almshouses generally failed to relieve the problem of prolonged
poverty or its symptoms. The profit from the labor of the residents generally went to the institution, preventing the inmates from accumulating
travel money or a nest egg for an attempt at a renewed life. The truly
depraved and corrupted among the poor avoided such institutions, as did
any children old enough to fend for themselves on the streets by working odd jobs, begging, or stealing. Gangs composed of young men and
women flourished while the almshouses filled to overcrowding with the
helpless, the decrepit, the abandoned, and the very young. The emphasis
on rehabilitation and personal reformation, initially a primary goal of the
antipoverty reformers, quickly became irrelevant as the most heartrending
members of the poor community were hidden behind brick walls. Gone
were any semblance of a comprehensive educational program and any

time for childhood play or frolic. A committee in New York reported in 1857 that the general conditions found in such institutions, after more than 30 years of operation, had degenerated into a cruel and punitive system of custodial care.

Common Schools

Today, a comprehensive education is seen as a pathway to a stable income and a successful career, but this was not always obvious. Antebellum education reformers noted that the centuries-old system of apprenticeship was quickly fading away in the wake of increased industrialization and mass production, and a more practical educational system was needed. The system they devised for all children, based largely on German and Swiss theories of education, emphasized accurate arithmetical and bookkeeping skills that could be applied to the factory and precise penmanship, grammar, and spelling for use in the business office. Ironically, the natural characteristic of children to run and play was also recognized by the inclusion of a specific and formal period of "recess" that would have undoubtedly been seen as sheer idleness a generation earlier.

The proposed curriculum was well meaning and forward-looking because it was designed to prepare children for life in a changing modern society, but it was unforgiving of various learning styles and abilities and marked by a strict adherence to propriety. Timeliness, regimentation, absolute silence, and a strict work discipline (similar to that imposed in a workhouse or prison) were highly valued. Any breech of classroom decorum was punished, often with physical force that ranged from a cuff on the ear to a whipping with a hickory rod. A generally inadequate, poorly trained, and underpaid teaching staff often relied on the threat of corporal punishment for motivation rather than on fostering intellectual curiosity among the students. Sadly, the educational atmosphere, especially at the schools frequented by immigrant children, was generally repressive.

One of the first groups formed to help provide schooling for the poor was the Free School Society of New York City, founded in 1805 (renamed the Public School Society of New York in 1826). Its first president was DeWitt Clinton, then mayor of New York. The members of the society were determined to offer an education to poor children by making private donations, soliciting subscriptions from the public, and requesting funds from the state. These schools were taken over by the New York City Public School Department, which was formed in 1842.

There were more than 200 public schools in New York City in 1851, and the number of pupils was more than 107,000. The whole annual expense of almost $275,000, $2.57 per scholar, was derived partly from the Common School Fund of the state and partly from a property assessment placed on the city residents. A similar public education society was founded for the poor of Philadelphia. By 1818, a citywide system was in place serving almost 50,000 scholars at a cost of almost $200,000, or $4.00 per scholar. Boston had a "free school" as early as 1635 and deserves an honorable place as the initiator of free public education in America. By 1851, Boston reportedly kept one-quarter of its population (approximately 35,000 children) in school all year at a cost of $183,000, or $5.23 per student. Differences in cost among these cities can generally be attributed to the length of the school year, the quality of the facilities, the availability of teachers, and the local cost of living.

Meanwhile, in 1837, a group of influential men led by Horace Mann pushed legislation through the Massachusetts Legislature creating a state system of education. Mann's efforts, based largely on the theories of Swiss educator Johann Heinrich Pestalozzi, generally resulted in a more centralized school system. Mann also introduced the concept of high schools and state teachers' schools into the Massachusetts system. At about the same time, Henry Barnard and John Pierce were making similar efforts in Connecticut and Michigan, respectively. These pioneer educators made great strides in the development of free public education.

Yet not everyone was convinced that universal public education was beneficial for America, and the concept was the topic of widespread disagreement, public controversy, and political debate. The ongoing development of a system of free public schools was paralleled by the institution of a Catholic school system in the immigrant-filled cities of New York and Boston, which tended to exacerbate the controversy and underpin the opposition. Whereas many Protestant groups in the Midwest gave strong support for the idea of public education, the owners of private academies, foreign-language schools (mostly German), and those institutions administered by minority religious communities generally opposed it. Questions of private versus state control of parochial and private schools were as prominent then as they are now. Such notions were seen by some as a threat to fundamental values and a clear danger to the social status quo that had to be avoided at all costs.[16]

Social conservatives, North and South, particularly deplored the development of free public schools that admitted children from many classes, ethnic groups, and family backgrounds. They feared that they would be exposed to a set of novel values that stressed social equality rather than republican principles. Alexis de Tocqueville, no opponent of the value of education in general, wrote in 1831 that he saw in the nascent system of American public education disturbing signs of a trend toward mass conformity that might suppress individual expression and personal talent. He envisioned a new kind of "social despotism" emerging, suppressing personal liberty by the power of intellect and by the force of emotion.[17]

The majority of school reformers were Northerners, and, because most Southerners felt that the public schools were at least partially responsible for the distasteful attitudes displayed by residents of that section of the country with regard to slavery and states' rights, they hesitated to embrace any institution that could produce such thinking. Largely because of these attitudes, basic public education in the South languished. As late as the 1830s, nearly one-third of white Southern adults were illiterate, and by 1860, only four Southern states and a few isolated communities had effective public school systems.

It was, nonetheless, thought essential by many that children should be prepared for the intellectual and technological challenges that 19th-century society would make on them. Senator Daniel Webster noted the connection: "The future life and character of a nation is to be seen in its system of schools."[18] Those living during the antebellum period witnessed major changes in the American system of education, many of the characteristics of which are still with us today, and public sentiment gradually became more favorable to a more egalitarian system of public schools. Thomas H. Burrowes, a contemporary educator noted, "People are beginning to see that their children can get a sound practical . . . education in our common schools."[19]

Children of Affluence

As the second quarter of the 19th century progressed, the movement toward community or common schools gained momentum, but many wealthy families avoided public education in favor of private institutions generally known as academies. These had flourished since colonial times. Based largely on similar institutions in France, Holland, and Scotland, the academies had been founded initially by those persons deemed dissenters from the established Church of England. Dutch Reformed, Baptists, Presbyterians, and Methodists all founded academies in America. Many of the Presbyterian academies founded by Scotch-Irish communities in the Southern backcountry maintained strong ties with major universities in Europe such as Edinburgh, Glasgow, and Ulster. In New Jersey, Pennsylvania, and Delaware, where there was little enforcement of the laws governing the established religion in colonial times, academies expanded in number, in the scope of their courses, and in the power they maintained.

The All Saints Summer Academy was typical of these religious academies. In 1832, the rice planters and their wives of Georgetown, South Carolina, joined forces to form a private school with the help of the Reverend Alexander Glennie of the Episcopalian faith. Six years later, under the direction of David D. Rosa, it was opened to both male and female students who could afford the tuition. Students over 12 years of age paid $20 per term, while those under 12 paid $10. Board and washing fees totaled an addition $13.50 per month, and the school expected students to provide their own furniture and bedding. The school provided a complete

This fine home from Central New York State at first looks like it belongs on a Southern plantation. It does exhibit several of the characteristics popular in the South, including classical columns, tall windows, and a railing along the top of the porch. It was used as a female seminary in the 1830s and 1840s.

English-style education as well as religious instruction. Classes in Latin, Greek, French, music, and drawing required additional fees. Although initially styled a summer school, the term started in January and ended with the onset of the malaria season in late summer or early fall.

Many academies in the antebellum period served as preparatory institutions for university studies on the grammar-school level. The nonconformists who ran these academies were receptive to the influences of intellectual and educational innovations, which taught classical literature, science, and politics in English rather than in Latin. "The academies were in their very nature alternatives to the established practice of higher education." The Albany Academy of New York was so highly rated that it was called "a college in disguise" by the president of Union College, Dr. Eliphalet Nott.[20] A few academies evolved into independent degree-granting institutions like the College of New Jersey at Princeton or the College of Rhode Island at Providence. The academy movement had evolved and diversified in format and emphasis, but the institutions retained their status as educational alternatives for parents who could afford them.[21]

The Richland School for Classical, Scientific and Practical Education near Rice Creek Springs, South Carolina, was typical of the boarding academies frequented by the sons of Southern planters in the antebellum period. A surviving school catalog from 1830 claims that the institution was organized along the lines of the most improved pedagogical principles to be found in Europe or America. The younger students, beginning as young as seven or eight, were taught spelling, arithmetic, grammar, and geography. Older students were offered three curricula: one for the business minded, one that led to a life as an engineer, and one for future planters. The courses of study included an appropriate mixture of mathematics, penmanship, bookkeeping, surveying, navigation, civil engineering, geology, chemistry, botany, mineralogy, and the principals of agriculture, depending on the curriculum the student chose to follow. All students studied Greek, Latin, rhetoric, and classical literature, and an appropriate regard for moral precepts and the general principles of the Protestant religion was impressed upon the students.

A few academies were open to both boys and girls, but generally the sexes were educated at separate institutions. A female academy movement swept the country, both North and South, in the early years of the century. Younger girls were offered courses in music, singing, drawing, painting, French, and the social graces. Older girls, generally too poorly prepared to undertake more advanced studies, concentrated mainly on refining their knowledge of etiquette and manners and their ability to manage a household. A few schools went beyond domestic subjects to offer academic studies. Emma Willard's Female Seminary founded in 1821 in Troy, New York, Catherine Breecher's School for Young Ladies founded in 1824 in Hartford, Connecticut, and Mary Lyon's Mount Holyoke Seminary founded in 1837 in South Hadley, Massachusetts, all attempted to teach academic subjects to young women; but they always did so in the guise of their application to domestic economy so that they would not be seen to threaten the male-dominated world of business and trade.

Parents viewed attendance at an academy differently, depending largely on the section of the country from which they came. The growing sectionalism that affected the rest of society was also affecting the educational choices made by parents. For Northern parents, the academy for young women was seen as an important step on the pathway to a college education or to a position in the emerging fields for women of school teaching, social service, or authorship. Well-disposed young women might have their educations augmented by lessons in mathematics, Latin, science, and the classics. The parents of young Southern women tended to view attendance at the academy as an end unto itself, preparing their daughters for their preordained role in the plantation culture as the mistress of the manor house and fitting them as well-read and socially acceptable wives and mothers for the Southern aristocracy. Historian Catherine Clinton has noted that "although mothers and daughters warmly greeted improvements in their education, these women of the planter class realized that their intellectual development would most likely wane with marriage, decline with housekeeping, dwindle with mother-hood, and at no time result in any measure of social recognition."[22]

As the century approached its midpoint, it became increasingly obvious that many of the women educated in the academies were the mainstays of the hated reform movements, particularly abolition and women's suffrage. Socially conservative parents viewed these institutions as contagious sources of social liberalism and began to turn their daughters away from them as an educational option. The female academy movement, already suffering from lagging enrollments due to repeated economic panics, went into decline in the 1850s. Oddly, during economic hard times it was more likely for Northern parents than their Southern counterparts to dispense with their daughter's education away from home. For upper-class Southern parents, time spent at the female academy had become an absolute necessity if they wished their daughter to secure a proper marriage. The Northern schools, therefore, suffered the greater declines when Southern students were removed from their roles, yet the schools did not disappear. Rather, the emphasis of the surviving institutions was shifted from intellectual pursuits to the development of social graces and ladylike decorum in order to attract continued patronage from the South. For their part, the academies located in the South carefully resisted any impulse to modernize their approach to education that might be seen as filtering down from the North. Because the doctrine of male dominance and female dependence remained pervasive throughout the country, an advanced education for women was not generally seen as crucial to a life devoted to caring for a husband and raising babies. Consequently, as the war approached, the curricula of many female academics came to be characterized as frivolous and superficial.

Tuition at male academies like Richland was almost $300 a year. This was no mean sum, but it included room, board, bedding, washing, mending, firewood, lighting, and health care. The cost of tuition was rather more for girls than boys because of the additional fees accumulated in taking courses in dance, music, drawing, and embroidery, as well as a preference for occupying private rooms rather than living in dormitories. Northern academies solicited Southern students because their parents could pay regularly and were generally ill disposed to public education, especially when the establishment of community schools required the use of their tax dollars. Most Southerners feared that free public education would create "ragged schools" like those filled with pauper children in England, and there was a belief that "poor whites" would swarm the free institutions of public education. Nonetheless, good academies, especially for boys, were difficult to find; many institutions were notorious for ignoring the education of the child as long as he or she refrained from causing an annoyance to the teachers. As the nation moved closer to the inevitable conflict, certain Southern parents with children in Northern academies found discomfort with their selection and withdrew their children from attendance. They even began to regret the fact that so many Northerners had been employed as teachers and tutors in the South.

Children of Slavery

Following biblical prescriptions and ancient Roman law, slave children did not belong to their parents but generally were considered the property of their mother's master. The father—and the father's master, should he be a different person—was denied any standing with regard to the offspring of a female slave. The offspring of a freeman with a slave woman was, thereby, a slave; yet, the offspring of a slave with a free woman was considered to be freeborn, even if the woman was black. Even the children of a white master by a slave mother were born slaves unless their father made them free. In the case of a dispute in this regard, with very few exceptions, whenever a slave's human rights came into conflict with a master's property rights, the courts invariably decided in favor of the master.[23]

It was thought to be unacceptable to have throngs of slave children milling around the plantation, and they were given tasks to accomplish as soon as they were old enough to understand. These tasks varied with the gender and age of the child, and usually dealt with agriculture, husbandry, or service duties like cleaning and cooking. The smallest children worked under the scrutiny of their mothers, grandmothers, or other aged females. Young boys and girls of 8 to 10 years of age were set to work picking cotton, hoeing farm fields, or caring for livestock. Teenagers were generally expected to carry the same workload as adults, and some were given specific training as coopers, woodworkers, leatherworkers, masons, or smiths. There were a number of gender-specific tasks distributed among the slave population in much the same manner that farmwork was divided among poor whites. Assignment of men to heavy tasks such as plowing, digging ditches, lumbering, cutting firewood, building, or moving bales and barrels was based more on the physical size and ability than their age. Work for women and girls included mundane daily routines such as tending the dairy operation, sewing, spinning, laundering, washing dishes, sweeping, and so forth. A number of tasks required the labor of everyone. Haymaking, harvesting, and the processing of pork and other meats required all ages and genders to work. The work of house slaves, liverymen, and personal servants was a very small proportion of the tasks carried out by slaves on a plantation.

Free blacks seem to have preferred to live in an urban setting and were twice as likely to live in cities than slaves, who were primarily agricultural workers. In cosmopolitan areas free blacks and slave craftsmen found opportunities for training, employment, exposure to black culture and religion, and the company of other freemen. However, the majority of free blacks lived on the margins of poverty, and they were subject to detention and questioning by the authorities without cause. In a society where slavery was based almost solely on race, the distinction between free blacks, black indentured servants, and black slaves quickly blurred.

There were no organized educational facilities for blacks in the antebellum South. In 1819, Virginia's General Assembly passed a law prohibiting the teaching of reading to Negroes, and many other states followed with similar legislation. There were, however, always masters and mistresses who ignored the statutory prohibitions and instructed those blacks with whom they had the closest relationships in some basic rudiments of education. Frederick Douglass, with his fine writing style and splendid speaking voice, was used by Northern reformers and antislavery activists as a prime example of the possible accomplishments that could be made by educated blacks. However, following the bloody slave insurrection led by Nat Turner, an educated black slave and local preacher, both fear of educated blacks and compliance with the legal prohibition against their instruction increased greatly. The violence of the Turner uprising of 1831, with up to 60 white deaths distributed among men, women, and children, severely stifled the desire of many moderate Southern whites to educate slaves and caused many other whites to question the wisdom of educating even free blacks.

The popularity of antislavery and abolition societies in the North spawned a number of efforts to provide formal educational institutions for blacks, but even the best-intentioned efforts proved to be sporadic and short lived. One of the best and oldest institutions in the region was the African Free School, begun in 1787 by New York's Manumission Society. In this regard, however, New England seems to have taken a lead during the period. Boston opened a school solely for black children in 1820. Salem, Massachusetts, was the first town to allow black and white children to attend school together, and it allowed black teachers to serve in the classroom. Nonetheless, when Prudence Crandall, a Pennsylvania Quaker, opened a school for black girls in Connecticut in 1831, the state quickly passed a series of "Black Laws" forbidding persons from outside the state to found a school for blacks without the consent of the local government. Crandall was arrested and convicted under these statutes in 1833. Although a higher court sided with her efforts, Crandall abandoned her school in 1834 and moved west. Although Amherst College and Bowdoin College had both graduated a black man by 1826 and the first black college had opened in Philadelphia in 1854, higher education at any level was simply not a realistic option for blacks, slave or free, before the end of the Civil War. Black education lingered in the 1840s and 1850s as activists focused more and more on the primary goal of abolition.

During the Federal occupation of New Orleans from 1862 to 1865, Northern researchers took data from hundreds of black residents of the city regarding their experiences as slaves. More than 500 marriages were recorded as having taken place while couples had been slaves. Of these, fewer than 100 remained unbroken. While some unions lasted 20 to 40 years, the average length of a slave marriage was only 5.6 years. Records indicate that 70 percent of these marriages ended due to death or personal choice, and only 30 percent were broken up by the action of slave owners. Many planters went to considerable length to avoid breaking up families because of the great unrest it caused in the slave community. Unfortunately, mortgage foreclosures, loan repayments, and inheritances brought many slaves to the auction block with no concern for the family unit. Executors of estates often divided slaves up into lots of equivalent value for distribution to heirs also without regard to family relationships. Additionally, planters often made gifts of slaves to their children, especially as wedding presents. The first activity of many refugee or escaped slaves was to begin a search for their missing mates, children, or siblings.

THE SCHOOLHOUSE

Youngsters fortunate enough to attend school spent a good deal of time in the schoolhouse. The little red clapboard schoolhouse of one room common to the folklore and anecdotal history of many communities may not have been as common in antebellum America as most people think. School buildings were constructed in a number of ways including in brick, wood frame, logs, and stone. According to period documents, 58 percent of school superintendents in Pennsylvania described their schools in negative terms. It was not unusual to see claims that the schools were "less fit for the purpose of schooling, than would be many modern out houses for sheltering cattle." One schoolhouse was described as "a crumbling, dilapidated, damp, unwholesome stone building with a ceiling eight feet high, room about twenty-six by thirty feet into which one and hundred seventeen are crowded, and placed at long, old fashioned desks, with permanent seats, without backs." One superintendent reported finding "the teacher and pupils huddled together, shivering with cold, and striving to warm themselves by the little heat generated from a quantity of green wood in the stove." Additional complaints included a lack of "outhouses and other appliances necessary for comfort and convenience." Concern was expressed over the fact that schoolhouses were "placed far off the road and buried in the wildest forest."[24]

The interior of this one-room schoolhouse in Norwalk, Connecticut, has been restored to its look in 1826. Note the sheet iron wood-burning heater, the dunce cap on the teacher's desk, and the small seats for young learners. This school was used until the early 20th century.

In many schools sufficient blackboards were also wanting. Many blackboards in poorer regions were just smooth wooden boards, painted black, and covered with chalk dust. "Chalking in" the wood provided a reasonably erasable surface. Well-supported schools had not only blackboards of real slate but also outline maps, spelling and reading cards, charts, and globes. The average school had only one or two of these instructional materials. Writing paper was scarce in rural schools and considered too valuable for scratch work and student lessons. Students commonly wrote on wood-framed slates. Although these were initially "confined to such as had made advancement in arithmetic . . . now we find the smallest scholars engaged with their slates."[25]

Furniture was, at best, sparse in most classrooms. "It is useless to complain of school furniture," lamented one superintendent. "It seems that people would sooner see their children have spinal or pulmonary affliction, than furnish the school room with proper desks and seats." A York

County, Pennsylvania, superintendent noted, "I witnessed a great deal of uneasiness, amounting in many instances to intense suffering, among the small children, from . . . being seated too high. In some instances, the desks are still attached to the wall, the scholars with their backs to the teacher."[26]

Nonetheless, there exists documentation of a number of new school buildings that were described in more favorable terms. One school superintendent described a "tasteful brick building 30 × 45 . . . furnished with first class iron frame furniture for 62 pupils." Other new buildings were built of wood, and one was "24 × 36 with four tiers of seats for two pupils each accommodating 64 pupils." Another superintendent boasted, "All the rooms are warmed by coal stoves, most of them have ceilings of proper height, windows adapted to ventilation; plenty of black-board surface; and they are tolerably well seated." A new schoolhouse was proudly described as having an "anti-room, closets and platform and in every respect is superior to most of the other [school]houses."[27]

School revenue was directly tied to the success or failure of local commerce. In an 1861 report, the county superintendents in Pennsylvania noted that the frosts of June and early July, resulting in a loss of much of the wheat crop, caused a "pecuniary embarrassment" that forced a shortening of teaching time and a reduction of the wages of some teachers to the point that some of the best educators left the county or became engaged in "other pursuits." Nonetheless, the remaining teachers were applauded for their self-denial and the manner in which they bore up during a difficult time. In the same year that some agricultural districts chose to suspend school for the entire year due to poor crop yields, lumbering districts were favored by high water that made the movement of lumber more efficient. These were favored by increased prosperity, and the schools were unaffected.[28]

Teachers

Most teachers received their pedagogical training at a normal school, an institution dedicated to the profession of education roughly equivalent to a junior college program today. In the antebellum period, graduates from normal schools were more common among public schoolteachers than college or university graduates, and many teachers trained in normal schools continued to serve into the middle of the 20th century. Rural districts were often unsuccessful in obtaining normal school graduates and had to settle for whatever reasonably well-educated persons they could find.

Although both men and women taught, male teachers were preferred. As the Civil War approached, many young men left the schoolroom thereby opening the door for more women to enter the field of education. Four-fifths of the teachers in Philadelphia were female. A county superintendent of schools noted the employment of female teachers with some dissatisfaction because they were believed to be "inadequate to the task of controlling a winter school." However, he also noted that the "superior cleanliness and arrangement of their rooms, the effect of their natural gentleness and goodness on the scholars . . . amply compensated for their want of physical force." These qualities were appreciated even more when it was found that the young women could be paid lower salaries than the generally older male teachers. The average salary reported in Pennsylvania in 1861 for a male teacher was $24.20 per month. Women were paid $18.11.[29]

School districts sometimes had to go far afield to find teachers. The Board of National Popular Education, a teacher preparation institution in New England, advertised the availability of its female graduates for rural teaching positions in the Midwest in the following aggressive manner in 1849:

> The Board collects its teachers in classes semi-annually at Hartford, Connecticut, and carries them through a short course of preparatory training. . . . It is desired that the applicants . . . for teachers . . . be made by letter. . . . The application should state the name of the town and county, where the teacher is wanted; the branches in which instruction is desired; the probable number of scholars; the rate of compensation, specifying whether with or without board; and the family to which the teacher may resort on her arrival. It is desireable that information should accompany the application in regard to the place—its population, healthfulness, and social and religious priviledges. If a special preference is felt as to the religious denomination of the teacher, let it be expressed in the application, and it shall, if practicable, be complied with. . . . As applications to the Board are becoming so numerous, teachers may not be expected to be sent unless a compensation of at least $100 per annum, besides board is offered. Instruction in the higher branches or in the case of very large schools, it is expected will command a higher compensation.[30]

Teaching in the common schools was a young person's profession largely because it was generally a part-time job with nominal annual rates of pay translating into one-half or less over the typically shortened school year. The teachers spent a good part of the remaining months attending academies and normal schools or taking on other work, including manual labor and housekeeping. The *Boston Directory* for 1859 lists the salaries established for administrators and instructors in the various schools in the system.

> The salary of the Master [principal] of the Latin, the English High, and the Girls' High, and Normal Schools shall be $2400 for the first year's service, with an increase of $100 for each additional Year's service till the salary amounts to $2800 per annum. . . . The salary of the Sub-Masters [vice principals] of the Latin and English High Schools, and the Masters of the

Grammar Schools shall be $1600 for the first year, with an annual increase of $100 till it amounts to $2000. . . . The salary of the Head Assistants in the Grammar Schools shall be $500 per annum; the salary of the other assistants in the Grammar Schools, and the Teachers of the Primary Schools, shall be $300 for the first year, with an annual increase of $50 till it amounts to $450 per annum.[31]

The majority of teachers were between 18 and 25 years of age, but some were little more than children themselves.[32] A school superintendent complained that it was "to be regretted . . . that parents will urge their sons and daughters to seek to become teachers at so early an age; and it is a great error in directors, as a general rule, to employ such young persons. Men engage persons of mature age and experience on the farm, in the shop or store, in the kitchen or dairy room; but they hire girls or boys of 15 or 16 to train up and educate their offspring."[33] Teaching offered moderately educated young persons, especially women who had no other professional prospects, the respectability of a professional calling without the expense and effort of lengthy studies at law or preparation for the ministry. Nonetheless, some parents preferred "to have there children work in the mines or learn a trade [than to] become qualified to teach school."[34]

Some school districts established examinations to ensure that teachers were competent to assume their duties. Most exams were a combination of written and oral questions. "They were held publicly, and attended by numbers of citizens, who had a desire to see and hear [the process] for themselves."[35] Emma Sargent Barbour's sister, Maria, wrote about the examinations given in Washington, D.C., suggesting little need for advanced preparation among aspiring educators. "[Hattie was] accompanying me as far as City Hall where I was to be examined, when she remarked that she had a good mind to try just for fun. She went in and passed an excellent examination and next Monday will take a position at my school."[36] Not all examinations were quite as simple as Maria seemingly implies. Many applicants failed the examination process and were turned away, and others, considering that many rural districts were lucky to find teachers at all, ultimately found employment without certification.

Institutes were held periodically to help teachers to improve their skills. Some occurred only once a year whereas others were held semimonthly on alternate Saturdays. The idea of professional development for schoolteachers had not yet taken hold. It was expected that any person who had successfully passed through his or her own formal schooling as a student could also teach effectively. Naturally, not all teachers performed to the satisfaction of the districts. A Wayne County, Pennsylvania, superintendent wrote of his teachers: "Two last winter had the reputation of being of intemperate habits, and some few are rough and rowdyish in their manner."[37]

Instructional Methods

Reading was always the main lesson of any school day. Traditional reading materials included the *King James Bible*, regarded by many as the central textbook for all education; the *Westminister Catechism*, the most popular of more than 500 catechisms available to be used with young students; and the *New England Primer*, used widely in the early decades of the republic. However, texts like these, which were generally grounded in a Calvinistic form of the Protestant religion, were falling into increasing disfavor among educators by the beginning of the antebellum period. Nonetheless, they continued to be used but were supplemented with works rooted in a more general morality. Popular nonsectarian materials from the period included *McGuffey's Eclectic Readers*, the *Peerlees Pioneer Readers* by the same author, Webster's "Blue-Backed" *Speller*, and *Ray's Arithmetic*. Spelling was just becoming standardized, and *Leach's Complete Spelling Book* of 1859 contained a "Collection of Words of Various Orthography" that included words of "common use, which are spelled differently by the three most eminent Lexicographers . . . Webster, Worcester, and Smart." Books like these represented a significant force in framing the mores and tastes of the nation and were outweighed only by the continuing influence of the Bible.[38]

Ironically, William Holmes McGuffey was himself a religious man and an ordained minister. He began writing the *Peerless Pioneer Readers* in 1826 because he was dedicated to the cause of secular education. He published the first volume a decade later, and received $1,000. In 1838, he released *McGuffey's Eclectic Reader*, the best-known title among his works. McGuffey was the first to attempt to arrange his materials for students of different ages and to select topics that generated their interest and enthusiasm. In 1845, McGuffey was appointed Professor of Moral Philosophy at the University of Virginia; until his death in 1873, he continued there, periodically revising his readers to suit the interests, abilities, and comprehension of the children who would used them. His books quickly became some of the most popular and effective teaching tools available in the United States at the time. Eventually, he evolved a series of six graded texts, a spelling book, and a high school reader. For most students, the level of the reader from which they could read determined their grade level in school. These readers passed through many editions and were adopted as standard texts by 37 states in McGuffey's lifetime. It is estimated that more than 120 million copies were sold.

Emma Sargent Barbour's letter from her young cousin Mary gives additional insight into the nature and varieties of period textbooks: "I am getting along first rate, at school. I don't always get 10—tough by any means. I always get 9 in writing. I study *Robinson's Arithmetic*, it is a very hard one. *Frost's United States History*, *Towen's Speller*, *Weld's Grammar*, the same almost exactly like the one I studied [in the] east, but the *Grammar* is not at all like it. I read out of *Sargent's Reader.*"[39] Many schools suffered from a lack of uniform class sets of texts, although the adoption of this practice was frequently a goal. One forward-looking educator wrote, "In time, however, as the old books, (some of which, carefully preserved, have descended from grand-fathers) are worn out, uniform class-books will be used, much to the advantage of teachers and pupils."[40]

Most lessons were done via rote memorization and recitation. In a time when paper was at a premium, teachers generally "heard" the lessons of their students. Poems, speeches, readings, arithmetic facts, and times tables were presented orally by the student before the class. Arithmetic and grammar exercises, for the youngest students, were done on a small lap slate or on the classroom blackboard. Older students were sometimes given "foolscap" (writing paper of poor quality) on which to do their mathematics and essays. To stimulate student motivation, less-interesting material such as geographic facts were sung to popular tunes and multiplication tables were often taught in verse, such as, "Twice 11 are 22. Mister can you mend my shoe?" or "9 times 12 are 108. See what I've drawn upon my slate." Mental arithmetic was still an innovation in learning, and more than one district supervisor reveled in the fact that it was taught in his schools. "Mental arithmetic has been extensively introduced during the past two years and will soon be considered an indispensable item even in our primary schools."[41] Rural schools were often ungraded and had no standard final examinations or report cards. Scholastic success was given a showcase via exhibitions, bees, and quizzes held for parents during which students demonstrated their expertise in spelling, arithmetic, geography, and history. In addition to adulation, winners were given certificates and prizes such as books or prints.

There were few educational standards at this time. There were no state or national norms, and all standards that did exist were local. The length of the school day and year varied as the individual community saw fit. The average length of the school term in 1860 was five months and five and a half days, almost exactly matching those months between harvest and planting when there was little for children to do on the farm. A typical school day ran from nine to four with an hour for recess and dinner at noon. The day often commenced with a scripture reading followed by a patriotic song. Emma Sargent Barbour received a letter from her sister, Maria, addressing her teaching duties: "I am a regular schoolmarm. School commences every day at nine o'clock when they write a half hour and the lessons follow."[42] A subsequent letter provides more details of a teacher's day. "School! School!—is the cry, my daily life may almost be embraced in the following programme; rise at seven, breakfast at half past, practice my little singing lesson and ready to start for school at half past eight. Direct the youths how to behave and hear lessons until twelve, then from twenty minutes to a half an hour, hear missed lessons and eat lunch, chat with the boys until one o'clock, then proceed as before until three; prepare for dinner and sometimes attend receptions or receive company in the evening."[43]

The subjects that were taught at any level of education depended on the competency of the teachers and varied greatly from place to place. In the annual report of Armstrong County, Pennsylvania, the superintendent boasted, "The number of schools in which geography and grammar are not taught is steadily diminishing. There is a considerable increase in the number in which mental arithmetic is taught. Algebra was taught in 11 schools; history in 4; natural philosophy in 2; Latin in 1; composition in 5 and in several there were exercises in declamation and vocal music."[44] In Connecticut, one of the more progressive places where state standards were dictated by the Legislature, incorporated towns with 80 families were required to have at least one school for young children that taught English grammar, reading, writing, geography, and arithmetic. Towns with 500 families were to establish an additional school for older students that offered algebra, American history, geometry, and surveying. Those places with larger populations might institute programs that included natural philosophy (physical science), Greek, and Latin as they saw fit.

In addition to the three R's, schools were expected to infuse a strong moral sense, foster polite behavior, and inspire good character. Another instructional objective, presented in a reading text, was "a desire to improve the literary taste to the learner, to impress correct moral principles, and augment his fund of knowledge."[45] There was no sense of separation of religion or morality from secular education. The report of the Beaver County, Pennsylvania, superintendent of schools noted, "The Bible is read in 140 schools; not read in 17. I trust that all our teachers may become so deeply impressed with a sense of their duty, in the moral education of their pupils, that we may soon report the Bible read in every school."[46] An introductory geography book contained the following extraordinary attestation in its preface: "The introduction of moral and religious sentiments into books designed for the instruction of young persons, is calculated to improve the heart, and elevate and expand the youthful mind; accordingly, whenever the subject has admitted of it, such observations have been made as tend to illustrate the excellence of Christian religion, the advantages of correct moral principles, and the superiority of enlightened institutions."[47]

Readers contained lessons emphasizing honesty, behavior, and good manners such as "The First Falsehood," the "Effects of Evil Company," a "Contrast between Industry and Idleness," and a "Dialogue between Mr. Punctual and Mr. Tardy." Stories, poems, and essays used in instruction drilled the messages that good triumphed over evil, frugality surpassed extravagance, obedience superseded willfulness, and family always came first. This can be seen even in brief multiplication rhymes: "5 times 10 are

50. My Rose is very thrifty"[48] or "4 times 10 are 40. Those boys are very naughty." The last was inscribed beneath a picture of two boys fighting.[49] Some texts published in the North, contained distinctly anti-Southern sentiments, whereas many from the South carried pro–states' rights and militant themes. Caroline Cowles Richards wrote in her diary just prior to the outbreak of war, "I recited 'Scott and the Veteran' today at school, and Mary Field recited, 'To Drum Beat and Heart Beat a Soldier Marches By.' Anna recited 'The Virginia Mother.' Everyone learns war poems now-a-days."[50]

Gifted students could pass through the entire local system of schools by age 14 or 15, but only the most well heeled could move on to college or university. Although college enrollments grew throughout the antebellum period, the slow development of high schools in the Northern cities provided for a less expensive educational opportunity than college or the academy for boys who wished to become merchants or mechanics. Most people felt that this form of higher education should not be part of the legal public school system. A high school education was seen as terminal at the time. Boston, a leader in educational matters, did not open a high school for girls until 1855. By 1860, there were only 300 high schools in the United States, 100 of which were in Massachusetts. High schools remained a uniquely urban institution until after the Civil War. Nonetheless, in the decade after the war, only 2 percent of the 17-year-old population had graduated from high school.[51] A foreign visitor to New England found that most middle-class American men had a basic education that stressed reading and writing, but that few exhibited the fine formal education available in Europe.

HIGHER EDUCATION

Colleges and universities in America have long been viewed as repositories of knowledge established to train the best minds to deal with advanced philosophical concepts, if not in technical and professional subjects. There were 11 major colleges established during the colonial period. Chief among these in the North were Harvard (1636), Yale (1701), Princeton (1746), University of Pennsylvania (1751), Columbia (King's College, 1754), Brown (1764), Rutgers (1766), and Dartmouth (1770). In the South there were William and Mary (1693), Hampton-Sydney College (1776), and Transylvania College (1780). Twelve more colleges were established from the end of the Revolution to 1800; 33 from 1800 to 1830; and 180 from 1830 to 1865. The oldest colleges in the East were established by private groups and chartered by their respective legislatures, but they were otherwise independent of government control. Those in the West and South were generally supported and controlled by their state government. From the early part of the 19th century there was some effort to offer higher education to women. Mount Holyoke Seminary in Massachusetts (1837) and Elmira College in New York (1855) were nearly equivalent to those schools reserved for men. Vassar in Poughkeepsie, New York, which styled the prototype of modern colleges of women, was not founded until 1865.

Some of these institutions such as the College of New Jersey at Princeton or the College of Rhode Island at Providence owed their existence to the academy movement from which they had evolved. Others were founded by sectarian groups. Columbia (King's) College, Queen's College, and Rutgers were founded by adherents of the Dutch Reformed Church. The College of Philadelphia was founded by the Presbyterian Synod of that city as the chief training school for its ministers. Harvard, in Boston, was established to provide a sufficient number of trained Anglican ministers for the pulpits of Massachusetts, and Yale, in New Haven, was established by Connecticut residents as a Congregational response to the perceived liberalism of the Harvard alumni. Other schools, like Reverend Eleazar Wheelock's college at Dartmouth in New Hampshire had a more involved evolution—moving from a frontier school for the Christianization of Indians to a distinguished, cosmopolitan university.

Yet the purposes for which these institutions had been founded were always broader than their anecdotal histories revealed at first glance. The idea that colleges were nothing more than religious societies for the training of ministers was "nothing less than popery" according to some contemporary observers.[52] The establishment of new institutions in America that lacked the ancient customs and traditions of European schools inevitably lead to the development of a university system rooted in a more general form of Protestantism. Unassociated, as most were, with the older universities of Europe, American colleges tended to humanize religious life, moderate intolerance, and bring the academic community closer to a less sectarian form free of most of the controversies over doctrine that plagued the older institutions. American institutions of higher learning came to be characterized by their relatively heterogeneous student bodies, their acceptance of a common worldview rooted in Christianity, and their openness to new ideas.

Only the Catholic institutions remained intolerant of criticism, unapologetically authoritarian, resolute, and unalterable in their structure. As the oldest and best-organized religion in the Western world, Catholics demanded the unquestioned obedience of their members to the will of the Pope, and expected the same from the teachers and students at their colleges. Nonetheless, Alexis de Tocqueville said of the Catholic institutions in Maryland: "These colleges are full of Protestants. There is perhaps no young man in Maryland who has received a good education who has not been brought up by Catholics." The Catholic Church in America began its educational system on a diocese-by-diocese basis in response to anti-Catholic legislation in New York that required the daily reading of the King James (Church of England) version of the Bible. The Catholic system included a number of colleges and seminaries, as well as high schools and grammar schools, but these were limited to regions with large Catholic populations wealthy enough to support them. In 1839, more than 5,000 students attended eight institutions in New York alone.[53]

Southern colleges and universities offered opportunities comparable to their Northern counterparts. The College of William and Mary in Virginia was well thought of even in the European academic community. The University of North Carolina–Chapel Hill, first chartered in 1795, remained a single building near the New Hope Chapel until 1860. Student enrollment at Chapel Hill increased steadily with only Yale boasting of a larger student body before the war. The University of Virginia, founded in 1825, was unequivocally cosmopolitan and academically ranked second in the nation in 1860, preceded only by Harvard. Although largely under state control, most of the South's colleges were supported by religious denominations. Presbyterians took the lead with Hampton-Sydney College (1776) in east Tennessee, Washington College (1782; it changed to Washington and Lee in 1865), and Transylvania College (1780). Episcopalians had established William and Mary and followed with St. John's College and the College of Charleston. The College of Louisiana was opened in 1826 in Jackson, and it expanded in size throughout the 1830s, adding a number of buildings. Nonetheless, by the mid-1850s it had closed due to declining enrollments. With 250 students and 11 faculty members, the Centenary College at Brandon Springs, operated by the Methodist/Episcopal Church South since 1839, took over the College of Louisiana buildings in 1856. Between 1856 and 1858, the Centenary College built a gymnasium, a 3,000-volume library, and a chapel/auditorium that seated 2,000 people.

Colleges also sprang up in the rural Southern countryside from the rootstock of older academies that were clearly offering college-level instruction. Clio's Nursery in North Carolina and the Newark Academy in Delaware were two examples. No fewer than 25 institutions like these were granted state charters before the end of the antebellum period, and several received considerable state aid that helped them to remain solvent despite declining enrollments. Nonetheless, the outbreak of the Civil War had a profound effect on most Southern colleges. Roanoke College in Virginia (1842) was one of the few Southern institutions to remain in operation throughout the conflict. Many closed for the duration of the war as young men streamed into the military units of the Confederacy. Federal or Confederate forces occupied some college buildings to use as hospitals, barracks, and headquarters during the war.

College studies everywhere were heavily laden with classical course content, which seems to have taken on the role of a puberty rite granting access to proper society through the pain and punishment of reading Livy, Cicero, Homer, Plato, Euclid, and other ancient writers in the original Greek and Latin. Instruction was based on the same fundamentals as those of the 17th century, and, as with primary education, oral recitation was the most common form of instruction. In much the same way that physical activity was preparation for the life of a laborer, the function of higher education was thought to be the training of the mind through mental discipline rather than instruction in specific course content. In the 1850s, an observer noted the system used at Yale: "The professor or tutor sat in a box, with his students before and beneath him, and the so-called education consisted of questions upon a textbook. Not questions to elicit thought, but simply questions to find out how nearly the students could repeat the words of the book, or, if it were a classic, to find out how little they knew of Latin or Greek grammar." Many students found it impossible to satisfy their instructors by thinking in Greek and Latin, and they were generally indifferent to the classical course content, hoping instead to learn more about the application of science, mathematics, and engineering, which, if treated at all, were given the same superficial attention that they are in grade school today. As late as the 1854, many of the professors at Princeton expressed their satisfaction with the traditional curriculum noting that no "experiments in education" had been given the slightest countenance.[54]

In the 1820s, George Ticknor, a professor of European languages at Harvard, proposed a program of college studies based on the departmental subdivisions and elective courses, but the institutions of higher learning in America were slow to adopt this structure. Nonetheless, by the 1840s medicine and law, the most frequently pursued vocations, were being taught as separate curricula. Work in the sciences, which covered physics and astronomy with some topics in chemistry and geology, consisted mostly of lectures with occasional laboratory demonstrations. Many important technological advances were initially considered "philosophical toys" created for the entertainment of those in the lecture hall. Mathematics explored algebra, geometry, trigonometry, and calculus and encompassed the strict memorization of rules with only a limited effort to apply them to practical problems. Rhetoric students studied composition as well as speaking. Other studies included natural and biblical philosophy and logic.[55]

The editor of the *American Journal of Education* wrote in 1862 a description of university education that well characterizes the state of higher education at the end of the antebellum period.

All branches of human learning may be embraced in the proper schedule of university instruction; but has any university given equal attention to all branches of education? What are called colleges in our country, all aim at fitting young men for the civil professions—Law, Medicine, and Theology. They therefore make the classics the principal branch of study, and are right, since Law, Medicine, and Theology have their foundation laid deep in the classic ages. Literature also is a part of professional knowledge, necessary to adorn and illustrate the history and theory of professional science. Hence, in those lines of instruction specially have run the studies of the college, and from these is derived the tone of college education.[56]

College professors were offered small salaries, and often found that at the end of the year they were reduced to dividing the assets of the college treasury because enrollment had not met expectations. There were no research facilities or grants, and there was no tenure, pension, or retirement plan. Instructors served at the will of the college president or committee. Many of the professors were elderly clergymen in failing health and unequal to the duties of required by an ordinary ministry. There was no special training for college instructors beyond what they knew, which was usually rooted in their own classical educations. Most institutions provided a number of tutors to assist the professors, but these were almost always young men in the early stages of training for the ministry.

Professorship at the university level evolved from a mere organizational model to one of a larger intellectual and pedagogical specialization, and the college lecture, like its civilian counterpart, soon came to be a device whereby the instructor could present and contrast his own ideas with those of others in a systematic and efficient form. Chester Dewey, a professor at Williams College and later at Rochester, was typical of the breed in the early days of the period. Well versed in the Bible—he was an ordained minister—Dewey was a tireless lecturer, giving more than 4,000 lectures in chemistry, mineralogy, and botany from 1810 to 1827. Each was peppered with biblical quotations and allusions like a well-rehearsed sermon. Nonetheless, Dewey was a serious scientist who enthralled his audience with demonstrations and pranks such as lighting alcohol with an electric spark, passing a current through his students, and making things glow in the dark by coating them with phosphorous.

Notwithstanding teachers like Dewey, as early as the first quarter of the century, educators had begun expressing concern over the direction of higher education. In 1820, Alden Partridge, an educator and later superintendent of the U.S. Military Academy at West Point, gave a lecture on his views concerning the deficiencies to be found in public colleges and seminaries of higher learning. His speech was subsequently printed and circulated widely throughout the pedagogical community. His main point was that the college years were an opportunity to prepare young students to correctly discharge the duties of any station in life in which they might be placed. The key weakness he found in the American system of liberal education was that it prepared students only "to become members of the college or university," calling for the study of Latin and Greek while giving "very slight attention" to English language and literature, the elements of arithmetic, and other practical matters. "Here they spend four years for the purpose of acquiring a knowledge of the higher branches of learning; after which they receive their diplomas, and are supposed to be prepared to enter on the duties of active life. But, I would ask, is this actually the case? . . . Has their attention been sufficiently directed to those great and important branches of national industry and sources of wealth—agriculture, commerce, and manufactures?"[57]

Partridge also found the system of higher education wanting in the areas of physical education, then popular among German educators and proponents of the gymnasium for producing "a firm and vigorous constitution." Beyond the superficial niceties of clean clothing and bedding, hygiene at most colleges was little regarded with few or no facilities for bathing and restrooms no more advanced than those of the outhouse found on most rural farms. Athletics were barely tolerated, and at some institutions running, jumping, climbing, and many other forms of physical exertion were considered below the dignity and deportment of the scholar. The lack of exercise produced a student body that was "sickly" and "desk-bound." In mid-century, Oliver Wendell Holmes described them as "a set of black-coated, stiff-jointed, soft-muscled, paste complexioned youth[s]," and Nathaniel Parker Willis described them as "hollow-chested, narrow-shouldered, [and] ill-developed looking."[58]

Partridge denounced the large amounts of idle time afforded students away from their studies and the quantities of disposable money available to those students from wealthy families "thereby inducing habits of dissipation and extravagance, highly injurious to themselves, and also to the seminaries of which they are members." Finally, he decried the requirement that all students follow the same course of study in a prescribed length of time. "All youth have not the same inclinations and capacities . . . for the study of the classics . . . the mathematics and other branches of science." By following a predetermined length of time for the course of education, "the good scholar is placed nearly on a level with the sluggard, for whatever may be his exertions, he can gain nothing in respect to time, and the latter has, in consequence of this, less stimulus for exertion."[59]

College students during the antebellum period seem to have been no better in terms of their decorum than modern scholars. Moreover, some of their activities went beyond pranks, drunkenness, and adolescent licentiousness to a level that was remarkably unrestrained and even violent. In general, student manners were good with boys doffing their caps to faculty and attending early morning religious services. Yet although there were long periods of peaceful coexistence on antebellum college campuses, faculty-student relations were often strained at the very best institutions and many disagreements resulted in the smashing of furniture, the use of explosives, and the effusion of blood. One institution in New York found it necessary to codify its regulations forbidding students to "blaspheme, rob, fornicate, steal, forge, duel; or assault, wound, or strike the president [of the college] or the members of the faculty."[60]

Rioting among the students was somewhat of a tradition at many schools. In 1807, Harvard students protested the quality of the food; in 1823, 43 of 70 seniors were expelled; and, in 1834, the entire sophomore class was dismissed for the remainder of the year. At Yale in 1830, Benjamin Silliman attended his laboratory with two loaded pistols during a period of student unrest that ended with the banishment of half the sophomore class, and in 1843, a tutor was fatally stabbed when he tried to subdue a window-breaking rioter. Four years later, protesting students shot and killed a New Haven fireman. Princeton experienced six major student rebellions between 1800 and 1830, many of which were related to drunkenness. In 1817, of an entire student body of 200 scholars, 125 were expelled after a pistol was fired through a tutor's door and a bomb was exploded in Nassua Hall, breaking the windows and cracking the walls.

Southern schools mirrored their social and cultural environment with frequent duels with pistols between students and outbreaks of physical violence toward the administration. In 1840, six seniors attacked the president of the University of Georgia, and in the same year, a student stabbed and killed the president of Oakland College in Mississippi. The faculty chairman at the University of Virginia was seized and whipped by a throng of rioting students before the state militia could restore order. The man later died of his wounds. A modern historian has noted of these incidents, "Granted they were exceptional and hence memorable; nevertheless they reveal a habit of mutiny that lay dormant from the mid-century to our own times. In the early days of the Republic violence was part of American life, on the frontiers and in the turbulent cities. The collegians did no more than follow the example set by their elders. They were subjected to a galling regime of restriction and repression, to a routine of hardship, to a curriculum of studies that was generally unwelcome. The explosions were likely to be thunderous."[61]

Military Education

Near the end of the 18th century, the young United States felt an immediate want for men trained in the best possible habits and principles of military science. As early as the Revolution, George Washington had recognized the inherent weakness of a country that had to rely on foreigners to shape his army and to plan his fortifications. For quite some time there was a struggle among competing ideas of just what balance of moral, intellectual, and physical disciplines were needed to provide for a corps of properly trained officers for the Army of the United States. The English author John Milton penned a pedagogical outline for military education that was very close to the one instituted in American schools. Milton's ideas were based on "virtuous and noble" principles designed to prepare the student "to perform justly, skillfully, and magnanimously all the offices, both public and private, of peace and war." His program of education included studies in a number of areas such as mathematics, surveying, engineering, navigation, and the art of fortification. He also suggested a dedication to physical education, a knowledge of geography, and any academic activity that helped the student contemplate "the serene countenance of truth in the still air of delightful study."[62]

In 1802, Congress established the idea of a national military academy at West Point, but the idea of making a separate institution for the scientific study of warfare had not yet fully matured. As a school, West Point, for many years, survived "an inchoate existence, without regular teachers, or limited studies, or proper discipline. . . . No professor of engineering or any other department was appointed before 1812 [and] in fact, there were no graduates prior to 1815."[63]

The curriculum chosen for West Point cadets in 1825 included, in their order of importance, mathematics, natural philosophy, mechanics, astronomy, engineering, chemistry, French, tactics, principles of artillery, mineralogy, ethics, and history. Some attempt was made to adapt the school to the tone of higher education in civil institutions, but the object of West Point was not civil, but martial life. Yet as late as 1840, a period newspaper, *Citizen Soldier*, found the U.S. Military Academy at West Point "monopolizing, aristocratic, unconstitutional, and worse than useless."[64] In 1862, Henry Barnard, editor of the *American Journal of Education*, noted of West Point, "It was not to be expected that schools of refined, scientific art should be found by small colonies in the wilderness of a new world. When even their clergymen must resort to Europe for education, and their lawyers for license, it was in vain to expect their soldiers to be accomplished engineers."[65]

The tone of education at West Point was characterized by "neither a metaphysical discussion, nor a hair-splitting argument on the law, in which they were expected to excel. They were to learn the sterner arguments of the battle-field; to arrange squadrons for the hardy fight; to acquire that profound knowledge of the science and materials of nature, which should fit them for the complicated art of war." These arts were stated under the unassuming headings of "Studies," "Physical and Moral Discipline," and "Military Exercise." The division of time during the school year alternated between study and exercise, "leaving the least possible time for idleness, or mere amusement." The problem of military education was thought not to revolve around simple ignorance, but rather around unequal development of the "co-relatively intellectual, physical, and moral. . . . There [was] not, as in civil colleges, the great fallow field of poetry, history, and metaphysics, in which [the student] may show his classical professor that he has acquired rich things, although ignorant of mathematics. It will not do to say that he has wandered with Greeks and Romans around the ruins of Troy, or by the waters of Babel. There [was] no such compensating principle in the system at West Point. The cadet must study what [was] set before him; must study it hard; must think upon it, and discipline his mind to systematic modes of thought."[66]

As part of his formula for the revision of all higher education, Alden Partridge had also dedicated a good deal of his thinking to the inclusion of military studies and discipline for all students. Although the course of academic studies that he proposed was as extensive as that of any academy or college in New England at the time, not everyone favored the inclusion of military topics and discipline. In 1820, Partridge opened an institution for almost 500 students organized under his own ideas at Norwich, Vermont, and in 1824, he removed the academy to Middletown, Connecticut, at the invitation of the citizens of the region. Here the school grew to house more than 1,200 pupils from every state and territory in the United States, many from Canada, Mexico, the West Indies, and several from South American nations. In 1834, he reopened his institute in Vermont as the Norwich University, and in 1839, he established a similar school at Portsmouth, Virginia, which came to be known as the Virginia Literary, Scientific, and Military Institute. In 1853, he opened at Brandywine Springs, near Wilmington, Delaware, another institution "in which he fondly hoped his ideal of a National school of education would be realized." His plan, as it developed, emphasized "physical training in connection with military exercises and movements [accompanied by] the acquisition of practical knowledge of the great principles of science that underlie all the arts of peace and war." The success of Partridge's schools in Vermont, Connecticut, Delaware, and particularly in Virginia led to the establishment of similar schools of military training throughout the nation and particularly in the South.

As early as the first decade of the 19th century, an unequaled interest in military education had been clearly manifest in the South, and by the final antebellum decade, the movement toward military education and the establishment of schools dedicated specifically to the martial arts had gained marked momentum. A military career became increasingly acceptable for the sons of the plantation aristocracy who reveled in a military mythology that traced their descent from the Cavaliers of the English Civil Wars who had ridden at Nasby. The success of Southern warriors during the Revolution and during the Mexican War of 1846 also greatly enhanced the prestige of a military education and career. In 1854, a Charlestonian noted that the South cherished a military spirit and wished to diffuse the precepts of military science among its young men so that they might defy the North should it take up arms against the South.

Notwithstanding the negative attitudes toward a Northern education, the "aristocratic" characteristic of military education at West Point certainly appealed to Southerners. So highly prized was the quality of this military and academy preparation that more than one-third of the student body at West Point had Southern roots. On the eve of the Civil War, it was found that 306 graduates of West Point had joined the Confederate Army as officers. This finding led U.S. Secretary of War Simon Cameron to remark in July 1861:

> The large disaffection at the present crisis of United States Army officers has excited the most profound astonishment and naturally provokes inquiry as to its cause. . . . The question may be asked in view of this extraordinary treachery displayed whether its promoting cause may not be traced to a radical defect in the system of education itself.[67]

Notwithstanding Cameron's remarks, public sentiment in the South had increasingly frowned upon a military education at Northern schools. North Carolina was among the earliest of the Southern states to initiate the study of the martial arts as a regular part of the course of study. Schools in South Carolina, Mississippi, and Alabama also showed interest in military education by the second quarter of the century. By the 1840s, a generation of young men had been trained in Light Infantry Tactics, Broad Sword Exercises, and Cavalry Evolutions on "the plan of the West Point Seminary" in schools based in the South.[68]

Most initiatives at established academic schools simply added to the ordinary branches of studies the science of camps and tactics—a modification that was found "agreeable" to the youth of the country. Nowhere did Southerners better understand this problem than in Virginia and South Carolina. In 1836, Virginians decided to substitute a military school for the company of state guards by diverting the financial resources of the state from the Lexington Arsenal to the Virginia Military Institute (VMI) in its stead. Virginians pointed to the development of VMI as "thoroughly and exclusively Virginian" and pointed with pride to the state patriotism engendered therein. South Carolinians attempted to combine the "enterprise and decision of a military character" with the acquisition of a scholastic education by converting the Arsenal at Columbia and the Citadel and Magazine at Charleston into military schools. Another major Southern school, the Georgia Military Institute, was opened in 1851.[69]

An important factor in the growth of Southern military schools was the zeal of those who graduated. The graduates of these schools, especially those of VMI, devotedly promoted military education throughout the South. Many VMI graduates went on before the breaking of the crisis to serve as instructors in newer institutions. When the war came, it was not surprising that two-thirds of the highest-ranking officers in the Confederate Army were from Virginia.

Nowhere else in the South were there any developments remotely approaching the success of schools like VMI. As the war approached, town after town in the South boasted a new "military academy." However, students attending these institutions generally saw only minor modifications in instruction and the addition of various military activities—riding, military drills, and tactics—incorporated into the routine academic curriculum. Companies of uniformed cadets were established in many places. Most prospered only briefly to be abandoned when the novelty wore off. State support was generally limited to providing the school with tax exemptions and as many antiquated muskets, artillery pieces, and other arms as needed for training purposes. Some military institutions received increasing public support as the sectional disputes tearing at the nation proceeded toward war.

Yet military education required more than mere financial support. Military schools enjoyed excellent public relations in the South, engaging in activities designed to excite the interest of the populace. Cadets made frequent off-campus visits to communities to display their skills at drill and their attractive, if rather gaudy, uniforms by parading in the town square or on the county fairgrounds. An unbridled martial spirit was abroad by the 1850s, and most Southerners regarded their military schools as among their most valuable regional assets. Moreover, a wider usefulness was recognized in having a cadre of military personnel that could quickly respond to possible slave uprisings.

Schools of Science

Not until 1827 would the term "technology" be coined to represent the application of the study of science to real-world situations. Jacob Bigelow first used the term during a lecture at Harvard. At most colleges and universities, only a few scientific lectures were given each year in addition to the classical curriculum. Williams College boasted of an astronomical observatory, but major schools like Dartmouth and Bowdoin adhered to a strictly classical curriculum. As late as 1845, at Yale the first two years of college were limited to Latin, Greek, and mathematics, and during the next two years students were exposed to periodic lectures on natural philosophy, chemistry, mineralogy, geology, and astronomy. There were two professors of science and three teaching assistants. Harvard offered essentially the same subjects, although some chemistry and natural history were studied in the first two years. Oddly, one of the weakest fields affecting science education was mathematics, which was so mired in the work of

Newton and Euclid that it could not easily expand into new dimensions of theoretical thought.

At the beginning of the antebellum period, no formal laboratory instruction existed at any school even though Amos Eaton had demonstrated its usefulness at Rensselaer College in New York as early as 1817. At Yale, Benjamin Silliman Sr. had a single basement room for experimentation that was enlarged only after the Medical School was established, and John W. Webster, author of the *Manual for Chemistry* (1826), founded a chemistry lab at the Harvard Medical School in that year. Nonetheless, Silliman and his son Benjamin Jr., who was also a teacher, had attracted a number of young men interested in chemistry and geology to Yale. In 1842, the younger Silliman was able to secure a workshop at the school in which to instruct a few students interested in the practical application of scientific or engineering principles.

The early teaching of biological science at Williams College ultimately affected not only the curriculum at Yale and Harvard but also that of Amherst College and the Rensselaer Institute. In New England, private medical schools were opened at Pittsfield, Massachusetts, at Woodstock and Rutland in Vermont, and at Fairfield near Utica, New York. Although their clinical facilities were primitive by today's standards, these rural schools were advanced for their day, successfully competing for students with Yale and Harvard. Yet by the beginning of the Civil War, most of the rural medical schools had disappeared, and their students had been absorbed into the major urban universities. The inspiration for these schools came from abroad where many American physicians had received their own training. It is interesting to note that the scientific school at Yale was founded largely by men trained in agriculture, whereas at Harvard it was founded by those rooted in industry. John Pitkin Norton started the School of Applied Chemistry at Yale in 1847.

Another of the weaknesses in American higher education was in the area of scientific agriculture. Southerners were much more expert in this regard than New Englanders. Many Southerners had formed or joined private agricultural societies in the 18th century in an attempt to better underpin the plantation system. The colonials had used seaweed, clam and oyster shells, fish, ashes, and bonemeal to improve their soil, but they did not spend a great deal of time using animal fertilizers. This may have been because virgin land was plentiful, but also because direct and purposeful fertilization was a new idea. It was not until several decades had passed that the earliest settlers noticed a change in the soil that they were farming. At first it had been dark, almost black, but with time its color became lighter, and crop yields fell. Scientific agriculturalists in England, like Jethro Tull, believed that active cultivation of the soil was the secret of its fertility. Deep plowing was his answer to diminished crop yields as this helped to dry out wet land and allowed the soil to better utilize rain-fall. Jared Elliot, a minister and doctor from Connecticut at the turn of the century, correctly believed that the fertility of the soil was associated with the organic matter that it contained. He showed that the addition of swamp mud to the soil increased the yield and improved the crops, and he was one of the first to note that certain crops rebuilt the soil. Ultimately, he was able to show that animal manures, cover crops of red clover and timothy, and a years' rest between plantings could significantly improve agricultural production. Later experiments showed that root crops such as turnips and carrots helped the soil. Moreover, turnips, in particular, could be used as winter feed for livestock.[70]

In the 1840s, many Southern planters abandoned their worn-out coastal land for new fields in Mississippi and Alabama, which promised to be more fertile. The rich black soil of these areas promised an abundance of cotton, if not tobacco. Yet, in just a decade, these "new" lands were also showing the effects of erosion and soil worn by extensive single-crop agriculture. This circumstance found the next generation of planters moving on again to Texas and Arkansas. Virginia Senator John Randolph, seeing fields gullied and rivers full of mud, called the farming techniques commonly used in his state "improvident." He warned his fellow planters, "We must either attend to . . . our lands or abandon them and run away to Alabama." Randolph, with a few concerned planters, sponsored programs that trained farmers and their slaves to use modern plowing methods. They introduced technological improvements to farming and encouraged soil experiments. Another planter and politician, Edmund Ruffin—best noted as the man who fired the first shot of the Civil War—served for many years as the head of the Virginia Agricultural Society. This group also fostered more modern farming methods, and from 1833 to 1842, Ruffin was the editor of the *Farmer's Register*, a publication dedicated to the improvement of agricultural practices.

PART II

Popular Culture

3

Advertising

All persons troubled with Coughs, Colds, Hoarseness, Sore Throat,
Etc. will find immediate relief by using these drops. Public Speakers,
Singers, Etc. are invited to try them. One of these drops put in the
mouth before going to bed, loosens the phlegm and causes the
patient to enjoy a comfortable nights sleep.
> —The first Smith Brothers Cough Drops ad, 1852

During most of the antebellum period, nationwide promotion of products
and services was impractical. Businesses, tradesmen, and professionals
such as doctors and lawyers generally operated locally. Much advertising was done with handbills, which were posted in public places such as
taverns and general stores. Advertising in this period was primarily used
by retailers, wholesalers, patent medicines dealers, and transporters to
inform potential customers of their services or to advise the public about
lost possessions, lotteries,[1] and runaways. It was not until after the Civil
War, when manufacturers began to seek larger markets, that national
branding and national advertising really came into being. Many retailers'
ads were little more than lists of newly arrived merchandise. The following 1859 ad for R.H. Macy was typical for the period:

SPRING RIBBONS now opening every day.
SPRING FLOWERS just received from Paris,
JUST RECEIVED, an invoice of Linen Handkerchiefs,
JUST RECEIVED, an invoice of New Lace Goods,
JUST RECEIVED, an invoice of Hosiery and Gloves,
JUST RECEIVED, an invoice Spring Styles Housekeeping Dry Goods.

LADIES CORSETS, 8s, 7s and 10s, Good Styles.
LADIES KID GLOVES 63c, all colors and sizes.
ALL KINDS EMBROIDERIES, very cheap, to close.
OUR GREAT SALE is still on the INCREASE.
Ladies please call. We sell good Goods.[2]

ADVERTISING PREJUDICES

Despite the fact that advertising provided necessary revenue for news-papers, little attention was paid to it. Advertisements were often sold at a fixed price per year and copy was seldom altered. A New York paper accepted advertisements "not exceeding one square, inserted three weeks for one dollar and for every additional insertion 25 cents, larger ones in the same proportion. To those who advertise by the year a liberal discount will be made."[3]

Early in the 19th century, newspapers commonly copied advertisements from other papers and ran them at no cost to the advertiser. They did this hoping to establish themselves as a prominent advertising vehicle. They would also contact the advertisers and see if they would like to purchase the space in the future. This seemingly neglectful attitude toward advertising was reflected in the resistance to advertising by editors of the media. Antebellum advertisements were generally confined to agate type size and single-column format. There was often a "no display" rule governing graphics. Some of these restrictions were supported by mechanical limitations and paper size, but some were just for the sake of constraint.

Advertising was considered rather ungentlemanly and crass. In some cases, early advertisements appeared under a section referred to as "Business Cards" or "Business Notices." The term "business notice" may well be the best description of advertisements during this time as they generally appeared much like legal notices or classified ads in modern papers. Ads were often as simple as Cyrus Prentiss's notice of "Flour—a few Barrels of Superfine Flour, just received and for sale by the subscriber."[4] Many were very succinct: "FUR CAPS & MUFFS—Just received at WRIGHTS, No. 23. State-st."[5]

USES OF ADVERTISING

In addition to the notification of the arrival of new goods, retailers used ads for related business purposes as well. In rural areas, it was not un-usual to find ads for stud services by the owners of well-bred stallions and bulls or notices about the return of strayed livestock. Subscribers placed want ads for teams, teamsters, post riders, laborers, and journeymen artisans such as blacksmiths, joiners, and cabinetmakers. Found amid of-ferings for "Boots and Shoes," "Books," and other merchandise was this ad seeking an apprentice: "Wanted, at this office an apprentice to the Printing business, a lad from 14 to 15 years of age. One of that age, of good habits, quick perception, and possessing a correct knowledge of the Spelling Book, may apply as above."[6]

Notices of a "Sheriff's Sale were squeezed in among ads offering overstocks of foolscap paper, barrels of flour, and revolving pistols and other firearms. Among other retailers' proclamations of "New Goods," "Fresh Supply," and "Clothing," this notice of a more private nature from Davis Price ran: "Caution. My son, JOHN W. PRICE, has left my employ, without any just reason. This is to caution all persons against harboring or trusting him on my account as I shall pay not debts of his contracting after this date."[7]

Many ads were headed "REMOVAL" and gave notice of business relocation; others reminded patrons to settle their accounts. Mr. D. Leary had a unique message to deliver: "Mr. L. deems it important to caution the public against placing any confidence in the reports which have lately been put in circulation by the proprietor of another establishment saying that the shop was closed, calculated to injure his business. As he can with confidence assure them that all work entrusted to him will be executed in style superior to that of any establishment in Western New York."[8]

Big-city newspapers like those in New York, Boston, or New Orleans ran whole columns of ads for competing companies. In a single issue of a Boston weekly in 1848, ads for the Boston & Worcester Rail Road, the Western Rail Road, the Norwich and Worcester Railroad, and the Providence and Worchester Rail Road were stacked in a single column of print with amazingly similar illustrations of steam engines and passenger cars. Surrounding these were ads for stagecoach and steamship lines and express companies, suggesting that this potion of the paper, at least, was arranged topically.

J. Whittlesey made good use of his advertising space when he ran this ad in *The Ohio Star*. Not only did he announce the change of his business address, but he also hawked his summer stock and threw in a mild reminder to those who owed him money to pay up.

REMOVAL
and
NEW GOODS
J. Whittlesey has removed his stock of goods into his new White
Building opposite the Court-House—where he is receiving his
supply of
Spring and Summer Goods
CONSISTING OF
Dry Goods, Groceries, Silk & Fancy Goods, Crockery, Glass and
Hard Wares, Paints and Dye Stuffs
Also, Nails, Iron, Hoes, Blood's Cast Steel Scythes, Harris

Grass and Cradle Scythes, Collins's and Simon's Cast Steel Axes,
Sole Leather &c. &c.
Those persons who neglected to pay their notes and accounts
previous to my going to New York are reminded that it would be
very acceptable, even at this time.[9]

Language in Ads

The language of advertisements was often quite formal. Although the high-sounding vocabulary seemed to be aimed at a generally upper-class consumer, it may in fact have been used to give a modicum of dignity to the advertiser and his business in an era when newspaper advertising might be viewed as lacking in delicacy or refinement. Joseph Carrol gave notice to his deadbeat patrons in a moralizing tone by saying that he "Takes pleasure in informing the public, that he continues his business in all its various branches at his shop, one door west of the office of D. Lyon, Esq.; and he hopes, by punctuality and good work, to merit and receive the patronage of the public. He would also remind those who have BOOK ACCOUNTS of long standing, that 'punctuality is the life of business,' and that payment must be made without further delay." The only mention of his merchandise was the heading "Boots and Shoes," which appeared above the copy.[10] Clock- and watchmaker, Robert E. Campbell, advised readers in the most formal terms that he "Respectfully informs the public that he still continues business at his brick shop, next door east of Z. Kent's store, in Raveena, where he will be pleased to receive favors in the line of his profession."[11]

Illustrations

Key words in the advertisement were often capitalized for emphasis and attention. On rare occasions, small woodcut illustrations were included. Quality printing blocks used for illustrations were difficult to make and, being of wood, did not last. The pictures used in ads therefore were often generic stock pieces much like clip art. Ads for piano makers Steinway & Sons and John B. Dalton ran only inches away from one another each bearing the same rough image of a piano.[12] Owners of the Portage Temperance House and the Raveena Public House might have been quite opposed, philosophically at least, to their advertisements running adjacent to one another, with both notices bearing the same vague illustration of a nondescript three-story brick building.[13] The same illustrations might be seen from issue to issue with no attempt to make changes. One field of advertisements that was likely to contain actual illustrations of products were new inventions such as washing or sewing machines, newly patented stoves and heaters, or unique items such as "Dr. Brown's Patent Baby Tender."

Handbills, posters, and broadsides were not similarly constrained by the limitations of columns and spaces; but they, too, often contained only text, and any illustrations that were used were generally very simple. The size of the type used in this format was often very large and varied. It was arranged in a seemingly incomprehensible pattern that bordered on randomness, and which may have reflected a shortage of uniform type in rural printing shops.

Toward the end of the period, some ads bore illustrations that incorporated the name of the business or product as part of the illustration much like a logo. Ads for the Central Park Skate Emporium contained a picture of a single skate with the business name within the skate blade.[14] Henshaw & Clemson sold cast-steel saws. Their ads featured a saw blade with their name and "Machine Ground" beneath.[15] William Clapp sold fancy goods.

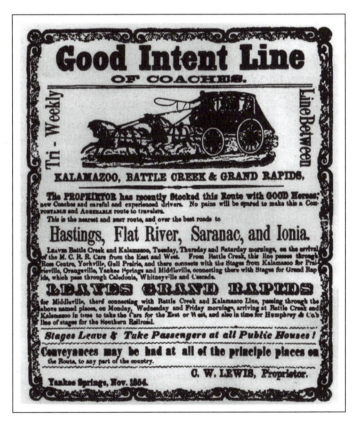

This 1854 newspaper ad for "Tri-weekly" stagecoach service from Grand Rapids to Battle Creek promises to "Leave and Take Passengers at all Public Houses!" It also promises good horses, new coaches, and "careful and experienced drivers."

The ads featured a glove resting horizontally. The hand portion displayed the name and address of the establishment. The cuff and each finger bore the name of merchandise sold, "dress trimmings," "thread," "gloves," "hosiery," and "fancy goods."[16]

The *Boston Directory* for 1859 contained 192 advertisements in addition to its alphabetical business listings. Because the book was made to be a reference for the entire year, the ads it contained were of a finer quality than those found on handbills or in the newspaper. These ads were not subject to column formats as in newspapers. They contained many different fonts of various sizes and styles, yet only 120 of the advertisements contained any type of illustration. Twenty-seven provided actual illustrations of the products offered. These were usually mechanical items such as furnaces, industrial scales, sewing machines, ranges, and machinery. Sixteen of the illustrations showed the building in which the establishment was located. Most of the remaining graphics contained generic illustrations of the types of products offered or vague representations of wares.

Creative Approaches

As the century wore on, American ingenuity came into play. Endeavoring to attract attention to his literary periodical, the *New York Ledger*, publisher Robert Bonner made a bold advertising move in 1856. He ran 93 identical advertisements, one under the other, filling up a complete column in the New York *Herald*. His simple ad read: "ORION, THE GOLD BEATER is the title of Cobb's sensational story in the New York Ledger."[17] He later used the same technique using full pages. Photographer Matthew Brady broke through newspaper industry prohibitions in the same year using inventive type to advertise his photographs, ambrotypes, daguerreotypes, and other photographic services. Nonetheless, the production of actual photographs in print would have to wait until later in the century.

Operating within the publishers' constraints, advertisers became creative in the manner in which their copy was laid out. Many began to form their copy into pyramids or even numerals of a business address in order to create visual interest. The text of an ad for B.T. Babbitt's Concentrated Soft Lard was bordered on both the left and right with the street address of the firm, "68 and 70," printed vertically and repeated for the length of the ad.[18] The copy of Frank Johnson's patent insecticide wasn't likely to attract attention with its witty copy, but the staggered text did make it an attention getter.

Frank G. Johnson's Patent Powered Coal Tar
    For exterminating
    INSECTS AND VERMIN
    IN FIELD AND GARDEN

It will save your Plants
It will save your Corn
It will save your Potatoes
It will save your Wheat
It will save your Cotton
It will save your Tobacco
It will save your Fruit Trees
It will save years Bushes
It will save every product of Field and Garden[19]

Repetition was a common technique. The ad for the *Water-Cure Journal* illustrates the degree of redundancy that could be found in some advertisements.

THE WARTER-CURE JOURNAL
If you are sick and desire to be well
   Read the Water-Cure Journal
If you are well, and desire to avoid disease
   Read the Water-Cure Journal
If you would know the true science of Human Life
   Read the Water-Cure Journal
If you would learn the injurious effects of drugs
   Read the Water-Cure Journal
If you would understand the condition of Health
   Read the Water-Cure Journal
If you desire to dispense with the services of a Physician
   Read the Water-Cure Journal[20]

An ad for E. Anthony's card portraits was quite an eye-catcher. It took the form of two concentric squares. The center contained the numeral 501, which was the address of the establishment. Each of the four trapezoids that enclosed the center square featured items sold such as "Photographic albums," "Card portraits of eminent men," "Foreign views for the stereoscope" and "American views for stereoscopes."[21]

ADVERTISING AGENCIES

By 1840, there were 1,400 newspapers in the United States. As the idea of advertising in the press spread and the number of publications increased, the solicitation of advertising became increasingly competitive. By mid-century, an estimated 11 million advertisements could be found annually in approximately 2,000 newspapers. Advertising in the *New York Tribune* alone doubled between October 1849 and October 1850.[22] Moreover, readers had begun to seek out advertisements in the newspapers. Advertisers wanted to know in which newspapers it would be most worthwhile to run their ads, and the newspapers were beginning to seek quality advertisers more aggressively.

Advertisers quickly came to the understanding that they needed more information in order to be competitive. Charles Mitchell published the *Newspaper Press Directory* in 1846. The directory listed newspapers, journals, circulation rates, and prices as well as information on copywriting and the laws governing advertising. This proved a great aid to individual businessmen, tradespersons, and professionals in creating and placing ads.

Some publications hired salespeople to solicit ads from local merchants. Volney B. Palmer was the first American to act as an advertising agent. He began in Philadelphia in 1841. Palmer did not offer the services associated with modern agents. He operated as an agent for the newspapers rather than for the advertisers, collecting 25 percent commission on any space he sold. As the advertising agent concept spread, agents began to buy space from the newspapers and then sold the space to advertisers at a higher rate.

COPYWRITING

S.M. Pettingill, a former employee of Palmer, struck out on his own adding a new dimension of service to his clients: copywriting. Professional writing, crafted for effect, stood out among the wordy, mundane, and moralistic prose of the amateurs. By mid-century innovative language began to appear in ads including the introduction of modern-sounding terms and the use of eye-catching phrases. Lyon's pesticides featured scientific-sounding "Magnetic Pills," which were guaranteed to be "sure death to rats and mice." The ad hoped to gain further attention with a parody of the "Night Before Christmas."

A MIDSUMMER MELODY
'Twas a night in the dog-days,
   And all through the house
Night prowlers were stirring—
   Roach, bed-bug and mouse.
The children, uneasy,
   Squirmed this way and that—
The bed bugs preferred them
   Because they were fat.
But at dawn, on each insect
   LYON's death powder fell;
And the rats and the mice, too,
   Succumbed to the Pill.[23]

Poems and verse were common in newspapers of this time. To fill additional space, papers relied on prose and poetry heavy with sentimentalism, reflection, and affectation of virtue in order to give the publication an air of sophistication. This appealed a great deal to the romantic nature of the period. Clever advertisers took advantage of the appeal of poetry and incorporated verse into their ads as with this poetic advice.

TO THE LADIES
The simplest things are always best.
    And so it goes in food;
The pastry used is very bad,
    But Ice-Cream's ever good.
In four minutes now 'tis had,
    By Torrey's patent plans,
And in Platt-street, number nine,
    Are too self-sealing cans
Then, charming ones! your rosy cheeks
    With pastry no more pale,
But get the FREEZERS, now so cheap;
    They're everywhere for sale.[24]

Patent medicine ads made some of the most outrageous claims in the newspapers, asserting superior quality, secret ingredients, or exotic formulas. Among the remedies for coughs and chest distress were Anderson's Celebrated Cough Drops, Turlington's Balsam of Life, and Hill's Pectoral Balsam of Honey. A number of "Anti-Dyspeptic" formulas were available for stomach ailments, including James' Formula, the Family Bibulous Formula, and the Cathartic Formula. Lee's Pills and Hooper's Pills were advertised for female trouble alongside Kennedy's Corn Plasters, British and Harlem Oil, and Godfrey's Cordial and Volitile-Aromatic Snuff. Dr. Shawl's Peptonic claimed to cure dyspepsia, sick stomach, headache, and constipation. Although its main ingredient was good old-fashioned alcohol, it was described as a great remedy for both adults and children. One ad from 1857 featured a rhyming conversation between Death and Disease over the effectiveness of a patent medicine pill.

DEATH   —   How comes it, friend, in every shape
                 You let so many folks escape?
DISEASE   —   Dread sire, I use all means I can,
                 To abbreviate the life of man.
                 I dog his footsteps from his birth
                 Till he returns to mother earth;
                 Changes of weather—hot and cold,
                 I give them colds—I give them pains
                 I rack their bones—I fire their veins
                 I poison them with rancid bile,
                 In place of the digestive chyle;
                 Yet all is useless—nothing kills.

DEATH   —   How's that?
DISEASE   —   They take Brandreth's Pills![25]

Household furnishing, drapes, bedroom suites, oil lamps, and furniture were all hawked in the press. So many ads were placed in print that advertisers feared that their ads would be lost among the others. Grover and Baker Sewing Machines hoped their ad in verse would be more memorable if it were linked to a popular tune.

AN APPEAL TO MANHOOD
(Tune "Yankee Doodle")
Fathers, sons and brothers all
Would you do your duty?
Would you save our precious lives
And help preserve our beauty?
(*Chorus*)
   Buy us the new Machine
   One to do our sewing;
   One of Grover and Baker's make,
It is the best one going.
Would you like our faces bright
As a sunny morning?
Would you see the rose of health
The cheeks you love adorning?
(*Chorus*)
Would you have the forms you love
Revealing the graces?
Help to make their labor light
For care will leave its traces.
(*Chorus*)
Now let each one do his part
To make our home sunny
Don't think that you'll accomplish this
Without a little money.
(*Chorus*)[26]

Compensated endorsements by persons of note, or those in their circle of friends or employ, were very common. The persons purported to be making statements of recommendation for products represented in the newspapers often did not exist, and many of those who did may not have had any real relationship with the product or service. Testimonials, even today, are incorporated into all kinds of ads, and unsophisticated consumers often fall prey to many spurious, fraudulent, and deceptive forms of anecdotal endorsement. Nonetheless, the readers of the antebellum press seemed to be easily influenced by moving tales of miracle cures, instant solutions to chronic problems, and wondrous machines and inventions.

The following example is trying to use the effect of an endorsement by someone near a celebrity, although there is no evidence offered of its truth.

GLENFIELD PATENT STARCH
Used in QUEEN VICTORIA'S LAUNDRY
and pronounced by HER MAJESTY'S LAUNDRESS
to be the FINEST STARCH she ever used
Sold by all respectable Grocers and Druggists
Throughout the Union.[27]

Not all testimonials and endorsements came from users of the product or service offered. The Graefenberg Company included two testimonials "from high authority in the literary and religious world" in an 1857 advertisement for their medicines. Just why the reader should consider these literary and religious gentlemen experts in the field of medicine is a mystery left unanswered by the advertiser.

My personal acquaintance with some of the members of the Graefenberg Company justifies me in expressing the opinion that their medicines are worthy of confidence.

—FRANCIS HALL
Editor and Proprietor N. York Commercial Advertisers

I hereby certify that I have examined a number of testimonials exhibited to me by the Graefenberg Company, relative to the merits of their medicines, and I take pleasure in saying that they present evidence of genuineness and are therefore entitled to the confidence of the public.

—N. BANGS, D.D.
of the Methodist Church[28]

THE FATHER OF ADVERTISING

Phineas Taylor Barnum was a best-selling author, distinguished speaker, outrageous showman, shrewd entrepreneur, and marketing genius. Although he is often remembered for his museum, his many hoaxes, and later as a coowner of a circus, Barnum's masterful use of the media has led him to be called the "Father of Advertising." P.T. Barnum knew that advertising could be a powerful tool. He wrote most of the ads for his projects himself. They were led by shocking headlines and filled with exciting, exaggerated copy. He would create entire histories for the attractions he touted. These compelling ads would titillate the readers' curiosity, focusing their attention on what they would see rather than revealing the attraction prior to debut. Intrigued by his claims, they would go and see for themselves if the promises were true. The crowds who flocked to his museum were directly proportional to the amount of mystery and hype that he generated in the press. This adept use of advertising copy has also earned him the moniker, the "Shakespeare of Advertising."

Barnum was an aggressive advertiser, an approach that had never before been attempted. In an 1843 letter to Moses Kimball, he wrote, "You must drive business. . . . I shall send you some lithographs to distribute about your whole city—especially in all public show windows—Hotels— P. Offices, etc."[29] He filled the news sheets with ads to show off his attractions. He managed to get editors to break with convention and allow him to run ads that were two columns wide and containing line illustrations of museum features. The advertising dollars he spent in the local press pleased editors who would in turn provide newsworthy accounts of his shows in their paper. As a result, he would often get twice as much for his money. In his autobiography, first published in 1854, he explained, "I was aware of the great power of the public press, and I used it to the extent of my ability."[30] Barnum encouraged merchants to advertise, cautioning them that if they did not advertise for themselves, the sheriff would do it for them when he auctioned off their goods to settle their debts.

Barnum employed every marketing tool imaginable at the time. He flooded the city with pamphlets, posters, and handbills. He draped his museum with gigantic banners and during the night hung transparencies to project lighted illusions of bubbling and boiling liquids on the building walls. He staged publicity stunts and used gimmicks knowing that anything that would break through the dullness of daily life would attract attention. One of his most famous stunts involved hiring a man to take a few bricks out to the corner of Broadway. The man was instructed to place the bricks on the ground and then to exchange them back and forth continually. Naturally, this attracted the attention of passersby. Every hour the man would pick up the bricks and walk into Barnum's Museum. Invariably, he was followed by a number of the inquisitive onlookers. Barnum later claimed that this stunt embodied his advertising philosophy. "It employed novelty, demonstrated ingenuity, and achieved free publicity."[31]

Many of Barnum's displays at his museum perpetrated frauds on the public. Even when one of Barnum's hoaxes was uncovered, he managed to use the media to his own benefit. In 1835, he put on display an elderly woman by the name of Joice Heth, advertising that she was 161 years old and a former nurse of George Washington. When interest in her began to dwindle, he started a rumor that she was not a real person at all but rather an automation. People flocked back to the exhibit in order to determine for themselves whether she was real or not. Upon her death, Barnum held a public autopsy in order to determine her actual age. When the doctors announced that Heth was no more than 80, Barnum planted a story in the *New York Herald* claiming that the body had not actually been Heth. Keeping the story alive and the public intrigued, Levi Lyman, a collaborator with Barnum, gave the *Herald* what he purported was the true story of Heth. In a series of six articles Lyman detailed how Barnum had found Heth and taught her to act the role. In reality, none of these stories was the truth. Barnum had merely bought the right to exhibit Heth from someone else who was already doing so.

On the heels of this, Barnum created the "Fejee Mermaid." His posters and advertisements depicted three beautiful mermaids, one holding a mirror while grooming long her locks. Despite having recently been defrauded by his display of Heth, the public streamed in to see the new display. They were met with a hideous, dried-out carcass. When scientists began to question the feasibility of a mermaid, Barnum again turned to advertising and invited the public to decide for itself. The "Fejee Mermaid" was one of the most talked about events of the year.

General Tom Thumb's career began as another of Barnum's deceptions. Charlie Stratton was a four-year-old, 25-inch-tall, 15-pound boy from Connecticut when Barnum realized his potential as an attraction. He soon dashed off a letter to Moses Kimball: "In a few days I will send you some fine lithography of him (Thumb) so that you can begin giving him notoriety." By Barnum's own admission, it "contained only two deceptions."[32]

The wedding picture of Mr. and Mrs. "Tiny Tim" and their wedding party. P.T. Barnum made "Tiny Tim" famous. This photograph is on a *carte des visite* from the studio of Matthew Brady, and it is signed by those in the picture.

Stratton was represented as an 11-year-old from England. Tom's personality seemed to leap from the ads and the public responded. Recognizing the potential profit in the public's fascination with photography and Tom's charisma, Barnum began to use photographs of Tom in advertisements. Barnum's ability to commodify people turned Tom Thumb into a cultural icon. Although Tom went on to be one of Barnum's greatest attractions, he also became one of Barnum's closest friends.

Barnum's most successful publicity event was the 1850 introduction of European singer Jenny Lind to America where she was virtually unknown. With this episode he truly made the transition from hoaxer to showman. Barnum filled the papers with stories of her marvelous accomplishments overseas and saturated the public with newspaper ads, handbills, and broadsides. He held auctions for tickets to her performances and planned a grand parade for her arrival. Such sensational interest was created by this advance hype that 40,000 New Yorkers met her at the dock. Lind's tour was a spectacular success.

Barnum summed up his marketing approach in a 1860 letter: "The Mermaid, Woolly Horse, Ploughing Elephant, etc. were merely used by me as skyrockets in advertising, to attract attention and give notoriety to the museum and such other really valuable attractions I provided for the public. I believe highly in advertising and blowing my own trumpet, beating the gongs, drums, etc. to attract attention to a show; but I never believed that any amount of advertising or energy would make a spurious article personally successful."[33]

The possibilities of advertising were just beginning to be understood during the antebellum period. Those who saw it as a powerful tool and were willing to test its potential broke down the social biases and cultural taboos that separated classes, insulated ethnic groups, and confined men and women to gender specific roles. As naive as their ideas seem to us today, they were bold in such an unsophisticated marketplace. When industry and manufacturing expanded after the Civil War, it was this new attitude that helped to create markets that stretched across the nation.

4

Architecture

What have husbands to do with housekeeping? If they furnish the
funds to supply the family, is that not sufficient?
—*Housekeeper's Encyclopedia*

HOUSING

Antebellum Homes

There was no single characteristic house style during the antebellum period, but the elegant plantation homes built in the American South, with
their central entrances, balconies, columns, and formal ballrooms, came
closest to representing a discrete architectural style for the period. The
focus on Southern architectural characteristics somewhat distorts the character of home building in the period. Actually, the majority of homes built
from 1820 to 1860 were Greek Revival, Classical Revival, and Federalist
style structures or some adaptation thereof. Moreover, surviving examples
of stately Northern mansions and palatial Southern plantation houses
reflect the power, idealism, and tastes of only the wealthiest Americans.
Unlike the homes of the wealthy, most of the functional and sturdy structures belonging to average Americans no longer exist in an unmodified
form, having undergone numerous renovations in the 20th century. Their
original contours and characteristics were seldom recorded except by accident in a photograph, painting, or sketch.

Although home ownership served as an ideal during the period, many
families, especially in the cities, had to settle for apartments, boarding
houses, and tenements. Even among individual homeowners, there was
a wide diversity of residences including mansions, villas, multistory

houses, cottages, cabins, and soddies. The Irish immigrants were noted by observers at the time for building "shanties"—structures that were virtual shacks. Yet the majority of homes built during the antebellum period were simple frame farmhouses. In the largely rural areas of a young America, a husband and wife might sit down, pencil and paper in hand, with thoughts focused on cornfields or pumpkin patches rather than on cornices or pilasters. These amateur architects tended to design plans for a practical house, a functional barn, a predator-proof chicken coop, or a well-drained pigpen. Fenced farm fields and properly planted orchards were far more important to the common farm family than symmetrical facades or grand staircases. Many of these plans were piecemeal and disordered, and few such drawings survived.

Yet in an odd custom among rural societies in 19th-century America, some of the best plans were rescued from obscurity. Prizes were sometimes offered for successful farmhouse designs by a number of agricultural improvement societies. Many of the most functional plans were submitted and displayed at county fairs or published in farm journals.

This illustration from a popular plan book is said to be of a simple rural farmhouse with a number of embellishments, including front and side porches, bow windows, columns, brackets, a broken roofline, and several chimneys.

Ordinary periodicals often carried house plans, and few illustrated magazines failed to carry a floor or building plan of the month. Evidence gleaned from sources like these have allowed historians to construct an accurate picture of the average farm home.

A number of architectural pattern books were published during the period that contained a variety of house plans of different sizes and prices. Among these was *Rural Residences*, published in 1837 by Alexander Jackson Davis. This particular architectural pattern book was thought to have introduced the Gothic Revival style to North America. In a similar manner, *Victorian Cottage Residences* and *The Architecture of Country Homes* were published by Andrew Jackson Downing in 1842 and 1850, respectively. Both emphasized the Carpenter Gothic style.

The Middle-Class Home

The typical middle-class home could be divided into three classifications of rooms: public rooms, private rooms, and workrooms. The common public rooms included the hall, parlor, dining room, and library, and the private rooms were the bedchambers and nursery, which were almost exclusively located on the second floor. The placement of a bedroom on the first floor of a two-story home, except in the event of sickness or infirmity among the occupants, was considered risqué in many circles. The final category of rooms included workrooms such as the kitchen, pantry, laundry, scullery, or cellar. These were often the haunts of servants, if the family could afford them, or places where the homeowners did not want to be seen doing the work of servants. Of course, every middle-class family hoped to support the fiction that they were wealthy enough to avoid doing their own hand labor.

The Front Hall

In addition to the practical purposes of providing a barrier against the cold or containing the mud and dirt from outside, the front hall of an antebellum home had a very important social function. Business dealings in these times were much more likely to be done face to face; and guests needed a place in which to be greeted when calling. The front hall provided a reception area where these dealings could take place without exposing the family's private quarters to the view of strangers. In the absence of a servants' entrance, shopping purchases were often delivered here, and in urban areas, mail might be delivered at any time during the day.

The front hall was the public face of the home, and it was important that it be decorated in a fashion that was appropriate to the social standing of the family. It was likely for the hall to be furnished with a pair of chairs for visitors, a mirror for checking one's appearance, and a table to receive calling cards. Upscale homes often had massive pieces of furniture that combined several of these features. Floors could be tiled for the practical purpose of accommodating the dirt of a high-traffic area, but more often they were covered with carpet or oilcloth. Elizabeth Blair Lee wrote, "I have enquired [sic] about carpets & oil cloth—the latter is much the cheapest for the Hall—the best quality costs $1.25 to $1.50 for a square yard—a poor carpet costs that & dust makes the oil cloth best in other respects." Oilcloth was often made of canvas coated with a thick layer of oil-based paint and decorated with a geometric design. The effect of these designs was often remarkably similar to that of real tile, marble, or carpet.[1]

The procedure known as "calling" was a social function that was required by proper society and governed by convention. On the topic of calling, *Martine's Hand-Book of Etiquette* stated, "Such visits are necessary, in order to maintain good feeling between the members of society; they are required by the custom of the age in which we live, and must be carefully attended to."[2] Martine counseled that ceremonial calls be kept brief. "Half an hour amply suffices for a visit of ceremony. If the visitor be a lady, she may remove her victorine [a type of veil], but on no account either the shawl or bonnet, even if politely requested to do so by the mistress of the house. Some trouble is necessarily required in replacing them, and this ought to be avoided."[3] Upon exiting the home, callers would leave a card identifying themselves, which would be placed in a cardholder in the front hall. Elaborate cardholders were made from silver or china. Ladies magazines contained patterns for handcrafted ones. "In leaving cards you must thus distribute them: one for the lady of the house and her daughters . . . one for the master of the house, and if there be a grown up son or a near male relation staying in the house, one for him."[4]

Socially conscious women kept a list of family members and business acquaintances who formed a basic calling circle. It would be expected that persons on this list would be visited at least twice a year. Failure to reciprocate in calling could be considered a grievous slight. Naturally, close friends and family would see each other more frequently. Martine warned, "Keep a strict account of your ceremonial visits. This is needful, because time passes rapidly; and take note of how soon your calls are returned. You will thus be able, in most cases, to form an opinion whether or not your frequent visits are desired."[5] Brides were kept particularly busy making rounds as they introduced themselves in their new social position. Women were reminded that "it is the custom for a wife to take her husband's cards with her, and to leave one or two with her own."[6]

The Parlor

The parlor was the most public room in the antebellum house. Parlors were common to both the North and the South and across the social classes. Some more affluent homes had a front parlor solely dedicated to formal visitations and a back parlor for family use, but a single parlor was most common. The parlor was the place where important visitors and relations would be received. Where the front hall was the public face of the home, the parlor was where the first impressions of the family were formed. Decorating decisions were made in a very calculated manner so as to project the image a family wished to portray. Parlors contained a family's "best" in every way. It would have the highest ceilings, the largest fireplace and most elaborate furnishings. The center feature of most parlors was a large circular table with a kerosene or oil lamp. Here the family would gather to write, read, converse, play games, or engage in needlework and crafts. The need to gather around the central light, which may have been the only one in the room, helped to foster a communal atmosphere. The parlor table allowed family members to be together, yet various members of the family could be engaged in a variety of pastimes. They were able to function as individuals, yet remain a part of the family community as a whole.

The second focal point of the parlor was the fireplace. The mantel was often heavily decorated with pictures, collections of natural objects, or mementos. What could not fit on the mantel might be contained on shelves or étagères around the room. An intense appreciation of nature prevailed during this time, leading to the collection of seashells, fossils, minerals, pinecones and dried flowers, all of which might be displayed in the parlor. It was felt that objects like these reflected a harmony between the natural world and the civilized one. Homes decorated with objects of nature were thought to demonstrate nature's beauty in family life. Additionally, using natural objects as decorative accents showed a wife's sense of economy, an attribute much extolled in women.

Other parlor furnishings might include an upholstered sofa, armchairs, and a pair of easy chairs, all covered in matching fabrics. Rocking chairs were very much in fashion during the period, and parlors were just one room in which they might be found. Common upholstering materials included brocades, silk damask, and tapestry, all adorned with tassels, cords, and fringe. It was not unusual for sofa ensembles to contain a large, gentleman's armchair and a smaller chair with half arms for the lady, which accommodated her wide skirts and kept her posture properly erect. The placement of chairs around the room allowed social groupings to change as activities varied. A person might move from the solitary activity of reading quietly to join a game with other family members at the table. Sofas were designed with slight curves to encourage conversation.

Ownership of a piano or parlor organ bespoke solid middle-class status. Parlor organs, as opposed to pianos, tended to be an outgrowth of domestic religious worship during which the family celebrated the Sabbath by singing hymns and playing ecclesiastic music. These were particularly important to homes that actively fostered the Christian development of family worship. The reed organ, which was perfectly suited to use in the parlor, was being produced in the United States by the 1840s. Pianos were rather more a status symbol than the organ in heralding the financial stability, educational accomplishment, and cultural propriety of the owner and his family. More than 20,000 pianos were being produced annually in America by the time of the Civil War. Advertisements for pianos and organs filled period newspapers and magazines. Retailers offered payment terms even for their least expensive models that sold for about $300.[7]

Families enjoyed singing and listening to pieces played on the piano. As with many of the activities undertaken by antebellum society, people followed their inclinations with little restraint. Consistent with this view was the growing popularity of piano concerts given in both public halls and private parlors. An 1853 editorial in the *Pittsburgh Evening Chronicle* gives a generally negative perspective on this phenomenon: "A hobby of society at this present day is to be music-mad, and the adulation and toddyism lavished upon every Piano Forte player of any talent is enough to disgust all sensible people with the instrument forever. . . . [O]ne would suppose that there was nothing else worth living for in this life but music and the Piano Forte player especially." The editors further noted that "Signor Pound-the-keys . . . fills his pockets for one night's work with as many dollars as three-fourths of the community earn in a year."[8]

The piano was generally considered a feminine instrument, and women actively cultivated their musical talents on it. "Young ladies are the principal interpreters of domestic music," stated *Macmillan's Magazine* in 1860. This association with the feminine led to the selection of many accessories that were generally thought to interest women to adorn the piano top.[9] Yet the pursuit of musical excellence may not always have been motivated by a love of harmonious tones. The piano provided a reason for courting couples to be in relatively close physical proximity during a time when proper behavior generally forbade such intimacy. By the piano, the couple could exchange glances as the young woman played, and the young man could bend closely, as he courteously turned music pages for the seated player.

The sheet music industry, aided by advances in printing and engraving, was already well established and flourishing at the beginning of the period. The sheet music itself was often beautifully lithographed, providing the additional bonus of an inexpensive piece of artwork for the parlor. Some families acquired so much piano sheet music that a separate piece of furniture, sometimes known as a Canterbury, was acquired by the family to hold it. Possession of such a piece of furniture was an additional status symbol.

Assorted small tables around the parlor contained additional bric-a-brac, a stereoscope with its 3-D photographs, or perhaps a gilded album that was used to collect *cartes de visite*. Filling albums with *cartes de visite* was quite a family hobby, popular with families across the middle and upper classes. Edwin Weller wrote to his fiancée, "I should be pleased to aid you in filling up your Album with nice Pictures, and will do so if I have an opportunity."[10] Some albums were elaborate and decorated with silver or brass clasps and covered with velvet, wood or mother-of-pearl. Inside, the album contained 20 or more pages of precut frames ready to receive the *cartes*. With time, the *cartes* became relatively inexpensive, and at least one photographer advertised on the back of his work, "CARTES DE VISITE, 6 for $1.00." Filling an album was an accomplishment likely to be made only by a middle- or upper-class families with incomes that allowed for a good deal of discretionary spending.[11] People generally stood for photographs at landmark times in their life, such as just after marriage or betrothal, following the birth of a child, or before leaving for war. *Cartes* could also be purchased, and collectors acquired pictures of famous people or *cartes* that contained a religious or poetic sentiment.[12]

The walls of a home were often covered in wallpapers that boasted large floral bouquets tied with ribbons, verdant foliage, or oversized fruit—a style that had started late in the decade of the 1840s and persisted into the 1860s. The walls were usually further ornamented with paintings and, for the less affluent, black-and-white prints or color lithographs. Attractive prints of good quality and color were readily available in the second half of the period, and many families took advantage of this new technology. Subjects included farmyard scenes, prints of famous racehorses, European riverscapes or landscapes, hunting vignettes, still lifes, and biblical tableaus. The popularity of farmyard pictures in homes decorated in brocade and tassels can be attributed to the passion for establishing a sense of harmony with nature and an underlying yearning, in an increasingly industrialized environment, for simpler times.

European subjects might be used as wall hangings to remind the family members of travels they may have made, a fact the family would have been desirous to publicize to visitors. Another popular subject was that of famous people, both historical and contemporary. These were chosen from among musical, literary, political, and military venues especially from the Revolution, the War of 1812, or the Mexican War of 1846. Representations of these people might take the form of a painting, a print, an engraving, or a bust. The public figures with which a family chose to decorate their home made a powerful statement about the owners of the parlor.

Not only did the selection of these works of art show good taste and education, but also they served as silent but concrete reminders of revered values. George Washington, for example, was admired as a selfless leader who put the public interest above his private preferences. The presence of his picture in the parlor showed that the family valued this attribute. A picture of Thomas Jefferson showed a respect for the law, and that of Andrew Jackson a certain egalitarianism. These pictures served as constant reminders to children of what was expected of them in adulthood. Many of the women depicted in this form were wives of famous men such as Martha Washington or entertainers like the singer Jenny Lind. The message for young girls was an expectation that they would be quiet movers, gently working behind the scenes.

Floors were carpeted with patterns that tended to be floral or of natural colors. However, carpets were sold by the linear yard and came in strips a little more than two-feet wide. They had to be pieced and sewn together much like wallpaper patterns. Susan Evans wrote to her sister, Emma Sargent Barbour, about the installation of new carpet. About a dozen women came to assist her in the installation. "I had to help cut the breadth, but we were not very experienced hands and consequently the carpet was cut wrong, or rather one breadth fell short. We measured it before hand, but could not seem to make the figures match any other way."[13] Nonetheless, extant examples show that carpets were often sewn with remarkable skill by professional installers who hid the seams and flawlessly matched the patterns. Mats often covered carpets in high-traffic areas or where fireplace sparks were likely. It was not unusual to take up the carpet in summer and replace it with sewn reed mats to make the home seem cooler and to save wear and tear on the generally expensive carpet. Elizabeth Blair Lee compared prices for a carpet from two merchants in Washington and Philadelphia, respectively, and stated that they ranged from $150 to $262 for a room.

Americans revered intellectual pursuits, and books were, therefore, a must in the parlor. Diary entries refer to reading more than any other pastime. Large, heavy Bibles were most often displayed on the central table as a symbol of the family's dedication to religion. Other books were frequently displayed on tables or on built-in bookshelves. Books brought learning and the world outside into the home. A parlor containing books showed that the owners valued knowledge and wished to better themselves. The information contained therein provided greater understanding of the natural world and the Lord's works. Antebellum Americans were fond of creating literary allusions in their lives, and they did not limit themselves to pictures of famous authors or samples of their works. Statues and ceramics containing scenes from literature were used to decorate the parlor. Images heralding the fight for Greek democracy or the history of the Roman Republic were popular in Southern homes, whereas the image of Spartacus, the great slave leader of Roman times, or more contemporary antislavery characters from Harriet Beecher Stowe's *Uncle Tom's Cabin* graced those in the North.

Windows were almost buried beneath a shroud of fabrics. Closest to the window would be a thin curtain, most likely made of lace, which served as both a barrier to flies and a window treatment. These would be covered with a second layer made of heavy fabric that could be closely drawn to block out the light entirely and prevent the fading of upholstery and rugs. The ensemble would be topped off with a valance fashionably trimmed with cords, tassels, and braid. Overall, the antebellum parlor was a place of abundant accumulation. It also gives insight into the spirit and the structure of the society of which it was a part.

The Library

Although it was common to see period house plans showing libraries—and many trade catalogs displayed library furniture—libraries were only affordable to the upper classes and the wealthiest among the upper middle classes. Although the antebellum home, in comparison to the home of an earlier century, was becoming increasingly dominated by feminine interests and decorations, the library remained largely a male domain. It was a place to which a man could retreat and engage in the kind of activities that did not coincide with the outward picture of the female-dominated home and hearth. Here a man could smoke, drink, and discuss money, politics, and war without exposing the rest of the family to such vulgarities. Libraries were usually on the ground floor and off to one side. Decorations were more subdued than in the parlor. Walls were paneled or covered in dark-colored paper. Heavy bookshelves filled with leather-bound volumes were a necessity, and other furniture would include a desk or writing table, large gentlemen's chairs, and various occasional tables. If a man had hobbies or interests, it would be here that he would pursue them. Gun cases and other weapons collections might be featured, and specimen cases containing fossils or insects might be displayed among accompanying magnifying glasses and other optical aids.

The Dining Room

The luxury of a room dedicated solely to the purpose of dining was another badge of middle-class status. Families of lesser means ate in kitchens or in areas adjacent to the parlor, set aside for dining. Dining room furniture tended to be massive, often of mahogany or other dark wood. Elizabeth Blair Lee wrote to her husband, "I have look[ed] at some furniture & find that dining room furniture alone will cost four hundred dollars of oil walnut which is as cheap as oak."[14] The standard number of chairs was eight. A sideboard was a common complement, providing an excellent place to display oversized serving pieces and candelabras. Walls tended to be dark to show up well under candlelight, the standard lighting for this room. Even during luncheons, it would not be unusual to draw the draperies and eat by candlelight. The formal dining experience was one of tremendous ritual and ostentation. Books of etiquette contained page upon page of rules guiding proper behavior while dining. Certain foods required highly specialized serving or eating utensils, and attention to proper form while dining was extremely important. Ten of the 30 pages that Martine dedicates to dining in his etiquette book pertain solely to carving meats at the table. Beginning in the mid-19th century, the upper classes developed a passion for complicating the dining process by introducing such superfluous table items as spoon warmers, cheese servers, and other odd serving pieces in an attempt to further ritualize the dining process and to distinguish those "in the know" from the common folk.

The Kitchen

The main utilitarian room in the mid-19th-century house was the kitchen. It was here that the most mundane, labor-intensive household duties took place. The kitchen was always located on the ground floor with a door to the outside, to facilitate deliveries. It was not necessary for it to be adjacent to the dining room, and in certain circles, distance was considered an asset, keeping odors contained. Very large homes might have a separate building that served as a summer kitchen. Kitchen furnishings were functional and simple. There was usually a large central worktable, a cupboard for storing dishes, and a "safe" for storing cheeses, breads, cooked meats, pies, or puddings. The safes were a kind of screened cupboard that protected kitchen items from insects, pets, and vermin, but they did nothing to regulate their temperature.

Miss Beecher's Domestic Receipt-Book advises, "The kitchen floor should be covered with an oil cloth. . . . Nothing is cleansed so easily as an oil cloth, and it is much better than a painted floor, because it can be moved to be painted."[15] In many homes, the kitchen was also the scullery and the laundry. In those cases, there would also be a deep sink with a drying rack for washing vegetables and pots. Indoor sinks generally had hand pumps but drains to the outside were a rarity. Dirty water often had to be bailed out and emptied outside. Dishes were washed in a large wooden bowl as a measure to keep down breakage. Pots were stored by hanging them from racks.

In this period, unlike in the previous century with its massive stone hearths, many homes had a single dominating feature in the kitchen—a wood-burning iron stove. Cast-iron stoves had become fairly standard in middle-class homes in the North by 1860. Many styles had been patented with special functions or unique characteristics. They ranged from simple cylinders for heating a small room to large, ornate contrivances for larger spaces. Iron stovetop and oven combinations for the kitchen were just becoming fashionable, and many were installed into existing kitchen fireplaces. Some had several levels for cooking, baking, and heating water.

Metal chimney pipes were often routed through the walls or ceilings to several other rooms in order to provide indirect heating from a single stove. Even elaborate systems of stovepipes were seemingly ignored in terms of the overall household aesthetics and were viewed as the price for efficient and modern heating. In rural areas and in much of the South, particularly among the lower classes, cooking was still done on an open hearth. There were those who resisted the kitchen stove solely because they felt that the hearth was the traditional heart of the home.

Kitchen furnishings might include an ice chest, which was a large double-sided wooden box with charcoal or sand sandwiched between the inner and outer layer of sideboards for thermal insulation. These became more sophisticated with time, but there was no attempt at true refrigeration. A block of ice was simply placed in the box to keep dairy products cool. The melt water was captured in a pan below. Ice was cut from ponds and lakes in winter and stored for future use in an icehouse. Commercial icehouses could be found in urban areas. Dry goods such as flour, sugar, and cornmeal were stored in crockery or in tinned iron or wooden containers. Rural kitchens, and those of families of lesser means, were also likely to be more family oriented than those found in the more wealthy homes, which had servants or slaves. These kitchens may well have been used for sewing or helping children with studies. Responsively, they would contain additional furnishings to suit their multipurpose functions.

The Bedrooms

The bedrooms of the late antebellum period were very different from those of the previous century. They were no longer the semipublic multiple-use spaces of the 18th century in which a person might receive close acquaintances. Bedrooms were now very private places and would not even be referred to in polite conversation. Beds retained the use of rope "springs" and feather mattresses, but the wooden frames had lost some of the mass of earlier times. The heavy bed curtains of former years had all but disappeared. Built-in closets were just beginning to come into vogue in 1860, and clothing or linens were stored in trunks, chests of drawers, and wardrobes.

After her husband sent her some cloth samples for bed linens, Elizabeth Blair Lee wrote, "The linen is wonderfully cheap—Cotton that width costs in the city $1.25 cts & not of the best quality—that linen here would sell for $1.50 to 60 cts. . . . You could not do better to buy than buy two pairs— they will take about 11 yards—I have 12 prs of double linen sheets & two prs single . . . & two pairs of Blankets—for we cannot get any blankets here for less than six dollars. I would like one pair."[16]

Beside the bed might be found a small table upon which to rest the chamber stick used to guide one to the bedroom upon retiring. Oil lamps were usually not found in bedrooms, and carrying an oil lamp with its liquid fuel from room to room was considered a major fire hazard. An overturned or dropped candle presented less danger of a quickly spreading conflagration. Therefore, store-bought candles continued as an important commodity through the end of the century. Many communities required that home owners have leather fire buckets at hand, filled with sand, to stop the spread of accidental fire. Some of these were imprinted with the commercial logos of fire insurance companies. People generally did not sit in bed and read before sleeping nor did they lounge about in their lingerie. Bedrooms were likely to be drafty places most of the year and cold in winter.

The Nursery

Cribs and cradles were frequently found close to the parents' bed to facilitate breast-feeding and as a precaution should the child take ill during the night. Older children in lower economic situations might also sleep in the same room. Families who could afford it had a nursery for the children, and children of particularly wealthy families might share the nursery with a nanny. As the decade progressed, children had come to be thought of as innocent beings in need of protection and of controlled exposure to the world outside. Accidents and common childhood diseases claimed nearly half of all children before the age of five. Although the nursery could limit the stimulations a child received, it might possibly protect it from the accidents and diseases that claimed so many less fortunate youngsters.

Modest households had a single nursery room often found on the third floor of the home. Affluent households could afford both day and night nurseries. These rooms were designed to withstand the abuse that children can sometimes inflict on furnishings. Walls were often whitewashed. Curtains were simple. There would be a table with several chairs. These might be simple pine furniture bought for that purpose or cast-off furniture from other rooms. There were shelves and cupboards for books and toys and perhaps an armchair or two. Nurseries also often doubled as schoolrooms and might also contain globes, maps, and perhaps a blackboard as needed for instruction.

The Necessary

Whereas wealthy families might have had inside plumbing and the accompanying bathroom facilities, most people had to make due with ceramic wash basins and pitchers on a washstand, and a chamber pot under the bed. Full-fledged baths were labor-intensive events that involved bringing up heated water from the kitchen to the bedchamber so that a compact metal tub could be filled. Only the lower classes bathed on the ground floor, if at all. This relegated total immersion baths even for the middle class homeowner to special occasions. Sponge baths were

This typical home from the antebellum period sat for many years overlooking the Erie Canal in western New York. It was moved to Rome, New York, and was restored by the Erie Canal Village museum.

the more common occurrence. Freestanding outhouses were the rule almost everywhere, but outhouses were not convenient at night. Most bedrooms contained a covered chamber pot. Some chamber pots were hidden in various pieces of furniture like chairs and stools, but some were merely stored beneath the bed until their contents were emptied into the slop jar in the morning and disposed of down the outhouse hole.

The Southern Plantation House

The mention of the antebellum South invariably brings to mind images of stately mansions with porticoes, balconies, and ballrooms. The grand, white-columned plantation house has become so symbolic of the antebellum South that many people think it was developed there. On the contrary, the South developed no distinctive style of architecture of its own, but it was very successful in adapting existing modes from Europe, and even from the North, to its own needs and inclinations. From colonial times, upland Southern homes continued an Anglo-Saxon building tradition. Southern structures can be found that show Tudor, Stuart, and Jacobean influences. It was, however, the Georgian style that really took hold during colonial times and reigned until the Greek Revival style came into favor during the 1830s. Later plantation houses still bear traces of a lingering Georgian influence. In the Deep South, with its historic ties to France and to Spain, a blend of European influences was adapted to the subtropical climate of the Gulf Coast and Mississippi Delta. This is particularly true of the existing plantation houses in Louisiana that survived the ravages of destruction during the Civil War due to the early capture of the region by Federal troops. Houses were constructed high off the ground, away from dampness and potential flooding. Walls were built thick to keep out the heat, and long, sloping roofs extending over two-storied porches provided a perpetual shade and comfortable space for outdoor living.

Regardless of their European antecedents, most Southern plantation houses exhibited a number of common architectural features. The facade was symmetrical with evenly spaced windows and central doorways both in front and in the rear. Rounded colonnades extended upward from the ground to support an elaborate band, called a "frieze," running above the doorways and windows but below the cornice. This provided a classical dignity to the home and was sometimes decorated with designs and carvings. The roof either was hipped, sloping down to the eaves on all four sides, or it was gabled, the slope of the roof forming a large triangle. The area supported by the columns was called the "entablature." Beneath this were the balconies and covered porches. Sometimes external staircases divided and curved gracefully from the upper balconies to the center of the house.

As the indisputably common feature of the typical Southern plantation house, columns deserve special mention. A column is an upright pillar or post that may be purely decorative or may serve as a structural support for the roof. With details reminiscent of the Parthenon, pillared homes reflected a passion for antiquity and classic style. They were introduced into the American South by Anglo-Americans who moved into the region about the time of the Louisiana Purchase (1803). The lower portion of the column is called the base, and the upper portion the capital. The classical names for five different types of columns were recorded by a Renaissance architect named Vignola in the 16th century in a book titled *Classic Orders of Architecture*. According to Vignola, three of these types were developed in ancient Greece: Doric, Ionic, and Corinthian. Two others were developed in ancient Rome: Tuscan and a combined style known as Composite. All five types can be found in surviving structures from the antebellum period.

Inside the Southern plantation home, there were frequently a large center hall and a grand staircase with large rooms to either side, allowing for good air circulation and ventilation. High-ceilinged rooms with full-length windows allowed for the circulation of the cooled porch air and gave the rooms a sense of dignity and scale unlike that seen in any other region of the country. When open, the windows sometimes served as walkways onto the porch. Sleeping chambers were generally kept on the second floor. Dormer windows, which added light to the attic, were also common.

Regularity of design was carried from the main house to the outbuildings that made up the entire plantation, creating a sense of symmetry and a pleasant arrangement of structures.Two pavilions frequently flanked the central building. A typical domestic complex included a detached kitchen about the size of a single-room house, a springhouse or root cellar for the cool storage of milk products, a smokehouse to preserve meats, a laundry, and sometimes an icehouse, a schoolroom, or a storehouse. Slaves and servants were often quartered in these work buildings, or they were provided with separate housing out of sight of the main building. Northern travelers often compared the scene posed by a plantation to that of a small village.

Greek Revival Houses

Stately, pillared Greek Revival homes reflected a passion among their owners for antiquity. Popular from about 1825, these homes commonly featured pedimented gables, a boxy symmetrical shape, a heavy cornice, a wide unornamented frieze, and bold but simple moldings. Many of these structures had entry porches with columns and decorative pilasters. Long, narrow windows often flanked the front door. Actually, the earliest example of note of Greek Revival styling was not a domicile but an office building—Latrobe's Bank of Pennsylvania, built in Philadelphia, in 1798.

Many architects, trained in Europe, worked in the Grecian style, and the fashion spread via carpenter's guides and pattern books. The style spread across the country, ironically, taking hold in the South more slowly, at first, then in the North, and penetrating the Deep South only in the very last decade before the Civil War. With its classic clapboard exterior and bold, simple lines, Greek Revival architecture was the most prominent housing style in the United States for seven decades, receiving a designation at one point as the "National Style."

The Greek Revival also came to be viewed as the embodiment of the paternalistic, chivalric, and aristocratic ideals of the South. It remained an integral part of the conservative Southern culture in a time when the industrialized North was moving forward. The Southern planter aristocracy considered the style a physical manifestation of the ideal of Greek democracy and of the independence of individual states. The new state capitol building in South Carolina, completed in 1860, was constructed in Greek Revival style, as were many of the Federal buildings planned for Washington, D.C.

The Federal capital at Washington was highly valued as a symbol by 19th-century Americans. Carefully laid out in a district allocated from within the boundaries of Maryland in order to salve the pride of the South, the nation's capital city had been under construction since the turn of the century. Americans pointed proudly to the imposing structure of the U.S. Capitol Building, as well as the General Post Office, the Bureau of the Treasury, the Smithsonian Institution, and the Executive Mansion, as representative of a vigorous young nation preparing to take its place among the leading countries of the world.

Unfortunately, Washington was also symbolic of other things. The plans for the city, like the basic founding concepts of the nation itself, were as pretentious as they were visionary, and in 1860 both lay unfulfilled and disordered. Sprawling along the banks of the Potomac with the "Old City" of Alexandria, Virginia across the water, the great buildings of the new capital remained incomplete even after the expenditure of vast sums of money and six decades of effort. The U.S. Capitol Building, an imposing architectural edifice, lay unfinished with its original dome removed—scaffolding and a towering crane representative of restructuring and rethinking. The wings of the building were "stretched bare and unfinished, devoid even of steps." The imposing obelisk of the Washington Monument, at that time, lay as a mere foundation. Blocks of marble, lumber, cast-iron plates, and the tools of workmen strewn about the district gave quiet testimony to the fact that the plan for the nation's first city, like the social and political plan for the American nation itself, was incomplete and open to revision. As the gap between Northern and Southern political beliefs widened during the antebellum period, the Greek temple form of architecture came more and more to symbolize stability and authority in the South at a time when its lifestyle, institutions, and political rights were under increasing attack.[17]

Cabins

Not all residents of the South lived in plantation manors. The vernacular architecture of the Upland South was characterized by the log cabin, constructed of horizontal courses notched together at the corners. This technology was brought to the area with the migration of the Scotch-Irish and Germans who came from central Pennsylvania in the early 19th century. Many of the cabins of white yeoman farmers varied little in construction from those of slaves. What set them aside were the unique additions and porches, which personalized these homes in a way that the uniformity of slave housing rarely permitted. Porches, an architectural concept imported from Africa, were used as extended workrooms for the house and to that end were generally furnished with tables and some kind of seating. One popular style of cabin was the dogtrot, which could be described as two,

two-room cabins joined together by a central breezeway onto which each section opened and that could be used for outdoor activity.

Wood was the characteristic building material in the Lowland South due to the abundance of timber, particularly yellow pine. Post and beam buildings assembled with basic mortise and tenon joints or notch joints were versatile enough to be used for outbuildings and farmhouses alike. Exterior walls were usually shingled or sided with planks. Interior walls might be finished in lathe and plaster. Wood framing, requiring the use of pit saws or water-powered sawmills, was generally reserved for larger homes. These building techniques changed little before the Civil War.

Gothic Revival Houses

It is said that Sir Horace Walpole began the Gothic Revival in architecture when he decided to renovate his English country home in the mid-18th century. In an attempt to get away from the boxlike symmetry of the more classical Georgian style, Walpole included arched windows, pseudo-Medieval battlements and parapets, and other Gothic details to the design. The new look was inspiringly Romantic, bringing to mind the style of storybook castles. Fanciful, romantic features that appealed to the emotion ultimately replaced the orderly classical ideals that appealed to the intellect. The Gothic style was also strongly suggestive of ecclesiastical structures like churches and convents. Some of the common features of Gothic Revival architecture were steeply pitched roofs, pointed leaded glass or clover-shaped windows, asymmetrical floor plans, grouped chimneys, pinnacles, crenulated battlements, and wide verandahs. Gothic Revival design became extremely popular in America in the 1840s.

Alexander Jackson Davis was one of the first architects to formalize the Gothic Revival style in his 1837 book *Rural Residences*. His design for Lyndhurst, a quarried stone country estate in Tarrytown, New York, was an archetype of the style. Wealthy home owners from all over the North attempted to reproduce at least some of the features of this romantic and imposing structure, although they did not follow the Gothic pattern blindly. An excellent example is the Lockwood-Matthews mansion in Norwalk, Connecticut, begun in 1860 and finished during the Civil War.

Little by little, houses throughout the country began to show the influence of a frivolous and romantic Gothic design. Andrew Jackson Downing helped to spread this trend by applying it to wood frame buildings. In both his pattern books, *Victorian Cottage Residences* (1842) and *The Architecture of Country Houses* (1850), Downing suggested the scrolled ornaments, lacey trim, and vertical board and batten siding made of wood that best characterized what is known as the "Carpenter Gothic" style. Many older homes of wood, brick, and stone had Gothic appointments layered on as an afterthought either in wood or in cast iron. The "Wedding

An illustration found in one of the many
books containing house plans. A clerk or
a mechanic who would earn a few dollars
a week could afford this small building.
Although inexpensive, the building has
some of the decorative embellishments,
like columns and brackets, found on
larger homes.

Cake House" designed by G. Bourne in Kennebunkport, Maine, is an excellent example of such a home. Basically a Federalist-style brick structure built in 1822, the Wedding Cake House had lavishly carved buttresses,
spires, and lacey spandrels applied to its facade, and a Palladian window
was set in above its main entrance by 1855. In the post–Civil War years,
the fanciful and overly elaborate details of the Gothic style lost popularity among home owners. Nonetheless, Samuel Sloan's pattern book,
Sloan's Homestead Architecture (1867), remained a popular source of architectural details inspired by the Gothic Revival.

The Gothic Revival may have experienced its best and most lasting
expression during the late antebellum period in ecclesiastical structures.
Arched windows made from leaded stained glass, pseudo-Medieval appointments, towers with gargoyles, and buttressed sidewalls adorned
these buildings. Trinity Church of Boston, designed by George Brimmer
and begun in 1829, is one of the earliest examples. Other examples of ecclesiastical structures in the Gothic style include: the First Unitarian (North)
Church of Salem, Massachusetts (anonymous architect, 1836), Trinty
Church, New York (Richard Upjohn, 1839), and St. Patrick's Cathedral,
New York (James Renwick, 1858). Although the Gothic style went out of

fashion, these churches were built over many decades, thereby keeping the style in the public eye well after the Civil War.

PARKS AND PUBLIC SPACES

As the antebellum period progressed, many traditional social concepts were apparently being washed away by rampant modernization and unrestricted urbanization. Prime among these endangered traditions was the concept of community. Lost among the teeming tenements, boarding houses, and grimy shanties, both the beauty of the natural environment and the freedom of open spaces seemed to be disappearing from the American way of life. In response to these changes, the concepts of domestic and civic tranquility were becoming closely identified among the middle and upper classes more with rustic, pastoral, and agrarian scenes than with the overcrowded neighborhoods, the outflows of sewers, or the thermodynamics of steam engines.

The cultivation and classification of garden plants, flowers, fruits, vegetables, trees, and shrubs first became popular among the upper class. Ultimately, interest in things botanical and horticultural spread to the general population. This development coincided with similar movements toward the representation and glorification of nature among artists, poets, and writers, but in a more tangible and authentic way that could be partaken of physically and experienced intimately. The development of public parks was the most obvious manifestation of a desire to develop user-friendly public spaces where urban dwellers and townsfolk might commune with nature without braving a mountain trail, spending a night under canvas, or even breaking a sweat. Both the poet William Cullen Bryant and the writer Washington Irving struggled to protect open areas from unrestricted urban development, and they were instrumental in saving a large and potentially valuable portion of Manhattan Island in a semblance of its natural state before the sprawling city overtook it. The result of their efforts was Central Park, the most extensive and elaborate public space project of the period.

Frederick Law Olmsted is probably best known as the landscape designer of Central Park. In 1857, Olmsted was appointed superintendent of Central Park, and in 1858, he and Englishman Calvert Vaux won the competition for the landscape design for the project. Olmsted and his associates went on to design New York's Prospect Park in Brooklyn, Riverside Park in Manhattan, the city parks of Hartford, Boston, and Louisville, and the grounds around the nation's newly restyled capitol in Washington, D.C. A well-traveled observer, Olmsted had toured New England, Great Britain, the Continent, and China, studying the largely rural landscape of popular travel destinations and recording his findings in *Walks and Tours of an American Farmer in England* (1852). Soon after the publication of this book, Olmsted was commissioned by the *New York Times* to write an unbiased impression of the overall condition of the South. His letters to the editor were very well received by the reading public and were published as a book, *A Journey in the Seaboard Slave States,* in 1856. A second tour on horseback took him through Texas, New Orleans, and Virginia. His reports on this trip appeared in two books: *A Journey Through Texas* (1857) and *A Journey Through the Back Country* (1860). These three works regarding the Southern states, written on the eve of the Civil War, were condensed and reissued in both America and England in 1861 under the titles *The Cotton Kingdom* and *Journeys and Explorations in the Cotton Kingdom.* They were heralded for their thoughtfulness, their calm examination of fact, and the fairness of the scenes that they presented of Southern life.

The movement toward the creation of parks and public spaces was particularly popular in New England and in the more populous urban centers of the North. Nonetheless, few towns, even rural ones, chose to bypass a chance to demonstrate their dedication to the aesthetics of nature by developing some sort of public space. The common open space in the center of a village, used for the grazing of livestock in former times, now became the village green or town park as small agricultural hamlets developed into more closely knit, semiurban communities. In most cases, plantings were made and greenery was maintained to provided shaded areas. Lawns were developed and maintained in place of natural pasture. These areas were often surrounded with wooden or cast-iron fencing to delineate the public space from private property. The green or park may have been provided with benches, street lighting (by gas lamps where feasible), and a public gazebo or bandstand. These structures often reflected the same type of fanciful and overly elaborate details then popular on Gothic-style homes. Antebellum parks often included ponds, streams, or other water features sometimes surrounded by a system of paved walkways, carriageways, or bridle paths. Bridges made from ornamental wood or cast iron were set in place over water obstacles.

Similarly, those homeowners with the financial means to do so erected summerhouses, gazebos, and garden archways on their property. These were often surrounded with formal walks and plantings in the geometric Georgian style of the 18th century or by curved pathways, flowered walks, and blossoming fruit trees designed in a more modern nonlinear mode. In either case, there was an attempt to make the backyard or other open space surrounding the home reflect the occupants' love of, and intimate contact with, nature beyond that commonly associated with the pursuit of agriculture. In so doing, antebellum home owners provided for themselves, and for visitors to their homes, a cool, shaded, and generally pleasant surrounding in which to read, write, paint, or pursue other leisure activities in the out-of-doors. This was a great change for middle-class home owners whose contact with the areas outside their homes had formerly been limited to

The movement to create open spaces in towns and villages often led to the building of a town bandstand. This highly decorated example from the 1840s has been restored at a country museum in central New York.

activities generally considered to be associated with their trade, housework, or the care of livestock. Nonetheless, it was not unusual for property owners to plant a small orchard or fence in an area around their homes for livestock in addition to any formal outdoor space they may have created.

Rural Cemeteries

During the 1830s, a phenomenon known as the "rural cemetery movement" began. The deplorable conditions found in crowded and neglected city graveyards created a desolate setting for surviving loved ones making their final farewells. Family monuments were the only man-made structures dotting the otherwise parklike landscape of rural cemeteries, which were specifically created as idyllic places where peace and calm would reign and the family bond could remain forever unbroken. The layout created a sort of garden of graves. Cemetery paths meandered over landscaped hills and valleys. Benches were placed at gravesites, providing an inviting place of contemplation. The landscape offered air and light, safety and nature, joy and optimism. It facilitated acceptance of the physical separation of the dead from the living. In the rural cemetery, death had been transformed from grotesque to beautiful.[18]

Rural cemeteries continued to expand into the 1850s. By the time of the Civil War, virtually every city of size in both the North and South had its own rural cemetery. They were created to provide a safe, secure resting place where the remains of loved ones would not be moved, abandoned, or vandalized. Bonaventure Cemetery outside of Savannah, Georgia, was considered extraordinarily beautiful. *Harper's Weekly* noted in 1860, "There is nothing like it in America or perhaps the world. . . . Its melancholy loveliness once seen can never be forgotten." One of the largest rural cemeteries, which still reflects many of its founding characteristics, is Woodlawn Cemetery in Bronx County, New York.[19]

Nonetheless, the primary concern of the rural cemetery was the burial of individual persons in a manner that maintained the ideal of family, and certain sections were designed to highlight family plots. The winding roads, constructed so that many family plots would be able to have the highly desired, roadside locations, were built wide enough to accommodate family carriages. Gravesite visitations were akin to afternoons in the park. A contemporary noted the quiet solitude of such a parklike setting, "By the grave of those we loved, what a place for meditation!"[20] The entire institution surrounding burial was designed to honor, strengthen, and maintain the family. *Frank Leslie's Illustrated Newspaper* carried a lead story on the increasing volume of mourners in cemeteries: "The cemeteries of New Orleans are very interesting places, for almost every day may be seen parties of mourning relatives and friends decking the grave of some loved one, who, by an early death, has been spared the pangs of regret."[21]

The Antebellum Period

5

Fashion

Dresses for breakfasts, and dinners and balls;
Dresses to sit in, and stand in, and walk in;
Dresses to dance in, and flirt in, and talk in;
Dresses in which to do nothing at all.

—"Nothing at All"

HAVING STYLE

A contributor to the *National Recorder* in 1829 made the following observation on women's fashion:

> The history of woman is the history of the improvements in the world. Some twenty or thirty years ago, when manual labour performed all the drudgery, some five or six or seven yards of silk or muslin or gingham would suffice for the flitting flirting of the most gay and volatile of the sex. But as soon as the powers of steam are applied, and labour is changed from physical to intellectual, the ladies, in their charitable regard for the operative class of the community, begin to devise means for their continued employment, and as the material is produced with half the labour, the equilibrium must be sustained by consuming a double quantity.[1]

Although the observer's remarks were made tongue-in-cheek, there is some basis here in fact. Industrialization had redefined the role of women in the home. Men were caught up in an economy where they worked outside the home and away from the household for an extensive part of the day. The same industry and commerce also brought increased wealth to a growing middle class, and a larger share of the families' dispensable income came to reside in the hands of the women of the household. New laborsaving inventions also freed women from much of the drudgery of household labor and increased the amount of free time they had. With both the time and the money to follow fashion, they anxiously awaited the arrival of the latest fashion magazines, which contained illustrations of the latest Paris fashions.

One of the greatest influences on American women's fashion during the period was *Godey's Lady's Book*. Louis B. Godey founded the magazine in July of 1830. In addition to serials, essays, poems, and craft projects, it featured engraved fashion plates. Each month, the magazine depicted morning dresses, promenade dresses, seaside costumes, riding habits, dinner dresses, and ball gowns. Such wardrobe depth was seldom needed for the vast majority of the magazine's readers, whose clothes could generally be categorized as public or social and domestic or work, with a few seasonal additions for summer and winter. As time progressed, *Godey's* began to show fashions better suited to the lifestyle and interest of the middle class American woman. By the 1860s, *Godey's* had become a fashion institution, setting the standard for fashion savvy. Other magazines

This illustration is from *Godey's Lady's Book*, where fashion plates were just beginning to appear during the antebellum period. The family group here is dressed in rather fanciful attire from the early part of the period.

such as *Peterson's, Arthur's, Graham's, Leslie's,* and *Harper's* began to follow suit or grew in popularity.

Fashions in the opening years of the 19th century, like the architecture
and furniture, echoed the past. Napoleon's campaigns in Italy focused the
attention of architects and designers on the ruins of Rome, and an almost
universal interest in politics further stimulated the revival of the republican ideals of ancient Greece and Rome. Artists drew inspiration from ancient history, and classic style became popular in every kind of decoration.
This strong classical influence in fashion lasted only briefly in the opening years of the antebellum period. After 1820, there was a reaction against
the high-waisted empire style and the togalike draping of fabric related
to Greco-Roman influences.

Women's Dress

The period 1820–1830 marked the transition from the empire style to a
new romantic look. Fashions reinforced the image of the affluent woman
of increased leisure. Skirts became increasingly fuller. Sleeves were set low
on the shoulder restricting movement and making them very impractical for household labor. Working-class and rural women wore garments
that were less hampering but that followed the basic style and silhouette
of the period.

The waistline moved gradually downward from just below the bust to
just above the anatomical waistline. The bodice during the 1820s and 1830s
generally had wide, V-shaped crossover folds draped from the shoulder
to the waist. This was often covered with an extremely wide capelike collar called a "pelerine." Made in either white or matching fabric, the extremely popular pelerine extended over the shoulders and across the
bodice. The fichu-pelerine was a variant that extended into two long strips
that crossed at the waist and passed under a belt. When the neckline was
open, a chemisette, or tucker, was commonly worn beneath to fill in the
opening. These fillers created the impression of an underblouse but were
actually sleeveless and sideless articles that were secured around the
waist. This construction created less bulk and could be easily laundered.
They could be varied to create a different look with the same basic garment. The neckline during this early part of the period was usually high
and crowned with a small collar or ruff. The pelisse-robe was another style
of day dress. Adapted from the outer garment of the same name, it was a
kind of coatdress that was secured down the front with buttons, ribbons
or hooks and eyes.

From 1825 to 1832 the exaggerated fullness of the sleeve was the most
striking feature of women's dress. Almost as much material was required
to make a pair of fashionable sleeves as for the skirt of a gown. The leg-
of-mutton sleeve, or gigot, was greatly puffed at the shoulder and

graduated into a long sleeve that fitted tightly at the wrist. The demi-gigot sleeve was full from the shoulder to the elbow then fitted from the elbow to the wrist frequently with an extension over the wrist. Some sleeves were a small puff covered by a sheer oversleeve. Another sleeve was full to the wrist but tied at intervals with ribbons or fabric bands. Yet another was extremely full from shoulder to wrist where it gathered into a fitted cuff. Sometimes the cuff was accessorized by a *santon*, which was a silk cravat that was worn around the neck.

Skirts ended at the instep until about 1828 when they became shortened to ankle length or just above. In 1836, they once again returned to the top of the foot. From the beginning of the period until 1828, the skirt was fitted through the hips with gores gradually flaring out to create fullness at the hem. Thereafter, skirts began to get fuller at the hips as the fabric was gathered or pleated into the waist. Popular fabrics included muslin, printed cotton, challis, merino, and batiste.

Evening dresses followed the same basic silhouette with a few alterations. Necklines were lower, and sleeves and skirts were shorter. During the 1820s, the neckline could be square, round, or elliptical. In the 1830s, they were usually off the shoulder. Evening dresses were usually made in silks, satins, gauze, or organdy.

Around 1836, the silhouette began to undergo a transformation, which moved fullness and extravagance from the top of the garment toward the bottom. Bodices usually ended at the waist but increasingly came to a point at the front. The "Y" bodice was most common. It had a fanlike appearance and remained in vogue through the remainder of the antebellum period.

Sleeves in this period were set low and off the shoulder, and the puffiness of the sleeve began to migrate down the arm. Bishop sleeves were loose sleeves that grew wide at the elbow, causing the sleeve to hang in a curve and creating the appearance of a slightly bent arm. They extended from a row of vertical pleats at the shoulder and fell into a full, relaxed sleeve that gathered at the wrist. A newer style also emerged that was fitted at the shoulder but widened about halfway between the elbow and the wrist into a bell shape. Because of this looseness, undersleeves, which would conceal the forearm from view, were worn for modesty's sake. Undersleeves were separate, straight sleeves that fitted closely at the wrist and extended to the upper arm where they were secured by a drawstring. Most commonly they were of white cotton or linen.

Skirts became increasingly fuller with excess fabric gathered into the waist. Many hems were edged with braid or other trim to reduce wear. Additional horizontal trim was added for balance, but overall the effect created a certain heaviness at the bottom of the garment. Trims included ruching, cording, scallops, and flounces. Most skirts had one or two flounces at the bottom, but some had row upon row down the entire length of the skirt. Others had a horizontal panel at the front of the skirt. An innovation at the time was the inclusion of sewn-in pockets. In the past, pockets were a part of a woman's underdress. They were separate articles that were suspended from a band tied at the waist and could be reached through slits in the outer skirt.

Evening dress continued to follow the same silhouette as in the day. Necklines were off the shoulder and either straight or with a dip at the center. Many had berthas, a wide neckline covering, which provided additional modesty for older or more conservative women. Fabrics included silk, moiré, velvet, and organdy. The use of trims increased greatly. Popular choices included lace, ribbon, and flowers.

The study of fashion during the last decade of the antebellum era is particularly exciting because this period represented the first time that there was widespread photographic documentation of what people actually wore. No longer is the study merely subject to interpretations of the hand-drawn or engraved fashion plates to which period women may have aspired. Whether or not a woman could afford the extravagances touted by the fashion plates of the day, it can be seen that the "look" that she was hoping to attain was the same. Women of this period wanted to create the appearance of a narrow waist. Virtually all lines of garments emphasized the smallness of the waist by creating the illusion of width at the shoulders and hips. This was further accentuated by foundation garments, which altered the body's physical appearance.

The dress bodices during the period can be classified by three basic styles. There was the "O" bodice, distinguished by the fullness of the fabric as it cascaded over the bust and gathered in around the waist. "O" bodices were especially popular prior to the Civil War. The bodice that was becoming fashionable at this time was the "V" bodice. This very fitted style was characterized by double or triple vertical darts extending from the waist. The darts, as well as the side and back seams, were usually boned. Stays could be made from whalebone, metal, or even wood. The third style bodice was the "Y" style from the prior decade. Like the "O" bodice, "Y" bodices were relatively loose fitting.

Regardless of style, bodices ended at the natural waistline. The bodice portion of the dress fastened at the center front by hooks and eyes whereas the skirt portion had a side-front closure. This created an awkward opening that extended vertically from the neck, then horizontally along the waist and then vertically again down a few inches along the left front skirt seam. The *armscye*, or armhole, was almost always diagonal or horizontal to give the shoulders a sloping and wider appearance.

Sleeves by this time were very full, particularly at the elbow, again imparting the illusion of the slender waist. Sleeves, too, came in three fundamental styles. Straight sleeves were simple, loose-fitting sleeves that gathered together into a cuff at the wrist. Bishop sleeves continued in popularity. Pagoda sleeves tended to be found on more elaborate dresses. This was a loose sleeve, which was widest at its hem and usually of bracelet length and worn with an undersleeve.

Often sleeves had sleeve caps. These were ornamental pieces of fabric that covered the top few inches of the sleeve supporting the image of the wide, sloping shoulder. Sometimes the impression of a sleeve cap would be created through the use of trim. Short cap sleeves, which revealed a women's arm, could only be found on ball gowns.

The necklines of day dresses usually came to the base of the neck. Many were trimmed by small, white collars, which were sewn flat and met in the front. Some had very short stand-up collars. Collars were basted inside to protect the garment from wear and soiling. They could easily be removed for frequent launderings from which the entire garment could be saved. The collars would be constructed of sturdy white or very light-colored fabric that could stand up to the repeat washings this portion of the garment required. Sometimes these collars had matching sets of cuffs, which were similarly attached and served the same purpose. Collars were frequently decorated with a broach at the center of the neck. If a bow were used, the tails of the bow would extend diagonally away from the center, continuing to proffer the illusion of the broad upper torso. Ball gowns often had wide, bateau necklines.

Many of the fabrics and dyes used at this time did not hold up to frequent laundering. Garments were often taken apart and resewn when cleaned. The *Household Encyclopedia* provided nine pages of instructions for washing various fabrics, such as "Take rice-water, and wash them quickly, without soap."[2] Other methods employed included the use of bran, ox-gall, salt, elixir of vitriol, and egg yolk. Most women's dresses were never totally laundered but rather spot cleaned as needed.

Skirt lengths were long but seldom touched the ground where they would have become exceedingly hard to keep clean. Hem tapes were common to many skirts. The tapes or trims were wrapped around the finished hem and could be removed for cleaning or replacement. Skirts were very full and were either fully gathered or pleated at the waistline. No effort was made to make the stomach area appear flatter because, once again, the fuller an area away from the waist seemed, the narrower the waist appeared.

Fabrics used for dresses and skirts included silk, linen, wool, and cotton. These were available in an almost infinite variety of weights and weaves, some of which are no longer available today. By far, cotton and linen were the most common choices for everyday wear. Silk was expensive. If the average woman owned a silk dress, it would be saved for very special occasions. Linen, because of its extreme durability and ability to be produced at home, was considered frontier or laborer clothing. This was particularly true in the South where it was in common use among the slave population. Wool continued to have its place because of its warmth and especially because of its fire-retardant qualities. Cotton, a status symbol earlier in the century, had become readily available and affordable for even modest households by the 1830s due to an extremely well-developed textile industryand the invention of the cotton gin. From time to time, there were movements in the North among abolitionist women to avoid the use of cotton due to their belief that cotton was produced largely as a result of slave activity, but this tended to be confined to relatively small groups.

The color palette available at this time was basically that which could be achieved by natural dyes. While Southern women tended to wear lighter hues, popular colors included browns, soft blues, greens, lavenders, and grays. Yellows and deep berry-toned reds were also in use. Black was a common color for trim and detailing. Even though chemical dyes had been introduced by the end of the 1850s, these colors were mostly found in decorative fabrics for the home. Although some showy young women in the North did wear them, proper ladies did not. *Peterson's* counseled against the use of bright colors saying, "though they may gratify the savage, will not please the educated eye." Readers were warned about wearing yellow and yellow-greens: "It is scarcely necessary to observe that, of all complexions, those which turn upon the yellow are the most unpleasant in their effect—and probably for this reason, that in this climate it is always a sign of bad health."[3]

Popular patterns included geometrics such as dots, checks, and stripes. Sometimes these were combined with small floral motifs or grouped into small clusters. Large florals were not in style nor were the very small floral calicos, which were not popular until later in the century. Patterns were also created by variations in the weave or with the use of shiny and dull threads.

Trim to dresses was generally placed in horizontal or diagonal lines continuing the illusion of the narrow waist. Day dresses had little trim except on the sleeves or bodice. Skirts, if trimmed, were done so near the hemline. The trims used included braid, piping, binding, or ribbon. Ribbons were commonly gathered, pleated, or ruched. Some skirts appear to be trimmed at the hem but had actually been fitted with a hem protector. This tape wrapped around the hem of the garment to protect it from wear. It was much less expensive to replace a worn hem tape than to replace the garment, and the process was less labor intensive than turning the skirt. Some ball gowns had flounces or even a series of ruffles along the skirt. Trims on gowns tended to be more expensive and elaborate than those on everyday dresses.

Accessories

Dresses were updated or embellished by the use of accessories. A dress might be given a different look by the addition of a "fischu." There were several styles of fischus, but, basically, they covered the upper back much like a shawl collar and extended over the front in long tails that either met at the waist or crossed over each other. Some extended down the skirt a foot or so. Fischus were often made of sheer, gauzelike fabrics. They were decorated with ruffles, ribbons, lace, and bows. These were particularly popular in warmer climates at a time when propriety dictated that a lady's shoulders be fully covered until evening. A cooler dress with a scooped neckline could be worn and covered by the lightweight fischu. They were also worn over ball gowns by Older women also wore fischus over ball gowns. Once again, practicality dictated that the fischu be a separate piece that could be cleaned more easily than the entire dress. This also allowed dresses to be easily changed to reflect new trends in fashion. Berthas served a similar purpose to fischus but were like oversized collars rather than wraparounds.

Sashes and waistbands were made of rich fabrics often embroidered or trimmed. They extended well down the length of the dress. Belts of many different styles were wornand some were quite elaborate. The Medici belt stands out as perhaps the most notable style. It was several inches wide at the sides and back but the front flared out into two exaggerated points that extended up to the area between the breasts and down to mid-stomach. The Bretelle corset was similarly shaped with shoulder straps almost like braces.

Ball gowns, naturally, would not have been found in the majority of women's wardrobes but their splendor and overstated nature demands some comment over and above the few aforementioned remarks. Ball gowns had scooped necklines, short sleeves, and extremely full skirts. Silk was the fabric of choice. Ball gowns were elaborately decorated with long sashes, tiers of laced ruffles, flower garlands, or whatever extravagance might have struck the wearer.

Skirts worn with shirts and jackets or with vests and jackets were popular among young women in their teens and twenties. It was not until the mid-1860s that the skirt and blouse unaccompanied by the jacket was seen. The jackets were similar to what is called the bolero today. Jackets frequently matched the skirt fabric. As the fashion grew more popular, the jackets became decorated with more and more black braid, which was often done in increasingly ornate patterns. Vests were generally of a solid fabric. Blouses were white and generally closed by buttons rather than the hooks and eyes that fastened dress bodices. The end of the blouse was sewn into a waistband as opposed to hanging loose.

Riding habits consisted of a skirt, jacket, blouse, and occasionally a vest. Hats were small and frequently had a veil. The fabric was closely woven to withstand snags on branches and dark colors were preferred for practicality. Of course, not all women rode for exercise. Some rode in parks to "be seen," and these ladies often preferred more elaborately decorated outfits. *Godey's Lady's Book* offers this description of an illustration: "Riding habit of black cloth with fluted worsted braid and large gilt buttons; white cashmere vest; scarlet cravat; black felt hat with black feather and scarlet bow."[4]

White wedding dresses came into fashion toward the end of the period; however, many women still followed past traditions and were married in their "best" dress. Those fortunate enough to be able to afford such a specialized garment tended to wear dresses that might be considered plain by ballroom standards. Expense was more likely to be put into the fabric rather than trim. Generally, weddings were held during the day. Wedding dresses were, therefore, day dresses with jewel necklines and long sleeves. In keeping with "the look" of the day, headdresses and veils tended to lie flat on the head to avoid adding height. Coronets of real or artificial flowers were arranged so that they framed the face and added width.

Undergarments

Quite possibly, undergarments reached the highest level of complexity and sophistication in fashion history during this period. Undergarments served to protect the outer garment from body soiling, molded the body to create the ideal "look," and served to distribute the weight of the full skirts over the hips. Like the previously discussed collars and cuffs, undergarments were constructed of serviceable fabrics that could be laundered repeatedly. They were usually white.

The garment worn closest to the skin was the chemise—a knee-length, loose-fitting shift. The body was almost triangular in shape due to the gussets on the sides. This basic garment had changed little in the previous 600 years. During this period, the neck was so wide that it was almost off the shoulder and the sleeves were short, "infant sleeves." Trim, if any, would be found at the neck or sleeve cuff. Sometimes the yoke would be decorated with small tucks. Its prime purpose was to help absorb perspiration and protect outer garments. It was sometimes affectionately called a "shimmy."

Drawers by this period had come to be worn by women of all classes. Commonly known as "pantalettes," they were constructed of two independent legs attached to a waistband and extended to just below the knee. Sometimes these were decorated with tucks, fancy stitching, or eyelet.

The corset was worn on top of the chemise. The purpose of this garment was to make the waist look small compared to other parts of the body and to shape the upper portion of the body upward and outward from the waist to the bust. Corsets were lightly boned and usually had steel clasps at the front while lacing up the back to allow for adjustment. Some had laces in the front with a "busk" inserted for rigidity. Busks were often made of whalebone. Light corsets were introduced to girls around age twelve and certainly by the age of puberty. Over the corset was worn a corset cover, or camisole. These were sleeveless and extended to the waist.

Early in the period women wore a small cotton- or down-filled pad known as a bustle. It was not as dramatic or highly structured as the bustle that was to reappear at the end of the century. The bustle was tied around the waist and located at the back. Worn in addition to multiple layers of petticoats, it served to create extra volume and further support the full skirt.

The crinoline, or hoop, was the major fashion innovation for women during the 1850s and is perhaps the single garment most associated with women's clothing during the antebellum period. The circumference of skirts increased steadily throughout the decade with some reaching 12 to 15 feet. This proliferation of fabric required the use of more and more petticoats to sustain the volume. *Peterson's Magazine* touted the crinoline as a solution to the problem.

> There can be no doubt, that, so long as wide and expanded skirts are to be worn, it is altogether healthier to puff them out with a single light hoop than with half-a-dozen starched cambric petticoats as has been the practice until lately. Physicians are now agreed that a fertile source of bad health with females is the enormous weight of skirts previously worn. The hoop avoids that evil entirely. It also, if properly adjusted, gives a lighter and more graceful appearance to the skirt.[5]

Crinolines could be covered or caged. Caged crinolines were a series of hoops of varying sizes suspended from strips of tape, which descend from the waist. Covered crinolines were fabric petticoats that contained casings to hold the hoops. Crinolines were worn beneath petticoats in order to make the skirt appear more full. They also helped in the practical task of distributing the weight of the skirt, which could become quite oppressive depending on the type and amount of fabric in it. Generally, day dresses had crinolines that were somewhat smaller than those worn for the evening. Atop the crinoline were placed one or more petticoats for added fullness and to soften the ridges that could be created by the hoops. Skirts tended to be so much greater in circumference than the crinolines that they tended to drape over this support in folds.

Even a small sampling of period photographs would indicate that few women actually wore hoops in the extreme proportions depicted in fashion plates of the day. The normal proportion diameter of the hoop was approximately 50 percent to 70 percent of the wearer's height. Women engaged in vigorous work would decline wearing them. The structural material that made the hoop was often of long thin strips of whalebone, called "baleen," turned back on itself in a circle. *Peterson's Magazine* offers insight into this distinctive fashion component.

This image from a *carte de vista* shows the tremendous fullness skirts reached toward the end of the antebellum period. As voluminous as they appear, these skirts are not nearly as wide as those depicted in fashion plates of the day. Both women are wearing undersleeves beneath the broad sleeves of their dresses.

Five years ago when hooped skirts were first introduced, every one predicted for them a speedy decline, and fall; but after encountering the shafts of ridicule and opposition in every conceivable form, they still not only remain a fixed fact, but have become a permanent institution, which no caprice of fashion will be likely wholly to destroy.

The reason of this constant and increased appreciation is found in the acknowledged principle of comfort and utility upon which the idea was based . . . ladies realized what they needed—something to extend their dresses to proper and becoming dimensions, and save the oppressive weight of a mass of clothing upon the hips.

When a mode, no matter how excellent in itself, becomes a fashion, the tendency is always toward an extreme, and it is not surprising that this was the case with hooped skirts, and that at a certain period the size became absurdly and preposterously large. At the present time a happy medium seems to have been reached.[6]

The nightdress was ankle length white cotton and approximately two and a half to three yards wide at the hem. The collar, cuffs, and yoke were often decorated with embroidery, lace, ruching, and tucks. Nightcaps, often decorated with lace and bows, were still worn. Prior to dressing, a woman might wear a morning robe over her nightdress.

Outerwear

Until the mid-1830s, the pelisse was the common outer garment. The pelisse followed the general silhouette of the dress and sleeve style of the day and was similar to the modern coat. After that time, when it came to outerwear, women had a wide variety of options, including capes, cloaks, shawls, jackets, and coats. Capes varied in length from just below the hip to just above the ankle, and they fit closely to the top portion of the torso. Some capes had arm slits for ease of movement. Cloaks were extremely full in order to accommodate the full sleeves and skirts.

Jackets and coats naturally followed dress lines, making them many times wider at the hem than at the shoulder. Jackets, or "paletots" as they were called, may have been more popular than coats because they were more lightweight. Even coats tended to be 6 to 10 inches shorter than the hem of the skirt.

Shawls were very popular, and retailers advertised the arrival of new shipments of them. They were oversized and extended well down the back of the skirt. Commonly, two-yard squares were folded into triangles. Double-square shawls could be 64 inches by 128 inches or more. Some shawls were knitted or crocheted; others were made from wool or lace. Many were decorated with fringe, ruffles, or lace, and paisley shawls were particularly popular.

"Mantel" was the general term used for other outer garments not previously mentioned. Mantels tended to be basically triangular in shape although the back could easily have a rounded "point." They extended over the shoulders and were slightly shaped at the arms. The long ends in front assumed a variety of shapes. For summer wear, the fabrics tended to be light and unlined. Winter mantles were made of heavier, lined fabrics. Evening mantels were made of luxurious fabrics such as velvet or satin and decorated with braid and other rich trims.

Headgear

Hats in the 1820s and early 1830s were either large brimmed with high, round crowns or bonnet style. They were commonly decorated with feathers or lace and tied beneath the chin with a large ribbon. The "capote" was a style of bonnet that had a soft fabric crown and a stiff brim.

The "coal scuttle" bonnet was popular during the 1840s. These bonnets fit the head closely on the sides and extended straight out on all three sides, creating an almost tunnel effect for the wearer. Over the next decade the bonnet brim shortened and widened somewhat, making it more attractive for wearers and improving their visibility.

Bonnets were popular throughout of the period. They were one apparel item that women could constantly update by reworking the trim or decorations to meet the current vogue. Favored decorative features included ribbon, lace, and clusters of silk flowers or berries. These were used on the outside of the bonnet as well as inside of the brim to frame the face. Huge ribbons several inches wide were tied in large bows beneath the chin. The outsides of bonnets were covered in silk or more commonly polished cotton, which was then pleated, ruched, piped, or quilted. A gathered flounce or skirt was often found attached to the base of the bonnet at the nape of the neck. For summer wear, bonnets were often made of straw.

When serious protection from the sun was needed, it was the slatted bonnet that came to the rescue. These work garments were made of cotton or linen and bore no decorations or trim. They had long back pieces that extended over the shoulders, and the front could be folded back or fully extended to shade the entire face. Women were seldom photographed in sunbonnets due to their unflattering appearance.

During the day women wore dainty caps made of muslin, lace tulle, and ribbon. These would never be worn outdoors. Crocheted nets were also worn, but they were generally not considered suitable for dress occasions. Some older, conservative women wore more substantial caps, often with lappets, which fully covered the head and were reminiscent of the caps more commonly worn during the previous century.

Ancillary Clothing

Aprons were an important item in a 19th-century wardrobe. The difficulty involved in cleaning garments made clothing protection an important step in household management. Early in the period, aprons covered almost the entire dress. The aprons fit closely at the top of the chest and tied at the back. They hung down loosely from shoulder straps to just above the hem.

As skirts widened, household aprons grew to accommodate them. Aprons became extremely large, enveloping almost the entire skirt from front to back and extending down to within a few inches of the hem. Often they had rectangular tops, which were known as "pinners" because they were held in place by pins rather than the neck strap common in the 20th century. Smaller aprons would be worn for mealtimes unless servants served the meals.

Aprons would often be made from fabrics with small plaids or checks that would help to hide stains. Although they could be solid, they were seldom white. Aprons were made from linen, flannel, wool, or cotton. Wool was greatly preferred for safety around fires. It does not burn as quickly as linen, and its odor when burning gave fair warning. Burns were the second leading cause of fatality for women at this time, surpassed only by death during childbirth.

Fancy, decorative aprons were sometimes worn only for show. These were made of fine quality fabrics and were sometimes decorated with lace, embroidery, or ruffles. These aprons would be much shorter than their functional counterparts, extending only two-thirds to three-quarters of the way down to the hem. Light-colored fabrics were often used, and many were made of polished cotton-type fabric. Ladies magazines of the period gave patterns for these as sewing projects. These aprons would be worn when doing needlework or when receiving guests at home.

Gloves were an essential of a 19th-century woman's wardrobe. Arthur Martine, in his *Hand-Book of Etiquette, and Guide to True Politeness* remarks, "When dancing is expected to take place, no one should go without new kid gloves: nothing is so revolting as to see one person in an assembly ungloved, especially where the heat of the room, and the exercise together, are sure to make the hands of the wearer redder than usual. Always wear your gloves in church or in a theater."[7]

Daytime gloves were short. Commonly, they were joined by a button at the wrist. Some were secured by short lacing. Kid leather was the most common material, but fabric and lace were also used. Fingerless gloves of netted lace or silk, known as "mitts," were popular during the 1840s and 1850s. Evening gloves were long, to the elbow, until the second half of the 1830s when they were shortened to wrist length. For day wear, gloves could be found in a wide variety of colors, but only white was proper for evening and formal wear. Some were embellished with decorative stitching or embroidery.

Footwear

Shoes were slipperlike with flat, square toes. After 1840, they began to have small heels of one inch or less. For ordinary wear, they were made from leather or cloth and were black, light brown, or gray. Formal day dress shoes would be made of fancier fabrics such as satin. Black satin shoes were the dominant evening fashion until about 1840. Evening shoes after that time came in a variety of styles. Some had ribbon ties, which wrapped around the ankle. Others displayed embroidered tops. Evening shoes were often in bright colors to match the ensemble.

Women's boots were ankle height and laced up the sides at the inside with elastic gussets at each side. Some buttoned at the sides. Dressy boots might be made from kid or satin. Congress gaiters, rather low-cut boots finished with a wide piece of elastic on the side, were made of cloth, came in a variety of colors, and were tipped in patent leather. Balmoral boots, which laced up the front, were considered very stylish and were widely popular. Rubber overshoes were introduced in the late 1840s.

House slippers were low-heeled mulelike foot coverings commonly done in Berlin work. The Berlin work was a form of needlework done on the canvas that made up the vamp, or upper part of the shoe, and many patterns were featured in ladies' magazines. The mule was a low, open-backed affair that covered only the front of the foot. Slippers were also crocheted in a low, bootie style.

Items at Hand

As with the previous century, fans remained a popular accessory. The traditional, semicircular fan was often covered in paper or silk. Some were beautifully painted. The average fan length of this period was 6 to 10 inches. Circular fans were also fashionable. These fans had handles that, when folded backward, revealed an accordion pleated, fabric fan. Round or spade-shaped palmetto or straw fans were less expensive and were sometimes homemade.

Umbrellas and parasols were two different accessories and each served a separate purpose. Umbrellas were for use in inclement weather. They were large and black and were meant to protect the carrier from the weather. Parasols were small, ladylike contrivances. Their purpose was to protect the carrier from both the sun and unwanted glances. When hats were very large in the 1820s and 1830s, the parasol was often carried unopened. Parasol frames were made of metal. Handles were ivory or wood. Parasols designed for carriage rides often had a hinge at the top of the stick, which allowed the top to tip in order to better fit the confined space. They varied from 16 to 22 inches. Parasols used for walking were generally larger, 22 to 26 inches. Silk was the most common fabric. Trimming was lace or ruching. Paper oriental-style parasols with cane ribs were used at the seaside or for informal occasions.

Purses came in a variety of styles. Patterns for crocheted, knitted, or Berlin work purses abounded in ladies' magazines. Purses were decorated with tassels, cording, and embroidery. Shapes were round or rectangular, but the six-inch-square bag was most popular. One of the most interesting kinds of purses was a long, thin, knit or netted cylinder closed at both ends with a slit in the center. These were called "miser purses" or "long purses" and were quite popular. Toward the end of the period, small bags, sometimes referred to as "waist pouches," were suspended from the waistband. Formal purses often had beading or were made with metallic thread.

Jewelry

In the 1820s and 1830s, gold chains with lockets or scent bottles were fashionable. *Chatelaines* were still being worn. Popular in the previous century, these ornamental chains were suspended from the waist and contained a variety of useful items many often related to sewing such as scissors, a thimble, a needle case, or a pincushion. They could also feature a scent bottle, a penknife, or anything else that a woman wanted to keep handy. Brooches, bracelets, and drop earrings were also popular. In the 1830s, it became fashionable to wear a narrow velvet ribbon or tress of hair around the neck. Known as a "Jeanette," this adornment often supported a heart of pearls or small cross.

The 1840s saw less jewelry being worn. Watch ownership, however, was fairly common by this time, even for women. Watches were worn on watch chains and were tucked in the belt or carried in a watch pocket at the waist. Patterns for crocheted, beaded, and braid work watch pockets appeared in period ladies' magazines. Watches were hung on a long, fine chain worn around the neck, which extended well below the waist. Some were suspended on a short chain from the belt.

Many photographs from the end of the period show women wearing some jewelry. Popular materials included jet, ivory, bone, onyx, jade, amber, garnet, and pearl. With its discovery in California, gold was the order of the day. Particularly fashionable was the brooch worn at the center of the neckline. Brooches varied in size from large to small and were worn both vertically and horizontally. They closed by simple C clasps without safety catches. Cameos were highly favored and often bore images of mythological figures. The female head, almost synonymous with the modern cameo, was just coming into fashion toward the end of the war. Cameos were made from sardonyx, shell, lava, ivory and coral.

The mid-19th century was a very romantic and sentimental era. It was a common practice to have a piece of hair as a keepsake from a loved one. Many period brooches contained a lock of a beloved's hair under glass in the center of the brooch. Other brooch materials included goldstone, agate, bog oak, enamel, horn, and mosaics. The mosaic pieces were very small and portrayed classical scenes or floral sprays. Enameled pieces were usually blue or black with a gold figure in the center.

Other neckline decorations included short necklaces of single-sized pearls or beads, especially jet. Long chains, popular earlier in the period, were still being worn by some. Both a beaded and a long chain necklace might be worn at the same time.

Bracelets were also stylish and often were worn in pairs, one on each wrist. These tended to be large, almost chunky, bangle style. Serpents were one motif much in vogue. Jet beads strung on wire were also worn. Dangling earrings with long ear wires were worn. These were usually shorter than those worn later in the century. Many earrings were made of hollow wear, an inexpensive rolled gold that appears almost puffed or was formed into hollow tubes. Naturally, this made the earrings very light in weight. Use of acorns as a motif was widespread. Often earrings and brooches came in matched sets.

The wearing of rings was widespread. Unmarried females would wear a ring on the first finger of their left hand no doubt in hope that they would soon be wearing it on the third digit of that same hand. A simple gold band was the prevalent sign of a married woman. Generally, diamond rings were not worn. The diamond mines of South Africa were not discovered until 1870, and it was not until this time that diamonds would become affordable to anyone but the most affluent. Rings were likely to bear garnets, amethysts, pearls, onyx, amber, jade, red coral, or cameos

Hairstyles

In the early 1820s, women generally parted their hair in the middle and had tight curls around the forehead and temples. The back was usually tied into a knot or bun. After 1824, elaborate plaits of false hair were often added. "La Chinoise" was a style that was popular in 1829. Hair was pulled from the back and side into a large knot atop the head while the hair at the forehead and temples was arranged in tight curls. By the mid 1830s, the hair was parted in the middle and pulled flat against the temples from where hanging finger curls, plaits, or loops of hair covered the ears. The hair at the back was pulled into a bun or chignon.

As with other fashion items, hairstyles of the late antebellum period were intended to emphasize a broad upper body. To that end, the center part is almost universal in period photographs. This allows for a wide, bare forehead making the face appear broad while creating no height on top. To continue this illusion, the fullest part of the hairstyle was at or below the ears. Most women had long hair, which they wore rolled, braided, or otherwise confined and pulled toward the back of the head.

If the hair was not confined, it was generally fixed in long finger curls and pulled to the side of the face. The variety of curls and hair rolls was as rich as the ingenuity of the women who styled them. Ladies' magazines of the period offered many suggestions for elaborate hairdressing for evening wear and suggested incorporating such items as flower blossoms, pins, combs, chains, feathers, and false curls.

DRESS REFORM MOVEMENT

The early 1850s saw an attempt to supplant women's dress with a practical alternative to the restrictive fashions of the era. The dress reform movement advocated that women wear full trousers gathered at the ankle under a short skirt that extended just below the knee. Elizabeth Smith Miller introduced the outfit to the women's rights community after seeing this type of clothing on a trip to Europe. It was, however, Amelia Bloomer who is best known for the costume. Bloomer was a lecturer and writer who supported the temperance movement and women's suffrage. After she published woodcuts of herself wearing a "freedom suit" in *The Lily*, a monthly temperance magazine, in 1851 the outfit became known as the "Bloomer Costume."

Bloomer defined the outfit as "a pair of Turkish pantaloons, wide, and nearly meeting the shoe, of such material and texture as the season demanded, and of a hue adapted to the taste of the wearer; and a garment neatly fitting the person, buttoned, or permanently closed on all sides, extending just below the knee . . . ornamented to suit the fancy of the wearer; and . . . headgear not subject to be crushed and destroyed by every slight contact." She asked, "What reasonable person could object to the substitution of such a costume for that worn now?" In addition to the practicality and comfort of the attire, Bloomer advised, "Yet the convenience of the thing is nothing when compared to the health and comfort. Small waists and whalebones can be dispensed with, and we shall be allowed breathing room; and our forms will be what nature made them."[8]

Dress reform had its followers although it did not gain momentum outside the suffrage movement. One of the most famous women to wear the attire was actress Fanny Kemble. Kemble generated much excitement in the local press. Bloomer reported, "There has been a great cry raised by the gentlemen from all quarters, about the male attire which Fanny Kemble is said to have adopted. . . . We have scarcely taken up a paper these two months but we have seen remarks on the subject."[9] The "Bloomer Costume" was an idea whose time had not yet come. The denunciation and ridicule that the outfit garnered eventually led to the abandonment of the dress reform movement, as the supporters felt that the derision undermined their attempts at social reform.

MEN'S CLOTHING

Martine, in his handbook of etiquette, remarks, "There are four kinds of coats which a man must have: a business coat, a frock-coat, a dress-coat, and an over-coat. A well dressed man may do well with four of the first, and one each of the others per annum. An economical man can get along with less."[10] Yet this was not reality. Just as the average woman did not have a specialized outfit for every task of the day, most men did not enjoy the wardrobe depth detailed by Martine. Like women's clothing, men's clothing in practical application tended to fall into formal and informal, summer and winter. New clothes would be considered best dress until they became worn, and they would then be relegated to work status.

A shirt, vest, and trousers would be the very least in which a man would allow himself to be seen in public. A man appearing with anything less was considered to be in a state of "undress." Even laborers and farmers would not allow themselves to go with less. The rare workman who would not be so attired, such as the blacksmith, would wear a heavy leather apron, which covered him somewhat above the waist.

Dress shirts were made of white cotton. Longer than the modern shirt, they were pullovers that buttoned from the midchest to the neck. Small vertical tucks commonly decorated either side of the buttons, but this became less favored as the decade progressed. Shirts had neck bands and detachable collars. Work shirts were made in a variety of colors and checks and could be made from cotton or linen.

For formal day wear, the collar was upright with a gap between the points, which just touched the jaw allowing for freer movement of the head and neck than had been the style earlier in the century. For informal wear, men wore either a shallow single collar with sloping points meeting at the center and forming a small inverted V-shaped opening or a shallow double collar similar to the modern collar.

Stocks or cravats were worn around the neck. Stocks were often black and fastened at the back. As the period progressed, they were abandoned in favor of the cravat. The cravat was a band of fabric passed around the neck and tied in either a bow or a knot with hanging ends. Sometimes they were fastened with a decorative pin. Silk was the fabric of choice, and it was one area where a man might be able to display his good taste even if his purse prohibited further extravagances. Ladies' magazines of the period, however, offered patterns for woolen and cotton knitted cravats. Even laborers would simulate the look, although they may only have been able to knot a cotton kerchief around their neck.

The suit ensemble consisted of a coat, waistcoat, and trousers. For dress occasions, tailcoats were worn. Tailcoats could be either double breasted with large lapels or single breasted with smaller lapels. Collars were cut

A *cartes de visite* portrait of a well-dressed man from just before the Civil War. Note the patterned vest and tie. The table, floor covering, and draperies are probably fixtures of the photographer's studio—in this case, that of Matthew Brady.

high behind the neck with a rolled collar, which joined the lapel in a V-
or an M-shaped notch.

Frock coats, which had a fitted torso, collar lapel, and skirt flaring from
the waist, were popular throughout the period. Prior to the 1830s, sleeves
were full at the shoulder and formed a puff at the top when the excess
fabric was gathered into the armhole. After 1830, the skirt became somewhat shorter and narrower and the coat became longer waisted. Early in
the period, the most fashionable coats had padding in the shoulders and
chest area, but this disappeared during the late 1830s.

Jackets were single-breasted garments with side pleats and no vent in
the back. The front closure was straight but curved back slightly below
the waist. Collars lapels, and pockets were small.

Toward the end of the period, the fuller suit seems to have been favored
by the average man. Perhaps this was due to comfort or the need for less-
skilled tailoring. The formal suit appears to have been the "look" to which
men of power aspired. Lapels sported a more modern single notch than
earlier in the century. Frock coats sometimes had velvet collars and
cufflink-style buttoning. Trousers had buttoned, full fall fronts or buttoned
"French" flies. Wool was the fabric of choice and linen was popular during the summer, especially in the South. Farmers seemed to favor tweeds
and more sturdy woolens. Generally, solids dominated, and browns and
grays were most common. Black was the choice of professionals who also
preferred fine woolen broadcloth, serge, and twill. These fabrics often had
a certain amount of silk woven into the fabric to give it a finer finish and
lighter weight.

Vests or waistcoats were worn under the suit coat. Early in the period,
they had straight standing collars or small, notchless, rolled collars arranged so that only the edge would be seen at the edge of the coat. They
were either single or double breasted, although single breasted was more
popular during the 1820s. Lapels narrowed and were less curved in the
1840s, but by the end of the decade they had widened again. They could
be made of the same fabric as the suit or they could be of a much finer,
dressier fabrics such as silk taffetas, embossed silks, or brocades. Patterns
ranged from tone-on-tone to stripes, checks, and paisleys. The neckline
cut came to lie flat and moved lower during the period. Watch pockets
were becoming common.

For outdoor wear, men wore overcoats that were referred to as "great-
coats." Between 1820 and 1840, these often reached down to the ankle and
had deep, rolled collars. The fit was very close to the body at the beginning of the period but this characteristic disappeared in the 1840s. The box
coat was a large, loose-fitting greatcoat with one or more capes at the
shoulder. Coats of this looser style became increasingly popular as the
period progressed. The mackintosh was a waterproof coat made of rubber cut like a short, loose overcoat. While their water-repellent nature was

welcome, many chose not to sport them due to the offensive odor they emitted. Capes continued to be worn and were especially the fashion for evening wear. They were cut in gores and fit smoothly at the shoulder. Some featured large standing collars; others had flat ones. Some had capes of varying lengths and even multiple capes at the shoulder. In the 1830s and 1840s, short, round capes lined with silk were the fashion for evening wear. Later in the period, some men wore shawls over their suits as outerwear.

Hat styles varied. The top hat was popular for both day and evening wear. Many Southern gentlemen favored what has come to be called the "plantation hat." This a low-crowned, stylish hat with a substantial, but not overstated, brim. The commonly found round hat had a round crown with a medium brim. This should not be confused with the derby, which was not developed until later in the century. Many men wore flat-topped straw hats in the summer. Rural men often wore wide-brimmed, high-crowned hats, which offered less in fashion but more in protection from the elements and a cool space above the head.

As with women, gentlemen wore gloves. These were made of leather, wool, or cotton for the daytime and silk or kid for the evening. Leatherwork gloves and riding gloves were also common. When "dressed," men carried canes often with fine detailing and gold or silver trim. In inclement weather, they carried large black umbrellas.

Shoes had low heels and square toes. Shoes with laces first became popular during the 1830s. Work shoes were often fashioned with the rough of the leather exposed. This allowed a cheaper grade of leather to be used, and the knap of the leather could be greased to help repel moisture. For formal wear, the shoe was made with the smooth side out. It was often open over the instep and secured with a ribbon bow. Leather or tarred canvas gaiters, which covered the shoe top and were secured by a strap under the shoe, were worn in bad weather. Spatterdashers, which reached to just below the knee, were longer versions of gaiters that were worn for hunting and other sporting activities. Knee-high boots were worn for riding. Later in the period, shorter, half boots with elastic sides or laced closings were also worn.

Male jewelry included cravat pins, brooches worn on shirtfronts, watches, jeweled shirt buttons and studs, and decorative gold watches and watch chains. Rings of all types were popular. They took the form of signet rings, seal rings, mourning rings, and commemorative rings. As the period progressed, jewelry lessened and was generally limited to rings, cravat pins, watches, and watch chains.

Braces or suspenders buttoned on to the trousers by means of leather tabs. It was quite the fashion for women to crochet them or decorate them in Berlin wool work. Once again, ladies' magazines featured patterns for doing this. Makers were cautioned, "This crochet should not be done too tightly, as a little elasticity is desirable."[11] Elastic had been invented by this time but its only apparel application was in wide panels in shoes. Men unfortunate not to have braces made by an attentive woman may have sported those made of linen cloth.

Throughout the period, men wore drawers that extended down to the ankle and had button fronts. These could be made of silk stockinette, cotton, or linen. In the early years of the period, some men wore corsets or padding at the shoulder, chest, hip, or calf in order to have a fashionable silhouette. Later, an undershirt, a long-sleeved pullover that buttoned to midchest, was added. However, one-piece "Union suits" with the trap door in the rear were not developed until after the war.

When it came to lounging in the privacy of one's home, gentlemen had several specialized items of attire. The lounging or smoking cap was an elaborate item made of rich fabrics and adorned with embroidery, beadwork, or braid. They generally came in three basic styles: the round, pillbox style; the fitted, six-panel cap; and the teardrop-shaped, Scotch style. The first two styles ended with a tassel on top. The last was finished with a narrow ribbon at the back of the cap at the point. Ladies' magazines carried patterns for making and decorating these. In addition to slippers, which greatly resembled the woman's slipper, a man might have preferred the dressing or lounging boot. These boots were made of fabric and were decorated with elaborate embroidery.

Nightshirts were made of white cotton and extended to the ankle. They had long sleeves and small turned-down collars. The nightcap was a bag-shaped item with a tassel on top. Some were knit or crocheted, but these were going out of style. Over his nightshirt, a gentleman may have worn a wrapper. This was a long, sack-style robe with a plain sleeve confined by a cord at the waist.

Men wore their hair parted on the side, in a short to moderate length often in loose curls or loosely waved but cut short in the back. Beards came into fashion around 1825 with a small fringe of whiskers. Facial hair continued to grow longer throughout the period, and many arrangements of facial hair became stylish. Men sported beards of all styles, lengths, and degrees. Mustaches were equally in favor. Photographs from late in the period show the tremendous variety that abounded.

CHILDREN'S CLOTHING

Children's clothing rivaled women's fashions both in complexity and ornateness. Some middle- and upper-class children were dressed in layers of clothing, often in impractical fabrics. *Godey's Lady's Book* carried the following description with an accompanying illustration "Child's dress of green silk with narrow pinked ruffles, corselet of green silk, white muslin gimp, white felt hat with white wing." Ornate as it sounds, this outfit is not classified as a "party dress." Gauze, silk, wool, and taffeta were common fabrics suggested for children's dress in ladies' magazines. Print fabrics tended to be small geometric or abstract designs. These kinds of designs allowed for economical use of material since it was easier to match such prints and there was less waste when cutting patterns. Braid or ribbon were popular trims even for the children.

In rural areas, children's clothing was considerably more practical, much the same as their parents. Muslin and cotton was the fabric of choice for country and poorer folk. In order to allow for growth, it was common for seams at the shoulders and under the arms to be folded in an inch each, so that they could later be let out as the child grew. Sometimes a waistband was added as the child grew. Several tucks of an inch or so were often made near the hems of skirts and trousers. These created an attractive detail that could later be let down to accommodate growth.

Little girls were dressed very much like their mothers. *Godey's Lady's Book* contained an illustration for a "corset for a little girl," which laced down the back only. Not everyone encouraged its use, however, as the editor of *Peterson's Magazine* points out: "Stays or tight bands about the ribs compress them readily, as these bones are not fully formed, hence readily cause deformities, and alter the natural and healthy position and action of the lungs, heart, liver and stomach, and produce a tendency to disease in these organs."[12]

The main difference between a woman's attire and a girl's was that a girl's skirt was considerably shorter, ending about midcalf. Pantalettes hung just below the edge of the dress. These would be plain for everyday and would be adorned with lace or eyelet for dressier occasions. These pantalettes differed from women's in that the crotches were sewn, and they buttoned at the sides. Like her mother, a little girl wore a chemise as the basic undergarment. Once the hoop made its debut, even young girls of age seven began to wear one, although it would likely have only one hoop ring at this time. Once again, like adult women, she would wear under- and over-petticoats. One popular style dress for Sundays and parties around mid-century was the bateau or "boat" neckline. This extremely wide neckline was another impractical fashion and many photographs show one sleeve slipping off the child's shoulder. Like their mothers, little girls wore undersleeves and chemisettes. They also wore tuckers. A tucker was a panel of crimped muslin secured by a tape and sewn on the inside edge of the neckline and sleeve edge. The purpose of this was to save wear on the fabric, and the tucker could be removed and laundered separately from the garment. Blouses and skirts were not popular for toddlers but were worn by young girls.

Fancy aprons for children were popular. These tied around the waist and covered almost the entire skirt portion of a dress. The top covered only part of the dress front and crossed over both shoulders on top. These were commonly decorated with flounces, bows, and other decorative details. Pinafores, which covered almost the entire dress, were more practical and much more common across all economic lines. They were constructed in such fabrics as muslin, calico, or linen. The pinafore fit closely to the chest and hung down loosely to the hem. Another layered style for young girls was the white dress covered by another jumperlike dress.

Children's jewelry tended to be modest and simple. Little girls wore strings of beads, lockets, and chains. Very young girls wore coral necklaces or pairs of coral bracelets. Infants were given elaborate coral rattles mounted in silver or teething rings also made of coral.

Boys wore a series of different types of outfits, each befitting a certain age group. Very young boys often had shirts that buttoned to the waistband of their pants and provided a neater look. From age one to four, boys wore a Nankeen suit. This was a dresslike costume worn over white underdrawers not unlike the girl's pantalettes, although they were likely to be less fancy. It was a blousy sack, often with a large sash or a cord tied around the waist.

Between the ages of four and seven, boys wore the French blouse. Essentially, it was a loose, dresslike tunic secured at the waist by a belt and large buckle or sash. This would have been worn over loose knee pants, although, it was also worn over skirts for very young boys. They may also have been attired in a loose jacket and waistcoat, once again with loose, knee pants. Boys may also have been clad in a suitlike outfit with a slightly cutaway jacket, gently rounded in front, and very loose trousers, which extended to about midcalf.

From 7 to 12, a boy may have worn what would be thought of as a suitlike outfit consisting of a loose, ankle-length trouser and waist-length sack coat with a ribbon tie fashioned into a bow. The pants might have "box pleats." At this time, suspenders became fashionable. Sailor suits were also popular for young boys 7 up to 14. Some boys in certain areas did not wear long pants until 14 or 15.

As older teens, boys dressed much as adult men. They wore pants, vests, and jackets. Jacket types included sack, frock, and a short, military style. Boys' undergarments included an undershirt and drawers that reached down to the knee. When boys graduated into longer pants, they wore longer, ankle-length drawers that fit the leg more closely.

For outerwear, children often wore coats, jackets, and cloaks similar to those worn by women. They also wore capes secured by buttoned tabs across the chest. Girls generally wore small hats. In summer they were usually straw for summer and cloth for winter. As with women, slatted bonnets were worn in rural areas. Brims tended to be small and they were very simply decorated. Boys wore caps and small hats with rounded crowns.

Girls wore leather or canvas short boots for day wear and slippers for dressy occasions. Some of the slippers had ankle straps. The boots either laced up the side or had elastic gussets on the side. Canvas boots often had toe and heel portions covered in leather for added protection and durability. Boys wore footwear similar to adult shoes or short pull-on boots sometimes decorated with a tassel on the front.

Girls wore their hair in a short, ear-length blunt cut, which was pushed behind the ears. Some wore their hair in long finger curls. The latter seems to have been more popular among girls of higher economic status. Occasionally, ribbons were used to keep the long hair out of their faces. Girls of about eight or nine began to wear their hair in hairnets. Sarah Morgan, at age 19, wrote in her diary, "The net I had gathered my hair in fell in my descent and my hair swept down half way between my knee and my ankle in one stream."[13] Like their mothers, the hair was center parted. Boys parted their hair to the side. The sides and back were usually short. Due to the fashions in which young boys were attired, often when looking at photographs, the part is the only clue to the sex of the child

Finally, the editor of *Peterson's Magazine* offers the following advice to mothers about clothing children:

> To guard against cold, the child should wear flannel, of varying thickness, according to the season of the year, next to the body, and fitting tolerably close, for, without this protection, the present style of dress, causing the clothes to project away, leaves the body exposed to sudden chills. The head should be lightly covered, so as to protect it from the sun, or sudden change of temperature; but it should never be covered with thick or heavy material. Anything causing fullness or congestion about the head will very commonly act by sympathy, as it is called, on the stomach, and cause obstinate and violent vomiting. . . . A pin should never be used about a child's clothes at any age; buttons and strings should always be the modes of fastening.[14]

Infants wore long gowns that were often twice the length of the child. This provided the child with greater warmth. Long gowns could not be cast off as loose blankets could. The gowns were generally white in order to withstand the frequent washings that infant clothing required and were of "soft material, entirely free from starch."[15] For the first few weeks after birth, infants wore long narrow strips of fabric known as "belly-bands." These were several yards long and were designed to protect the navel. In addition to diapers, or napkins as they were called, infants wore a shirt, a pinner that contained their lower limbs, a skirt or skirts, and a dress. Babies also wore caps for which women's magazines frequently carried patterns.

The *Housekeeper's Encyclopedia* details the order of operations in dressing a baby:

The first article put on, after a napkin, should be a flannel band, from four to four and a half inches wide; pin it snugly, but not tight enough to bind, and make the babe uncomfortable; the little shirt is the next article of dress to be put on the child; this should be open at the front, and folded smoothly, so as to leave no wrinkles; the pinner comes next; lay the infant on its stomach, fold the shirt smoothly on its back, fasten the shirt and pinner together with a small pin, leaving the point covered, so as to prick neither child nor nurse; wrap its feet in the pinner, and pin it as close as possible without cramping its limbs; then take the flannel skirt . . . fold the shirt over, and fasten shirt, band pinner, and skirt, together with two pins, near the arms, being sure to have the points hid in the clothing. . . . Fasten the dress, and the little one is ready for presentation.[16]

As the child grew older clothing adjustments were made. Mothers were commonly advised to "keep socks on after the child is two months old; before this, its pinners will be sufficient protection. . . . When a child shows a disposition to creep, shorten its clothes that it may have free use of its limbs, and protect its feet with stockings and shoes."[17]

The antebellum era was the first era to provide students of fashion with an abundance of pictorial documentation. Ladies' magazines and their fashion plates achieved tremendous popularity during the period and had a wide readership among members of both the upper and middle classes. The fashion plates provide a monthly history of changes in styles and supply tremendous detail. Even though the fashions depicted in these magazines may have been extreme, they show the ideal and provide insight into the styles to which many aspired. The development of photography later on in the period documents what was actually worn and provides insight into adaptations of the fashion plate exemplars. Unfortunately, documentation of working-class clothing remains sketchy, as what few pictures these people might have had taken always showed them in their best clothing.

6

Food

Game's good as any relish and so's bread; but pork is the staff of life.

—James Fenimore Cooper, *The Chainbearer*

FOOD PRESERVATION

Despite movements during the period toward modern foods, the single most important controlling factor of diet remained the food that was availability. For most people, the majority of fresh food choices were governed by regional and seasonal availability. Certainly a person's economic situation provided the means for wider choices, but even these were limited. The storage of food in the mid-19th century was problem for everyone, regardless of economic status, and this reality colored the types of foods that people ate, how they were prepared, and their very quality. In addition to recipes for cooking and suggestions on maintaining the household, books like *Miss Beecher's Domestic Receipt-Book* invariably contained suggestions on how to make slightly spoiled foods palatable. "If meat begins to taint, wash it and rub it with powdered charcoal and it removes the taint."[1] To restore rancid butter, Miss Beecher advised putting "fifteen drops of chloride of lime to a pint of water, and work the butter in till every particle has come in contact with the water."[2]

Many foods, such as grain, root crops, and cooked and smoked meats, would last for a reasonable amount of time if kept in a cool, dry place. This was not a major problem during the winter months when the temperature and relative humidity were low, but hot and humid weather posed a significant problem, especially in the South with its difficult climate. One of the earliest solutions to keeping food from spoiling during warm weather was the icehouse. Originally, farmers used axes and long saws to harvest ice. The ice was cut from frozen ponds or lakes in large blocks. This could be an individual or community operation in rural regions, but there were a number of ice companies that hired large crews to cut ice and transport it to the cities and commercial storage facilities.

Regardless of its source, ice was most often stored in wooden or brick structures known as icehouses, which were usually constructed partially below ground level or into a bank of earth or cliff side. The temperature a few feet into the ground rarely becomes warmer than about 45 degrees Fahrenheit even on the warmest days. Icehouses were owned by individuals or were cooperatively owned by a group of farmers living in close proximity. Most icehouses were located near a pond or other source of quiet water where thick ice was likely to form and a minimum distance was needed for transportation. Licenses were issued to local communities to cut ice from frozen canals as early as the 1840s. It could then be moved many miles by sledge along the frozen canal with little effort. The ice was usually cut in late January or early February, when it was thickest, and brought to the icehouse where it was stacked in layers with spaces between filled with sawdust or straw to permit melting and to keep the cakes from freezing into a solid block. Once the structure was filled, the top layer of the ice was covered with a canvas tarp and sawdust or straw for insulation. Melting in the icehouse ranged from 25 percent to 50 percent annually, but the ice could last through the following October if conditions were favorable. By the dawn of the Civil War, the icehouse had become an indispensable component on the rural farm.

Thomas Moore patented the first domestic icebox in 1803. The icebox gave individual homes and city residences a means of keeping food cold. Fresh meat, dairy products, and perishable fruit could be kept in good condition for much longer if kept cool. Household iceboxes, many of which were homemade, consisted of a wooden box inside another, separated by some insulating material, with a tin container at the top of the interior box. The exterior of the boxes were made of oak, pine, or ash wood and were lined with zinc, slate, porcelain, galvanized metal, or wood. Charcoal, cork, flax straw, ash, or mineral wool provided the insulation between the walls. Irregularly shaped ice blocks were sold to consumers in baskets. Even with the icebox, the frozen blocks would only last for about a day. Boston families could obtain 15 pounds of ice per day from an iceman for two dollars a month just prior to the Civil War. By 1850, *Godey's Lady's Book* called the icebox a "necessity of life."

In 1825, Frederick Tudor and Nathaniel Wyeth solved the problems of preserving ice and made ice harvesting a commercial interest. Commercial ice harvesting was conducted in the months of January, February, and

March in the New England and Middle Atlantic states. Holes would be driven into the ice to determine its thickness, which varied from as little as 6 inches to as much as 30. After clearing the ice of any snow cover, rough ice would be planed. The field was then marked off in squares using a narrow blade, which was steered by plow handles drawn by a horse. An ice cutter, which cut approximately two-thirds the depth of the ice, was then employed to cut the ice into sheets of approximately 12 blocks. The sheets would then be channeled to the edge of the pond by long-handled ice hooks, and from there they would be transported to the storage facility. An icehouse that could hold 25,000 tons of ice would require nearly 100 men with 10–12 teams of horses to fill it. The entire process would usually take 15–30 days.[3] Ice was not only provided to city residents in the North, but it was also shipped to Southern cities and even to the West Indies. Between the 1825 and 1860, New Orleans alone increased its demand for ice seventyfold.[4] In the 1860s, a rudimentary refrigeration system was invented, but American ships were carrying ice to such far away places as Calcutta and Bombay in India for another 40 years.[5]

Modern Advancements

By mid-century, the railroads had become the prime cause of increasing the diversity of food for the American table. Perishables such as milk, oysters, and lobsters were transported by rail to urban areas in large cars filled with ice. The railroad not only augmented the diet, it also served to improve the quality of the food that was eaten. Beef was fatter, more tender, tastier and less expensive. The cattle no longer were driven to market on hoof, and hence, they developed less muscle. The cattle were fed on grain that was also shipped via the railroad, thus improving the flavor. Finally, the entire cost was reduced because there was less weight loss between pasture and market. A similar situation arose with pork. Prior to railroad transportation, a desirable breeding characteristic among hogs was their ability to walk to market. This made long legged varieties superior to short legged ones. With the advent of rail shipping, breeders began to focus on more portly hogs and tastier meat.

The processing and preservation of food had always been a domestic activity, until Frenchman Nicholas Appert invented vacuum-packed, hermetically sealed jars early in the 19th century. In 1818, Peter Durand introduced the tin-plated can to America. The following year, Thomas Kensett Sr. and Ezra Daggert began canning oysters, fruits, meats, and vegetables in New York. In 1825, Kensett filed the first American patent for tin cans, but it was not until 1839 that tin cans came into widespread use. In 1821, William Underwood, who would go on to be famous for canned meat spreads, established a canning plant in Boston. He canned a variety of vegetables, fruits, and condiments, producing grape and mushroom catsup, jams and jellies, and mustard. In 1849, Henry Evans was granted a patent for a machine that limited the amount of hand labor needed to produce tin cans. It increased worker production from 5 or 6 cans an hour to 50 or 60 per hour, stimulating the processing of food as a commercial endeavor. Lobster and salmon were the first foods to be commercially canned. The canning of corn, tomatoes, peas, and additional varieties of fish rapidly followed. Gail Borden obtained a patent for condensed milk in 1856, and although his earlier attempts at canning were less successful, the condensed milk met with great success.

By 1860, 5 million cans a year were being produced. Canned foods were welcomed because not only did they permit consumers to eat out-of-season products but they also provided a certain consistent quality. Americans living in isolated western territories particularly welcomed the profusion of canned foods. The line from the song, "My Darling Clementine," which describes Clementine's footwear as "herring boxes without topses," refers to the oval-shaped fish tins that were plentiful in mining towns.

Putting up the Harvest

Food preservation was an essential household activity. The harvest season came but once annually, and if a family were to live comfortably through the year, careful attention had to be paid to "putting up" harvest surplus until the next growing season. Families generally ate well through most of the winter as the household was still enjoying the abundance of the harvest. Spring, and even early summer were generally the hardest times. Fresh produce was not yet up and stored foods were often becoming limited. Catherine Beecher cautioned housewives, "One mode of securing a good variety in those months in spring when fruits and vegetables fail is by a wise providence in drying and preserving fruits and vegetables [in the fall]."[6]

Produce was preserved by a number of methods and much of it was stored in crocks and jars. Instructions for sealing these vessels included a number of methodsfro a variety of containers: "[S]oak a split bladder and tie it tight over them [jars]. In drying, it will shrink so as to be perfectly air tight."[7] "[C]over each tumbler with two rounds of white tissue paper, cut to fit exactly the inside of the glass."[8] "[S]ecure [jars and crocks] with paper dipped in brandy and a leather outer cover."[9] Finally, "cement on the covers [of stone jars] with a composition of bees-wax and rosin melted together, and thickened with powdered brick dust."[10]

Hundreds of men and women obtained patents for jars that would ease these time-consuming processes. Perhaps the most famous of these was John Mason who patented his Mason jar in 1858. These threaded glass jars had zinc lids with threaded ring sealers. Newspapers often carried notices of patent jars for sale. One such ad boasted "Tomatoes, green corn, peaches or any other fruit or vegetable may be preserved without sugar, by using Spratt's Patent Cans, which are acknowledged to be the only reliable self sealing cans to market." Immediately below this statement followed another notice which asserted, "Few things will be found more delicious in Winter than finely flavored apples and pears, kept fresh in 'Arthur's Self-sealing Cans and Jars.' Let every housekeeper try a dozen or two. . . . She will thank us for our advice next Christmas if she follows it."[11] Jars such as these were a welcome improvement for both city and rural homemakers who had to preserve nature's bounty until the next harvest season.

FOOD ATTITUDES

Modern issues of vitamins, salt, fiber, and fat content were virtually nonexistent for most people during the antebellum period. A few groups emerged during this time urging people to refrain from eating meat or to increase grain consumption, but generally their followers were thought to be eccentric by most Americans. Some women's magazines and receipt books did urge balance and moderation in diet. *Peterson's Magazine* contained the following statement on corpulence: "Dr. Radcliffe recommends that the mouth should be kept shut, and the eyes should be kept open; or, in other words, that corpulent persons should eat little food, and that the quantity of sleep should be diminished. These precautions may be followed with discretion, but it may be dangerous to carry them too far."[12] Most meals at this time contained meat, which was likely to be high in fat content, and bread in one form or another. Frances Trollope, a visitor to the United States in the 1830s, was shocked by the American diet. She remarked on the extraordinary amount of bacon and other meats eaten in American homes. "Ham and beef steaks appear morning noon and night." Equally astonishing to her was the way eggs and oysters, ham and apple sauce, beefsteak and stewed peaches, salt fish and onion were eaten in combination.[13]

COMMON FOODS

Pork was the most common kind of meat consumed, particularly in the Southern diet. Pork might be served three times a day in some households without engendering comment, however, it was not likely fresh pork. Salt-pork and smoked pork were the staple varieties during most of the year except during the harvest season. The abundance of pork was mainly due to the fact that pigs were relatively easy to maintain. They required little space and tolerated a wide variety of foodstuffs, including leavings from household food preparation. Pigs did not have to be put to pasture and consumed less feed than cattle to add the same amount of weight. They could be, and often were, set to fend for themselves in the brush along the margins of the family farm.

Pork could be easily preserved in a number of ways, including pickling, salting, and smoking. Salting and drying retarded the growth of bacteria, as did pickling, smoking, and sugar curing. It was a common practice among farmers' and upper-class planters' wives alike to sell their cured hams as well as surplus lard butter and eggs. In 1856, the mistress of a Georgia plantation recorded the selling of 170 pounds of ham.

James Fenimore Cooper summed up the feelings of many in *The Chainbearer* when he wrote: "I hold a family to be in a desperate way when the mother can see the bottom of the pork barrel. Give me children that's raised on good sound pork afore all the game in the country. Game's good as any relish and so's bread; but pork is the staff of life."[14]

Beef was popular in the North especially after the expansion of the railroads to the West. With its commitment to the cash crops of tobacco and cotton, the Southern planter was not inclined to set aside large portions of land for the grazing of cattle. Many households preferred their beef relatively fresh. During the deep winter, cuts of beef were stored for months in barrels packed with snow. "Hung beef" was another preference where the beef would be hung for several weeks in a dry place to allow it to age. Beef could be preserved by drying or smoking or in brine, but it was not as versatile as pork. Most farmers did keep enough cows to provide their own supply of dairy as well as some beef in the form of male calves.

Lamb was eaten less often but it was popular, particularly in Kentucky, where it remained a mainstay of the local diet. Lamb was only available in the spring and early summer. Once the lamb matured, its meat, now known as mutton, proved to have a strong flavor that was not favored by the American palate. The main disadvantages of mutton were that the animal was more valuable as a source of wool than of food and that the meat was not easily preserved.

Chickens were also an important source of meat. Once again, they required little space but were difficult to preserve. Like other domesticated fowl, chicken was generally eaten fresh. Chickens had the additional appeal of being egg producers while they lived. Eggs were another good source of protein. Eggs were preserved in several ways. Receipts instructed homemakers to "pack them in fine salt, small end down . . . [or] pack them small end down, and then pour on them a mixture of four quarts of cold water, four quarts of unslacked lime, two ounces of salt, and two ounces of cream-tartar." They could be "preserved for two or three months by greasing them all over, when quite fresh, with melted mutton suet, and then wedging them close together [the small end downward] in a box of bran or charcoal." Hard-boiled eggs were sometimes pickled in vinegar.[15]

In the South and rural areas, hunters would supplement the cuisine by bringing home such victuals as geese, rabbits, squirrels, wild turkeys, partridges, pheasants, deer, and reed birds. The meat supplied in this manner was particularly important for poorer families. Even youngsters of 10 or 12 might be experienced enough with firearms not to waste a shot in haste. Defending against predators alone made knowledge of firearms and their use imperative, and it helped to fill the larder in times of want.

Fish and seafood were eaten in abundance in shore communities. Relating a visit to the island of Nantucket, Herman Melville's Ishmael observed, "Chowder for breakfast, and chowder for dinner, and chowder for supper, till you began to look for fish-bones coming through your clothes."[16] Freshwater fish included bass, cod, sturgeon, pickerel, perch, pike, whitefish, and catfish. Fish could be salted or smoked but much of it was eaten fresh or made into chowder or stews. Oysters were extremely popular. They were eaten fresh but were also pickled and canned. Oysters were also made into catsup. Catsup was the general name for a paste that was bottled and used as a sauce. Lobster and anchovies were also made into catsups.

Salt

As can be seen from the previous discussion, salt was indispensable to the rural family. Besides its use in preserving foods, heavy doses of salt were needed to maintain the health of horses, cows, and other livestock, and for use in tanning leather. Common salt could be mined or retrieved by evaporating seawater. The North relied extensively on the salt works at Onondaga Lake near Syracuse in New York State for this important substance. There, the brine (saltwater), which welled up naturally from the floor of the lake, had provided an extensive source of salt made by evaporation for decades. Even Native Americans had used the site to provide themselves with salt. More than 9 million barrels of salt, worth in excess of $30 million were produced in New York State annually in the 1850s. In 1860, a new source of salt was found west of the Appalachian Mountains at the Saginaw River site in Michigan. This resource yielded more than 500, 000 barrels of salt annually for the residents of the Ohio Valley and Great Lakes region. Previously, residents of the region had relied on a small supply of salt laboriously boiled from the mud of salt licks. So successful were the commercial domestic sources that the North did not need to import any foreign salt.[17]

Southern salt works were not nearly as productive as those that served the North. Besides hundreds of coastal evaporating operations that utilized seawater, there were only five principal Southern sources of salt located in Louisiana, Alabama, Virginia, and Kentucky. The major production centers, making 3,000 bushels of salt a day, were in the Kanawha Valley of western Virginia, and at Saltville, Virginia. Salt brine was pumped up from among the salt-bearing layers beneath the earth and air-dried until it became a thick white sludge. Completely drying the salt at its place of origin was found to be inefficient and uneconomical. Most of this salt was transferred to railcars for transportation to Northern and Southern cities. On the eve of the Civil War, the Southern government apprehended a major shortage of salt.

Milk Products

Dairy products were difficult to keep in the warm Southern climate. Milk provided an inviting medium for bacteria, a very real problem in an age when unsanitary conditions abounded. A visitor to the South in 1838 reported that milk was a "rarity" and that she found it plentiful only in

Among the necessities found in an antebellum kitchen were all types of "safes." This is a cheese safe used to dry and store a selection of hard cheeses made by the housewife. It also kept away flies and rodents.

Kentucky. Cheese also suffered in the South due to the presences of high humidity. Making hard cheese was a good way to preserve dairy products for long periods, and those in Northern climates commonly did so. In the South, the only cheeses readily available were simple cottage cheeses and cream cheeses, which did not require the long curing of hard cheeses. Some hard cheeses were imported and could be found in coastal cities.

In 1851, Jesse Williams of New York revolutionized commercial cheese making. He began to purchase milk from other farmers. By combining the milk and producing large cheeses he could achieve a uniform taste and texture. Up until this time, commercial cheese makers would buy up batches of cheese curd from farmers to make into cheese, but the quality and taste varied greatly. Initially Williams's cheese factory would produce four cheeses daily, each cheese weighing 150 pounds. This "store cheese" quickly became popular, and central New York, Vermont, and New Hampshire quickly became cheese-making regions.

Greens and Root Crops

Vegetables were eaten fresh in season, and, in the very Deep South, were they available during the winter. Vegetables such as beets, cabbage, carrots, cauliflower, onions, parsnips, potatoes, radishes, rutabagas, sweet potatoes, turnips, and winter squash were stored in root cellars, where the climate allowed. The optimum temperature for the storage of root crops ranges between 50 and 55 degrees. This is fairly easy in the summer and early fall but could be most difficult during cold Northern winters. Root cellars were insulated with straw and an insulating layer of snow was welcome. In some cases certain vegetables were packed in straw and stored in barrels. The straw acted as a barrier to prevent the spread of spoilage to the entire barrel. Carrots were often buried in sawdust boxes. Other vegetables such as corn, beans, and peas were dried and used in cooking. Onions that were harvested when their "necks" were long were braided and hung in the cellar. Green corn was preserved by turning back the husk leaving only the last, very thin layer and then hanging it in the sun or a warm room to dry. When it was needed for cooking, it was parboiled and cut from the cob. Sweet corn was parboiled, cut from the cob, dried in the sun and stored in a bag that was kept in a cool, dry place. Sweet corn was also dried in the husk and then buried in salt. String beans, squash, and, in the South, okra were strung on thread and hung to dry. String beans were strung whole and other produce was sliced thinly and dried in strips. Cabbage was made into sauerkraut. Cauliflower, cucumbers, green peppers, mushrooms, onions, red cabbage, string beans, and tomatoes could be pickled. Sometimes, assortments of vegetables were pickled together. In addition to those just mentioned, carrots, radishes, cherries, green grapes, and nasturtiums might also be included. Vegetables could also be preserved by making them into catsups and relishes. Mushroom, tomato, and walnut catsups were popular.

Southern cooks seemed to have especially favored fresh "greens" as they are frequently mentioned in diarists' accounts. Some slave owners encouraged their slaves to grow their own vegetables in order to supplement the basic diet of cornmeal, salt pork, and sweet potatoes provided to them. It was observed by at least one man that the addition of fresh vegetables seemed to lessen disease. During the winter, a small supply of vegetables could be grown in hot frames that utilized the heat of manure and sunshine to keep temperatures warm enough to produce plants year round as far north as Virginia.

Fruits and Berries

Although most fruits and berries were made into jellies, jams, and marmalades, or preserved in sugar syrup for off-season consumption, they were also eaten fresh when seasonally available. Apples, peaches, and pumpkins could also be sliced thinly and dried. Peaches and plums could be what was called "half dried" and packed closely in stone jars with a thick layer of brown sugar in between them. Cherries were dried whole. Apricots, cherries, grapes, and peaches were sometimes preserved in brandy. Some fruits, mainly apples and peaches, were mashed, boiled, skimmed, and dried into what were called "leathers" which were stored in boxes. Apples and pumpkins were also stored whole in barrels much like vegetables. Apples were frequently wrapped in newspaper prior to being placed in the barrels. Apples were also made into apple butter, a seasoned saucelike condiment that could be spread on bread. Squashes and pumpkins were also preserved whole. While still on the vine, they were placed on boards to keep them off the ground. At harvest, the stems would be cut long and tied off at the ends. They were then cured in the sun before being stored indoors.

Bread

American housewives had extreme pride in their bread making. Catherine Beecher devoted an entire chapter of her book *Miss Beecher's Domestic Receipt-Book* to bread making. She counseled, "A woman should be ashamed to have poor bread, far more so, than to speak bad grammar, or to have a dress out of fashion. . . . When it is very frequently the case that a housekeeper has poor bread, she may set herself down as a slack baked and negligent housekeeper."[18] She reminded housewives to be "aware of their responsibility in reference to the bread furnished to their family. As this is the principal article of food, there is no one thing on which the health of a family, especially young children, is more dependent."[19]

Commercially produced bread was one area in which modern convenience was strongly resisted until the early years of the following century. Many believed as Beecher that "Baker's bread [was] often made of musty, sour or other bad flour, which is made to look light, and the bad taste removed by unhealthy drugs. Of course, to the evil of unhealthy flour, is added unhealthy drugs, and there is no mode of discovering the imposition."[20]

Beverages

From colonial times most meals were served with beer or cider. Rural housewives brewed what was known as small beer "every week or so and it was consumed shortly after brewing. Receipt books contained recipes for spruce beer, ginger beer, sassafras beer, and molasses beer. "Strong" beer was brewed annually in October from roasted malt barley and hops and in most cases was made by those with expertise in the craft. English brewing techniques did not translate well to the humid American climate. Wild yeasts were often picked up from the air and ruined the taste of the product. The influx of German immigrants in the second quarter of the 19th century brought new brewing methods that yielded better beers and ales.

The Eagle Brewery, a commercial operation later to be known as the Yuengling Brewery, opened in Pennsylvania in 1829. Many others soon followed. During the period, beer became an increasingly more popular public beverage choice, and beer gardens opened outside large cities attracting both immigrant and native-born citizens. The beer garden was more than a place to drink under the shade of a tree; it was a social center. Some places were very fancy and built ponds or offered entertainment. By 1850, 431 breweries were producing 750,000 barrels of beer. Ten years later, the number of breweries grew to 1,269 and were producing over 1 million barrels of beer, 85 percent of which was consumed in New York and Pennsylvania.

Cider was an excellent way to preserve the apple harvest. The liquid from the pressed fruit was allowed to ferment naturally in the cellar until it was mildly alcoholic. Hard cider that was served in taverns had a slightly higher alcohol content because sugar was added during the fermentation process.

Fruit wines were also made in the home. Receipt books often contained recipes for blackberry, blueberry, currant, elderberry, gooseberry, and raspberry wines. Shrubs and bounces were also made from fruit harvests but required the infusion of a brandy or whiskey. Nonalcoholic versions of these fruity beverages were also made. Currants, cherries, and fox grapes were commonly used in these recipes. Commercially produced wine was generally found only on the tables of the wealthy because tariffs added to already high import costs. Commercial wine making efforts using European grapes met with repeated failure. There were some successes with native grapes such as the Catawba. German vintners from the Rhine Valley used Catawba grapes to make wine on the islands of Lake Erie and in the Ohio Valley. Lawyer Nicholas Longworth planted Catawba grapes in Cincinnati in 1825. By 1842, he had planted 1,200 acres and had produced the country's first sparkling wine. By the late 1850s, Ohio was the leading wine-making state until the vines were destroyed by disease shortly before the Civil War. California made wines prior to the gold rush, but it was not until 1857, when Agostin Haraszthy successfully planted classic European grapevines, that the roots of California wine growing really began.

Traditionally, Americans drank a good deal of whiskey and other hard liquors. The rate of heavy drinking in the 1820s was much higher than today. Men of all social classes met regularly for a friendly drink in local the tavern. On Sunday, taverns often opened during the noon hour so that men could get a drink before returning for the afternoon service. Tavern keeper Ezra Beaman of West Boylston, Massachusetts, kept a detailed record of the food and drink purchased during the 1820s and 1830s. He kept his bar well supplied with brandy, Holland gin, and New England rum. For those who preferred milder alcoholic choices, there was Lisbon wine, "strong" beer, and hard cider. Popular drinks at the time included flips, slings, and toddies.

As attitudes changed and the temperance movement took hold, consumption of strongly alcoholic beverages declined. Some motion toward temperance began in the 18th century, but the movement truly became aggressive in the 19th century. Activists began demonstrating and demanding legislative action. Supporters of the movement wanted new rules for American behavior that made public drinking less acceptable and generally restricted access to liquor in many states. In 1829, the American Temperance Union was created and membership quickly climbed to a 100,000 members. By 1833, membership in the nation's 5,000 temperance societies reached 1.25 million. In 1846, Maine passes a prohibition law. In 1852, Vermont, Massachusetts, and Rhode Island followed suit. Prohibition was voted for in Michigan in 1853 and began in Connecticut in 1854. Many of these laws were repealed during the wartime turmoil of the 1860s.

Many country innkeepers gave up serving liquor to become temperance barrooms that served coffee or lemonade. A number of New England towns had a "Temperance Hotel" as well as a traditional tavern. Beecher even included a chapter titled "Temperance Drinks" in her receipt book, which contained recipes for sarsaparilla mead, effervescing fruit and jelly drinks, and ginger beer. She introduced the section with an explanation of various positions held by temperance supporters that ranged from those who "will not use any kind of alcoholic liquors for any purpose [and] such [who] will not employ it in cooking, nor keep it in their houses." To those who shared Beecher's more moderate view on alcoholic consumption, Beecher said that she thought "it proper to use wine and brandy in cooking and occasionally for medical purposes." Beecher further speculated that "the cause of temperance [would] be best promoted by going no further."[21]

Beginnings of Modern Snacks

Mineral springs abounded in many regions and Americans had long believed strongly in the health benefits of "taking the waters." Pharmacists reasoned that they could improve upon the curative powers of the waters by adding a variety of natural ingredients such as birch bark and dandelion. The flavors that emerged as most popular were ginger ale, root beer, sarsaparillas, lime, and strawberry. Pharmacists and scientists continued experimenting with the natural fizz of some waters and developed a way to artificially carbonate water. By the 1830s, both artificial and natural mineral waters were welcomed as refreshing and healthy beverages.

French-fried potatoes had been an American favorite ever since Thomas Jefferson brought the recipe back from France and served them at his home in Monticello at the turn of the century. They were on the menu at the stylish Moon Lake Lodge in Saratoga Springs, New York, in 1853 when a dinner guest complained that they were cut too thick. Chef George Crumb prepared a thinner batch and presented them to the patron who still found them objectionably thick. Crumb returned to the kitchen, planning to spite the complaining guest by making a batch so thin and crisp that they could not be skewered with a fork. To Crum's amazement, the diner was delighted and other guests began to ask for the crispy potato chips. They were added to the menu as "Saratoga Chips," a house specialty, and soon thereafter were sold locally in small packages.

The graham cracker first made its appearance as a health food. Originally, the unsalted, unleavened biscuits of whole grain flour were touted by New England preacher and self-proclaimed nutritionist Sylvester Graham in the 1830s. Graham encouraged the use of whole grains in baking and advised homemakers to boycott commercially baked bread. At a public appearance in Boston, a group of his supporters dumped slacked lime on a group of resentful bakers who assailed the gathering. The movement had strong supporters in certain parts of the country and certain stores carried Dr. Graham's flour, bread, and crackers.

The early Dutch settlers and the Pennsylvania-Germans introduced doughnuts to America. The deep-fried cakes were a special treat on Shrove Tuesday, prior to the Lenten fast. The inclusion of a hole in the center is said to date back to 1847 when Hanson Gregory of Maine complained that his mother's doughnuts were raw in the middle. He tried poking holes in the center of her next batch and liked the results, and the modern doughnut was born.

COOKBOOKS

It was not until 1796, when Amelia Simmons published *American Cookery*, that the first cookbook written by an American author was published. Prior to that, American cooks referred to English works for culinary guidance, and the few cookbooks that had been published in the colonies were wholesale reprints of older English works. Although certain American ingredients such as turkey, tomatoes, chocolate, and vanilla had made their way into English works by the mid-18th century, their appearance in cookbooks was in no way in deference to American tastes. It merely showed the evolution of English epicure. Simmons's book started a vogue for recipes in the United States. Over 160 receipt books, as they were called, appeared during the first half of the 19th century. Receipt books contained far more than recipes. They were commonly divided into three sections, cooking, medicine and household management. These books provided information on how to deal with household emergencies and day-to-day trifles. Some contained philosophical guidance on household management.

One of the most prolific food writers of the antebellum period was Eliza Leslie. Her first book, *Seventy-Five Receipts for Pastry, Cakes and Sweetmeats*, printed in 1828, was so popular that it was even included as an addendum to other 19th-century cookbooks. Her *Directions for Cookery*, which was published in 1837, is considered to be the most popular cookbook of the 19th century with 60 editions published by 1870. Leslie followed these works with the *Lady's Receipt-Book* in 1846 and the *Ladies New Receipt-Book* in 1850. Other popular receipt books of the period included Lydia Marie Child's *The American Frugal Housewife* (1832), Sarah Josepha Hale's *The Good Housekeeper* (1841), and Catherine E. Beecher's *Domestic Receipt-Book* (1846).

Just as the South had developed a separate culture, it evolved its own particular style of cooking that was recorded in its cookbooks. In 1824, Mary Randolph published *The Virginia House-Wife*, which is said to be the first regional American cookbook. A cousin of Thomas Jefferson, Mrs. Randolph represented the old Virginia aristocracy. Lettice Bryan's *The Kentucky Housewife* (1839) came from an area much more rural. *The Carolina Housewife*, written by Sarah Rutledge in 1847, included numerous recipes for rice breads, cakes, and pilaus (rice-based dishes). Eliza Leslie's *Miss Leslie's New Cookery Book,* published in 1857, was widely used throughout the South.

DINING OUT

Nearly all Americans in the early 19th century ate their meals at home or in the homes of their hosts. In rural areas, eating a meal in public was an unusual event. Public dining was offered only in taverns or ordinaries with the exception of community outdoor dinners on special occasions such as the Fourth of July. Travelers were forced by circumstances to take their meals at taverns and inns. Although local men also frequented these establishments to drink, they generally did not eat there unless the establishment had been catered for a dancing or sleighing party or for a ball.

Meals at these establishments were not brought on demand, but were served only during specified times. Englishman Isaac Wald complained, "At each house there are regular hours for breakfast, dinner and supper and if a traveler arrives somewhat before the appointed time for any one of them, it is in vain to call for a separate meal for himself; he must wait patiently 'til the appointed hour, and then sit down with the other guests that may happen to be in the house."[22] The food served in taverns could be considered home cooking. It was unpretentious and very much in the style of the region. Both food quality and portion sizes varied greatly. Perhaps because diarists seldom recorded average or acceptable meals or innkeepers took advantage of travelers with no alternatives, journals abound with reports of horrid dining experiences. After eating at a tavern in Shelborne Falls, Massachusetts, in 1838, Nathaniel Hawthorne remarked that the meal "was about the worst [he] ever saw . . . hardly anything . . . to eat . . . at least not of the meat kind."[23] Baynard Rush Hall detailed his breakfast at a stagecoach inn while traveling through the Midwest in the 1830's: "[T]he coffee was a libel on diluted soot. . . . Eggs, too!—It certainly was not without hazard to put them in the mouth without first putting them to the nose . . . a sausage coiled up like a great greasy eel [and] hot rolls . . . a composition of oak bark on the outside and hot putty within."[24]

Although some offerings were incredibly meager, Hawthorn recalled seeing a group of young college students being served what was typically a children's breakfast of bread and milk "with a huge washbowl of milk in the center, and a bowl and spoon set for each guest."[25] Other meals were reported as being quite substantial. An 1832 diary claimed that a full-scale New England breakfast at an inn included ham, beef, sausages, pork, bread, butter, boiled potatoes, pies, coffee, and cider.

By the 1820s, many taverns had become hotels, which offered guests breakfast and supper. What could be termed the first "luxury" hotels first came about in 1829 when the Tremont House opened in Boston. This was followed in 1836 by the Astor House in New York City, which was considered by many to be the best hotel in the country at the time. Initially, hotels continued the custom of supplying set meals at fixed hours for all paid guests whether they chose to consume them or not. In the 1830s, the new, larger eastern hotels began offering table d'hôte meals from a menu of items. This became a common feature in major hotels by the 1850s. French cuisine was frequently featured, although a number of establishments offered American-style meals.

A growing number of city restaurants began to open serving midday meals to businessmen, and they began to compete with the high quality cooking found in the hotels. Brothers Giovanni and Pietro Delmonico opened an ordinary cafe in 1827. In 1830, they opened up a "Restaurant Francais" next door. Delmonico's was soon recognized by the New York elite for its culinary excellence. In 1826, the Union Oyster House restaurant opened its doors in Boston. At this time, the nation was seemingly in the throws of an oyster craze. Virtually all principal towns and cities had some type of oyster parlor, oyster cellar, oyster saloon, oyster bar, oyster house, oyster stall, or oyster lunchroom. The owners of the Union Oyster House installed the fabled semicircular oyster bar where Senator Daniel Webster was a regular customer. Webster had his daily tall tumbler of brandy and water with a half-dozen oysters. He seldom had fewer than six plates. In addition to oysters, clams and scallops were served in season. The Union Oyster House is also famous for having been the first place where the commercially produced wooden toothpick was used. Charles Forster of Maine imported the picks from South America and hired young men from Harvard to dine at the Oyster House and to ask for toothpicks as a promotional gimmick. The toothpick fad quickly spread beyond Massachusetts, and it was not unusual to see scores of young dandies with the slim stick of wood protruding from their lips in cities everywhere.

COOKING APPLIANCES

Although an iron stove had been invented by Benjamin Franklin in the 18th century as a room heater, cast-iron ranges for cooking were a rarity in homes until the 1830s. Until this time, the stone or brick fireplace dominated the kitchen, and it remained common in Southern kitchens until after the war. Around 1830, economical iron stoves were being produced as factory-made commodities for the home. These early iron stoves, like the pots and kettles used on them, were cast directly from the raw molten iron as they passed from the smelting furnaces to the sand molds on the ground in a process that had its technological roots in the 15th century. The impurities left in the iron during this process caused stove parts to be generally brittle and not very durable or long lasting. Jordan Mott began casting stoves from purer pig iron in New York about 1835, and experiments with cast-iron stoves continued throughout the remainder of the century with stunning results. Tinned iron stovepipes, almost identical to those used today, were also developed. Wood and coal were the principal fuels used in these stoves, but tar, sawdust, and kerosene were all tried. A gas-fired range appeared around 1850, but it was considered dangerous and was extremely expensive.

The antebellum period was a period of transition in food availability, preservation, preparation, and consumption. America was moving from a society whose diet was solely the result domestic industry and cooked on the hearth to one that had expanded to include commercially prepared food, tinned consumables, and manufactured ranges. Industry generally took men away from the home during this period and eating out became more than a traveler's necessity. Transportation improved and products, which were once only locally available, were now sent to markets across the nation. It was the dawn of the period of modern convenience and accessibility, which was to explode following the Civil War.

7

Leisure Activities

Whoever is made warm by this quilt, which I have worked on for six days and most of six nights, let him remember his mother's love.

—A Southern women, 1860

OPTICAL NOVELTIES

Optical novelties were very much in vogue in the antebellum period. Americans seem to have enjoyed a wide variety of optical phenomena in their drawing rooms and parlors. The simplest forms of these devices used candles to throw shadows on a dark wall. Cutout cardboard shades in many forms could be used much like hands to produce interesting shadows. These had an ancient history of public performance in the far-off Orient, probably brought to America through contact with the expanding China trade of the 1830s and 1840s. Children were encouraged to cut their own shades and give their own shadow shows with rod-operated or finger-operated shades. Instructions for cutting particular shades and erecting stages and screens were sometimes included in books and magazines. Some of the shades were very complicated images of public figures and national heroes such as George Washington or Napoléon Bonaparte.

Lenses and mirrors were used to help create abstract patterns of light and color. The "anamorphosis" was a curved mirror used to make sense of elongation or otherwise apparently warped images on flat paper or cardboard stock. The most enduring form of the reflective devices was the *kaleidoscope*. Developed by David Brewster in 1816 as the "polyscope," a tube of cardboard or tin plate containing two long mirrors set at 60 degrees to each other formed a colorful design of beads or small piece of glass set in the end away from the viewer. The entire tube could be rotated to change the pattern. The number of reflections and their complexity depended upon the angle between the mirrors with small angles producing many more images. The "chromoscope" was another device used to form interesting or colorful patterns. Two glass discs having radiating lines or colorful painted bands were mounted together and counter-rotated with a geared handle. The interacting rotating patterns gave the impression of expanding and contracting, and the translucent colors mixed to produced shades and tints. An earlier device, the "eidoscope," used punched tin discs and a magic lantern to produce stunning and hypnotic effects on a wall or screen.

The camera obscura dates back to the 1500s when it was composed of a pinhole in a dark shutter closing off all the light to an enclosed chamber. Pictures of the outside world were thereby projected on the far wall of the room, but they were inverted and of poor quality. Schoolchildren today use the same characteristics of light used a pinhole camera in art or basic photography classes. The phenomenon of projecting images in this manner may have been recorded by Arab desert dwellers who saw similar inverted pictures through tiny opening in their tents. Early experiments showed that a darkened box fixed with a focusing lens and inverting mirror could improve the quality, brightness, and definition of the image. Viewing usually required the observers to insert their heads into the box and cover them with a dark cloth. Later examples were made with ground glass or translucent paper instead of an opaque screen so that the picture could be seen from outside the box. Although the portable box camera obscura was the most common form, large rooms were sometimes adapted with special white screens so that small groups of people could enjoy seeing the world magically transformed into a picture filled with motion. Views from hilltops and high towers through the camera obscura were characterized by brilliant, natural color.

Artistically minded showmen incorporated the basic idea of the camera obscura into panoramas and dioramas. Long panoramic views were sometimes passed from roller to roller before a seated audience and sometimes the audience walked through the panorama as in a rotunda or gallery. The large format panoramas, especially the circular ones, could not easily be reduced to domestic proportions, but a miniature roller version soon became available as a toy for children. The subject matter often revolved around a trip through the countryside or a journey along a river or roadway. Dioramas were invented by J.M. Daguerre, the photographer, who first exhibited one in 1823. Semitransparent paintings were viewed by a mixture of reflected and transmitted light that was controlled by the exhibitor, allowing the viewers to see through one painting into the next. This gave an acceptable illusion of depth. Dioramas were also available in miniature, but they were not as effective as large displays. Professional exhibitors often combined panoramas and dioramas for group viewing, but they were cumbersome, expensive, and difficult to set up.

Photography

As a direct ancestor of the photographic camera, the camera obscura could be used to record a likeness of the image by tracing it with a pencil. Art teachers during the period sometimes encouraged their students to use the camera obscura when rendering landscapes, architectural subjects, or well-lighted still lifes in order to obtain a natural proportion, proper perspective, and depth of field. Quite passable pictures could be made in this manner. Another device used for copying pictures and prints was the camera lucida, a double horizontal pallet—one for the original and one for the copy—separated by a vertical plate of glass. This simple device allowed the artist to trace the partial reflection of the original with remarkable detail. Of course the image was reversed from left to right. From a practical point of view, photographs almost completely replaced optical wonders such as the camera obscura and camera lucida with regard to capturing likenesses, but such novelties remained parlor curiosities into the 20th century.

Hundreds of antebellum photographs are available today, and, periodically, new ones are found to exist. During the period, photographs of cities, scenic wonders, and personalities were shown in galleries for a fee in many major cities. The photographic galleries in New York and Washington, in particular, were very popular and admission was expensive. The pictures were made with a wet-plate process that was very slow and painstaking. The subjects needed to remain very still for many minutes, thus making inanimate objects a favorite topic. The process precluded any action shots.

Matthew Brady is possibly the best-known photographer of the period, and people flocked to his studios to have photographic portraits taken in their best clothes. *Cartes de visite*, photographs a little larger than modern business cards mounted on thick cardboard stock, were possibly the most popular form of civilian photograph. Thousands of such photos exist. Several "cabinet photos," of a size on the order of five-by-eight inches, are also known to exist. However, very few Brady photographs were taken by him. Brady was practically blind and wore dark blue glasses to protect his eyes from the light. Therefore, his assistants, sent out in photographic wagons with their wet glass plates, took most of the extraordinary pictures that were credited to his studio.

The technology of reproducing photographs for the print media was almost nonexistent. The usual way of reproducing a photograph for a newspaper or magazine was to have an artist redraw it and make a woodcut or engraving as with battlefield sketches. This process neutralized most of the advantages of photography for the newspapers. Only original prints were available to the public, and because enlargement equipment was as yet in a formative stage of development, prints were almost always made by placing the glass plate negative in contact with the photosensitive paper and exposing them to the sun. This resulted in a "contact print" the same size as the glass plate negative.

Some photographs were stereotypes, two similar images set side by side giving a three-dimensional view when seen through a viewer, called a stereoscope or stereopticon, designed for the purpose. The original device, invented by David Brewster in England, dates back to 1816, but the first stereoscopic pictures were in the form of line drawings representing simple objects with one rendering done with the right eye and the other with the left. When viewed together through the stereoscopic device, well-wrought drawings seemed to merge together to form a solid picture with depth. Simultaneous photography with two lens forming similar images made the novelty more practical. Stereotypes of period places, buildings, monuments, and naval vessels predominate in the extant photographic collection. Although right- and left-eye pictures are necessary for a true stereoscopic effect, it was discovered that a single well-defined picture

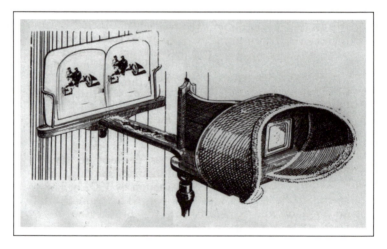

The antebellum period was one of great advances in visual technology. One of the more impressive optical fads was that of the stereoscope, made possible by the development of photography. The double image cards, taken simultaneously at different angles from the subject, gave a remarkable 3-D image that is still impressive today.

viewed through a large magnifying glass also took on an apparent quality of depth. Once again, photography made this phenomenon practical. Devices known as "monoscopes," which held a picture or print fixed before a high quality magnifier, soon became popular. Very few stereotypes of the poor or of the squalid condition of the America's slums are known. Photographers understood that to sell their pictures, they would have to appeal to a financially well-heeled public that did not wish to be reminded of the nation's failures.[1]

Magic lanterns had been around for over 200 years, in use by showmen and hucksters to beguile audiences with mystical images. As early as 1820, the phantasmagoria lantern was used to project pictures and drawings on translucent scenes. The earliest images were often of ghosts, skeletons, or demons, and commercial exhibitors used them to produce shows to excite or terrify their audience. Each form of lantern consisted of a metal box into which an oil lamp or candle was placed. A polished metal reflector focused the light on a painted glass slide, and the light was projected through a hole with a lens onto the screen or sometimes onto clouds of smoke. These lanterns were notably improved as a result of photographic discoveries that allowed for a positive image on glass, and their use thereafter became widespread. Lanterns, often used by lecturers to enhance their presentations, also became very popular as parlor toys to show comic pictures. The Smithsonian Institution has recently restored a number of hand-colored glass slides of the Civil War.

Other optical curiosities mimicked motion pictures through the natural phenomenon of persistence of vision. Discovered by Isaac Newton in the late 1600s, persistence of vision is a property of the eye where a visual impression continues to be seen for a fraction of a second. The bright spot left on the eye after a flash photograph is an example of how the eye can be thus overwhelmed, but a much more delicate effect is always present. The first moving picture novelties were simple drawings that, when seen one after the other, left the impression of motion, but photographs increased the sensation dramatically. A simple cardboard disk with complementary drawings on either side could be mounted on a string so that it would spin back and forth. This was called the "thaumatrope" by its inventor Dr. J.A. Paris in 1827. Classical examples are pictures of a bird that appears to be in a cage and a cannonball that appears to exit a cannon.

The "phenakistiscope," or Magic Disc, invented in France in the 1830s by Joseph Plateau, used a series of as many as a dozen pictures drawn about the edge of a continuous circle and viewed through a number of openings as the circle rotated before a mirror. In this way, a more complicated cycle of motion could be produced than on the thaumatrope, which used only two images. It was important that the first image in the series also serve as the last so that the motion was smooth and without apparent interruption. A similar but more precise device than the phenakistiscope was the "phantascope." This simple contrivance consisted of a cardboard disc with a series of thin slits equally spaced around the center and a handle that acted as a pivot, around which the phantascope was rotated. The reverse side contained a series of pictures set between the slits. When the operator held the device in front of a mirror and rotated the disc, the pictures appeared to be moving.

The most common form of a device for producing motion in pictures in the period was the "zeotrope," or Wheel of Life, invented in England in 1834 by William Horner. This had a series of slits cut in the sides of a rotating drum with a strip of pictures or drawings fixed inside. Any number of strips could be made for use in the same drum as long as they recorded a complete cycle of activity. Viewed through the side of the drum in normal light, the quickly changing pictures formed a realistic impression of motion. Moreover, because many people could view it simultaneously in a normally lit room, the zoetrope enjoyed great popularity as a parlor amusement.

The devices intended to produce motion pictures could be used with a series of sequential photographic images, but the quality of the photographic images of things in action was severely limited before the Civil War due to the slow speed of the photographic process. More commonly, drawings or prints were used, and it was the ability of artists to capture the discrete changes in position that rendered a believable motion that made mechanisms like the zeotrope and phantascope most popular. Walking men and running horses were the most common subjects, but tumblers, jugglers, cats chasing birds, steam engines belching smoke, turning windmills, whirling machines, and dancing couples were all popular. Ironically, the zeotrope renderings of running horses by artists raised a controversy about whether all four of a horse's feet broke contact with the ground at one time as they galloped. This question was answered in the affirmative after the war when a series of photographs were taken by a bank of still cameras actuated by trip wires.

LECTURES

The Greeks had their tragic drama, the Italians their opera, and the English their Shakespeare, but the Americans had the lecture. Lectures on science, medicine, agriculture, and politics were particularly popular among ambitious young men, and women favored those on music, painting, literature, and the arts. Public lectures enjoyed tremendous popularity from about 1840 forward. By the coming of the war, Northerners were demanding that lecturers make their concern matters related to the political chaos affecting the nation and the looming possibility of conflict. Topics sought by lecture audiences included denunciations of the South, glorification of Union causes, narrations detailing the reforms that might follow a Northern victory, and abolition. Popular speakers included Senator Charles Sumner, Major General Cassius Clay, Theodore Tilton, and Wendell Phillips. To some extent, politics hijacked the lecture circuit, and the serious nature of the lecture topics led to the establishment of less formal literary societies, study clubs, and reading groups, which better filled the need for less-stressful cultural entertainment.

CULTURAL INSTITUTIONS

There were an abundance of cultural institutions in the North and West in the antebellum period, but the declining plantation economy and general poverty of the population retarded similar developments in the South for many years. The interest in art, music, literature, and nature that permeated the antebellum parlor surged forth into the social mainstream and stimulated the creation of museums, concert halls, libraries, and parks. These, in turn, engendered a plethora of ancillary institutions such as literary societies, study groups, and reading clubs to which affluent antebellum Americans flocked. In addition to the obvious activities such organizations could conduct, they created a venue that was ripe for the founding of additional social projects and reform movements.

These cultural organizations were generally gender specific. Male organizations attracted businessmen, professionals, and politicians, and the distaff versions provided activities for middle- and upper-class women beyond domestic and church endeavors. The clubs furnished an unparalleled arena for women to pursue their intellectual development. Study clubs met twice monthly for 10 months a year to discuss such topics as literature, history, and art. Meetings commonly were held in members' homes and consisted of conversation, presentation of papers, and subsequent discussions.

Reading Clubs

Many readers, particularly those women with substantial educations and no profession to follow, found reading one of the few sources of entertainment available to them. Many people read in groups and met regularly to do so. Books were frequently read aloud making it possible to share the books and newspapers that were "all too scare in the print-starved Confederacy." Even in the North where books were widely available, oral presentation, with an articulate reader, often enhanced the literature and allowed the majority of the women to do other chores such as sewing and embroidery. Reading aloud became an activity with many of the characteristics of theater. Books provided women with an almost pure escape from the realities of an idle lifestyle, suffering, and death. More importantly, oral presentation discouraged continual gossip among the women, and the camaraderie of the group helped to alleviate depression and gloom among those who were separated from loved ones, displaced from their homes, or anxious about their own futures.[2]

TOYS AND GAMES

Antebellum parents provided a limited number and variety of toys for their children that were almost indistinguishable from those of the previous century. Hoops, rings, pins, and balls were arranged in various configurations and sizes to facilitate the expression of youthful creativity and to release the children's natural exuberance. Molded lead and tin soldiers, animal figures in metal and wood, marbles, tops, and dolls in many sizes were popular. Oddly, surviving examples of antebellum toys seem to be uniformly made of "hard" materials like metal and wood. Soft and cuddly animals and dolls are almost totally missing from the prewar record. This does not seem to be a matter of a lack of extant examples. Soft toys simply were not popular until the second half of the 19th century.

A *Godey's Lady's Book* illustration showing a family group, including several children with their toys. Included among the toys are a cricket bat, a small ball, a wooden hoop and stick, a teeter-totter-like toy that goes with the "driver" in the smallest girl's hand, and a large ball (right) that defies description and, seemingly, gravity as well.

Games have always been popular in America. One popular game was solitaire, a game for one player that was played on a circular board containing 33 holes. Marbles or pegs were placed in all but the center hole. A peg was moved forward, backward or sideways, but not diagonally, over an adjacent peg, which was then removed from the board. The game ended when the remaining pegs could not make a move. The object of the game was to have only a single peg remaining, preferably in the center hole.

During the prewar years, board games were just coming into their own in America. Most board game publishers were located in the Northeast, particularly in Boston and New York. *The Mansion of Happiness: An Instructive Moral and Entertaining Amusement* is generally acknowledged as the first board game published in the United States. This 1843 game closely resembles the formerly imported *The Game of Goose*, but it had a distinctly moral message. Players landing on squares marked "gratitude" or "honesty" advanced more rapidly toward their goal. However, *The Game of Goose* was a board game distinguished by an elaborate spiral containing 63 squares. Players rolled the dice and advanced along the board, incurring a variety of changes in fortune involving a variety of penalties and bonuses. The game dated from the previous century and served as inspiration for a host of imitators.

American board makers copied other games as well. *The Game of Pope and Pagan, or the Siege of the Stronghold of Satan by the Christian Army* and *Mohamet and Saladin,or the Battle for Palestine* were both based on the centuries-old game, *Fox and Geese*. Other published games took the form of card games and included, *Dr. Busby, Yankee Trader, Uncle Tom's Cabin, Heroes, Master Redbury and His Pupils*, and *Trades*. The last of these consisted of lithographed people cards that depicted such tradesmen as shoemakers, farriers, and tax gatherers as well as occupation cards that contained the symbols of their trades. The object of the game was to collect tricks that matched the trade and person. It is thought that this game served as the inspiration for the very popular English game, *Happy Families.*

Other popular games included cribbage, checkers, tangrams, and lotto. A forerunner of modern bingo, Lotto was played with cards in three horizontal and nine vertical rows. Five numbers from 1 to 90 appeared on the cards, with the remaining spaces blank. Children's versions of the game were developed to teach spelling, multiplication, botany, and history.

The dominating vice of the antebellum period was gambling. Wagering was an exciting way of spending leisure time. In the early days, gambling among the social elite was essentially private. Isolated wagers would be made on a cockfight, the turn of a card, a steamboat race, or a horserace. Many of these activities were also orchestrated for public wagering, but no formal wagering authority existed. Steamboat racing was particularly popular, but the strain placed on the boats was blamed for boiler explosions and other river disasters.

Horseracing was much favored by those of the upper classes, and regular courses were maintained for its prosecution. Andrew Jackson won thousands of dollars on a match race between the horse Greyhound and his own horse, Truxton. The race was the last event of the public racing season in middle Tennessee. Truxton sired an entire line of racehorses for Jackson's stable, and Jackson maintained his interest in racing horses throughout his presidency and into his old age.

Virtually every known game of chance was available for wagering. As cities grew in population, wealth-wily entrepreneurs began to operate games that were open to the public. Special gambling rooms were fitted up in hotels, clubs, and coffeehouses, providing gaming tables for the convenience of their customers. As these gambling houses became more numerous, they also became a focus for crime and disorder. The local authorities at first attempted to suppress these establishments but quickly gave way to regulation and licensing, which seems to have provided a good deal of cash for the municipal pot in the form of fees, fines, and assessments.

Professional gamblers, who were considered social pariahs in this period, rarely frequented the gambling houses, and those who did were drab fellows when compared to the sharp-witted and gaudy river gamblers who established riverboat gambling as a recognized institution. These sometimes reckless and spectacular players were the stuff of which legends were made on the Mississippi River. Few of them relied on their luck and skill at gaming. Rather, they were generally adept at palming and marking cards; dealing seconds; and using cheating devices such as holdouts, poker rings, and stripped decks. They were often in league with unscrupulous bartenders, waiters, or other professional gamblers traveling the river.

Some of the favorite antebellum card games were poker, faro, twenty-one, and old sledge. Sleight-of-hand affairs such as three-card monte and shell games were saved for the traveling sucker and not the serious gambler. Roulette wheels and dice (craps or hazards) tables were commonly provided. There were no limits in the gambling houses of this period, and sometimes the stakes were very high, especially in the private rooms to which the gentry retired. Tens of thousands of dollars were won and lost in a single evening; plantations and crops were wagered; and slaves, or anything of value, were accepted in forming a wager.

There were a number of outdoor physical activities popular with antebellum Americans. These included a number of activities that were performed as a normal part of everyday rural life, such as walking, horseback riding, hunting, and fishing. However, city dwellers were quickly losing contact with such rural matters, and they came to view many of the ordinary activities of life as sports or vehicles for recreation. Bridal paths were established in city parks so that urbanites could ride their horses. City dwellers were warned, however, to "never appear in public on horseback unless you have mastered the inelegancies attending a first appearance in the saddle, which you should do at a riding school. A novice makes an exhibition of himself and brings ridicule on his friends."[3]

Antebellum Americans would travel to the mountains and foothills near their homes to hunt, fish, and camp in the outdoors. Trout fishing, in particular, became a fad during this period, and city dwellers resorted to the scenic freshets of the piedmont to stand in the gushing waters and land a fish with a rod and reel. Resorts in the Adirondacks, Berkshires, and Appalachian foothills became destinations for all sorts of outdoor activities, and northeastern locations such as those in central New York and along the streams entering the Hudson River were made popular by a small army of authors and artists. The New Jersey seaside became a magnet for those interested in water sports such as swimming, rowing, and sailing. The beaches in New Jersey, New York, Connecticut, Massachusetts, and Maine became destinations for Northerners and Southerners alike.

Recreational boating took on an etiquette of its own as antebellum Americans, both men and women, took to canoes and rowboats for "wholesome and vigorous exercise." Whereas young men took to paddling their canoes among the mountain lakes and rock-strewn streams, rowing became a great fad with the ladies, but only on the quiet waters of meandering rivers and private lakes. If they ventured into more-frequented waters, women were advised to find the protection of a gentleman who would give them preferential seating in the boat and do all of the rowing. When venturing out with the ladies as passengers, gentlemen were advised to do nothing foolhardy or frightening. They were especially warned not to splash the ladies when dipping the oars. In all cases, women were advised to wear a proper costume that would allow for freedom of movement. "Corsets should be left at home, and a good pair of stout boots should complete an [outfit] in which a skirt barely touching the ground, a flannel shirt, and a sailor hat are the leading features." Men were to wear flannel trousers, a rowing jersey, and a straw hat. "Peajackets are worn when their owners are not absolutely employed in pulling the oar."[4]

Outdoor winter activities included sledding, ice skating, and sleigh rides. Ice-skating parties were held on frozen ponds and lakes, but both New York City and Boston had ice skating rinks—New York's on Fifth Avenue. The Erie Canal, like other waterways, was used for ice skating, sledding, and sleighing in many towns along almost all of its frozen 300-mile length. Horse-drawn sleighs were all the rage in the period not only for winter transportation, but also for seeing and being seen about town. Young gallants might race their sleighs along the streets and by-ways in order to impress their female companions. Such activities, of course, were generally restricted to the North as there was not enough snowfall to warrant maintaining a sleigh in the South. Gentlemen were warned

This is an 1859 photograph of ice-skaters on Central Park Lake in
New York City. Normally, action shots were hard to take with the
slow photographic chemicals of the day (see blurred figure
in center), but the bright light reflecting off the snow and ice
allowed this shot to be taken.

against racing and cautioned to "not drive too fast if the lady accompanying him is timid, or objects to it. He should consult her wishes in all
things, and take no risks, as he is responsible for her safety." Poor conduct by a man while driving a carriage or sleigh was considered "dis-
respectful of the lady."[5]

Team sports did not gain popularity until the 1840s. English-style cricket
seems to have been played in America, but the breadth of its popularity
is questionable. Nonetheless, period illustrations sometimes show cricket
bats among children's toys. There was a rudimentary form of football
adapted to any terrain or number of players popular among the college
set. These antebellum football games were "splendidly unorganized and
offered a fine spectacle of players scrimmaging in stovepipe hats." The
first recorded intercollegiate athletic contest was a boat race held between
the rowing clubs of Harvard and Yale in 1852 on Lake Winnipesaukee in
New Hampshire. The event was organized by an opportunistic railway
agent who sold train tickets to spectators from both Boston and New
Haven.[6]

The first truly organized team sport was probably baseball. American
baseball may trace its origins back to 1825 when a local newspaper editor,

Thurlow Weed, organized a baseball team in Rochester, New York, at Mumford's Meadow. However, Abner Doubleday, who would later serve as a Federal General in the Civil War, is generally credited with beginning the sport at Cooperstown, New York, in 1839. The Mills Commission (1905) relied heavily on the anecdotal testimony of an old mining engineer when reaching the conclusion that Doubleday had indeed "devised the first scheme for playing baseball." However, many of the old man's musings later proved inaccurate. Doubleday was in attendance at West Point Military Academy in 1839, making it highly unlikely that he would have time to organize the sport.[7]

Notwithstanding arguments about its origins, by the 1840s, baseball had evolved into a recognizable sport with teams and rules closely resembling those of modern times. Nonetheless, the game was not reported in the newspapers until the 1850s when William Trotter Porter, editor of the *Spirit of the Times*, began giving baseball extensive coverage. Porter is credited with recognizing baseball as the "national game," and having invented the box score format for reporting results. Shortly thereafter, Frank Queen and Harrison Trent founded the *New York Clipper*, which devoted so much space to baseball that they hired Henry Chadwick as the first full-time sports journalist. Chadwick soon became the leading authority on baseball in America, and, as chairman of the National Association of Base Ball Players, he was instrumental in creating many of the rules of the game, including the "Infield Fly Rule." Although many players resisted the new rule, Chadwick refused to relent. He thereby saved thousands of fans from witnessing repeated rally-ending triple plays. In 1859, he also made the precedent-setting decision that baseball games could not end until a tie was broken, thereby formulating the extra innings format. His influence on the game gained for him a place in the Baseball Hall of Fame at Cooperstown, New York, and the appellation of "The Father of Baseball."

Some obvious differences between the modern and antebellum forms of the game are the latter's lack of baseball gloves, catchers' masks, and other protective equipment. Of course, the ball itself was not as hard and did not carry as far as modern ones. In fact, instead of the present caught-on-a-fly rule, a ball caught after one bounce in the outfield the 1840s was also considered an out because so few hits traveled that far in the air. While baseball remained an amateur sport throughout the period, heavy betting on the outcome of baseball games was not unusual. As early as 1858, as much as $100 was wagered on whether a particular player would hit a home run during a single appearance at bat. The National League with uniform rules governing the game was not adopted until after the Civil War, at which time Henry Chadwick considered the move a "sad blunder."[8]

LADIES' CRAFTS

Women engaged in a variety of needlework crafts including tatting, knitting, crocheting, and netting. Ladies' magazines carried a profusion of patterns for trims, fashion accessories, and small household items that utilized these handicrafts. Patchwork quilts were another popular activity. Women worked on quilts alone for their families and in group quilting bees as community activities. Prior to the war, groups of Northern women used their quilting talents to raise money for the cause of abolition. They renamed some traditional patchwork patterns to draw attention to the cause. *Job's Tears* became known as *Slave Chain*. *Jacob's Ladder* became *Underground Railway*. *North Star* was so named after the star that guided runaway slaves to freedom. Once the war commenced, Northern women mobilized relief efforts and began to produce quilts that could be sent to soldiers in need. U.S. Sanitary Commission records show that an estimated 250,000 quilts were distributed during the war. In Hartford, Connecticut, alone 5,459 quilts were collected during 1864.[9]

Many of the quilts were more utilitarian than those their makers had made in the past, but it is likely that they were made with no less love. To one quilt was pinned this note: "My son is in the army. Whoever is

A hard-to-find example of the Jenny Lind paper doll set brought out during her acclaimed tour of America in the 1850s. This toy, made of lithographed costumes printed on card stock might have been the favorite treasured item of some little girl.

made warm by this quilt, which I have worked on for six days and most of six nights, let him remember his mother's love." Confederate women also made quilts for soldiers. The Southern blockade, however, severely limited the availability of the requisite materials. Confederate quilts made during the war were made from whatever makeshift materials were available, including old sheets stuffed with newspaper.[10]

POLITICS AS USUAL

The most modern element in American life in the first half of the 19th century was a vigorous interest in politics. Politics became a great national pastime, almost a hobby, shared by both the North and the South. This interest crossed many of the old social and economic lines to engage devotees from many classes in sharp debates on an almost daily basis. This widespread participation almost certainly added to the furor for war.

Unfortunately, restraint was conspicuously absent from the political process. Antagonists on all sides assailed their opponents with arguments taken from the law, the Bible, literature, pamphlets, election speeches, and the press. When unprepared to rebut these arguments on an equal footing, the opponents often resorted to ridiculous remarks and unsupported allegations. A Southern observer wrote of the period: "The hot headed politician and preacher seemed to be molding public opinion without any regard to the country as a whole. Both North and South proving, from their point of view, the righteousness of their positions by resorting to both the Bible and the Constitution."[11]

Politics became increasingly characterized by intemperate and abusive language, or even fisticuffs, especially when the subject turned to inflammatory issues such as slavery. When Senator Sumner, a man of "wicked tongue" and "intemperate language" with regard to slavery, was physically beaten with a cane by Congressman Preston Brooks in the nation's legislative chamber, the blows were struck not only in the halls of Congress, but in the barbershops, parlors, and taverns of every small town and city. Yet these attitudes cannot fully explain how the geographic sections of the nation could share so many important cultural and political characteristics and still be mutually antagonistic to the point of shedding blood. The actual causes of the war are both sophisticated and multidimensional, and any discussion along these lines inevitability remains academic. It is clear that the nation did not go to war because of slavery any more than it did over disputes involving temperance, urbanization, poverty, politics, or economics. Possibly, historians should look to the cumulative effect of all the various disputes as a cause of the war.[12]

During the 1840s, the Whigs and Democrats, the two oldest political parties in America, had reached agreement on several issues that had plagued the early republic. The tariff, the National Bank, and the regulation of internal commerce ranked highly among these divisive issues. Americans celebrated their limited form of Federal government and considered any of its remaining weakness essential to the safeguarding of personal and political freedom. The decade before the war was one of rapid economic and social change in America; and politics was gaining a more general audience than at any time since the Revolution. The Whigs and Democrats were searching for new issues that would mobilize the voters behind the old party structure. This attempt to underscore the meaning of the old parties was to have far-reaching consequences as political and social agendas began to attract the interest of the common man and woman. One unforeseen consequence of trying to bolster the old parties was that, ironically, it would lead to their virtual dissolution.

The 1856 election proved to be the death knell of the old two-party system. In the presidential race, the newly formed Republican Party championed the slogan, "Free Speech, Free Press, Free Soil, Free Men, Fremont and Victory." John C. Fremont may have been made a national hero for his role in mapping and exploring the West, but he was an unacceptable presidential candidate in the South. The governor of Virginia warned that if the antislavery Fremont won the 1856 election, his state would secede. Consequently, the Democrats decided to run the more moderate James Buchanan of Pennsylvania. Buchanan won the election against Fremont due to the entry into the race of a weak candidate from the American Party, former President Millard Fillmore. Saddled with a cabinet split over a number of issues, including antislavery, that he could not control, Buchanan was fated to follow the country to war rather than lead it to a resolution of its problems

As a major third party, the Republicans had not had time to organize an electoral victory behind Fremont. Nonetheless, by the end of the decade, the Republican Party had become the foremost instrument of antislavery sentiment in the country. Its condemnation of the Slave Power forces, coupled with the passage of the Kansas-Nebraska Act and the Dred Scott decision, brought it adherents. The events, both real and fabricated, taking place in "Bleeding Kansas" and the schemes of fanatical abolitionists, like John Brown, to forcibly liberate slaves and promote slave insurrections, tended to radicalize even the most moderate politicians. "Both North and South seemed to be swayed by the demagogue," observed William Fletcher, who would go on to fight as a Southern private.[13]

Northern office seekers began calling for an assault on the traditions and honor of the South with all the enthusiasm that their rhetoric could convey. Such attacks fueled Southern indignation, created a desire for vindictive satisfaction, and retrenched the positions of Southern moderates. In a letter to a moderate Northern friend, Dr. Richard Arnold of Georgia expressed a widely held opinion with regard to slavery: "The abolitionists . . . have by their intemperance, united the whole South against them as one man. . . . I will observe that with you slavery is an abstract question, with us it involves life and property, safety and security. Its abstract right I do not argue for . . . the institution of slavery, although indefensible on the grounds of abstract rights, can be defended and well defended upon this, that so intimately is it mingled with our social conditions, so deeply has it taken root, that it would be impossible to eradicate it without upturning the foundations of that condition . . . for without a population of blacks the whole southern country would become a desert." Arnold warned, "To carry their plans into effect [the abolitionists] would have to wade knee deep in blood. . . . The two races are so separated, that the one now lower, will never be allowed to mount to a perfect equality, except over the prostrate bodies of the upper."[14]

Prior to the nullification crisis of 1828, the shadowy line between state and Federal authority had not been problematic. A contemporary observer noted that the diverse character of state governments had clearly "originated from the people" by their own "choice and formulation" and that the states "had virtually managed by themselves" without Federal interference. After the final nullification crisis of 1832, however, Southern radicals urged the defense of state rights and began to call for disunion as the best means of protecting sectional interests. The threat of secession came to dominate the rhetoric of many Southern politicians, and the concept of state rights was raised to the level of political gospel during the decade of the 1850s. Many Southern leaders espoused secession only sporadically, and usually only during an election campaign. Those who did otherwise did not achieve lasting prominence. However, among these were the Southern radicals called "fire-eaters," who were conspicuously in the forefront of the clamor for secession and served as consistent and effective proponents of disunion. What they started as an intriguing political device, however, soon got out of hand as common Southerners took the concept of a nation independent of the North to heart and were swept up in a reckless euphoria for secession and the establishment of the Confederacy.[15]

There is little doubt that secession was a widely popular movement supported by a vast majority of Southern whites. Secessionist sentiment pervaded the churches, the shops, and even the schools. Prosecession radicals smashed unfriendly presses, banned books, and fought duels with Unionists. The "fire-eaters" turned every news article, pamphlet, sermon, and play into a propaganda piece for secession. Even minor confrontations with the Unionists, or with the abolitionists, were declared crises upon whose immediate resolution rested the very survival of the South. Warfare in Kansas, the publication of *Uncle Tom's Cabin,* and the antislavery raid of John Brown at Harper's Ferry gave credence to the tales of the "fire-eaters." When there was no crisis, the radicals were fully capable of fabricating one. Southern leaders in Congress proposed the reopening of the transatlantic slave trade in 1859 without hope of the question being resolved in their favor so that the radicals might use the issue to good effect as propaganda.

Both the Southern "fire-eaters" and the Northern reformers were aided by a highly partisan and radical press. Public orations, electoral debates, and harangues were popular instruments used to drive public opinion, and they were well attended. Nighttime assemblies of placard-carrying zealots in streets lit by burning torches and oil lamps were particularly attractive to many people simply because of the spectacle they provided. Yet these forums addressed only those who could be present, producing a somewhat transient enthusiasm for the particular topic of discussion. Therefore, the 19th-century citizen favored the newspaper as a more individualized and enduring form of information. Newspapers gained influence steadily during the first half of the century. An incredibly large number of local publications appeared along with topical news sheets like the antigovernment *Citizen Soldier*, the antislavery *Liberator*, and the antialcohol *Temperance Recorder*. Speeches were printed in these papers in their entirety within a few days of their presentation. Political arguments, essays, letters to the editor, and discussions among dedicated readers—both genuine and planted for effect—flowed in the wake of every issue.

Reform Movements

It was socially encumbent on the well-to-do or those from the idle middle class to join a reform movement, and many well-educated Americans, especially young women lacking a venue to express their political will, were active in pursuing the objectives of the societies and organizations that they joined. The majority of the reform movements initiated prior to the Civil War were essentially benevolent, and they were characterized by the of activism of the "haves" for the "have-nots" rather than by a demand for reform from those who were oppressed. Personal protest would not become popular until late in the century. Philanthropic reforms in the antebellum period focused almost solely on the destitute or visibly degraded elements of society, including paupers, drunkards, orphans, widows, illiterates, Indians, slaves, prostitutes, and prisoners. Reform activities were characterized by a laudable urge to remedy visible social ills, alleviate suffering, and discourage behavior that was considered immoral. The planter aristocracy was remarkably intolerant of social reform and disdainful of activism. Southerners were particularly incensed by Northern reformers working in the South, and repeatedly expressed a frustration with those that crusaded for or against what they termed the "-isms" (abolitionism, alcoholism, feminism, pauperism, republicanism, etc.).

The dangers of immoderate drinking, for example, were real, and alcoholism could end in disaster. Strong drink was often cited as the cause for eternal damnation and earthly licentiousness, as well as spouse abuse and rape. In fact, the temperance movement was very closely allied with women's rights issues such as suffrage and abandonment. This may have mirrored a rising tide of female discontent with their place in the social order. Women took up the temperance struggle by forming prayer groups and railing against saloons and their bottles, mirrors, and portraits of reclining nudes.

The temperance movement was set back for a time in the 1850s by the defection of many activists to the cause of abolition. Yet the temperance reformers increased the stakes of their game and insisted on total abstinence from alcohol in any quantity or strength and supplemented their demands with calls for its legal prohibition. This shift from moderate and sometimes symbolic goals to conclusive ones, carved into the legal fabric of the nation, was typical of many of the reform movements of the 19th century.

Besides their well-known intolerance for abolitionists, social conservatives in the South particularly deplored the development of free public schools, and they worked to rid their communities of the destitute Indian population by removing them to the western wilderness. Moreover, they exhibited a remarkable toleration of prostitution—at least in private. Southern antipoverty reforms emphasized a faith in the efficacy of the kinship system (a responsibility that they took quite seriously) preferring to succor the abandoned members of society in their homes rather than to consign them to some anonymous agency. Of course, the needy were much less conspicuous and more sparsely concentrated in the largely rural areas of the South than they were in Northern cities.

Many in the North were no more fond of reformers than those in the South, and it should be remembered that reform activists remained a minority even among the population of the North. Much of the resistance to reform was based in a natural social inertia, but some of it was caused by the inability of the activists to articulate the scope and righteousness of their agenda to the public. Moreover, as the war approached, the activists became increasingly acrimonious, alienating, and violent in their rhetoric and called for the abandonment of the Constitution and the dissolution of the government if their ideas were not immediately implemented. Many of them disrupted religious services at "proslavery" churches and castigated the clergy and the antislavery moderates as conspiring with Southern "Slave Power." Those that espoused such sentiments were widely viewed as interventionists, anarchists, or worse. The activists proved most controversial in their insistence on immediate and total reform, and in their unwillingness to compromise. This was particularly true of the radical abolitionists who demanded that the government supplement intellectual persuasion with legal coercion in many areas.

The dimensions of the schemes put forth by the reformers of the early 19th century were outweighed only by the depth of their failure. This may have been due to their adoption of an overly confrontational style and their inability to admit to any good in the Southern way of life because of its association with slavery. Despite the incongruity between the reformers' utopian ideals and the consequences of reality, mindless social tinkering and disgraceful forms of public altruism persisted and proliferated until well after the Civil War. Nonetheless, the majority of social reformers worked through a genuine sense of moral obligation and national pride.

8

Literature

One book, wisely selected and properly studied, can do more to improve the mind, and enrich the understanding, than skimming over the surface of an entire library.

—Reverend Doctor Joel Hawes, 1835

"LET NOT MY BONES REST IN ENGLAND"

America's literary independence was not achieved simultaneously with its political separation from Britain. The development of a cadre of American authors, nationalistic themes, and an independent writing style "could not be realized until the instruments of culture were sufficient to produce trained writers, sensitive critics, and receptive readers." Schools and colleges, libraries, and publishing houses needed time to evolve and establish themselves. It has been observed that six of the America's greatest authors were born within 16 years of one another during the first decades of the 19th century: Ralph Waldo Emerson (1803), Nathaniel Hawthorne (1804), Edgar Allan Poe (1809), Henry David Thoreau (1817), Walt Whitman (1819), Herman Melville (1819). Certainly the list could be lengthened, but it does indicate that America was not ready to produce its own literature until its spirit of democracy and nationalism had had time to coalesce and take root. Prior to the beginning of the antebellum period, American writers tended to imitate European styles even when they were working on nationalistic topics. "As the turning point, one might well designate the years 1819 to 1821, when Washington Irving published his *Sketchbook* of essays and stories, when William Cullen Bryant's first collection of poems appeared, and when James Fenimore

Cooper, after one false start, won acclaim for *The Spy*, a novel set in the Revolutionary period."[1]

Prior to 1820, more fashionable and less-expensive English texts had almost closed the literary market to American authors and publishers. In 1820, Sidney Smith, an eccentric clergyman, wrote in the *Edinburgh Review*: "In the four quarters of the globe, who reads an American book? or goes to an American play?"[2] In 1834, fewer than 500 American titles were published in the United States. However, by 1862 this number had grown to almost 4,000.[3] The literary pendulum in authorship and publishing had begun to swing from the theoretical, intellectual, and theological writing that had dominated the Revolutionary and Federalist periods to the more emotional, physically stirring, and mystical writing of novelists, romantics, and the socially conscientious. The two great literary movements of the period were romanticism and transcendentalism. The transcendentalists, who gave the pursuit of literature a meaning normally reserved for the practice of religion, were always outnumbered by the romantics, but they exerted an influence out of proportion to their number largely because they occupied the halls of academia, particularly at Harvard University. Romantics, on the other hand, "fleeing from utilitarianism and the culture of nascent industrialism, often found shelter in medievalism, chivalry, Gothic tales, and the idealization of primitive peoples like the Indians" that so fascinated the general reading public.[4]

ANTEBELLUM LITERATURE

Taken against the devastated backdrop of the Civil War, American tastes in literature during the antebellum period seem frivolous. Students studying the period, blessed with the knowledge of the coming civil crisis, often expect that its literature, journalism, poetry, and plays might exhibit an overwhelming dread, a foreboding, or a sense of impending tragedy. Yet contemporary American readers and writers were generally unaware of the coming cataclysm. Even if they sensed that a major civil disturbance was on the way, they had no way of foretelling the extent of the disaster. America had not yet passed through the crucible that would change a group of states united by a common political system and revolutionary history into the United States. Generally, America's attention was drawn to other things: the opening of the West, the war with Mexico, the development of the railroads and the system of canals, the politics of nullification and self-determination, or the reform of urban society.

It is difficult to find a looming American tragedy in antebellum literature. Certainly, it cannot be found in the entertaining stories of Irving or the adventure novels of Cooper, two of the most popular American authors of the period. Nor can it be found in the introspection of Whitman, Emerson, or Thoreau, or in the melancholy, gloom, and horror mongering of Hawthorne, Melville, or Poe. Most Americans simply did not choose to read literature that proclaimed the imminent dissolution of the union. Only in the South did a secessionist press flourish, and it found only a small audience. In fact, most readers outside the halls of academia preferred the wildly popular romances, escapist adventures, and Gothic tales written by lesser-known American authors and published in the penny press. No doubt the momentum for a new realism concerning the fate of the nation was beginning to well up here and there, especially in the anti-slavery movement, but no clear and unmistakable portent of disaster appeared in print.

Literacy

One measure of literacy in a society is the extent to which writing and reading replace oral communications. "Literacy . . . makes practical the maintenance of a communication network wider than one's locality."[5] If only the ability to write one's name is used as the standard for literacy, documentary evidence suggests that most Americans were probably literate. If the ability to read for comprehension is added, drawing a valid conclusion as to the general literacy of the antebellum population becomes more difficult. The difference between signing one's name and a true literacy, where theoretical concepts and political strategies are being shared or modified in written or printed form, has enormous implications. It is almost certain that most native-born Americans, as opposed to recent immigrants, possessed a basic reading literacy. However, simple comprehension is a great deal different from the sophisticated skills required to read difficult prose, political and philosophical treatises, theoretical works in languages other than English, or the Greek and Roman classics.

Literacy was first measured as a separate category in the census of 1850, but informal surveys and anecdotal evidence suggest that the ability to write, and particularly to read, was quite high. An analysis of legal documents, letters, and journals of the period suggests that as much as 90 percent of free white men in New England were literate. This proportion shrinks to 70 percent among those on the frontier where there were few books available beyond the Bible. The planters of the aristocratic South seem to have mirrored the high literacy rates found among their social and economic peers in England. In the South, at least 70 percent of the white male population could read, and the planter aristocracy probably owned the most extensive personal libraries in the nation. This does not mean that Southern males read constantly. Although Southern planters were well educated, Aristotle, Caesar, and Cicero were more likely to be the names of slaves laboring in their fields than those of books on their nightstand. These authors were the stuff of schoolrooms, and adult reading preferences resided in more practical works.

In 1800, Americans across the nation read more for purposes other than a mere schoolroom recitation of Greek and Roman classics. Although it was common to see period house plans showing libraries, only the wealthy classes could afford to devote an entire room to books. The classical titles on the householder's bookshelf were more often for display than for everyday reading, just like the specimen cases filled with fossils and insects or the magnifying glasses, stereoscopes, and other optical curiosities that resided there. Four types of reading material have been identified as popular with readers of the antebellum period. In order of their volume of production these can be grouped as: newspapers and magazines; novels written for a variety of purposes, including entertainment; purposeful or instructive texts; and religious tracts. These categories, while somewhat arbitrary, can serve to describe the majority of the printed materials sought by 19th-century readers.[6]

The Cheap Press

Much of what Americans read was considered literature of the lowest class at the time and has come to be most closely associated with the paperbound volumes of Irwin P. Beadle's dime novels—advertised as "a dollar book for a dime." These, however, were not being published before 1860. Technological improvements in publishing and printing were initially made in the 1830s, but they were largely limited to inexpensive newspapers, magazines, and pamphlets. Nonetheless, in the 1840s, they were applied to the fantastically popular hardcover novels, causing the price of the genre to fall from several dollars per bound volume to as little as 50¢ or a quarter dollar. Unbound and paperback editions were available for as little as 6.5¢, although the better works generally brought an average price of a quarter dollar. Thereafter, the emergence of a new popularity in reading and writing among the American middle class underpinned a growing national interest in publishing and professional authorship.[7]

Conspicuous among the publishers of this inexpensive form of reading material were Rufus Griswold and Park Benjamin, who started a weekly magazine called *Brother Jonathan* in 1839. This publication concentrated on reprinting popular British novels without paying royalties to the authors. Another weekly called *The New World* concentrated mainly on reproducing the works of American authors. The remarkable steam-powered rotary press, invented in 1847, made paperbound publishing, in particular, remarkably inexpensive, and there was an enormous demand for "cheap" imprints among political parties, states' rights proponents, antislavery organizations, temperance and reform movements, and advertisers. Victor Hugo's *The Hunchback of Notre Dame* and Edward Bulwer-Lytton's *Last Days of Pompeii* were among the hundreds of British novels pirated by the

American cheap press. Although both sold for $10 in deluxe leather-bound editions, they sold for a mere 10¢ in paperback, making them available to a whole new segment of the reading population.[8]

At these prices, few Americans failed to read the work of Charles Dickens, Walter Scott, Washington Irving, or James Fenimore Cooper. The power of this literature to govern the minds of 19th-century readers should not be underestimated. The young were warned at the time that in the choice of books there was a "great need of caution," and the potency of literature to govern the minds of readers proved inestimable.[9] Fictional characters possessed a remarkable ability to influence society. Uncle Tom, Topsy, Ivanhoe, Hawkeye, Hester Prynne, Ichabod Crane, and Ebenezer Scrooge were incredibly familiar characters to those that read as much as antebellum Americans did. They often seemed to become nearly as real and as influential to the reader as actual friends and relations.[10]

Romanticism

Most American intellectuals of the prewar period were widely read in the literature of European romanticism, and they used romantic allusions freely in their writing. A romantic movement that emphasized feeling, imagination, and nature swept the nation in the decades before 1860. It embraced the past, drawing strongly on the styles and ways of ancient civilizations and medieval times. Romanticism could be found in architecture, painting and decoration, and even in the institutions of government. The South, in particular, felt that its pastoral society with its ruling elite and slavery-bound servants more closely matched the ideal of ancient Rome than the industrialized society of the North with its venial politicians attempting to rule the urban centers by manipulating the teeming immigrant millions.

Lacking, for the most part, true aristocratic roots, Southern planters invented a social mythology for their entire class, and they came to believe in it. The foundation for much of what they did was based directly upon what they read. Largely isolated from the reality of European aristocracy, they lionized the stratified but benevolent social order portrayed in the romantic novels of authors like Walter Scott and always strove to maintain a romanticized version of the old "aristocratic" order as they believed it to be before the American Revolution. They behaved in a haughty manner reminiscent of the old nobility of Europe; taught their sons an aristocratic code of social behavior; and married off their daughters as if they were sealing dynastic treaties between feudal estates. Individual liberty, manliness, and respect for authority and position were held in such high esteem that a man might put his life on the line like a medieval champion in shining armor from *Ivanhoe* (1819) or *The Talisman* (1825).

Northern intellectuals held many beliefs that were unknown to the old aristocratic families of Europe. Democracy in America had destroyed many old social and political relationships and replaced them with new ones. Many aspects of American life had been altered in forging the United States. Besides politics and social structure, family relationships, education, the role of women, speech, literature, science, entertainment, and many other areas of life changed. Although most Americans avoided the study of social philosophy in the traditional sense, they were, nonetheless, possessed of a number of assumptions with regard to the new nation, its population, and its society. Foremost among these was a restless ambition born of a faith in the concept of universal equality among all free white men.

The number of those that tried to cultivate a sense of letters, the sciences, and the arts in the egalitarian North was immense. However, a foreign visitor to America in the 1830s, Alexis de Tocqueville, feared that "the absence of great patrons, of schools for instruction, of time to develop and refine talent" might inhibit Americans from achieving the highest quality of work in these areas. De Tocqueville correctly predicted that American democracy would produce "mediocre writers by the thousands" and an "ever increasing crowd of readers . . . continual[ly] craving for something new." De Tocqueville was convinced that this would ensure "the sale of books that nobody much esteems." However, he failed to predict the greatness that other writers might achieve. Indeed, James Fenimore Cooper and Washington Irving were already captivating many European intellectuals at the time of de Tocqueville's visit.[11]

Writing as a Profession

Literary pursuits were deemed a gentleman's avocation prior to the first quarter of the 19th century. American gentlemen "loved their books and often acquired a polished literary style, but they seldom ventured into print." To write a treatise on surveying, mining, or husbandry and share it among ones social equals was one thing, but to publish them for the common people to read often offended their "sense of propriety."[12] The language of antebellum writing was therefore filled with socially acceptable catchwords such as "Nature," "Reason," "Wit," "Honor," "Virtue," "Prudence," and "Sense." Its style was utilitarian and conversational, and it seemingly excluded the stiffly artificial, indirect, and abstract forms of earlier years for a style that more closely resembled modern prose.

Washington Irving was one of the first Americans to find dignity in the role of a professional author. He is best known for the short stories that introduced the Headless Horseman, Ichabod Crane, Rip Van Winkle, and Dietrich Knickerbocker (his own pseudonym) to American readers. Although he has been called the father of the American short story, Irving ventured into essays, poems, travel books, and biographies. One of his greatest works, written in the later years of his career, was *The Life of George Washington* (1855–1859). Irving was the first American author to achieve international fame.

Washington Irving at first studied law in private schools and was admitted to the New York bar in 1806. He started his writing career in 1802 by making contributions to the *Morning Chronicle*, a newspaper edited by his brother, Peter. He later joined with his other brother William in writing a magazine-like publication known as *Salmagundi* (1807–1808). From 1812 to 1814, he was the editor of a similar magazine, *Analetic*, which circulated in both New York and Philadelphia. The first of his works to achieve lasting fame was his comic history of old Dutch New York called *A History of New York* by Dietrich Knickerbocker (1809). Although the stories in this book quickly became part of New York's folklore, it was the success of Irving's *Sketchbook of Geoffrey Crayon* (1819) that allowed him to become a full-time writer.

The *History* and *Sketchbook* were the first American works to gain widespread attention in Europe. Irving noted, "Before the appearance of my work the popular traditions of our city [New York] were unrecorded. . . . Now they form a convivial currency and . . . link our whole community together in good-humor and good fellowship." Moreover, the stories contained in these works of literature helped to forge a link between writing and art. John Quidor and Albertus Browere, both naive artists from New York, gloried in producing illustrations of Irving's Dietrich Knickerbocker characters; and Asher B. Durand, Thomas Cole, and William Sidney Mount, all noted landscape painters, produced works based on themes found in *Sketchbook*. Literary and artistic journals like the *New York Mirror* (1823 to 1842) and *The Knickerbocker* (1833 to 1865) provided the public with engravings of the artists' paintings. "At no other time in the history of American art was the writer so closely allied to the artist."[13]

Ironically much of the work for which he is best known, filled as it is with Americana, was actually written by him in Europe where Irving lived from 1815 to 1832. He lived in London, Paris, Dresden, and Madrid. While in Spain, he worked for the U.S. Embassy, served as a secretary for the American Legation under Martin Van Buren, and had a brief romantic liaison with the writer Mary Shelley. From 1828 to 1832, when he returned to New York, he wrote several works with Hispanic themes. These included a number of histories that concerned the history and legends of Moorish Spain, including *Columbus* (1828), *Conquest of Granada* (1829), *The Champions of Columbus* (1831), and *Alhambra* (1832). Upon his return to America, he toured the West and South, producing travel books titled *The Canyon Miscellany* (1835) and *A Tour of the Prairies* (1835). From 1842 to 1845, Irving was the U.S. ambassador to Spain.

Irving's home in Tarrytown-on-Hudson in Westchester County, New York, is called Sunnyside. It is a small unimposing Gothic Revival–style cottage open to the public as a historic landmark home. Although it is nestled in the heart of the Hudson Valley that Deitrich Knickerbocker so loved, Irving lived there only briefly from 1836 to 1842 and again from 1848 to 1859, when he died. During the last decade of his life, Irving served as the president of John Jacob Astor's Library, which later became the New York Public Library. He published a 15-volume set of his own major works (1848–1851). Besides the five-volume life of George Washington that he finished during this period, he wrote a careful presentation of the life, beliefs, and teachings of the prophet Mohammed called *Mohomet and His Successors* (1850). After his death, his major works were collected and published in 21 volumes that were made available to the public in 1860 and 1861.

The Romance Novel

Beginning in the second decade of the century, the novel—the most popular form of antebellum escapism—gained a growing acceptance and appeal among the general reading public. Middle- and upper-class women have long been recognized as the chief consumers of this literary form. They consumed a flood of paperbacks filled with melodramatic situations, thrilling crises, and unspeakably evil villains. So great was the popularity of the novel that it drew criticism. As late as 1856, the Code of Public Instruction for the state of New York recognized the "necessity" of excluding from all libraries "novels, romances and other fictitious creations of the imagination, including a large proportion of the lighter literature of the day." The propriety of such "a peremptory and uncompromising exclusion of those catch-penny, but revolting publications which cultivate the taste for the marvelous, the tragic, the horrible and the supernatural [is without] the slightest argument." The code also expressed an "obvious" disgust for works dealing with "pirates, banditti and desperadoes of every description."[14] A published guide to propriety for mothers, written by Mrs. Lydia Child in 1831, decried "the profligate and strongly exciting works" found among the novels in the public libraries. "The necessity of fierce excitement in reading is a sort of intellectual intemperance," producing in the estimation of the guide's author "weakness and delirium" in women and young girls. The works of Lord Byron, Camden Pelham, Edward Maturin, Matthew G. Lewis, and Ann Radcliffe were all identified as having "an unhealthy influence upon the soul" that should be avoided.[15]

For modern audiences, the only recognizable name in Mrs. Child's list of forbidden authors is that of Lord Byron (George Gordon). Mrs. Child does not identify her reasons for including Byron in her list of authors to be avoided, but his collected works along with his letters and journals were available at the time to most American readers in a multivolume edition. Byron, Scott, Shakespeare, and Dickens were probably the most famous British authors known to those outside of Britain in the antebellum period. Byron was certainly the most notorious of the romantic poets and satirists. His influence on European poetry, music, novels, opera, and painting was immense. His 1814 work, *The Corsair*, sold 10,000 copies on the first day of its publication.

Byron typified the romantic movement in literature, and politically he was a "genuine and burning liberal." His advanced political views may have made him suspect, but his liberal and unrestrained lifestyle was widely condemned on moral grounds by his contemporaries. Byron led an open love affair with Lady Caroline Lamb, fathered a child with his half-sister, Augusta Leigh, and delved into homosexuality. He boasted of having made love to 200 different women on as many consecutive nights. He was made a member of the House of Lords in 1809, but left England permanently in 1816 to travel throughout the Mediterranean and came to reside in Italy. He died in 1824 at the age of 36.[16]

The "Pelham novels" referred to by Mrs. Child may be the works of Camden Pelham who wrote *The Chronicles of Crime*, a series of memoirs and anecdotes about British criminals "from the earliest period to 1841." These were illustrated by H.K. Browne, the famous illustrator of some of Dickens's works who went by the pseudonym "Phiz." The historical novels of Irish American author Edward Maturin were particularly steeped in the romantic. They included *Montezuma: The Last of the Aztecs*, a brilliant, if overly impassioned, history; *Benjamin: The Jew of Granada*, set in 15th-century Moslem Spain; and *Eva, or the Isles of Life and Death*, a romance of 12th-century England. One of his more fiery books was *Bianca*, a story of a passionate love between a woman and a man from Italy and Ireland, respectively.[17]

Ann Radcliffe's novels were primarily "time-fillers for a literarily [sic] inclined young woman who had no children and did not care for society." Although she died in 1823 and many of her works were written in the late 1790s, Radcliff was the main source of "horror stories with a twist" that circulated among 19th-century readers. The significance of her "horror-mongering" on later romantic literature cannot be over estimated. Terror connoisseurs found her heroines melancholy, easy to weep, and endearingly practical. In the *Italian*, she created a romantic villain who brought the physical aspects of terror to perfection. This villain, repelled by the enormity of his crime but fascinated by the looming tragedy of his fate, was the basis for similar characters used by Maturin, Byron, Lewis, and Scott. Her last novel, released in 1826, was *Gaston de Blondeville*. Actually written in 1802, this work preceded Scott's first historical novels and attempted for the first time to paint an authentic historical picture while telling a fictional tale.[18]

Almost totally forgotten today, Matthew G. Lewis was a follower of Radcliffe whose writings "ran heavily to the florid romantic." His first novel, *Ambrosio, The Monk,* was universally read but widely condemned in Britain and America. Lewis was charged with being immoral and irreligious when it was discovered that he was recommending that certain passages from the Bible be kept from the young. His work was considered "vicious" and "terrible." Often referred to as the "immoral monk Lewis," he was a man of genuine philanthropy and humane instincts. After inheriting a plantation in Jamaica with a complement of more than 500 black slaves, Lewis instituted a series of humanitarian reforms that were "regarded as mad" by his contemporaries. He attested to the effectiveness of these in *The Journal of a West India Proprietor,* which was published just before his death from yellow fever. Besides several dramas, Lewis produced two romantic novels: *The Bravo of Venice* and *Feudal Tyrants.* He also wrote a number of short pieces included in *Tales of Terror* and *Romantic Tales,* which were based on German and Spanish legends. In collaboration with Scott, Lewis produced a collection of ballads, *Tales of Wonder.* His work is generally neglected today, but he had tremendous influence on the romantic writers of his day.[19]

"He Is Dead Who Called Me Into Being"

The horror genre, initiated by Ann Radcliffe, was changed for all time in 1818 by the introduction of the character of the monster in Mary Wollstonecraft Shelley's *Frankenstein, or the Modern Prometheus.* After almost three years of developing a story based on a chance challenge issued by Lord Byron and her husband Percy Bysshe Shelley, Mary Shelley's horror novel was finally made available in print when she was just 21. Her work gave rise to a whole new type of writing. With her husband's encouragement, Shelley based her plot on the galvanic experiments in electricity, then popular in Italian medical universities, which sent shocks into the limbs of dead frogs and seemingly reanimated them. In fact, the muscle tissues were simply twitching under the influence of electric current. Similar experiments were later done with human cadavers with astonishing results.

The first edition of *Frankenstein* was widely accepted as the work of Percy Shelley. Many readers could not accept that any young woman could write such a shockingly repellent horror story. Yet the tale was a huge success. In the 1831 edition of the book, Mary Shelley clearly acknowledged her authorship and wrote that she got the idea for the story from a dream in which she saw a hideously formed dead man stir to life after being worked upon by a powerful machine. Although begun as a ghost story, the completed novel contained no supernatural elements, and the creation of the monster by Dr. Victor Frankenstein was based on a logical, if impractical, sequence of scientific concepts.

Inspired by a combination of an occult philosophy, the growing physics of electricity, and a number of advances in the science of medicine, Shelley has Dr. Frankenstein assemble and reanimate a man from body parts rescued from dissecting rooms, charnel houses, or the gallows. The creature (unlike that portrayed in mid-20th-century movies) proves intelligent and highly articulate, and becomes embittered when his "creator" turns from him in disgust and horror. The tale becomes a personal trial between the increasingly philosophical monster and the doctor, who is quickly approaching madness under the influence of guilt and frustration. The plot leads to a final confrontation in the Arctic wastes during which both antagonists are presumed to die.

Sir Walter Scott

Among the most popular books of the antebellum period were the works of Sir Walter Scott. As a writer and poet Scott was a born storyteller, a master of dialogue, and the chief architect of the historical novel. His influence as a novelist was profound, and his work inspired many other authors including Edward Bulwer-Lytton, George Eliot,[20] James Fenimore Cooper, and the Brontë sisters. Scott wrote 27 historical novels during his career. These can be grouped into three broad categories: those set in Scottish history; those set in the Middle Ages and the Reformation; and finally, all those that defy simple chronological classification.

The several works known as the Waverly novels received their name from the first of the series regarding Scotland, published in 1814. Annually thereafter followed a number of major works.[21] Most of these novels were written under pseudonyms, but Scott had already gained recognition in literary circles for his epic poems, among them *The Lay of the Last Minstrel* (1805) and *The Lady of the Lake* (1810). A financial crisis at a printing house, which he owned in partnership with his friend James Ballantyne, destroyed his anonymity as an author of historical novels in 1826. Scott had accumulated enough wealth from his writing alone to pay a cash bond of 130,000 pounds sterling—a fabulous sum worth millions today. His wealth and popularity can be compared to that of the top professional athletes, musicians, and actors today.

The Waverly novels found their theme in the Scottish struggle of 1745 to throw off the dominance and oppression of the English. *Rob Roy* (1817) sold out its first edition of 10,000 copies in two weeks. Scott's theme of Scottish independence, his use of romantic characters, highland warriors, lords and ladies, knights in armor, and grand estates was particularly resonant with the self-image of many Americans in the South. So familiar was Scott's work to Southerners that in later years Mark Twain only half-jokingly listed Scott as a cause for the Civil War.

The Adventure Novel

Second only to Sir Walter Scott's works in popularity were the American adventure novels of authors like James Fenimore Cooper. Inspired by Scott's historical novels, Cooper drew many mutually exclusive stereotypes, characterizing Indians as good and evil, male characters as wise or foolish, and female characters as fair or dark both physically and temperamentally. His first novel, *Precaution* (1820), was poorly accepted by American readers, largely because it imitated the British form of Jane Austen's *Pride and Prejudice*. Cooper's second work, *The Spy* (1822), was an outstanding success. Cooper is said to have started writing because he needed money, and the success of *The Spy*, which sold 8,000 copies in the first month after its release, seemed a satisfactory means to that end. Still, many male readers considered novels to be "trivial, feminine, and vaguely dishonorable" because they appealed to the emotions and aroused the imagination. Nonetheless, Cooper found that there was a great demand for adventure tales derived from the Revolution; and his writing was sufficiently manly and moral to find acceptance by a wide audience. His work successfully emphasized American incidents and scenes as interesting and important, but they were popular among men mainly because of their masculine adventure themes. He also wrote a series of American sea tales, starting with *The Pilot* (1824), which featured the person of Captain John Paul Jones.[22]

Like Scott, Cooper promoted a social vision of a stable and genteel society governed by its natural aristocracy, "perpetuating property, order, and liberty" as represented by a reunited American gentry. That this view resonated with the Southern image of itself would have upset Cooper with his very Northern attitudes. *The Pioneers* (1823), Cooper's third book, was dedicated to the proposition that the American republic, poised on the verge of "demagoguery, deceit, hypocrisy, and turmoil," could be transformed into a stable, prosperous and just society. It sold 3,500 copies on the first day of its release.[23]

"Few storytellers in all history have enjoyed so wide a popularity as [James] Fenimore Cooper."[24] Cooper's novels were often read aloud to eager audiences. He hammered out one adventure after another, acting out exciting plots against the lush and unforgiving scenery of the American wilderness. He introduced the first classic American fictional hero in the person of Natty Bumpo, the character known as Hawkeye in the five adventure novels that make up his Leatherstocking Saga. The history of Bumpo, who may have been based on an old hunter that Cooper knew in his boyhood at Cooperstown in western New York, was not at first planned, and the series was not written in chronological order. Bumpo is introduced in *The Pioneers* (1823) as an angular, irritable 70-year-old who deplores the advance of civilization upon the wilderness. He then appears in his best-known incarnation in his thirties in *The Last of the Mohicans* (1826); in his eighties in *The Pairie* (1827); again in his thirties in *The Path-finder* (1840); and finally in his 20s in *The Deerslayer* (1841).

Cooper seems to have grasped the process by which the old frontier came to be dominated by a civilization with European roots, and he communicated it clearly to his readers. "He had a realistic understanding of many facets of pioneer life: the romance, the heroism, the lawlessness, the crudity, the simplicity, the provincialism, the honesty, the corruption."[25] His portrayal of the settlement of the old New York frontier as a spiritual adventure resonated well with a public interested in westward expansion and religious revival. Cooper's depiction of the frontier can be criticized in that he filled his plots with "improbabilities." His pages are filled with random encounters, idle young women wandering in the wilderness to serve as the objects of rescue, and eligible young men to furnish suitors for the women. However, Cooper never claimed to be a realist, only a "romancer."[26] It was the succession of adventurous episodes, not the overall plot that riveted his readers. The same "cliffhanger" formula can be found in the cinema available to early 20th-century moviegoers or the more recent TV miniseries format. Once Cooper had hit upon a money-making formula, he maintained it, writing over 30 novels. He considered *The Pathfinder* and *The Deerslayer* his best works.

In 1826, Cooper took his wife and went to live in Europe, and he did not return until 1833. He had written four best-sellers among his first six novels. He then set about making it eminently clear that he was uneasy with what he considered American vulgarity and lack of manners by taking his countrymen to account in a series of books in 1838—*The American Democrat, Homeward Bound,* and *Home as Found.* Like a parent correcting a child, Cooper lectured Americans on their lack of decorum, condemned the tone of their politics, and criticized their press. He made it clear that he was offended by the seeming pushiness and familiarity of the lower classes, and expressed a belief in limiting suffrage to men of good breeding who might direct the fortunes and culture of the rest of America. The newspapers were quick to denounce him, and he became the target of unrestrained personal criticism even though his work remained popular. He launched a legal and literary counterassault on those editors and politicians that disagreed with him; yet when he died in 1851, many literary greats attended or spoke at his memorial including Daniel Webster, Washington Irving, and William Cullen Bryant.

The fact that he grew up in a region of New York from which most Native Americans had been removed colored Cooper's depiction of

Indians. His knowledge of Native life was almost completely acquired from his own reading of personal narratives and histories of Indian peoples written in the previous century. Cooper neglected to derive certain elements of Native American life from these sources. Except for a few chapters at the end of *The Last of the Mohicans*, Indians appear as individuals with personal traits rather than as communities or tribes with a social organization. His Mohican allies and friends, Chingachgook and Uncas, are clearly idealized portraits possessed of every virtue and no vices; almost all other Indians are depicted as evil, villainous, and untrustworthy. However, "to wish that Cooper had been more realistic and scientific in his portrayal of the forest, and frontiersmen, and the savage, is to wish that he had been a different kind of writer, and to miss his true achievement." Although many of his novels are not highly regarded today, the best of them can still enthrall both young and old readers. Three of his Leatherstocking tales have been made into major motion pictures, and one of these, *The Last of the Mohicans*, has been remade several times and has come to characterize an entire period of American history.[27]

Juvenile Literature

Youngsters were expected to read the Bible, their lessons from their schoolbooks, and little else in the way of entertaining literature. Like Lydia Child, who advised young women to avoid novels, the Reverend Doctor Joel Hawes warned young men that in the choice of books there was a "great need of caution." He believed that a person's character could be "ruined by reading a single [ill-advised] volume." Yet he confessed that one book, "wisely selected and properly studied" could "do more to improve the mind, and enrich the understanding, than skimming over the surface of an entire library."[28]

Several publications surfaced during the antebellum period to attempt to fill the gap between dry religious tracts and scandalous romance novels. In 1827, a weekly literary magazine was founded in Boston with the purpose of providing appropriate reading material for youngsters. Known as *The Youth's Companion*, the magazine remained in publication for more than a century and received contributions from many famous authors including Alfred Lord Tennyson, Thomas Hardy, Rudyard Kipling, Louisa May Alcott, John Greenleaf Whittier, Robert Louis Stevenson, and Jules Verne. In 1830, Sarah Josepha Hale published another work, *Poems for Our Children*, that included classics such as "Mary Had a Little Lamb." In 1853 and 1854, Nathaniel Hawthorne published his tales for children: *A Wonder Book* and *The Tanglewood Tales*.

School readers made their first appearance in the schoolroom during this period. The *Peerless Pioneer Readers* containing stories of interest to children, were first introduced in 1826 by William Holmes McGuffey, and the first of a long list of McGuffey's *Eclectic Readers* was published in 1836. Six readers in this series appeared between 1836 and 1857 with their sales reaching a peak during the Civil War. Literally millions of copies found their way into schoolrooms and children's nurseries during the antebellum period. In 1846, Epes Sargent's *School Reader* made its appearance. Elijah Kellogg's blank verse *Spartacus to His Gladiators* appeared in Sargent's first edition and became a standard exercise in classroom declamation of young students for decades.

"All for One, One For All"

The popularity of the adventure novel was not reserved for those authors writing in English. The work of French author Alexandre Dumas also gained a great deal of attention in America. Read both in its original French and in English translations made possible by increasingly inexpensive printing, Dumas's fast-paced adventure novels and historical tales became foundation works of the popular literature. Chief among these were *The Three Musketeers* (1844) and *The Count of Monte Cristo* (1845). Through his careful blending of historic fact and fiction, Dumas had revitalized the historical novel in France by midcentury. He wrote constantly, producing a steady stream of novels, plays, and short stories. Between 1845 and 1850, he completed the final two books in the Musketeers trilogy: *Twenty Years After* (1845) and *The Vicomte Bragelonne* (1850), better known as *The Man in the Iron Mask*.

Dumas was a man of African heritage, but he did not generally define himself as a black man. He seems to have encountered little overt racism in his life. Nonetheless, in *Georges* (1843), Dumas directly attacked the question of race and colonialism in print. There is evidence that his works were particularly popular with 19th-century African American freemen, who saw in the false imprisonment of Edmond Dantes in *The Count of Monte Cristo* and of Louis XIV's twin brother in *The Man in the Iron Mask* parables of emancipation for their people. His success was somewhat due to the rapid spread of inexpensive newspapers, in which his stories initially ran in serial form. The serial novel, a format also utilized by Charles Dickens and Harriet Beecher Stowe, attracted subscribers to the newspapers. Everyone read them, or had them read to them, creating a huge popular base of dedicated story followers. Although Dumas produced more than 250 books, he did so by maintaining a staff of 70 assistants. His expenses generally outran his income, and he was forced to constantly avoid his creditors.

Dumas's works, including more than 15 plays, created a romantic history for France that was largely fictional but so compelling that many

American readers found difficulty in separating the facts from the romance. His lesser-known works also included a number of supernatural elements and characters like the Siamese twins, separated at birth, in *The Corsican Brothers* (1844) who maintained a psychic knowledge of each other's experiences. Among these are *The Chateau D'Eppstein* (1844), a ghost story; and *Le Vampire* (1851), a dark tale of a bloodsucking night stalker; and *Le Meneur de Loups* (1857), in which a man makes a pact with the devil. In many ways, Dumas foresaw the popularity of the superheroes of the next century.

Escapist Literature

Americans were quick to record in their letters and journals the completion of *Nicholas Nickleby*, *The Pickwick Papers*, *The Deerslayer*, *Ivanhoe*, or other works of obvious quality, but they also read a great deal of low-quality material, much of which they did not mention. Nonetheless, many of these works have been identified. They include such masculine titles as *Con Cregan, Son of Eric, Gold Friend, The Quadroon of Louisiana, Son of the Wilderness, Scar Chief of the Halfbreeds, Wild West Scenes,* and *Our Own Heroes*. Other popular works were *Lady Audley's Secret, The Mystery, Macaria,* and *Louisa Elton*. Captain Mayne Reid, a friend of Edgar Allan Poe, published *The Rifle Rangers: Adventures of an Officer in Southern Mexico* in 1850, and Ann Stephens, the first author published in Irwin Beadle's dime-novel format, wrote *Malaeska: The Indian Wife of the White Hunter* in 1860.

Each of these publications was unquestionably escapist literature of the lowest sort. Yet books of this type sold well. An American author like Reid was able to follow his first success with other successful titles such as *The Scalp Hunters, The War Trail,* and *Forest Exiles*. In 1853, Reid wrote a novel inspired by his 15-year-old spouse, appropriately titled *The Child Wife*, and in 1856 he wrote a popular play called *The Quadroon* that combined a theme of tragic love between a white man and a free mulatto women with a knife duel, a steamboat explosion, a slave auction, and two murders. The success of *The Quadroon*, which was transformed into a popular stage play in the North, reflected the extent of the involvement of the reading public in the slavery controversy.[29] Another young American author, distinguished before the outbreak of hostilities, was John W. DeForest. From 1851 through 1859, DeForest wrote several books including the *History of the Indians of Connecticut*, and the novels *Witching Times, Oriental Acquaintance, European Acquaintance,* and *Seacliff*. DeForest went to war as a captain with the 12th Connecticut volunteers, and many of his battlefield reports were printed by *Harper's Monthly*. In these, DeForest shared the simple truth of life in the Army and on the battlefield.[30]

Social Commentary

The works of the English novelist and social commentator Charles Dickens were widely read in America. In Dickens's very popular works, readers found some character, situation, or condition that seemed to bolster the many different views of modern society held by Americans. Social reformers in this period generally championed the cause of the poor, but Dickens was generally unconcerned with the economic aspects of social reform, choosing rather to deal with an increased appreciation of the value of the human being. Ignorance, for him, was the great cause of human misery. In 1843, he gave a speech in the city of Manchester, England, in which he pleaded for a heightened sense of humanitarianism and an improvement in the system of public education in Britain. In contrast to the "ragged schools," that had been set up by well-meaning, but untrained, volunteer teachers to give England's poor children the rudiments of education, Dickens proposed that the surest improvement in the nation's future was tied to a public investment in education sponsored by the government.

Dickens's stories emphasized the need to enlighten traditional ways of thinking. However, many in the American South misread Dickens's message and saw the misfortune, destitution, and disease that filled his works as characteristic of all urban life. Modernization and urbanization were the great evils haunting the romantic domains of the Southern imagination. For these, Dickens's novels mirrored the inevitable bleak future of America if Northern concepts of social progress continued to be implemented as English ones had for decades without noticeably improving society. Southerners despised such ambiguous social remedies as the poorhouses and the workhouses that filled Dickens's pages. The debtor's prison of *Little Dorrit* and the orphanage of *Oliver Twist* were obviously not sufficient to solve the social ills characteristic of an urban society. Southerners were left with a portrait of cities, like those of the North, veritably teeming with the exploited masses from which they chose to be separated.[31]

Although thoroughly English in its settings and personalities, the interactions of Scrooge with characters from *A Christmas Carol*, first published in 1843, seemed to embody the very limitations of modern society in midcentury. Stripped of its sentimentality, the story portrays a secular, rather than a traditionally religious, attitude toward the holidays. The spirits and ghosts of Christmas are remarkably worldly in their appearance and temporal in their outlook. The awakening of a social conscience in Scrooge is uppermost in their endeavors. Ultimately, it is the specter of an unlamented death, a topic of great concern to persons of the 19th century, that brings Scrooge around. Yet even a morally awakened Scrooge refuses to devote his life to social work. Instead, he acts out his reformation on a very personal level. Apologists for the Southern way of life proclaimed that Scrooge's treatment of Bob Cratchit emphasized the abuses possible in an age governed by the "work for wage" system that so lacked a sense of personal involvement and family dedication. The personal responsibility, which many Southerners felt toward their neighbors, their workers, and even their slaves, seemed noble in contrast to the socially anonymous caretaking for the unfortunates found in Dickens's works.[32]

Nonetheless, Americans North and South loved Dickens's works, and all his writings were instantly read and eagerly put into print. Because much of his work was published in England in serial form, it was sometimes reprinted without the permission or knowledge of the author by the American press. Within hours of their arrival in the United States, many of his works were reprinted and available for sale. His *American Notes*, generally critical of the republic and much of New York society, sold 5,000 copies in New York City in two days at the price of 12.5¢ a copy. In Philadelphia, 3,000 copies sold in just 35 minutes. It was estimated at the time that 400,000 sets of Dickens's works were sold in the United States before the war. Many of these were published by the paperback press and brought no money to the author.[33]

In 1842, Dickens and his wife toured America, and thousands of citizens turned out to welcome them in New York City. Thousands more greeted them in Boston, Philadelphia, Cleveland, St. Louis, and Richmond. Dickens, described as a small but intelligent looking man with a fashion of dress approaching that of a dandy, was a stark contrast to his quiet and unassuming spouse. He came to America believing that the United States was the hope and promise of the world, but he found New York filthy, crowded, and unsophisticated. In his *American Notes*, written upon his return to England, he left a generally stark verbal description of many American cities as they appeared in the middle of the antebellum period.

Dickens described those Americans he saw in New York as crude, violent, and lacking in the manners expected of middle-class Englishmen. He was particularly taken aback by the widespread acceptance of the offensive habit of chewing tobacco and spitting the results into any convenient curbside. He was also aghast at the conditions he found in American tenements, prisons, and places of recreation. He considered the tenements hideous, the prisons loathsome, and the taverns low and squalid. He also expressed a strong aversion for the American press, calling it a "foul growth" upon America's utilitarian society. He found the American form of republican government polluted by political trickery and underhanded tampering during elections, and fettered by shameless greed and veniality among its highest officials.[34]

Dickens liked the city of Richmond, but he was much dismayed and distressed by the ever-present reminder of slavery everywhere in the South. The city was the third largest in the South and had proven an elegant state capital with fine buildings and traditional architecture. Dickens proclaimed the city the most picturesque in America. Despite his personal hostility toward race-based bondage, which he made obvious at every opportunity, Dickens and his wife thrilled the residents of Virginia with their visit. Ironically, he was also impressed by the excellent morale exhibited by the slaves in the factories and warehouses he visited, and he expressed that he greatly enjoyed their spirituals and tunes.[35]

He was struck by the absence of a festive air in the Quaker-dominated city of Philadelphia. He wrote of it in comparison to his native London:

> How quiet the streets are. Are there no itinerant bands, no wind or stringed instruments? No, not one. By day there are no Punches, Fantoccini, dancing dogs, jugglers, conjurers, orchestrinas, or even barrel-organs? No, not one. Yes, I remember one. One barrel-organ and a dancing monkey. Beyond that nothing lively, no, not so much as a white mouse in a twirling cage. Are there no amusements? Yes, there is the lecture room and evening service for the ladies thrice a week, and for the young men the countinghouse, the store, the barroom and the filthy newspaper urchins are brawling down the street. These are the amusements of the Americans.[36]

The author also toured toward the West. He found Cleveland, Ohio, unacceptably dirty and unsophisticated. He reported that the Indians, who were so highly esteemed by the authors of romantic literature, were actually "wretched creatures . . . squatting and spitting."[37]

Dickens felt better about the French quarter of St. Louis, Missouri:

> In the old French portion of the town, the thoroughfares are narrow and crooked, and some of the houses are very quaint and picturesque; being built of wood, with tumble-down galleries before the windows, approachable by stairs or rather ladders from the street. There are queer little barbers' shops and drinking houses, too, in this quarter; and abundance of crazy old tenements with blinking casements; such as may be seen in Flanders. Some of these ancient habitations, with high garret gable-windows peeking into the roofs, have a kind of French shrug about them; and being lopsided with age, appear to hold their heads askew, besides, as if they were grimacing in astonishment at the American Improvements.[38]

At the end of his *American Notes*, Dickens tried to soothe the disappointment and the anger that he anticipated his comments would engender among his American readers by declaring at least the upper classes of society "frank, brave, cordial, hospitable, and affectionate."[39] Indeed, many among the social and literary elite viewed Dickens's comments with sympathy and found them rooted in a reality that they themselves saw every day in many urban centers. Most attributed the starkness of Dickens's criticism to the author's own exaggerated expectations for the "noble course" that had begun in the United States. Hoping to see an American Zion inhabited by the stately scions of the founders of the American republic, Dickens was devastated by the realities of the American lifestyle, the frailties of its population, and the political bickering that had no meaningful bearing on the operation of the world's great republican experiment. This was a factor in the formation of his judgment of America to which Dickens himself admitted in later years. Nonetheless, when *Martin Chuzzlewit*, Dickens's American novel, appeared shortly after his return to England, it proved especially offensive to some of the residents of New York City, and many citizens were loath to forgive him for his characterizations. One man wrote that Dickens had written "an exceedingly foolish libel upon us, from which he will not obtain credit as an author, nor as a man of wit, any more than as a man of good taste, good nature, or good manners. . . . Shame, Mr. Dickens!"[40]

Transcendentalism

While romantics focused on the heroic and objective elements of America, Northern writers came to be dominated by the transcendentalists of New England who contemplated its philosophical and metaphysical meaning. The transcendental movement treated literature as a religion of sorts, and it arose from the remnants of New England Puritan theology left behind when democracy swept the country in the last quarter of the 18th century. It was a form of personal intellectualism and self-culture that highly valued the religious inner light of the common man. In transcendentalism the Puritan heritage, wildly distorted by 19th-century authors and historians into an intolerant theocracy, was blended together with a sense of American individualism, Classical mysticism, Teutonic idealism, and Oriental occultism. The transcendentalists reveled in a secular democratic consciousness. They were refugees from a brand of Calvinism that had suddenly grown too harsh for them to endure, and they turned to transcendentalism and the cult of Nature to escape the devastating realities of American urban life.

The movement started at Harvard University in the 1830s as a digression into German romantic philosophies and a number of social theories including the communism of Karl Marx. Transcendentalism reached its apex with the founding of Brook Farm by newspaper editor George Ripley in 1841. Brook Farm was a utopia of sorts, set in the hills of Massachusetts, that reached out into the intellectual community of New England through the publication of *The Dial*, a literary newsletter. Although the editors of the established press found *The Dial* a magazine for "Zanies," in fact it compared favorably with those in England and the United States "containing articles more pertinent to life" than many of its contemporaries. However, the Brook Farm contributors, agitating to humanize and resocialize America, had their literary energies diverted into the slavery question, and the opening of the Civil War checked for decades the strong drift of the movement toward radical socialism.[41]

The transcendental movement took its name from Immanuel Kant, who proclaimed that an intuitive knowledge of the moral order in the universe was superior to that gained by the mere physical experience of practicing the ceremonies and rituals of traditional religion. The metaphysical aspects of the movement viewed each individual as eminently perfectible, and it exalted the imaginative, the emotional, and the idealistic over the coldly intellectual, the strictly symmetrical, and the unyieldingly utilitarian. Every man might master his environment and transcend his personal weaknesses to share in a wider divinity than that offered by traditional churches—a universal soul imbued with the spirit of God and shared by all. Truth was to be had not from a careful reading of the scriptures but from nature itself, from the stars, the mountains, the waterways, and trees—a sort of "anthropomorphic divinity."[42]

Transcendentalism valued personal conscience above man-made laws and religious or political institutions. Individuals had a responsibility to realize their divine capabilities by their inner experiences—a sort of divine self-revelation. For persons living in a new democratic era where all men were created equal, this type of idealism and self-aggrandizement was a heavy stimulant. As such, it was a fitting philosophy for antebellum reformers impatient to build vast social utopias, free those in bondage, and perfect the common man in their own image. As religious thought became more secularized for the transcendentalists, man's degraded condition seemed less due to the predestination and original sin of Calvinist theology, and more dependent on environmental, political, and societal factors. An implicit faith in the perfectibility of man left many among the socially conscious movement with the notion that the continued existence of societal ills was due to the systematic reluctance of the older order to change—particularly if that order was in the South. The natural consequence that followed such thinking was the rise of social activism in the form of antislavery societies, temperance and universal suffrage movements, school and prison reformation, urban revitalization, and social experimentation, all quite properly directed toward perfecting the common people by perfecting the environment in which they lived.

Those who accepted transcendentalist thinking formed a sort of reform elite armed with enough conceit to decide the course of reform and the fate of the nation. Dorothy Lynde Dix spent her life trying to relieve the ills of paupers, criminals, and the insane. In 1845, she published a significant reform work titled *Prisons and Prison Disciple*. In the same year, Sarah Margaret Fuller wrote a scathing exposé of the female lot in life in America called *Women in the Nineteenth Century*. Yet some of what the transcendentalists envisioned was not quite reputable by the standards of the general antebellum population, and only one or two accomplished any meaningful reform (and then only briefly).

Historian Bernard DeVoto, less sympathetic to the transcendentalists than some commentators who focused solely on their literary accomplishments, wrote, "Brook Farm [was] the association of literary communists who had withdrawn from the world to establish Utopia a few miles from Boston. . . . The Brook Farmers were not political adventurers, conspirators, or opportunists: they had formally announced their refusal to adhere to the American political system." The "smock wearers" and "literary amateurs," as DeVoto calls them, "were making an experiment in economy, and they were very happy." With goals based largely on a reading of the *Theory of Human Passions* by Charles Fourier, they sought "to soften and regulate the temperature and increase the warmth at the poles, correct the heat at the equator, bring on eternal springtime, fertilize the desert, and prevent the drying up of streams. Moreover, [they] would domesticate the beaver and the zebra to man's uses and increase the fish in the lakes and rivers some twenty fold."[43]

Adherence to religion spawned many utopian societies in the antebellum period, but the transcendentalists attempted to reach the same goal by replacing the grace of God with the light of right reason and beautifully written sentiments. They "[gave] up Christ in favor of refined passions and virtuous labour." Its members promised a different perfection for America and the world, "perfect justice as an outgrowth of perfect cooperation—the cooperation, that is, of literary people." However, effective social reform required the least common denominators of society, not its loftiest ideals. In 1846, the community died because it could not pay its bills with the labors of its members. Nathaniel Hawthorne, who had invested $500 in the farm, sued for the return of his money. Ralph Waldo Emerson wrote that the Brook Farmers could not accomplish "anything good or anything powerful [with regard to literature] . . . with a pen in one hand and a crowbar or a peat-knife in the other."[44] Ripley founded Brook Farm because he believed that mankind was dwarfed and brutish and needed reform, but "the literary will accept no hybrid of brute and angel; they desire Utopia and will not settle for the human race. They love the people but they hate the mob." In that paradox ended all that the Brook Farm association had to say.[45]

Ralph Waldo Emerson

If the individual was one with God, as the transcendentalists believed, then Ralph Waldo Emerson was their high priest. Emerson led a group of like-minded literary types found among the Bostonian intellectual set, including Bronson Alcott, Sarah Margaret Fuller, Henry David Thoreau. Elizabeth Peabody, and Theodore Parker. Emerson began as a Unitarian minister, but left the pulpit in 1832 because he felt that the institution of the Church separated man from direct communion with God. "I am part and parcel of God!" he exclaimed in describing his discovery of the divinity within himself. "We but half express ourselves, and are ashamed of that divine idea which each of us represents."[46]

Emerson held a deep belief in self-reliance and extreme individualism. Unlike the romantics, he lamented America's cultural dependence on Europe and despised foreign travel as a means to true self-education. In a speech before Harvard's Phi Beta Kappa Society in 1837, Emerson declared America's intellectual independence by calling for courage and originality among American writers and scholars. Although his philosophy was based largely in the German and Oriental ideals, his essays and poems were basically Christian and democratic in their flavor, but they were too lofty to allow him to descend into open activism. Not until the decade before the Civil War did Emerson openly align himself with any social reform other than antislavery. He cautioned his contemporaries that the recent discoveries of science and technology, if applied to a progressive democracy, might not fix the social order, but he was open to the concept that they might be used to continually change it.[47]

Viewed as a founder of the "Church" of transcendentalism, Emerson might be thought a curiosity of antebellum history. However, he was also America's foremost man of letters, a figure who dominated the literary scene more than any other writer of the period. "In a sense everything in the literary line starts with Emerson," wrote historian Paige Smith. He gave preeminence to the academic professor in the lecture hall that had previously been reserved for the political orator in the halls of government. Emerson "heralded the virtual eclipse of Utilitarianism as a potent intellectual and religious movement [and] laid the foundations for a new alliance between literature and morality. It elevated the poet and, perhaps above all, the lecturer, to a new priesthood. It called for a fresh and vigorous religion of literature. Prayers were metamorphosed into poems and sermons into lectures."[48]

Emerson's followers at Brook Farm were thrilled by his work. Fuller, a leading feminist, found his words "more beneficial to me than that of any American."[49] He seemed to rediscover the power of the simple declarative sentence, "a sentence in which the weight and quality of each word [was] as carefully considered as a gem on a jeweler's scale."[50] After reading some of Emerson's essays, Sidney Fisher noted in his diary, "It seems to me that everything I ever thought is in Emerson's writings and a thousand things besides that I never thought. . . . Physical science, history, mathematics, philosophy are in his hands instruments and illustrations, which he uses with the ease and grace of a master."[51]

Though no one person can be credited with the invention of the lecture format, Emerson certainly perfected it. Bronson Alcott wrote, "There was no lecture till Emerson made it. . . . Everything is admissible, philosophy, ethics, divinity, criticism, poetry, humor, fun, mimicry, anecdotes, jokes, ventriloquism, all the breadth and versatility of the most liberal conversation. . . . Here is a pulpit that makes all other pulpits tame and ineffectual. . . . I look upon the Lecture room as the true church today."[52] An observer of Emerson's career has noted that "Emerson was the great liberator of the imagination for his age; his words came with thrilling power to thousands of young men and women who felt cramped and thwarted by ancient dogmas and turned to him as to a stream of living water." His work was "the private record of the New England soul turned into art."[53]

Henry David Thoreau

Upon his graduation from Harvard, Henry David Thoreau turned to the management of his father's pencil factory with the goal in mind to make a superior pencil. This accomplished, and his fortune assured at a young age, he lapsed into a great despondence over what he might do with the rest of his life "and not be ashamed of it." Emerson was his friend and spiritual mentor, but Thoreau chose not to join the transcendentalists at Brook Farm. He briefly served as a tutor for the children of Emerson's brother but soon returned home tormented by a sense of guilt in that he had not chosen a loftier goal for his life. He wrote after the death of his brother, "It surely is some encouragement to know that the stars are my fellow-creatures, for I do not suspect but they are reserved for a high destiny." Finally, in 1845, he decided that it was time "to begin to live." He built a little cabin at Walden Pond on a piece of property recently purchased by Emerson. Here he planned to live worshipping Nature and striving to discover its essence while still within walking distance of his home.[54]

This patently ridiculous and rather silly episode in the life of a 27-year-old Harvard graduate, was turned to greatness by Thoreau's epic journey into self-discovery and his quest to unravel the ethical laws of the universe by a journey into holy living. Free from encroaching social inhibitions, he strove at Walden Pond to live "a life of simplicity, independence, magnanimity, and trust."[55] Unlike the transcendentalists at Brook Farm, Thoreau came to recognize that without a religion or devotion of some kind, nothing worthwhile might be accomplished. During the long hours of hoeing his small field of beans or splitting firewood, Thoreau thought, and his thought slowly pulled him toward a number of causes. During his stay at Walden, the United States declared war on Mexico, and Thoreau was bitterly opposed to it. "When a sixth of the population of a nation [the United States] which has taken to be a refuge of liberty are slaves, and a whole country [Mexico] is unjustly overrun and conquered by [our] army and subjected to military law, I think it is not too soon for honest men to rebel and revolutionize." By refusing to pay his poll taxes, the author protested and was hauled off to jail, where he remained only a single night. The episode, brief as it was, produced his master essay "On

Civil Disobedience," a work of political philosophy so profound that it reached the minds of Mahatma Gandhi and Martin Luther King Jr. more than a century later. Also during this period, Thoreau wrote the first draft of *A Week on the Concord and Merrimack Rivers,* an incredible failure in terms of sales. More than 9,000 of the 10,000 copies that Thoreau paid to have printed remained unsold. The wood that he split while at Walden Pond had a greater value than the few volumes that he sold.[56]

Ironically, Thoreau did not write his masterpiece, *Walden* at Walden Pond, but began it in Emerson's home where he stayed for two years after his sojourn at the pond. The work was not finished until 1854. Thoreau was a writer of sentences, not finished and proper essays. He needed to revisit, reorder, and revise his thoughts many times while producing a finish work. Indeed, all of his works are the product of a young man's thoughts, one who refused to grow up, who prolonged his adolescence and his dependence on his mother and sisters. Yet by his loving observations of the natural world that surrounded his little cabin, Thoreau brought the transcendentalists' fascination with nature to its logical conclusion. He wrote, "[T]o be a philosopher is not merely to have subtle thoughts, nor even to found a school, but to love wisdom."[57]

Although Thoreau continued to write after 1854, he published no more books in his lifetime. Eight more works were published after his death in 1862, but it took 30 years for all of them to appear in print. Therefore, they had little effect on the culture of the antebellum period. Emerson spoke Thoreau's eulogy, "The country knows not yet, or in the least part, how great a son it has lost. . . . But he at least is content. . . . Wherever there is knowledge, wherever there is virtue, wherever there is beauty, he will find a home."[58]

Walt Whitman

If Ralph Waldo Emerson was the high priest of the literary religion, and Henry Thoreau its political philosopher, then Walt Whitman was its poet-hero. Described as a moody and untidy young man, Whitman first gained notice as an editor for New York's *Brooklyn Eagle* in 1848. He was generally interested in the cause of the oppressed, but seems to have identified himself most closely with the cause of temperance. When he denounced the Northern Democrats for refusing to face the slavery issue, he was dismissed from the paper. He thereafter adopted the clothing and manner of a workman and for a time made a living as an independent building contractor. He seems to have undergone a metamorphosis after reading some of Emerson's works. John Taylor Trowbridge, Whitman's friend and himself an author of books for young boys, reported, "All that had lain smoldering so long within him, waiting to be fired, rushed into flame at the touch of those electric words." Whitman himself recorded that Emerson's work "brought me to a boil."[59]

In 1855, Whitman completed *Leaves of Grass*, a quarto volume expensively bound in green leather with gilt titles. It contained 12 poems and a photograph of the author. The initial response to the volume was uniformly hostile among the critics. The *Boston Intelligencer* called it "a heterogeneous mass of bombast, egotism, vulgarity and nonsense." Most booksellers refused to carry the work, considering it indecent. Thoreau found some of the poems disagreeable and too sensual, but noted that "a man might read what a woman could not" without harm. However, Whitman sent a copy to Emerson who somewhat cautiously gave it a positive response in a return letter to the author. Whitman used Emerson's comments to promote the work, and in the next year brought out an enlarged edition containing 32 poems.[60]

Meanwhile, the author made no secret of his view of the state of American literature: "formulas, glosses, blanks, minutiae. There is not a single History of the World, there is not one of America, or of the organic compacts of the States, or of Washington, or of Jefferson, nor of Language, nor any dictionary of the English language. There is no great author; every one has demeaned himself to some etiquette or some impotence." Whitman also attacked many of the characteristics of contemporary American life. "The churches are one vast lie; the people do not believe them. . . . [They do] the most ridiculous things . . . no one behaving, dressing, writing, talking, loving, out of any natural or manly tastes of his own, but each one looking cautiously to see how the rest behave, dress, write, talk, [or] love." In the five years between its first edition and the Civil War, Whitman expanded *Leaves of Grass* again to include 123 poems. He continued to supplement and rearrange these for decades thereafter, "becoming its editor and custodian as though it had its own independent life."[61]

Nathaniel Hawthorne

A graduate of Bowdoin College, Nathaniel Hawthorne seems to have decided to be a writer from the first. Although he spent some time at Brook Farm, Hawthorne was wary of the transcendentalists with their bright outlook for the development of man. His forte was the darker side of the human being and the deep recesses of the Puritan conscience: ignorance, vanity, ego, decadence, corruption, veniality, and vulgarity. He "dissected the conduct of the great and good, the high and respectable; with unerring accuracy he portrayed the pillars of society as executioners of unjust causes."[62] He mined the history of New England for his subject matter. Under the pseudonym of Peter Parley, Hawthorne's short stories began to appear in the *American Magazine of Entertaining and Useful Knowledge*, for which he served as an editor. In addition to adult literature he wrote several children's stories. His first major literary success was *Twice Told Tales*, a collection of short stories. Not surprisingly, Edgar Allan Poe praised it, but many other critics found it dismal, dispiriting, and somewhat gruesome.

Convinced that most American literature ran too close to the British style, Hawthorne devoted himself to a uniquely symbolic and allegorical form. *The Scarlet Letter*, published in 1850, quickly became familiar to American readers, and its author was proclaimed a literary giant by his peers. The intolerance of 17th-century Puritans was the focus of his plot. Social lapses were often punished by condemning the offender to a pitiless form of public scrutiny such as the "A" on Hester Prynne's dress that attested to her adultery. Similar punishments were common for soldiers in the Army who were often forced to stand before their comrades with crude signs hung about their necks declaring them a "Thief," "Deserter," or "Drunkard."

In 1851 and 1852, respectively, Hawthorne wrote *The House of Seven Gables*, which sold well, and *The Blithedale Romance*. The latter was a study of failed utopian efforts to improve society and was possibly based on the failure of Brook Farm. Hawthorne managed to make a financial success of his writing, but he was troubled by the greater success of sentimental novels that were outselling his own work. "Is American now given over to a damned mob of scribbling women?" he asked his publisher.[63] Hawthorne's writing was good and his attack on Puritan asceticism was well received by the literary community. But his persistent dark emphasis on guilt and sorrow ran counter to the popular tastes and present religious sentiments of many Americans at mid-century. Hawthorne served as the U.S. Consul at Liverpool, England, for four years and traveled throughout Europe. He was particularly impressed by Rome, which served as the setting for his final novel, *The Marble Faun*. His final years were troubled by financial constraints brought on by the Civil War. He died in 1864 at the age of 60.

Antislavery Literature

The abolition of race-based slavery became a theme for novels early in the antebellum period, but it found little popularity beyond those dedicated to the antislavery movement until the 1850s. In 1836, Richard Hildreth, a Massachusetts jurist and historian, published the first of the antislavery novels called *The Slave, or, Memoirs of Archy Moore*. The work was immensely popular in New England, and it was reprinted in the decade before the Civil War under a number of titles. Although it did much to further the cause of abolition, Hildreth's work appeared too early in the development of the antislavery movement to have the effect of later works. However, when Harriet Beecher Stowe published *Uncle Tom's Cabin* in 1852, the book sold 300,000 copies in America and Britain in one year.

Stowe's work was one of total fiction, but it stressed the evils of slavery and presented a picture of total brutality. The author had no personal knowledge of slavery, but her brother, Edward Beecher, was an antislavery activist. The factual basis for the story was found in Theodore D. Weld's radical abolitionist tract titled *Slavery as It Is: The Testimony of a Thousand Witnesses,* which was published in 1839. *Uncle Tom's Cabin* was immensely more effective in preaching the antislavery message in the form of a novel than the earlier tract had ever dreamed of being. The book was made into an equally popular play, which found audiences well into the end of the century.[64]

Stowe provided two divergent accounts of the origins of her own book, but it seems quite certain that the death of Uncle Tom was written first and the surrounding details of Little Eva and other characters were added at a later date. The character of Eliza Harris, who crossed the icy Ohio with her baby in her arms, seems to have been based on the experiences of an actual person, and Stowe seems to have been made familiar with the story through her brother. She wrote in the preface of the 1852 edition:

> The object of these sketches is to awaken sympathy and feeling for the African race, as they exist among us; to show their wrongs and sorrows, under a system so necessarily cruel and unjust all to defeat and do away the good effects of all that can be attempted for them, by their best friends, under it. In doing this, the author can sincerely disclaim an invidious feeling towards those individuals who, often without any fault of their own, are involved in the trials and embarrassments of the legal relations of slavery.[65]

The South considered *Uncle Tom's Cabin* a slander and regarded it as abolitionist propaganda. A Southern women, familiar with slavery and slaves, wrote that she could not read a book so filled with distortions as it was "too sickening" to think that any man would send "his little son to beat a human being tied to a tree." The same women goes on to suggest, using other literary references, that Stowe's work portrays as much fiction as Squeers beating Smike in Dickens's *Nicholas Nickleby* or the gouging of the Gloucester's eyes in Shakespeare's *King Lear.* "How delightfully pharisaic a feeling it must be, to rise up superior and fancy [to] we [who] are so degraded as to defend and like to live with such degraded creatures around us . . . as Legree."[66]

Nonetheless, amicably disposed Northerners found the passages describing the murderous brutality of Simon Legree indicative of the typical behavior of Southern slave owners. A letter to the editor of *Frederick Douglass' Paper* wrote, "What a Book! It is, in its line, a wonder of wonders. . . . My nonresistance is of the Douglass, Parker, and Phillips school. I believe, as you do, that it is not light the slaveholder wants, but fire, and he ought to have it. I do not advocate revenge, but simply, resistance to tyrants, if need be, to the death." Another writer, this time to the editor of *The National Era*, said, "It was a noble effort—it is a splendid success. The God of Freedom inspired the thought." The editor of the *New York Independent* pronounced the book, "The Greatest Book of its Kind ever issued from the American Press." Other papers, almost exclusively in the North, carried similar sentiments. In answer to her critics, Stowe produced *A Key to Uncle Tom's Cabin* in 1853 and, in 1856, followed with a sequel to the original work, *Dred: A Tale of the Great Dismal Swamp*, which almost immediately appeared as a stage play in the New York theaters.[67]

The significance of these stories, as with many of the attacks on the institution of slavery, lay in their ability to dramatize and emotionalize the issue. Writing and speech making on the subject of slavery, in particular—and of the Southern culture, in general—was becoming increasingly stereotypical, and the stereotypes, even when presented in novels, were taking on a reality in the minds of the people.

Hinton Rowan Helper was born and educated in North Carolina. In 1850, he was attracted to the gold fields of California where he remained for three years. Here his observations led him to a firm belief in the value of free labor. In 1855, he wrote a book about his California experiences, *The Land of Gold,* initially muting his strong criticisms of slavery because of the fears of his publishers for their personal safety. In the following year, he moved to New York and wrote *The Impending Crisis of the South: How to Meet It,* an economic discourse in behalf of the nonslaveholding whites of the South.

The Impending Crisis contrasted the economic condition of the slave states and the free states, and it attributed the backwardness of the South and the impoverishment of Southern white labor to the competition of raced-based slavery. Although he showed no consideration for the plight of the Negro, Helper attacked the owners of a large number of slaves using the threat of a slave uprising to destroy the slave labor system from within. "Would you be instrumental in bringing upon yourselves, your wives, and our children, a fate too horrible to contemplate?" Helper's 11-step program to abolish slavery formalized a growing feeling that Southern economic and social welfare was being sacrificed on the altar of continued plantation slavery.

The Impending Crisis created a greater sensation than *Uncle Tom's Cabin,* and it has been described as a contributing cause of the Civil War. Men were hanged for merely possessing a copy of the book in some areas of the South. The book was furiously attacked in the South, and a good deal of effort and propaganda was put into casting doubts on Helper's integrity. In the North, it was a great success. One hundred thousand copies where printed and distributed for the Republican campaign of 1860. An appreciative Abraham Lincoln appointed Helper as American consul in Buenos Aires in 1861, a position he kept until 1866.

Poets

A contemporary observer of the antebellum scene noted that "we have no national school of poetry. . . . We've neither a legendary past nor a poetic present." This observation may help to explain America's fascination with stories of the Revolution like Cooper's, with tales of medieval times like Scott's, or even with whimsical anecdotes of the New York Dutch like Irving's. But George Templeton Strong, who wrote the comment, was clearly mistaken. The antebellum period began the golden age of American poets, which, although interrupted by war, continued throughout the 19th century. An anthology of American poems published in 1842 sold over 300,000 copies at $3 a copy.[68] It has been pointed out that William Cullen Bryant was the period's newspaper editor-poet, John Greenleaf Whittier its abolitionist-poet, Oliver Wendell Holmes its doctor-poet, James Russell Lowell its gentleman-poet, and Henry Wadsworth Longfellow its professor-poet. Each was a poet and something else, but it was Longfellow who became the great popular poet of the century.[69]

William Cullen Bryant began life as a lawyer, but in 1814 he published "The Yellow Violet," which combined a praise of nature with a moral principle, thereby setting the mode of American poetry for the century. One year later he wrote "Thanatopis" and "To a Waterfowl." He started his life as an aggressive Federalist, became the editor of the *New York Evening Post*, turned Democrat, and ended as an antislavery Republican. Much of Bryant's work exhibited strains of the traditional Puritan ethic: propriety in one's private life, devotion to the task at hand, a deep interest in public affairs, and a faith in the American citizen. Many of his poems engaged the concept of unmourned death, a 19th-century preoccupation. Both the devoted Christian and the transcendentalist could read his work with pleasure.[70]

Of all the literary figures of the time, John Greenleaf Whittier, the son of Quaker parents, was the one most closely identified with antislavery. Even William Lloyd Garrison, premiere antislavery activist and newspaper editor, took note of him in *The Liberator*. In the late 1820s, Whittier worked feverishly for several abolitionist newspapers, finally becoming editor of the prestigious *New England Weekly Review*. His early works— *New England Legends in Prose and Verse* and *Justice and Expedience*—urged immediate emancipation for all blacks. In 1846, Whittier published *Voices of Freedom*, a book of antislavery poems. He served as a speaker and lecturer for the cause and supported the rising Republican Party in the 1850s. His work praised nature and looked to the pleasure of common things. A contemporary described him as "a breath of air from a world of purity and beneficence." Although many of his verses have become mere historic curiosities with the passing of slavery, his rhymes caught the manners and morals of the common people. His famous poem "Barbara Frietchie" was written during the war.[71]

The works of Oliver Wendell Holmes and James Russell Lowell were almost indistinguishable to the casual reader. Both were Harvard graduates, but it was Lowell who became the leader of their literary circle called the Fireside or Schoolroom Poets. This group included Whittier, Holmes, Longfellow, and sometimes Emerson. Lowell's work was blatantly moralistic, making him seem conservative by modern standards, but, being an ardent abolitionist and temperance advocate, he was hardly considered so in his own time. His poem, "The Present Crisis," was written in 1844, and it made a deep impression on Northern audiences. Four years later, Lowell published four volumes: *Poems, Fable for Critics, The Biglow Papers*, and the *Vision of Sir Launfal*. Of these, only *The Biglow Papers* was political. The *Vision of Sir Launfal*, with its emphasis on the value of heartfelt charity, was America's contribution to the Arthurian Holy Grail legend. In 1857, Lowell became editor of the *Atlantic Monthly* magazine, and during the war he helped edit the *North American Review*.

Holmes left Boston after Harvard to study medicine in Paris, and he returned to find that the aging frigate *Constitution* was rotting in its mooring. Energized by a report that the heroic ship from the War of 1812 was to be demolished, he penned the immortal poem "Old Ironsides" that appeared in the *Boston Daily Advertiser* in 1830. The poem helped to save the vessel from destruction and prompted its preservation. It quickly became the subject of classroom recitation everywhere. One of Holmes's most famous poems was "The Chambered Nautalis," which drew an analogy between the ever-expanding shell of the creature and the need for constant spiritual growth. His work in the decades after the Civil War made his reputation as a poet extraordinary.[72]

Henry Wadsworth Longfellow was a born storyteller, producing romantic tales of the far away and long ago much like the other successful authors of the period. He was "perfectly democratic" in his poetry, and his work needed little scrutiny to make its point.[73] Longfellow held the chair of literature at Harvard. His most popular poems among those available during the period were "The Village Blacksmith," "The Song of Hiawatha," "The Wreck of the Hesperus," and "The Courtship of Miles Standish." When published in 1855, "The Song of Hiawatha" sold 50,000 copies in five months at $1 a copy. "The Midnight Ride of Paul Revere," appeared in Longfellow's *Tales of the Wayside Inn*. Written in 1860, this largely inaccurate and romanticized version of Revolutionary history became popular during the Civil War, but it ignored many of the facts of the encounter at Lexington in 1775, including the capture of Revere and the contributions of other alarm riders. The poem became the subject of classroom recitations and American history lessons into the 20th century. For generations of Americans, Longfellow was their poet, and he lived for three-quarters of a century, thereby fixing his place above all the others in the minds of most Americans.

Ironically, though little poetry of value was produced below the Mason-Dixon line at this time, Southern life served as the inspiration for some of the most original and endearing of American lyrics. Frances Scott Key's "The Star-Spangled Banner" is undoubtedly the most famous. The earliest Southern poet considered to be of any merit is William Crafts (1787–1826), who celebrated the sporting passion of his native Charleston in "The Raciad" and later penned "Sullivan's Island." William Grayson (1788–1863) authored several volumes, but only "The Hireling and the Slave" (1856) gained any notice because it purported to show the superior condition of the unpaid slave to the paid hireling.

Naturalists

The same advances in the printing process that made illustrated magazines possible facilitated the publication of books illustrating the flora and fauna of America. Alexander Wilson of Philadelphia was one of the great naturalists of the early 19th century, and he was the first to paint and describe the birds of America for publication. An immigrant, Wilson had been impressed by the richly colored birds of North America that were so different from those of his native Scotland. Strongly influenced by the naturalist William Bartram, Wilson toiled over his drawings of American birds. When he died in 1813, he had finished seven illustrated volumes called *American Ornithology*. During the two decades after his death, Wilson's friends and admirers, using his outlines and notes, added six more volumes to the original set.

Bartram's Botanical Gardens in southeastern Pennsylvania were known to naturalists all over Europe for their collection of flora, and naturalists, sketch-artists, and illuminators flocked there to do their work. Bartram, like his father John who had begun the collection on a 45-acre site on the Schuylkill River, had a strong sense for nature. Even the rattlesnake had a certain "magnanimity" for William "as animals in general for him were benevolent and peaceful, and he felt life in trees and plants." William Bartrum embodied these feelings in his own illustrated work called *Travels*, which describes the natural beauty of the South, his love of natural things, and his ardent belief in the natural goodness of man. The book was said to have positively influenced a number of romantic poets and authors including William Wordsworth and Samuel Coleridge.[74]

Meanwhile, a young man born in the West Indies had arrived in the United States in 1803. Although John James Audubon was not the first to draw and paint the birds of America, for the next half century he was the nation's dominant wildlife artist. He had been born on a Haitian plantation, the son of a French officer and his island mistress. Although island-born, Audubon lived a large part of his early years under the tutelage of his stepmother at a country house near Nantes in France. Here he developed a love of natural beauty and a talent for drawing, illustrating, and painting. He first focused on the birds of France, but on his father's farm at Mill Grove, Pennsylvania, he began to draw American birds, watching them closely and capturing their characteristic stances, habits, and ways of flying. He also conducted a good deal of scientific research, conducting the first bird-banding in North America, and discovering that many bird species returned to the same nesting sites each year.

After returning to France for about a year, Audubon sought out a means by which he could make a living from his work. He moved with his wife, Lucy, to the French colony at Louisville, Kentucky, and floated down the Mississippi River with an assistant, living hand-to-mouth while his wife served as a tutor to a wealthy plantation family. During this time, Audubon became totally familiar with the life of the river and its inhabitants, both animal and human. From Kentucky to the Gulf of Mexico, the region proved an ornithological paradise with egrets, herons, bitterns, warblers, and other birds. Moreover, the valley was teeming with other objects of interest to the naturalist. In later years, he traveled to such contrasting environments as Labrador and Florida, shared the details of American frontier wildlife with Meriwether Lewis and William Clark, and hunted with an aged Daniel Boone in the forests of Kentucky, Tennessee, and North Carolina.

Audubon passed 20 years on the frontier before he set out for England with more than 400 drawings ready for the engraver. *Birds of America* was first published in 1826 in Edinburgh, Scotland, and later in London. Audubon's ability to draw life-sized and highly dramatic bird and animal portraits hit just the right note for the romantics of the period, and his illustrations were an immediate financial success. He then collaborated with Scottish ornithologist and president of the Royal College of Surgeons, William MacGillivray, on the *Ornithological Biographies*, the life history of each of the bird species in the work. In 1843, he made a trip to the American West to research his final work on mammals, *Viviparous Quadrupeds of North America*. He wrote of the trip, "I left home . . . accompanied by my son, Victor. I left all well, and I trust in God for the privilege and happiness of rejoining them all sometime next autumn, when I hope to return from the Yellowstone River, an expedition taken solely for the sake of our work on the quadrupeds of North America. . . . It was no desire of glory which led me into this exile. I wished only to enjoy nature." The completed work contained 150 press-printed, hand-watercolored plates that sold in 30 parts of five plates each by subscription. Each part brought $10; or $300 for the entire work. A single plate today can fetch more than $30,000. Although Audubon died in senility in 1851 at the age of 65, his two sons continued his work through the rest of the century.[75]

Historians

During the antebellum period, there appeared an incredible dedication among amateur historians and antiquarians to gathering the papers, folklore, and objects of colonial and revolutionary life that seemed to be slipping away in a newly industrialized America. In colleges, libraries, state archives, and private collections, there was preserved the work of a thousand hands. Among these was George Tucker of Virginia who produced a Southern gentleman's history of the Old Dominion; Timothy Smith, who did the same for Mississippi; and Timothy Wight, who produced four massive volumes of historical observations concerning New York and New England. Between 1818 and 1865, more than 400 titles were published on the history of Illinois alone.

The growing interest in former times among amateurs was usurped by a cadre of professional writers of history dedicated to the laborious and scientific style of historical writing then popular in Germany. A remarkable number of the historians who achieved lasting reputations in the field were connected with Harvard University. The massive *Life of George Washington* and the Spanish histories assembled by Washington Irving, who was not a Harvard man, have already been mentioned. However, Irving's biography of Washington came late in the antebellum period (1855), and other historians of note had already been at work on similar projects.

However, it is clear that many of the Harvard historians harbored moralistic, anti-Catholic, anti–Native American, and pro-Protestant prejudices in their writings that have gone largely uncorrected in many 20th-century textbooks. All were well-to-do men of letters who were largely unable to deal with American history without including the backdrop of Spain, Britain, or France. Beyond the struggle for independence, America, in isolation from European history, seemingly had too few significant experiences in its short existence around which these men might pull their histories together as literature. The coming cataclysm of the Civil War would resolve this problem and lead to the publication of thousands of historical works concerning the details of the conflict. The separate opinions of the antebellum historians, given form by a common regard for recording the colonial history of America as they thought it should be, were also reflective of the popular literature and poetry of the day. Nonetheless, the group's reporting of factual events was detailed and their labor exhaustive. Their works, taken collectively, remain a foundation for all future study in this area.

Harvard graduate William Hickling Prescott was one of the first to achieve literary success by writing history. Taking his style from European historians like Edward Gibbon (*The Decline and Fall of the Roman Empire*), Prescott amassed a monumental pile of printed material and documents from which he fashioned the three volumes known as the *History of*

Ferdinand and Isabella (1838). This was an immediate success on both sides of the Atlantic, and it was followed by *Conquest of Mexico* (1843) and *Conquest of Peru* (1847). However, Prescott considered the production of histories a form of literary entertainment for the reader, not the stuff of serious scientific research.

George Bancroft followed his graduation from Harvard with a stay at the University of Göttingen, where he learned to write history in the German style by including an intensive and systematic analysis of all the available data. He began to distribute his 10-volume *History of the United States* in annual installments in 1834. From the founding of the colonies to the adoption of the Constitution, Bancroft wove his way through long and arduous researches somewhat prejudiced by his own New England origins and Democratic politics. His work portrays early America as an unblemished utopia to which the nation needed to return.

At approximately the same time, Richard Hildreth, the Massachusetts jurist and antislavery novelist, produced a six-volume work detailing American history from the Federalist point of view. His first volume appeared in 1849, but with the final volume of the work, completed in 1852, it spanned the period from the Age of Discovery to the Missouri Compromise of 1851. Hildreth was an abolitionist and temperance crusader, and his desire for reform bled through in his historical writing, costing him some readership. He had first come to attention as an author by writing antislavery tracts. His later work, *Despotism in America* (1854), described the sociological and psychological effects of slavery on American history. Both of his American histories contained some inaccuracies based in their author's politics, but they represented a great treasure of data concerning the social evolution of America.

Foremost in the field of precise historical scholarship were Jared Sparks and Peter Force. Sparks, president of Harvard and editor of the *North American Review*, produced a 12-volume compilation of the *Diplomatic Correspondence of the American Revolution* in 1830. He followed this with 12 volumes of the *Writings of George Washington* (1837), and 10 volumes of the *Works of Benjamin Franklin* (1840). In 1853, he produced a four-volume compilation of important letters between prominent Americans and George Washington known as *The Correspondence of the American Revolution*. These massive collections are still used for historical research today. In his editing, Sparks corrected the 18th-century grammar and spelling of the documents he researched to reflect the new American standards being developed by men like Noah Webster. Unlike Force, Sparks was more than a mere collector. The documents and letters he compiled were always accompanied by his commentary on their value and meaning.

Peter Force was a publisher, politician, and editor of *The National Journal*. Together with Matthew St. Clair Clarke, the secretary of Congress in 1833, Force undertook the task of compiling an extensive library of American

documents with the financial support of the Federal government and succeeded in publishing 20 volumes before loosing his grant of $22,500 per
800-page text. The first volume of his monumental work, *Documentary
History of the American Revolution*, appeared in 1837. By this time, Clarke
had retired from the project after calculating that the research cost to himself and Force was $11,000 per volume. Having lost his financing, Force
nonetheless continued the work for three decades. His research was conducted in the best traditions of scientific historical scholarship. Unlike
Sparks, who was working on similar projects at the time, Force offered
no interpretation of his collection and was thereby able to collect an incredible mass of paperwork. His collection remained unhampered by the
inclusion of any political editorials or romantic intrigues to tempt the
palates of contemporary audiences.

In 1867, the entire Peter Force Library (more than 22,000 unbound volumes, 40,000 pamphlets, and 129 bound works) was purchased by the
Library of Congress for $100,000. The collection began chronologically
with Spanish documents written in the late 15th century (1490), but the
majority of the documents date from 1750 to the end of the Revolution.
Represented herein were 18th-century American newspapers, imprints,
pamphlets, manuscripts, maps, atlases, official reports, private papers, and
colonial correspondence. Taken together, they are today known as the
American Archives. So massive was Force's work that some parts of it have
yet to be indexed.

Few people at the time would have chosen Benson J. Lossing from
among a list of eminent American historians, yet his dedication to capturing the words and memories of the last survivors of the American
Revolution before they faded away led him to the publication of a large
two-volume work known as the *Pictorial Field-book of the American Revolution* (1851). Beginning in 1847, Lossing traveled more than 8,000 miles
through the original 13 colonies making sketches of historic places and
relics from the Revolution and jotted down the reminiscences of the war
taken from those whom he stumbled upon during his visits. Interspersed
in his own narrative of the Revolution were the accounts of these eye-
witnesses to history and tales of his own travels. Although his interviews
were based on hearsay and anecdote and done in a random rather than a
systematic manner, Lossing made a record of unmatched scope and
variety that most contemporary readers found interesting.

Although he was personally excited by American history, Lossing's
career as a woodblock engraver, and the New York engraving company
that he founded, took up most of his time. Although he did much of his
research in his spare time, Lossing was no neophyte historian. He had
experienced modest success as both a writer and an illustrator before
undertaking his monumental task. In 1840, he had published and illustrated the *Outline History of the Fine Arts* and had earned some literary

distinction with a series of short illustrated paperbacks called *Seventeen Hundred and Seventy-Six*. Moreover, Lossing was one of the first historians to grasp the benefits to the reader of matching fresh and authentic illustrations with his text, and he included 1,100 woodcut engravings, original pen and pencil drawings, and watercolors with his 700,000-word text.

Lossing's *Field-book* began appearing in monthly paperback installments in July 1850. Thirty were printed while the enormous two-volume edition of almost 1,200 pages was being prepared. This was released in two parts in 1851 and 1852, respectively. These works sold well among history buffs, but academic historians were critical of Lossing's journalistic approach to history, which they thought had "sacrificed academic standards on the altar of popularity." Nonetheless, Lossing had measured the pulse of the public correctly. Most readers found the stiff academic style of the period frustrating and boring, whereas Lossing's histories were interesting and stimulating. Possibly for this reason Lossing found that his work was in great demand. His subsequent illustrated articles were published by *Harper's Magazine*, almost one every month throughout the 1850s, and the publication of his *Pictorial Field-book of the War of 1812* (1868) was only delayed in its release by the outbreak of the Civil War. He later published a three-volume *Field-book of the Civil War* (1868) based on his studies of both Confederate and Federal war records. All of Lossing's work was done with a fervor that matched his love of history. By 1890, he had written and published more than 40 books and hundreds of magazine articles. His purpose throughout was "to lure readers into history."[76]

Much like Lossing, Francis Parkman actively sought out the scenes of his histories by camping, hiking, and exploring America's rivers and mountains in an attempt to bring the ethic of Nature into his writing. After graduating Harvard with a degree in law, Parkman set out in 1846 to gather firsthand information about the American Indian. The results of his travels can be seen in the vivid and authentic-sounding descriptions of Native Americans included in *France in the New World*, *The California and Oregon Trail*, or *The History of the Conspiracy of Pontiac*. All of these were published between 1849 and 1851. His post–Civil War works, including seven volumes written between 1865 and 1892, left an indelible stamp on all subsequent writing about the period of the wars for control of North America between France and England. Parkman's research was prodigious, and very few errors or omissions have been detected by subsequent researchers. Moreover, his easy narrative style, popular with antebellum readers, failed to attract negative criticism from the academic historians.

Parkman visited French-speaking Canada and the Adirondack region of New York to do much of his research, and he actually traveled the Oregon Trail in 1845. However, for his own *Conspiracy of Pontiac*, Parkman drew heavily on the earlier work of Alexander Henry, a New Jersey adventurer and author of *Travels and Adventures in Canada*. Henry's work was a classic tale of the Canadian fur trade that recalled the days of the French and Indian War. Because he had traveled the northern forests and toiled up the rivers in his own canoe, Henry understood the life of the French coureurs de bois and native trappers. Thoreau called Henry's book a "classic among books of American travel . . . that read like the argument to a great poem, on the primitive state of the country and its inhabitants."[77]

Newspapers

There were millions of newspaper subscribers in the country before the Civil War.[78] European visitors to Brooklyn, New York, were amazed that the English speaking population of the town of about 300,000 supported a newspaper circulation of 70,000, about one paper for each family. Newspapers gained influence steadily during the first half of the 19th century as education spread the power of reading across the population. Alex De Tocqueville noted in 1831 that Americans had settled the continent with the Bible, the ax, and the newspaper. Many news sheets had their foundation in the colonial press, but new papers were constantly being founded. The weekly *Philadelphia Register and National Recorder* appeared as early as 1819, and the *Springfield Republican* was founded in Massachusetts in 1824. In 1825, the *Boston Traveler* was founded as a daily, and in 1833 *The Sun* was founded as a penny daily in New York. In 1834, the *New Yorker Staats Zeitung* was founded as a German-language weekly. James Gordon Bennett launched *The New York Herald* in 1835, and the *Philadelphia Public Ledger*, the *Blade* of Toledo, Ohio, and the German-language *Volksblatt*, all daily newspapers, began publication in 1836. In 1837, the *Connecticut Courant*, the country's oldest weekly (begun in 1764), became *The Hartford Daily Courant*. In the 1840s and 1850s, the *Boston Herald*, the *Chicago Tribune*, the *Chicago Times*, the *New York Times*, and the *Sacramento California Union* were all founded as daily news sheets.

Although *The Baltimore Sun* and *The New Orleans Picayune* were prestigious dailies, Southern papers were slower to develop than those in other parts of the country. They were almost completely dependent on Northern sources for type, presses, and newsprint—a weakness that was sorely felt during the Civil War. Nonetheless, an incredibly large number of local publications appeared as citizens came to favor the newspaper as an individualized form of communication.

Newspapers printed speeches in their entirety within a few days of their being given. Political arguments, essays, letters to the editor, and discussions among dedicated readers—both genuine and planted for effect—flowed in the wake of every issue. Persons read alone, or in small groups, with the leisure to reread and analyze what was printed. Many extraordinary pieces of literature first appeared in the press. Many of Dickens's

The ability of newspapers to form opinions in the United States during the 19th century is remarkable. People read and reread their newspapers, and those who could not read had the paper read to them by willing citizens. Newspapers sparked public debates, served as outlets for dissatisfaction, and were used to build consensus.

works and Stowe's *Uncle Tom's Cabin* first appeared in newsprint as serials. In 1823, *The Troy Sentinel* of New York printed an anonymous Christmas poem by a learned biblical author, Clement Clarke Moore, titled "A Visit from St. Nicholas," which later became better known as a book called *'Twas the Night Before Christmas*. However, in the estimation of the publishers, the most important articles to be printed were the official proceedings taking place in Washington, D.C., often with biting editorial preambles. Even routine congressional debates were reported in painstaking detail.

The power of the press to influence a wider audience than that which could be assembled at any one place and time was not to be underestimated. Some papers tried to remain neutral, but others sought out political alliances either because of the agenda of the editors, or, more commonly, in order to attract a lucrative trade in political advertising and public printing. Neutrality on any topic of public interest often doomed a newspaper to failure. At times, the papers were so full of scandal and untruth, that their publishers were prosecuted for libel; and more than one duel was fought over the comments made in the press.

The papers that sprang to the side of Andrew Jackson in his 1828 presidential campaign—and they were too numerous to be counted—bitterly assailed the administration of John Quincy Adams. In this way, they became an organ of the political party; and, in an era of slow-moving news and uncorroborated sources, they became an effective tool for convincing the party voter of the universal appeal of its candidate or position.

One of the earliest influential newspapers in the South was *The Courier*. Begun in Charleston, South Carolina, in 1803, it quickly became one of the most influential and popular of Southern papers. Its editors refused to give in to public pressure during the tariff nullification and secession crises, reporting only the activities of the conventions without adding any editorial support for their positions. As early as 1828, Robert B. Rhett used his Charleston-based newspaper, *The Mercury*, to urge resistance to the unrestrained rule of the Federal government. Rhett pleaded with his readers for the Southern states to secede en masse in defense of states' rights and Southern culture. *The Mercury* continued to plead the case of disunion right up to the eve of the Civil War.

The Richmond Whig was a leader when it came to strong opposition to disunion. *The New Orleans Crescent* opposed any form of violence. *The Memphis Eagle* portrayed peaceful secession as an absurd pipe dream. Many papers, including *The Natchez Courier, The Nashville Banner* and *The New Orleans Bulletin*, reminded the South of its intense reliance upon the North and warned that before any drastic measures be taken, the South had best make itself independent first.

Other papers foresaw and accepted the inevitable conflict. *DeBow's Review*, a monthly commercial publication located in New Orleans, urged the South to diversify its economy and build railroads, factories, and canals and thereby free itself from any dependence on the North. By mid-century, *DeBow's* was increasingly seen as a vehicle for secessionist propaganda. The *Hornet's Nest* of Charlotte, North Carolina, published a list of Northern businesses that did not support the South's position and urged other editors to print the list in their publications, a counsel that

The Southern Confederacy, one of the most vehement of secessionist papers, applauded.

The secession press was most intense in South Carolina and Mississippi. Besides the Charleston *Mercury*, several other newspapers actively stressed Southern independence. Some, like *The Natchez Free Trader*, plainly recommended secession as the only recourse for Southern grievances. Southern nationalism was hawked by the respected *Southern Literary Messenger*, once edited by Edgar Allan Poe; and even the *Southern Quarterly Review* was pleading the cause of disunion. Virginian papers tended to be less unanimous in these opinions. Yet the *Richmond South*, edited by Roger A. Pryor, and its sister paper, the *Enquirer*, edited by Henry A. Wise, both sported prominent secessionist themes. The Richmond *Examiner* and the *Dispatch*—once neutral and conservative—threw all their powers, and their large circulation, into the cause of secession by 1860.

Although there were many local news sheets, most people looked to illustrated newspapers such as *Leslie's* or *Harper's*. A number of American engravers made a living during the early antebellum period by circulating prints of early artworks. These sold well, and many antebellum inns and parlors were decorated with the likenesses of Washington, Hamilton, Jefferson, or Jackson. Alexander Anderson was an American woodblock and copper engraver who produved his earliest work for mass publication near the end of the 18th century. Anderson was forced to improvise his own tools and methods, even hiring a blacksmith to make thin sheets from copper pennies for his first engravings. His first financially successful copper plate engraving was of American naval hero John Paul Jones.[79]

New York publisher Frank Leslie produced amazing moving woodcut illustrations for his *Illustrated Newspaper*. The combination of stark black-on-white graphics and terse prose to interpret ongoing news events was a new concept in the American newspaper business that was quickly adopted by other news agencies. Leslie, whose true name was Henry Carter, had emigrated from Britain in 1848. There he had worked as an engraver for the *Illustrated London News*, which was the first newspaper to employ graphics. In London, Leslie learned the processes for turning pencil sketches into woodcut engravings that could be transferred to newsprint economically. In 1852, P.T. Barnum, the famed American showman, developed a process by which the sketch was divided into several pieces to be engraved on as many blocks by individual engravers and carefully assembled into a single printing surface.[80] Barnum hired Leslie as a supervising engraver for the short-lived *Illustrated News*.

Leaving Barnum, by 1854, Leslie had set up his own organization and published the first issue of *Frank Leslie's Ladies' Gazette of Paris, London, and New York*, one of the first illustrated fashion magazines in America. The *Illustrated Newspaper* quickly followed in 1855. Leslie employed more than

130 engraving and print artists as well as a substantial number of roving sketch artists. He introduced a number of different papers to American readers: the *Illustrated Zeitung*, a German-language edition aimed at the Germanic immigrant population of the North; the *Budget of Fun*, a whimsical publication featuring cheap fiction; the *Ten Cent Monthly*; the *Lady's Illustrated Almanac*; and the *Lady's Magazine and Gazette of Fashion*. All of these bore his name, beginning their titles with "Frank Leslie's."

In a day when a partisan press was the rule, *Leslie's* stood apart. Except for tolerating an anti-Irish sentiment and portraying Negroes in a stereotypical and condescending manner, *Leslie's* condoned little that was political. Within four years of Leslie's first publication, two independent graphic newsweeklies were launched in competition with his newspaper empire: *Harper's Weekly* and the *New York Illustrated News*. Fletcher Harper, the well-financed publisher from Harper and Brothers, actively tried to recruit Leslie's artists and engravers and aggressively tried to exceed Leslie's circulation. Leslie provided poor and erratic pay for his artists, many of whom he lost to competitors. By the opening of the Civil War, the two newspapers were within 10,000 copies of one another, with the *New York Illustrated News* a distant third.

Two of the best sketch artists of the period were the brothers William and Alfred Waud. Ironically, each served with a different paper: William working for *Leslie's* and Alfred for *Harper's*. William proved particularly adept at ingratiating himself with the social elite of South Carolina during the secession crisis. Because of the paper's uncommitted stance, wherever Waud traveled, he found individuals to be cooperative and helpful. Leslie instructed him to use the utmost care in making his sketches and to avoid giving any indication of political sympathies toward one side or the other. Nonetheless, Waud left *Leslie's* in 1863 to work at Harper's with his brother Alfred and another fine artist Theodore Davis. William Waud's genius and discretion were matched by an army of artists who continued with *Leslie's*, including Eugene Benson, Arthur Lumley, Henry Lovie, C.S. Hall, F.H. Schell, and Edwin Forbes. Forbes, a mere 22 years old, drew so well that readers "scanned the drawings in *Leslie's* for familiar faces."[81]

The quality of the sketches drawn by these artists was not always reproduced faithfully by the engravers, and, in viewing these graphic scenes, great care must be taken. What the artist drew was not so much reproduced as copied. The field artists were often in a hurry to get their work back to the engravers. Unfinished sketches of prominent figures in the scene with backgrounds and lines of soldiers "roughed in" and labeled as "trees here" or "Capitol building here" were often sent off to the engravers to be filled by hands whose eyes had never witnessed the scene. In many cases, this made the illustration more one created by imagination than reality. The results were sometimes unfortunate. Engravings of historic episodes from the American Revolution, popular in the press at the time, were often wildly inaccurate as to the cut and design of uniforms and equipment from the 18th century as engravers dressed Washington's soldiers in Federalist era uniforms.[82]

The South was generally dependent on Northern publishers to print its books and newspapers. In the entire South, there was only one type factory, no facilities for printing maps, and an entire inability to make inexpensive wood-pulp paper. A well-illustrated magazine, such as *Harper's* or *Leslie's*, could not be published in the South. The *Southern Illustrated News* and other papers were often limited to a single sheet of newsprint. These made an attempt to mimic *Harper's* and *Leslie's* with crude engravings but were obviously not comparable to the Northern news outlets.[83] Nonetheless, patriotic Southerners bombarded their newspapers with so much unsolicited poetry on nationalistic themes that some publications began charging to print it. Newspapers like the *Montgomery Daily Advertiser* were particularly successful in creating a wide public identification with the stirring events of the winter of 1860 and the spring of 1861.[84]

AVAILABILITY OF READING MATERIAL

The upper classes were particularly well positioned to enjoy the pleasures of the realm of books and writing and had a greater access to the printed word than the rest of the population. The plantation aristocracy and the upper classes of the North came to share a sense of cultural commonality through their newspapers and popular literature while the rest of the population received its information chiefly from conversation, verbal discussion, and religious exhortation.[85]

What people read prior to the war was dependent on what was available. In the Northern urban centers, there was an almost unlimited amount and variety of reading material, so that what was read in the South becomes more interesting to those researching the prewar period. Southern newspapers printed what was available, including advertisements, political tracts, the transcripts of lectures and speeches, and sordid social gossip that provided "some spicy reading" for the ladies.[86]

Books were read, reread, and loaned between friends and acquaintances. Many women and men turned to instructive reading, spending time reading books on history, geography, painting, foreign language, surveying, and needlework. A number of books were available on etiquette, manners, propriety, the rearing of children, husbandry, and oratory. There was a renewed interest in the Bible and religious tracts, the plays of Shakespeare, and the novels of Dickens, Scott, and Cooper. Secessionist literature like *The Partisan Leader*, written by Judge Nathaniel B. Tucker in 1830, had a plot dedicated to Virginian secession. The novel portrayed a unionized but unhappy Virginia in the evil grasp of Northern masters while a newly seceded and independent Southern nation enjoyed freedom and prosperity. Although the author did not survive to see disunion, his novel became the subject of a popular Southern literary revival.

SOUTHERN LITERARY DEVELOPMENT

The first three decades of the 19th century were marked by a cultural transition in America from the dominance of French classicism to the rule of German-style romanticism. This change can be seen clearly in the evolution of literature during the period. Literary development in the antebellum South was stunted by a social structure whose slavery and feudalistic ideals weighed it down in a time when native literature sought a loftier spirit. As the issues of slave and free states brewed, many Southern writers became mired in answering the charges of the Northern abolitionists and assumed defensive postures or attempted to romanticize the institution of slavery. The largely rural nature of the South and its weak educational system inhibited the opportunity for the exchange of ideas and the intellectual stimulation that abounded in larger population centers. The absence of effective Southern publishing houses left the Southern writer at the mercy of the tastes of Northern editors.

As a Southern consciousness emerged so did magazines written by and for a Southern audience. Periodicals such as *Niles' Weekly Register* (1811), the *Southern Literary Messenger* (1824), the *Review* (1828) and *Literary Gazette* (1834) rose to defend the aristocratic sentiments, chivalric loyalties, and feudal virtues that most Southerners held so dear. Most of these were outgrowths of the few literary communities that did emerge in the South. One center was in Lexington, Kentucky, sometimes referred to as "The Athens of the West." Another crystallized around William Gilmore Simms of Charleston, South Carolina. These circles were mainly composed of lawyers who met to discuss political issues and wandered off into literary discussions. As the antebellum period moved forward, the political rather than aesthetic perspective of their work gained increasing prominence. Unfortunately, professional writers were held in low esteem, especially in the South. Southern magazines, which had to struggle to survive, paid little to contributors. Many Southerners failed to patronize the work of their own sons whether in books or periodicals.

Edgar Allan Poe

The one writer to emerge from the South who attained lasting national recognition was Edgar Allan Poe. Although born in Boston, Poe often referred to himself as a Virginian and, in fact, spent most of his life in Richmond. He defended Southern institutions and traditions, and his writings seldom challenged social issues like slavery or secession. One of Poe's greatest contributions to Southern literature was his short tenure as editor of the *Southern Literary Messenger*. He encouraged the work of Southern writers, and, under his hand, the magazine emerged as one of the most important periodicals of its time. Orphaned in Boston at age three, Poe was adopted by a Richmond merchant, John Allan, and educated in private schools in the South.

Poe was the most renowned poet and short-story writer from the South, and the only Southern writer of the antebellum period to make a lasting national impression. What made Poe different from his regional contemporaries was the fact that he never became an apologist for the Southern way of life. Politically Poe was a Whig, but he rarely let his politics interfere with his writing. Today, Poe is best known for his macabre short stories. In his own time, however, his critical essays attracted a great deal of attention. Poe was committed to raising American literary standards by introducing an objective method of reviewing books rather than employing a solely moral standard. He employed rhetorical methods to evaluate the language and meter of poetry and demanded tight plots, functional details, and limited length in other works. The *Southern Literary Messenger*, the only periodical from the South to attract significant Northern subscriptions and contributions, flourished during Poe's tenure as editor.

Poe's personal life was filled with great frustration and sorrow. He had little patience with editors who were intimidated by his aggressive journalistic style and refused to work with those who did not share his vision. Financially, this translated into only four years of regular income for Poe out of an 18-year career. He lamented that some of his inferior work commanded greater fees than what he considered his best efforts, a frustrating fact of life for any writer. Poe's frequent lapses from sobriety, due both to opiates and alcohol, caused additional problems throughout his career. When his young wife, Virginia Clemm Poe, passed away, the author was devastated and had to be nursed back from total collapse by friends. He longed to publish his own magazine, but his *Broadway Journal* lasted only two months. In fact, Poe was on his way north to pursue backing for another magazine, when he fell ill and died in Baltimore, Maryland.

The Failure of Southern Literature

Horace Greeley, the powerful editor of the *New York Tribune*, refused to recognize Edgar Allan Poe as a Southern writer. Influenced by his disgust with the Southern lifestyle, Greeley recognized only a few Southern literary successes: William Gilmore Simms, the only Southern novelist of merit; Richard Henry Wilde, its sole poet; and Hugh Swinton Legaré, its only essayist. Notwithstanding Poe's success, William Gilmore Simms was perhaps the only other Southern writer of significance during the antebellum period. He was more typical of the mindset of the region and his political beliefs paralleled the South's evolution of thought. Simms was a major player in proslavery and secessionist circles. He collaborated with other authors to produce the *Pro-Slavery Argument* (1852), glorified the chivalric traditions of the South at every opportunity, and offered the idea that Southern government was little different from that of ancient Greece with its equal opportunity for freemen and assured security for its slaves. These positions made him unacceptable to Northern audiences.

Simms produced more than 20 full-length novels and almost 60 short stories, histories, and biographies. His single volume *Geography* earned him very little financially. His historical romances were typical of the romanticism that evolved out of Sir Walter Scott and James Fenimore Cooper and touched on both national and sectional themes. Simms was quite successful with them among Southern audiences. Readers liked his style and appreciated his Southern frontier and borderland scenes. In *Guy Rivers,* Simms set his adventure in the gold fields of Georgia from which the Creek and Cherokee had been recently driven. In *The Yemassee,* he realistically recounted the episodes of the Yemassee [Yamassee] Wars of the colonial period in South Carolina. The mixture of Indians, poor whites, mining-town toughs, gamblers, and hard-hitting heroes elated readers.

Many Southern authors of the 1830s and 1840s deftly avoided the antislavery and secession arguments, but Simms's efforts to establish a flourishing Southern literary magazine of his own failed mainly because he could not separate his literary interest from his pro-slavery politics. Nonetheless, during the 1850s Simms served as the editor-in-chief of the *Southern Quarterly Review* and battled with John R. Thompson, the editor of the *Southern Literary Messenger*, for recognition as the premier literary magazine in the South. Both men ultimately admitted that their magazines lacked stature in comparison to Northern journals simply because Southerners failed to patronize their own literature. Shortly after the release of *Uncle Tom's Cabin,* Thompson wrote, What Southern periodical, established for the development of Southern intellect, for the defense of Southern institutions, for the creation of a Southern literature, has not languished for the want of adequate encouragement?[87]

Black Authors

The first examples of writing in the formal genres by blacks were seen in the 1820s. Some marginal works appeared as poetry, but the slave narratives that began to be published in the 1830s had the greatest effect and popularity. While the influence of antislavery editors was clearly visible in some narratives, others were clearly the work of the avowed author. Frederick Douglass's 1845 *Narrative* has perhaps garnered the most lasting fame. Other significant works were penned by William Wells Brown, America's first black novelist; Josiah Henson; and Henry "Box" Brown.

Slave narratives sold very well in the North supplying sensationalism and sentimentality to an audience who relished both.[88]

From 1841 to 1860, Frederick Douglass was the most prominent black abolitionist. Douglass's *Narrative of the Life of an American Slave Written by Himself* (1845) was filled with noble thoughts and thrilling reflections. Douglass was a slave in Baltimore for more than 20 years; and his book, published by the American Antislavery Society, was replete with the physical abuses of slavery, including whippings, rape, unwarranted punishments, and cold-blooded murder. The work appealed to a wider audience of reformers than just those who favored emancipation. Proponents of women's rights, temperance, public education, and immigration reform all found something to stir them in Douglass's work.

Southern readers pointed with incredulity to many of Douglass's childhood memories of the whipping and murder of his fellow slaves. Because the editors carefully omitted corroborating details from the incidents, many whites were convinced that the stories were patently false. His accounts of two slaves being murdered in unrelated incidents by individual masters on adjoining plantations within hours of one another rang false to all but the most dedicated of abolitionists. Nevertheless, between 1845 and 1850 the book sold more than 30,000 copies and was regarded by many in the North as a true picture of slavery in Maryland. The reviewer of the *New York Tribune*, himself an abolitionist, praised the book upon its publication for its simplicity, truth, coherence, and warmth.

Emancipation advocates declared that only the great weight of slavery had deteriorated the natural goodness and intelligence that the Negro had brought from Africa. "It has a natural, an inevitable tendency to brutalize every noble faculty of man." Douglass served as a favorite symbol of the ideally regenerated freeman and was portrayed as a victim of slavery with a "godlike nature" and "richly endowed" intellect. Douglass was showcased as a naturally eloquent "prodigy—in soul manifestly created but a little lower than the angels." He was a favorite speaker on the lecture circuit, and hundreds of abolitionists flocked to his addresses.[89]

However, Douglass was not satisfied with the limits of such audiences. He reached out to the black community of the North to support its brethren in bondage. One of the more effective means that he used the 1850s was *Frederick Douglass' Paper*, later renamed *Douglass' Monthly Magazine*. Unlike the other black papers that were locally popular and short lived, Douglass's work was circulated throughout 18 states and two foreign countries. It had more than 4,000 subscribers and survived for more than 13 years.

Once the war commenced, Douglass altered his agenda from ending slavery to having blacks accepted in white society as equals. In this regard, he agitated constantly for the establishment of black regiments of

Federal soldiers feeling (optimistically in light of future events) that those who fought to save the Union would find an equal place in it after the war. At first he met with stubborn resistance, but finally he was successful in creating all-black infantry units from among free black volunteers. Two of Douglass's sons volunteered for this duty and served with distinction. Ultimately, black troops were placed in combat roles where their performance proved laudable and, at times, heroic. The best-known black unit was the 54th Massachusetts Colored Infantry with which Douglass was closely associated.

Born in Kentucky, William Wells Brown was taken by his owner to Missouri in 1816 where he remained a slave under three successive masters. On the first day of 1834, Brown slipped away from a river steamer that was docked at Cincinnati, and, fearing discovery every step of the way, made his way to Cleveland and freedom. Brown thereafter worked in the print shop of Elijah Lovejoy, who was to become the first abolitionist martyr, and eventually turned to the study of medicine. His intellectual development, and literary and oratorical skills, however, made him a stellar candidate for the antislavery lecture circuit. Here he distinguished himself, and was later equally eloquent for temperance movement

In 1847, the *Narrative of William Wells Brown, Fugitive Slave, Written by Himself* was published. His book was one of the most widely circulated and acclaimed of all the many slave narratives that appeared in this period. *The Anti-Slavery Harp: A Collection of Songs for Antislavery Meetings (1848)* followed. Brown's *The Escape: or, A Leap for Freedom* is acknowledged as the first play written by a black American writer. His most noteworthy literary effort may well be *Clotel* (1853), the first novel by a black American to be published. There are four editions, and several spellings, of *Clotel*. It was first published while Brown was living in London where he sought safety from the fugitive slave laws. Although the four versions differ in details, they essentially tell the same melodramatic tale of a beautiful female slave. Even though it contains a scathing rebuke of Southern racial attitudes, the novel endorses integration rather separatism. Brown was a diverse writer who also produced a collection of letters from his European travels and four notable works on black history. Ultimately, Brown returned to America and was able to practice as a physician. He spent most of the last quarter century of his life practicing medicine in Boston.

Southern Female Authors

Although Southern women were frequent writers of letters and diaries, writing as a profession was not one to which the Southern woman aspired. *Eliza Wilkinson's Letters,* detailing the British invasion of Charleston in 1779, were published in 1839, but even periodicals of the day contained few female contributions. One notable exception was Caroline Howard Gilman. Although born in Boston, Gilman spent her adult life in Charleston, where she wrote a number of stories, poems, and novels. Her 1837 *Recollections of a Southern Matron,* like other women's fiction in the North, was highly sentimental. It tells the story of a plantation girl as she grows into womanhood, and it was noteworthy as the first Southern work on that theme. Additionally, Gilman founded a children's magazine, *Rose Bud,* in 1832.

The literary product of the South's female writers was largely written in private documents that were never meant to be made public. In recent years several diaries and journals by Southern women have been rescued from oblivion. The quality of the writing, the insight it provides, and the dedication of the authors to accurately recording the events of their day comes through to the modern reader. Among these are the wartime journals of Dolly Sumner Lunt, Mary Chesnut, and Sarah Morgan. Also interesting is the journal of a Georgia plantation mistress, Frances Kemble, who as a displaced Northerner brought a different perspective to the reports of Southern life.[90]

9

Music

So much new music is now issued, that the sale of each piece is exceedingly limited, unless it is a particularly striking or original in its character. . . . Not one piece in ten pays the cost of getting up; only one in fifty proves a success.

—An 1859 notice from the publishing firm of Oliver Ditson & Co.

EARLY AMERICAN MUSIC

The earliest years of the 19th century offered little of note in the way of American popular music. Since the time of the earliest settlements in America, sacred singing and other forms of liturgical music were used during worship, but church music simply did not have much popular appeal. With the exception of tavern tunes, popular music was almost unknown in colonial times, and formal gatherings for the singing of nonliturgical pieces were rare and in some colonies illegal. Much of the popular music that was heard in America was drawn from traditional English, Irish, and Scottish sources that had accompanied the waves of immigrants who populated the country before the revolution. Classical works abound for the sophisticated ears of the upper classes, but even the social elite was fed a steady diet of European compositions. Many of these were performed in the parlor by family members on harpsichords, violins, and recorders. Opera was almost unknown in America until late in the period.

The antebellum period witnessed an almost complete musical transformation as the availability of American popular music and its performance for the middle classes increased throughout the period. The demand for church music and Sunday school songs, fueled by the Second Great Awakening, was tremendous, but it was patriotism and politics that were the key inspirations to the secular songwriters of the young nation. Nonetheless, until 1825, few songs of permanent significance emerged from America, with "Yankee Doodle," "Hail, Columbia," "The Star-Spangled Banner," and "Home, Sweet Home" being notable exceptions. From 1825 to the Civil War, however, there was a steady growth in the quality and number of native popular pieces. Musical societies were emerging, most with such lofty purposes as improving the quality of sacred singing or cultivating an appreciation for refined classical music. Even opera, initially unsuccessful when first introduced, experienced a popular renaissance in the 1840s and 1850s.

Lowell Mason

One of the earliest and most important American composers to emerge from this period was Lowell Mason. A banker with a strong musical background, Mason was particularly interested in hymns, which he collected and composed, but his efforts were to bridge the traditional gap between sacred and secular music. He saw untapped musical potential in the young nation and sought to expand the musical experience for Americans. By the time Mason was 30, he had amassed a substantial portfolio of original pieces. Following a number of unsuccessful attempts at publication, Mason's work came to the attention of the Handel and Haydn Society in Boston, a group dedicated to the appreciation of classical works. Published in 1822 under the title of the "Boston Handel & Haydn Society's Collection of Sacred Music," Mason's work became an enormous success and netted a profit of over $60,000 over the next 35 years, a very impressive amount for its time. Mason was responsible for many collections of hymn-tunes but is probably best known for five hymns that would have been easily recognized by his antebellum contemporaries: "Nearer, My God to Thee" (also known as "Bethany"), "From Greenland's Icy Mountains" ("The Missionary Hymn"), "Blest Be the Tie That Binds," "Work for the Night Is Come," and "My Faith Looks up to Thee" ("Olivet").

Mason also played a key role in the development of the song "America." The Reverend Samuel France Smith wrote the words to this renowned tune in 1831. Mason had given the young minister a collection of German music suggesting that he apply the melodies to new works, a common procedure at the time. Smith wrote the words to "America" and applied them to an old German tune, not realizing that the melody was already known as "God Save the King," the British national anthem. Smith reported that he wrote the words to "America" at a single sitting, without the slightest idea that it would ever attain the popularity it has since enjoyed. He added, "If I had anticipated the future of it, doubtless I would have taken more pain with it "[1] Mason introduced the song on July 4, 1831, at a children's celebration in a Boston church. It was well received and became an immediate success.

MUSIC EDUCATION

Lowell Mason was the first native-born American composer to make a commercial success of his creative efforts, and he sought to build upon his initial successes. One of his most enduring contributions to American music was his commitment to the practical teaching of music to children in public schools and to the training of teachers to deliver the instruction. He believed that the same techniques used in psalmody and sacred singing during worship could be applied outside the liturgical realm. He contended that class instruction could encourage the artful use of the voice and teach the rudiments of note reading. He encouraged the development of secular songbooks much like hymnals.

Mason asserted that all children had the right to receive basic music instruction as part of their public education, but this was not a view that was shared by everyone. Not only was he attempting to blur the lines between the religious and secular worlds, but also he was overtly supporting the concept of public education. Organized public schools were just beginning to be established as an American institution in Northern schools in the 1820s and 1830s. In the South, they were almost completely unknown. Many educators, unsure of the acceptance by society of universal public education, feared that music instruction would distract students from their other studies, affect their achievement in the fundamental areas of reading, writing, and arithmetic, and reflect negatively on the entire concept of public schools. In response to these apprehensions, Mason founded his own school, one of the earliest to include singing instruction for children. The youngsters were given free instruction provided that they promised to attend for an entire year. When he felt that the children were ready, he arranged for them to sing at a public lecture given by the noted educational reformer, the Reverend William Channing Woodbridge. The audience was spellbound by the performance. An observer later wrote, "A deep and lasting impression had been made on the public mind and the public heart."[2]

Along with George J. Webb, Samuel A. Eliot, and others, Lowell Mason helped found the Boston Academy of Music for the instruction of both secular and sacred music in 1832. School board members from the city of Boston began to take note of Mason's accomplishments at the academy. The board passed a resolution that "one school from each district be selected for the introduction of systematic instruction in vocal music."[3] The inclusion of music instruction in the city was formally authorized in 1836. Unfortunately, the board failed to release any funds for the program, but

Mason's commitment to the cause was so deep that he taught for an entire year without remuneration, buying needed music and materials out of his own pocket. Finally, in 1838, the board voted to appropriately fund music instruction.

Mason knew that if music education were to be successful, teachers had to be trained to properly deliver the instruction. In 1834, he offered his first music convention for educators, and 12 teachers participated. By 1849, attendance was up to 1,000. The conventions generally lasted for two weeks and taught singing mainly by rote. It was reported that some teachers traveled as far as 100 miles in order to attend. Participants returned to their home districts to become teachers of music. Mason's music conventions were so popular that he traveled around the Northeast to present them, and they form a bridge between the itinerant music teacher and the growing number of music schools. They also led to the development of annual music festivals and summer schools for teachers.

SACRED MUSIC

Liturgical music enjoyed widespread and enduring popularity in the antebellum period especially among religious revivalist and evangelicals. William B. Bradbury was enrolled in Mason's Academy of Music, sang in one of his children's choirs, and continued his legacy. As an organist and choir leader in New York City, Bradbury instituted singing classes for children much like Mason's. In 1841, he published a songbook, "The Young Choir," which was followed during the succeeding decades by many similar publications. Bradbury is best known for his tune, "China" (often called, "Jesus Loves Me! This I Know"). The song typified the childhood innocence extolled by antebellum Americans. The catchy refrain was easy to learn and hauntingly memorable:

Yes, Jesus loves me.
Yes, Jesus loves me
Yes, Jesus loves me The Bible tells me so.

Many composers of sacred music experienced immediate commercial success. Some of the more prominent names in this field include: Sylvanus Billings Pond, who compiled the "United States Psalmody"; Henry Kemble Oliver, who published "Oliver's Collection of Hymn and Psalm Tunes"; Benjamin Franklin Baker, whose "Haydn Collection of Church Music" contained tunes selected and arranged from the works of Haydn, Handel, Mozart, Beethoven, Rossini and other classical composers; and Isaac Baker Woodbury, whose music has been described as having been "used in churches more than any one of his contemporaries."[4] Finally, there was William Walker, known as "Singing Billy," who published "The

Southern Harmony and Musical Companion." This collection of hymns may have served as a connecting link between the hymnology of Lowell Mason and the religious music of many black spirituals. Over 600,000 copies of Singing Billy's songbooks were sold, and it quickly became the standard hymnal of many Southern churches from all denominations.[5]

PUBLIC PERFORMANCES

Urban areas abounded with opportunities for musical entertainment during the early 19th century. In many major cities, serious musicians formed prestigious organizations such as the Musical Fund Society of Philadelphia; Boston's Philharmonic Society, Handel and Haydn Society, and Boston Academy of Music; and the Philharmonic Society of New York. A search of music references in New York newspapers yielded the availability of 70 concerts in the city during 1839. Ten of these were dedicated to sacred music. Some were performed by the New York Sacred Music Society with the support of local church choirs. Ten presented operatic selections from the Italian repertoire performed by Arthur and Ann Seguin, Madame Albini, Madame Vellani, and Signora Maroncelli. Six were essentially instrumental recitals. Fourteen were a combination of instrumental and vocal offerings, and the largest category, with 30 selections, was composed of ballad concerts.[6]

Concerts were offered by both foreign and native artists. The performances were sometimes held for the benefit of the individual performer, and sometimes they were held for charity. Newspapers often carried notices for performances such as one held in New York in 1839, "A Vocal Concert for the Benefit of the Respectable Aged and Indigent Female Assistance Society." In New York City, concerts were held at the City Hotel, Niblo's Gardens, the Lyceum, the Apollo, and the Broadway Tabernacle as well as at some less lofty locations like restaurants and eateries. The *New York Herald* (January 7, 1839) advised readers, "A musical party will meet this evening, at 8 o'clock, at Davies' Hot Pie House, No.14 John Street. A professor will preside at the Piano Forte. Admission 12 1/2 cents."[7]

SHEET MUSIC

The flourishing middle class of the antebellum period rarely overlooked an opportunity to display its newfound social dignity or to demonstrate an air of culture and finesse. Increasingly, middle-class homes included a room that was neither a work area nor a sleeping chamber, known as the "parlor." Spurred by social aspirations and artistic appreciation, families embraced an emerging movement toward having music performed in their homes. The parlor emerged as a place where the family would gather to engage in musical pursuits as well as other leisure activities. The need to fill leisure time suggested that the family had reached a certain level of financial success, and conversely, provided an opportunity to pursue the time-consuming study of music. Ironically, formal musical training became more affordable in the wake of Lowell Mason's efforts to provide universal music instruction in public schools. Changes in the music publishing business also made sheet music, which was considered a luxury prior to 1825, increasingly more accessible during the second quarter of the century. The flourishing sheet music business, in its turn, had a profound influence on the musical instrument business. By the 1830s, the piano was replacing the harpsichords, violins, and recorders of the previous century as the instrument of choice for the home.

The growth of the sheet music business during this period was both an effect of and an impetus toward the playing of music at home. Prior to 1787, all sheet music in America was imported from England. In their early years, domestic publishing and the selling of sheet music were mainly done by musicians who sought to make contributions to the evolution of music. At the close of the 18th century, composer and publisher Alexander Reinagle composed two pieces of music. One was a piano sonata and the other a song titled "America, Commerce and Freedom." The song went into print almost immediately, yet the sonata remained in manuscript form for nearly 200 years. During the early years of the 19th century, publishers of music came to realize that songs, which were short, melodious, and easy to perform, held greater appeal for the amateur performer. Piano sonatas and similar classical pieces required a good deal more skill and dedication. Music publishers started to capitalize on the mass appeal of such songs.

Much of the early music published in America was printed as single sheets known as "broadsides." Music was also published in book form in songsters that contained lyrics without music or in anthologies that contained musically annotated songs. All of these forms continued into the 19th century, however, sheets in unbound folios came to dominate the home music market during the antebellum period. The economic incentive that drove the sheet music business in this direction lay with the publishers. Broadsides sold for a few pennies whereas the book forms brought 25 to 35 cents; yet bound books were expensive to produce. The two-page music sheet, which could be stored in a rack in the parlor, sold for 25 cents and cost little more than the broadside to produce. With such an opportunity for profit, sheet music publishers realized that satisfying the taste of the consumer could be very lucrative.

Even so, music publishers complained about the difficulty of maintaining their profits. Title pages were often beautifully lithographed as they were generally displayed in the home. The cost of engraving 100 copies of a two-page song could range between $12 and $17, requiring break-

A page of "music" published in 1846—but there are no notes. Music pages like this were supplied only to the singers, who followed along as someone else played the music or led the tune. This is an Irish tune praising the shamrock.

even sales of 48 to 68 copies. Few pieces ever sold 100 copies. First-time composers were often required to purchase a certain number of copies in order to defray set-up costs and to aid in the marketing of the work. An 1859 notice from the publishing firm of Oliver Ditson & Co. stated,

"So much new music is now issued, that the sale of each piece is exceedingly limited, unless it is a particularly striking or original in its character. . . . Not one piece in ten pays the cost of getting up; only one in fifty proves a success."[8]

Copyright laws also guided publishers in their musical decisions. The first copyright laws governing music offered protection only to American citizens or residents. Publishers had to buy a composition outright or pay a royalty based on the number of copies sold. The standard royalty was 10 percent of the retail price or a fixed amount for each copy sold, typically 2 cents. This was not true for foreign music, and publishers saw an opportunity to increase profits by publishing foreign songs and foregoing the payment of royalties. They also went out of their way to reinforce the prevalent idea that European music was superior to the domestic variety.

THE PIANO

From colonial times, the upper classes had showcased finely made virginals and harpsichords in their homes. Both were key-activated stringed instruments with wooden frames, but the virginal produced its sound by hammering the strings whereas the harpsichord used a complicated system of "jacks" to pluck the strings much like a harp. The harpsichord, unlike the simpler virginal, was capable of played trills and other repeating ornaments so common to 18th-century music. Both could produce a volume of sound appropriate for the typical colonial room, but they were grossly overmatched for any space larger than a very small concert hall. Moreover, even the finest of these instruments needed constant retuning and adjustment. Most keyboard instruments were imported from Europe, but New Englanders, who were by far the largest American market for them, found that they were not suited to the severity of the Northeastern weather with its great fluctuations in temperature and humidity. During the antebellum period, these instruments were all but displaced by the pianoforte, which became an essential of the cultured parlor.

The popularity of the pianoforte at this time was largely due to a series of technological advances. In 1825, Alpheus Babcock of Boston received a patent for a one-piece metal piano frame. Babcock believed correctly that his metal frame would be "stronger and more durable" than wood and would be less affected by temperature as it expanded and contracted in concert with the metal strings. Similar attention to the varying rates of expansion among metals had been applied to the manufacture of more accurate pendulum clocks with great success. With the availability of a piano better suited to the American climate, there came an increased demand. Jonas Chickering, also of Boston, began to mass-produce metal-framed instruments based on Babcock's patent. Chickering was making approximately 9,000 pianos per year by 1851.

So great was the demand for pianos that after the Chickering factory burned down in 1852, the replacement facility was second in size only to the Capitol in Washington.[9]

In 1855, a German-born American piano maker, named Henry Steinway, began to manufacture a piano with a cast-iron frame that, coupled with improved trip hammers and dampers, gave the sound of his pianos much greater brilliance and power than earlier forms. Each string in the instrument might have a tension placed upon it of more than 400 pounds to produce a volume that would fill a concert hall. Only the strength of cast iron could withstand the tremendous crushing force of almost 20 tons produced by the hundreds of wire "strings" in the piano. It was during this period that the familiar arrangement of 88 alternating black and white keys was standardized. There have been no fundamental changes in the design and construction of acoustic pianos since that time. This improvement heralded a widespread interest in piano concerts and musical compositions for them.

ORGANS

Just as the growing middle class sought to have music in their homes, increasing numbers of congregations wanted organs for their meeting-houses and churches. As the affluence of a congregation increased so did the desire for bigger and better organs. The reed organ, or melodeon, was being produced in the United States by the 1840s, but this type was functional only for small congregations. In 1846, Henry Erben, one of New York's leading organ builders, completed a huge organ for Trinity Church at a cost of $10,500. The Trinity organ was the largest pipe organ in the country. A visitor to Erben's shop joked that the organ was "big enough for a small family and room for boarders."[10]

Congregations vied for accomplished organists. Many Anglican churches continued the 18th-century tradition of obtaining their organists from England, while other sects sought out talented Americans. Organists of great skill were able to exert great influence over the worship services. On the other hand, mediocre organists were openly criticized not only for incompetent performances but also for their personal vanity. Psalmodist Thomas Hastings noted the fascination with organs, claiming that they served as "an object of splendid attraction, that the vacant seats of a congregation may be the more readily supplied by wealthy occupants; or as an instrument upon which the performer is to advertise the liberality of the donors, the ingenuity of the builder, or the marvelous powers of the executant."[11] Despite Hastings reservations, the fervor for organs did much to raise the musical aesthetic of the public because churchgoers were increasingly exposed to the compositions of European masters.

OPERA

The introduction of Italian and English ballad operas as well as adaptations from works in other languages goes back to the mid-18th century with Colley Cibber's *Flora*. In 1750, the English ballad opera known as *The Beggar's Opera* opened in New York after having been performed by the same company in Philadelphia. A late 19th-century observer noted that these were the first performances of ballad operas on the North American side of the Atlantic and that the people of New York—a city in which opera would ultimately take a firm foothold—initially seemed oblivious to the nature of operatic music. The Park Theater opened in 1798 with a musical afterpiece, *The Purse, or American Tar*, and for more than two decades the theater figured prominently in local opera history.

For several years, translations from German opera were the rage in New York. A German orchestra leader by the name of Pfeil (or Fyle) produced a tune called the "President's March" that later came to be called "Hail Columbia." William Dunlap, the playwright and manager of the Park Theater in New York, supported numerous imitations, alterations, adaptations, and translations of foreign operas, particularly those of German authors. Described as "a slovenly writer, discursive, untidy and garrulous, but a modest, honest, and tireless collector of facts," Dunlap translated and produced Friedrich von Schiller's *The Robbers and Don Carlos*, and more than a dozen works by Augustus Kotzebue. Dunlap also figured prominently in the transformation of many novels into operatic form. Charles Brockden Brown, owner and editor of *Monthly Magazine*, was also taken with German composers and filled the pages of his periodical with essays on German playwrights and anecdotes about German opera.[12]

Italian opera did not find an understanding and sophisticated audience with an appreciation of operatic music of its type until the opening in New York of Rossini's *Barber of Seville* as adapted by George Colman in 1825. This production starred the great Spanish singer Manuel Garcia and his prima donna sister, Maria. Almost immediately thereafter, Signor Garcia departed for Europe, but his 18-year-old sister, now using her married name, Madame Eugene Malibran, remained in New York developing her vocal powers in local theaters and in the cloister in Grace Church. Maria's performances were unequalled in America at the time, and the critics supposed her to be one of the most gifted and accomplished singers of the period. Unfortunately, her career was brought to a halt tragically when she fell from a horse while visiting England in 1836.

In the 1830s and 1840s Baltimore, Philadelphia, New York, Williamsburg, and Charleston hosted more than a score of foreign-language operas. Unlike most new plays, many operas were published in pamphlet form, and they continued to be played in later years. Among the adaptations were *Pygmalion, Devin du Village, Nina, L'Amant Statue, Deserteur, Zemire et Azor, Fausse Magie, The Marriage of Figaro* and *Don Giovanni.* These were almost invariably sung by English performers who toured with the repertory companies based in London. In terms of English ballad operas, the *Beggar's Opera*—a continuing favorite—was joined by Thomas Arne's *Love in a Village* and Isaac Bickerstaff's *Maid of the Mill.* All three saw a number of revivals in the first quarter of the 19th century as repertory pieces. Few English operas, either with original music or music adapted from ballad tunes, were heard in London without quickly making an appearance in New York. Among these were arrangements based on Shakespeare's plays. *Macbeth* was played with music by Matthew Locke and *The Tempest* found a new life as *Inkle and Yarico.* Even the legendary *Robin Hood* was adapted into a comic opera. The success of opera with the American middle class may have been based on the desire to be seen in attendance at indisputably cultured events; yet they seem to have enjoyed the performances for their own sake, even though the basis for their judgment may have been that of an American musical ear considered immature in European circles.[13]

PARLOR MUSIC

Much of the parlor music popular during the period tended to be sentimental and emotional. This was due in part to the fact that, with the emergence of industry and commerce in the 19th century, men became enmeshed in an economy where they worked outside the home. Men commuted to work and were away from the household for an extensive portion of the day. The same industry and commerce that brought increased wealth and laborsaving inventions into the home drove men away from their families. Women were thus progressively being freed from basic survival tasks by economic and technological advances and began to assume the responsibility of directing domestic matters rather than being wholly consumed by physical toil. They became entrusted with the socialization of the children and with the creation of a home atmosphere that provided a cultural haven. The home came to be viewed as a center for family shelter from the harsh realities of the outside world. The parlor and its furnishings were considered to be part of a feminine domain. Music publishers, who were male, produced pieces they felt would be pleasing to women, and the market was flooded with tunes that were thought to appeal to their sensitive and delicate nature.

Popular tunes were often reworked into fantasies and variations that could capitalize on the success of the original. Parlor music was performed more for its social pleasure than for its artistic value. The music was performed "live" and people enjoyed hearing favorite tunes. An old melody that raised sentimental feelings in the players and listeners was more likely to produce revenue than originality and artistic integrity.

Music publishers, therefore, tailored their inventory of sheet music to what they believed to be the feminine tastes of largely amateur pianists.

Love Songs

Parlor songs fell into several genres. The most pervasive were love songs, but patriotic, religious, and humorous tunes were played as well. Even minstrel tunes and operatic pieces were played in the home as well as on the stage. Songs based on chivalric love were very fashionable during the first two decades of the 19th century. Inspired by popular writers such as Sir Walter Scott, composers used themes and images that drew upon medieval lore and courtly codes. Benjamin Carr used a setting by Scott about Robin Hood's minstrel, Allen-a-dale, in his "Rokeby" in 1813. John Hill Hewitt"s "The Minstrel's Return'd from the War" published in 1833 bears a remarkable likeness to Scott's "The Crusader's Return."

> The noise of the battle is over.
> The bugle no more calls to arms,
> A soldier no more but a lover,
> I kneel to the power of thy charms.[14]

Although the images of archaic romance continued into the1830s, the music was coming to bear a strong Italianate influence. Italian opera brought a new sense of grace and intensity to American songs. Hewitt's "The Bridesmaid" is an example of a work that features the elevated Italianate melody and abounds in medieval imagery.

> Be still—be still my throbbing breast,
> I hear the bugle sounding.
> I see a warrior's snowy crest—
> A war steed proudly bounding.
> He comes—I know his gallant mien,
> His helmet, sword and spear;
> I know him by his doublet green
> My own brave Cavalier![15]

As music in the home became more affordable to the middle class, the images of archaic romance were exchanged for more down-to-earth sentiments. Separation in the form of physical distance, differing social class, and even death replaced the theme of courtly love. Most songs were written from the point of view of the male lover. They portray a very pure and unselfish love and focus on the emotional pain of separation. Few ever culminate in the lovers actually coming together. The theme of a "joy that's now no more," revealed another type of separation and yearning that inspired the songwriters of the period. This theme can be traced back to Irish poet Thomas Moore, who was an extremely popular literary figure with 19th-century Americans.[16]

Almost everyone had some unfulfilled dreams or a set of disappointments that they could relate to the words of such a love song, and songwriters tapped this universal frustration for inspiration. Songs of longing and loss such as "Ben Bolt," "I'll Take You Home Again Kathleen," "Listen to the Mocking Bird," "Lorena," "Sweet Genevieve," "When I Saw Sweet Nelly Home," and "When You and I Were Young" were pervasive.

Stephen Foster

The master of the newly transformed love song was Stephen Foster. His first musical work, "Open Thy Lattice, Love," published when Foster was a teenager, was set to a poem by George P. Morris that he found in the *New Mirror*. The song was a serenade in a genre that harkened back to the Middle Ages. The poem told of two lovers separated by society's code of conduct. The man stood beneath a woman's window and dreamed of the two lovers sailing off into the sunset. Even at such a young age, Foster seems to have embraced the more traditional courtship convention, yet he brought to it his own special touch. For "Sweetly She Sleeps, My Alice Fair" Foster set to music the text of a poem by Charles G. Eastman wherein a man gazed adoringly at his sleeping love and reveled in her beauty. Foster managed to capture the static nature of the scene in his music. One of Foster's most enduring and best-known songs in the courtship genre, "Jeanie with the Light Brown Hair," dealt with the theme of permanent separation. Herein the grieving lover laments the loss of his Jeanie, who is either dead or gone from him forever. He is left only with his memories of his lovely lost love.

Listeners to Foster's songs were invited to escape from the materialism and aggressiveness of an increasingly industrialized society. They were reminded of such timeless states as childhood, old age, and the good old days. The tender feelings of these times found popular expression in Foster's music. "The Voice of Days Gone By" typifies this desire for the past:

> Youthful fancy then returns,
> Childish hopes the bosom burns,
> Joy, that manhood coldly spurns,
> Then flows in memory's sweet refrain.

Many of Foster's songs strike a sad note. There is a subdued longing, nostalgia, or melancholy in such pieces as "Massa's in de Cold Ground," "Old Memories Under the Willows," "She's Sleeping," and "Summer Longings."

Foster is considered by many to be one of America's greatest melodists. His gift was his ability to pen melodies that were understood and embraced by people of all walks of life. His natural charm and simple, direct writing might have been lost had he been a more formally trained musician. Foster was responsible for making a classic contribution to the South's antebellum image of the contented slave, the kind-hearted master, and the white-columned plantation. "Old Folks at Home" or "Swanee River" captured the emotions of Southern life. His lyrics probably did more to underpin positive attitudes toward the South and its "peculiar institution" than any proslavery lecture or treatise of the time, an ironic situation considering his pro-Northern sympathies.

DANCE MUSIC

A large portion of the compositions available for the piano could be categorized as dance music. Unlike other forms of parlor music, dance music emphasized rhythm over melody. Perhaps the dance that created the greatest flurry during the period was the polka. Originating among Bohemian peasants, the polka made the rounds of European capitals beginning in 1835 and arrived on the theater stage in America in May 1844. Lawyer and diarist, George Templeton Strong, recorded his first impression of the dance in 1845: "It is a kind of insane Tartar jig performed to disagreeable music of an uncivilized character." He complained that "like an evil spirit," it haunted him and disturbed his sleep.[17]

Strong's negative reaction to the polka, however, was not that of the majority of Americans. Music publishers turned out thousands of polka tunes to satisfy the public's passion for the dance. Their marketing strategy was to give the polkas a variety of whimsical and exotic titles. Some titles, such as "Polka artistique," "Polka gracieuse," and "Polka sentimentale," suggested culture and sophistication. Other publishers incorporated the names of flowers, birds, and jewels into the titles in the hope of appealing to feminine interests. Women's names from A to Z were also popular additions to polka titles.

MINSTREL SHOWS

Theatrical impersonations of blacks by white men began onstage in the 1820s, and, although they degenerated following the Civil War, minstrel shows continued, in some form, for much of the century. "Blackface" acts, as they were sometimes called, affected two stereotypes—one, in ragged clothes, was modeled after the Southern plantation slave, and the other, dressed as a dandy, mocked the Northern black freeman emulating a cultured style and attitude. These shows fixed key images of blacks to the plantation tradition. They also demonstrated an allure of black culture for whites.

Minstrel shows were part of theatrical performances that featured a variety of short dramas and farces, dances and songs, all on a single program. The "Ethiopian Delineator," as the playbill was likely to herald them, was popularized by such men as Thomas Dartmouth (Daddy) Rice, who is credited with starting the idea; Bob Farrell; and George Washington Dixon. In between the songs and dance steps there was always time for gibes about the political issues of the day.

In the 1830s, solo performances by banjoists and dancers in blackface became popular. Joel Sweeney and Billy Whitlock became famous as banjoists, and John Diamond gained equal fame as a dancer. The music used by these performers was already common among frontiersmen and river boatmen and had Irish and Scottish roots. The blackface dancer mixed jumps and heel-and-toe moves with gestures mimicking plantation blacks. These evolved in the 1840s into small ensembles that included banjoists, fiddlers, singers, and dancers in various combinations. There were also short plays billed as "Ethiopian Operas" that featured a larger cast and were an outgrowth of the English ballad-opera. They included spoken dialogue and songs, which featured choral refrains, duets, and dances.

This late-period advertisement was for a vast minstrel show having dozens of persons on the stage at the same time. Minstrelsy, in blackface, is abhorrent to society today, but it was very popular both before and after the Civil War.

Female roles were played by men who specialized in playing "Negro wenches."

The Virginia Minstrels, the first successful minstrel band, appeared in 1843. Led by "Old Dan Emmit," the composer of "Dixie" who played the fiddle, the group included Billy Whitlock on the banjo, Frank Brower on the "bones" (a kind of castanet), and Dick Pelham on the tambourine. The banjo, fiddle, and bones were popular slave instruments. The tambourine, in combination with the fiddle, had been popular with river boatmen, who also served as an inspiration for the minstrels. Sitting in a semicircle, the ensemble's program included songs, choral refrains, banjo solos, dances, jokes, and comic banter. Throughout the next decade, the size of minstrel bands increased, numbering as many as a dozen members.

Initially, the songs used by these minstrels borrowed heavily from British folk music and Italian operas and then adapted the lyrics to slave dialect and inflections. In time, the works became more original, although it is often difficult to trace a particular tune to any specific author. The most prominent minstrel song composers of the period were Stephen Foster and Dan Emmett.

Foster's works in this genre were usually designed for solo performers and were often performed during the first part of the minstrel show, which was less racially focused in its theme and more oriented toward plantation life than the second portion, which more freely lampooned both black slaves and freemen. Foster hesitated to have his name appear on his "Ethiopian songs" for fear that the prejudice against them by some would injure him as a writer of another style of music. He carefully avoided "trashy" and "vulgar" lyrics commonly found other works of that genre. He reconsidered his anonymity when he found that a more refined audience enjoyed his songs. Foster's popularity spread through the minstrel troupes, which greatly favored his works. Some popular pieces were "My Old Kentucky Home," "Old Dog Tray," "Old Black Joe" and "De Camptown Races." For a number of years E.P. Christy had the privilege of being the first to present Foster's works.

Dan Emmett usually composed the end of the performance for the entire company. He was responsible for some of the most popular songs of the three decades prior to the Civil War. His 1840s hits include "Twill Neber Do to Gib It up So," "Gwine Ober the Mountains" and "Old Dan Tucker." "Root Hog or Die" and "Jordan Is a Hard Road to Trabel" were popular in the 1850s. "Walk-arounds" were performances that were sung and danced by a few soloists backed up by a chorus of six or eight men. In these years, walk-arounds were performed in virtually all minstrel shows. Emmett was responsible for many popular pieces for this venue, including "Billy Patterson," "Johnny Roach What o' Dat," and "Dixie's Land." Emmett is best known for writing the words to "Dixie," which was an immediate success. Various arrangements and lyrics followed the song as other performers latched on to it. Although Emmett received little money from it, "Dixie" was perhaps the greatest lyric success in America up to that time.

THE SINGING FAMILY

The family concert was another musical institution that had a significant effect on the songs of the period. Commonly referred to as a "singing family," the members of these musical troupes were presumably or actually related to each other. Each troupe was usually composed of four singers, including one or two women. The program generally included both vocal and instrumental pieces, which were performed as solos and ensembles. They sang in simple harmonizations and closely blended voices. Their material consisted mainly of ballads, which embraced a variety of moods from sentimental to realistic and from dramatic to comic. The songs performed by these troupes often became the popular tunes of the day. Often, the family members composed the material, writing new verses to old tunes and at times writing new music as well. Performances were given wherever an audience could be gathered, from concert halls and churches to barns. Singing families were at the height of their popularity in the two decades before the Civil War.

There were many singing families touring the country during this time. One of the best known of the early groups was the Hutchinson Family from Milford, New Hampshire. Their theme song was "The Old Granite State," which they adapted from a popular hymn, "You Will See Your Lord a-Coming." While the song celebrated their native state, the Hutchinson's also sought to advance the cause of abolition. One verse professed:

Equal liberty is our motto
In the "Old Granite State."
We despise oppression,
An we cannot be enslaved.[18]

In 1843, the Hutchinsons joined prominent abolitionists, William Lloyd Garrison and Wendell Phillips and the former slave Frederick Douglass at an antislavery rally in Boston. An observer at the event remarked, "Speechifying, even of the better sort did less to interest, purify and subdue minds, than this irresistible Anti-slavery music."[19] One of the Hutchinson's most potent antislavery songs was "Get Off the Track," which was sung to a snappy old minstrel tune, "Old Dan Tucker." Published in 1844, the sheet music identified the work as "A song for Emancipation." The sheet music's cover, depicting a locomotive named *Liberator* ringing its liberty bell and pulling a car jammed with passengers, was titled "Immediate Emancipation" and was proudly displayed in the parlors of those sympathetic to the cause of antislavery.

A contemporary account of a performance of "Get Off the Track" by the family at the New England Anti-Slavery Convention in 1844 captured the intensity engendered among the largely receptive audience.

> And when they came to that chorus-cry, that gives name to the song, when they cried to the heedless pro-slavery multitude that were stupidly lingering on the track, and the engine "Liberator" coming down hard upon them, under full steam and all speed, the Liberty Bell loud ringing, and they standing like deaf men tight in its whirlwind path, the way they cried "Get off the track" in defiance of all time and rule, was magnificent and sublime. ... The multitude who heard them will bear witness, that they had transcended the very province of music.[20]

The Hutchinsons were not averse to promoting a wide range of their social beliefs. They also advocated temperance, revivalism, religious socialism, and spiritualism. Their efforts in these areas were less a crass self-promotion and more a reflection of the times in which they lived. During the first half of the 19th century, many long-standing and formerly acceptable social customs, such as slave owning, excessive drinking, and the abusive treatment of women, were being reevaluated, and reform movements to remedy these social ills gained momentum steadily.

An antidrinking, or temperance, campaign took hold in the 1830s. The Hutchinsons included antidrinking songs in their concerts from very early in their career. "King Alcohol" featured their original verses set to the tune of "King Andrew." The dangers of immoderate drinking were real and alcoholism could end in disaster. Strong drink was often cited as the cause for eternal damnation and earthly licentiousness, as well as spouse abuse and rape. In fact, the temperance movement was very closely allied with women's issues and may have mirrored a rising tide of female discontent with their place in the social order.

MARTIAL MUSIC

There is a long history of the appeal to the public of military bands. American militias of the Revolution and early Republican years followed the British custom of providing military field music, mainly composed of fifes and drums and used for lifting morale, controlling troop movements, and regulating the daily rhythm of camp life. Another form of American martial music was known as "Harmoniemusik," which added to the standard fifes and drums instruments such as oboes, horns, bassoons, and possibly clarinets. Harmoniemusik was employed in recreational and ceremonial situations that involved both the troops and the public. These traditions continued into the 19th century.

An article that appeared in the *Boston Journal of Music* in 1838 recalled the effect martial music had on a man in his youth in the early 1800s. "Full well do I remember when I first heard the sound of the Clarinet, French Horn, and Bassoon. . . . [T]he company came in front of the public house, when it halted, and Capt. Taylor gave orders for Yankee Doodle. This fairly bewitched the crowd, and they rent the air with huzzas."[21]

As the 19th century progressed, the sound of the military fife-and-drum band was enhanced with the addition of other instrumental families. By the 1830s, cymbals, tambourines, triangles, and the bass drum had become standard pieces. Brass instruments, which were undergoing a technological development that included the development of slides, keys, and valves, allowed more notes in the scale to be played and capitalized on the instruments' bright resonance. The notes played by early horns could be modified by hand-stopping, "a weirdly beautiful technique with the horn held downwards and one hand in the bell which gave music the classical style of the horn" found in the works of Mozart and Brahms. In contrast, trumpets and bugles could only be modified by changing the player's lip pressure.

The Permutation Trumpet, invented by Nathan Adams of Lowell, Massachusetts, in 1825, was the first rotary valve instrument of which the details are accurately known. However, a contemporary observer noted that "brass instruments for the army . . . [with] rotaries proved rather delicate for cavalry musicians, though infantry bandsmen are able to take better care of their instruments . . . especially smaller instruments such as cornets and high trumpets. . . . The tone is freer . . . than with the . . . deeper instruments like trumpets, horns, tenors horns, [and] tubas."[22] The invention in Paris of the rotary valve Saxhorn by Adolphe Sax and of the first modern piston valves by Francois Perinet in the 1840s further enhanced the ability of the brass to play a wider variety of tones. In 1848 and 1850, Thomas D. Paine of Rhode Island designed additional improvements to the rotary system that made the valves quiet and efficient. By this point, most of the technological advances in brass instruments had been made. The remaining changes that determined the configuration of modern instruments were "almost wholly concerned with compensating arrangements or extra valves in order to overcome intonation defects of valve combinations."[23]

By the 1850s, the military brass band had evolved into the typical American band of no more than a dozen pieces, and many were completely independent of the military. Bands supplied much of the social music for the country. The concept of the orchestra, with the exception of that of the New York Philharmonic Society, had not yet developed in America. The closest things to orchestras were the ensembles of a few pieces that played in theaters for operas and theatricals. Band performances were held in theaters, halls, hotels, churches, and parks and at sporting events, fairs, parties, meetings, and almost any type of public gathering.

The repertoires of these bands encompassed nearly all genres of music. The historical connection to the military lent itself to the inclusion of marches, and these were extremely popular. Marches evolved during this period from showy parade pieces to more lighthearted melodic pieces, particularly the quickstep that came into vogue in the 1830s. Marches were played as dance music in country dancing. Patriotic pieces have also been perennial favorites for brass bands. Building upon popular songs from the early part of the century, such as "Yankee Doodle" and "The Star-Spangled Banner," brass bands continued to add patriotic songs such as Johann Lobe's "Song of America" to their repertoire through the Civil War.

Popular songs played in parlors also made their way into band programs. "My Old Kentucky Home" as well as traditional favorites such as "Auld Lang Syne," "Home, Sweet Home," "The Last Rose of Summer," and "Annie Laurie" were popular Some band programs included narrative pieces such as "The Night Alarm" or "An Alpine Storm." These pieces musically depicted scenes form a particular event. "The Battle of Prague" was a particular favorite. Through a series of short pieces it conjures scenes of camp maneuvers, the call to arms, a cavalry charge, combat, the moans of the dying, and the victory call. "Wood up Quickstep" represented the refueling of a wood-burning steamboat.

Bands also performed arrangements of orchestral, symphonic, and operatic works from Mozart, Verdi, Mendelssohn, Haydn, and others. Dances were also an important part of the band repertoire. Dance songs were included in concert performances as well as for dances. It was naturally expected that the bands would keep up with the latest dance tunes.

MUSIC MANIA

Mid-19th-century America was bursting with technological and social change. These were followed by the growth of leisure time that brought about an increased interest in music and musical training. All of these elements crystallized to form an ideal setting for the marketing of entertainment. The 1840s witnessed a deluge of entertainers giving concerts, lectures, and even acrobatic performances. European impresarios seized upon this ripe market and managed a number of foreign virtuosi who toured the country and then returned to their native lands. While their stays may have been brief, the impression they made upon society cannot be ignored. Some of the most prominent European visitors included violinist Ole Bull, pianists Henri Herz and Sigismund Thalberg, and singers Maria Malibran and Henriette Sontag.

Louis Antoine Jullien

French-born Louis Antoine Jullien had garnered fame in Europe before coming to America with an entourage of 26 professional musicians. Once in New York, he hired another 60 players, including singers and dancers. Jullien's aim was to popularize music, and he did so by having the largest band, the best performers, and the most interesting selections. A subscriber to the "bigger is better" theory, Jullien's preliminary advertisements for his 1853 concert series covered nearly a full column on the front pages of newspapers for a week. It announced in part that

> The program, [which will be changed every evening] will be selected from a Repertoire of TWELVE HUNDRED PIECES and will include a Classical Overture and two Movements of a Symphony by one of the great masters, a grand Operatic Selection, together with Quadrilles, Waltzes, Mazurkas, Polkas, Schottisches, Tarantelles, Galops, etc. In addition to the above arrangements, M. JULLIEN will each evening, introduce one of his celebrated NATIONAL QUADRILLES as the English, Irish, Scotch, French, Russian, Chinese, Indian, Hungarian, Polish, &c.: and at the beginning of the second week will be produced the AMERICAN QUADRILLE which will contain NATIONAL AIRS and embrace no less than TWENTY SOLOS AND VARIATIONS, for twenty of M. JULLIEN'S solo performers, and conclude with a TRIUMPHAL FINALE.[24]

Jullien's flashy approach to conducting also caught the public's attention. His jeweled baton and white gloves contributed much to the total effect. The *New York Courier and Enquirer* maintained, "Other conductors use their batons to direct their orchestras. Not so with M. Jullien. His band is so well drilled at rehearsal that it conducts itself at performances, while he uses his baton to direct the audience"[25]

No one, except perhaps P.T. Barnum, approached Jullien when it came to showmanship. The *Courier and Enquirer* article described the staging of one of his spectacles.

> Exactly in the middle of the vast orchestra was a crimson platform edged with gold, and upon which this was a music stand, formed by a fantastic gilt figure a desk, and behind the stand a carved arm chair decorated in white and gold, and tapestried with crimson velvet, a sort of throne for the musical monarch, He steps forward, and we see those ambrosial whiskers and moustaches which Punch has immortalized; we gaze upon that immaculate waistcoat, that transcendent shirt front, and that unutterable cravat . . . the monarch graciously and gratefully accepts the tumultuous homage of the assembled thousands, grasps his scepter, and the violins wail forth the first broken phrase. . . . The music is magnificent, and so is the humbug, as M. Jullien caps its climax by subsiding into his crimson gilded throne, overwhelmed by his exertions, a used up man.[26]

Perhaps the most outrageous spectacle of Jullien's American tour came at the Crystal Palace in New York. Prior to the Fireman's Quadrille, he announced to the audience that something unusual might happen. The piece started quietly when suddenly the clanging of fire bells could be heard from outside. Three companies of firefighters dragging fire hoses and squirting water raced in as real flames lapped down from the ceiling. Despite the warning, women in the audience fainted and ushers rushed up and down the aisles assuring concertgoers that it was all part of the program. When Jullien felt that the audience had seen enough, he signaled for the firemen to leave, and the orchestra burst into the doxology, which the audience joined in singing.[27]

In addition to his showmanship, which did much to cultivate a concert-going public in America, Jullien made other contributions to the nation's music. He frequently played the works of American composers, giving them recognition that they were often denied elsewhere. American composers were on the brink of developing a national consciousness and such exposure helped them realize that they had a right to fight for their place along with European composers. Jullien also started a custom whereby men in the orchestra sang as they played. This format can also be seen in modern jazz bands.

Jenny Lind

The most famous performer to visit America was without a doubt, Jenny Lind. Known as the "Swedish Nightingale," Lind's grand tour of the United States (1850–1852) was widely promoted by the great showman and huckster P.T. Barnum, who offered a prize of $200 for the best song written specifically for her. Barnum combined her performances with his own lectures on temperance. His daughter, Caroline C. Barnum, went along on the tour as a companion for Lind. Caroline kept a journal for part of the year 1851 in which she describes the tour.

Lind was known as a young woman of very great musical taste with a brilliant and precise voice. She had established her reputation in Europe and was particularly popular in America. A crowd of over 40,000 admirers greeted her when her ship docked in New York City in 1850. Theater owners demanded and received as much as $225 for a seat at her performances. She added to her own popularity by reportedly contributing half of her salary to various charities. At one point in her Southern tour it was suggested that she had made a donation to an abolition group in Boston—a rumor that P.T. Barnum emphatically denied.

Besides performances in Northern cities such as New York, Boston, Philadelphia, Baltimore, and Cincinnati, Lind also toured many of the major cities of the South. In Richmond, she sang at the Marshall Theater. She spent 10 days entertaining the social elite of Charleston, and about a week in Wilmington, North Carolina, before sailing to Havana, Cuba. Returning to the United States through the port of New Orleans, she gave 12 sold-out performances at the St. Charles Theater in that city. Thereafter, P.T. Barnum chartered the steamer *Magnolia* to sail up the Mississippi

The Swedish singer Jenny Lind was one of the first "superstars" of the antebellum period. In this illustration from Currier & Ives, Lind is surrounded by an adoring audience. Her rendition of "Home, Sweet Home" at the New National Hall before President Millard Fillmore was so moving that both tears and sentiment swept the audience.

River with stops at Natchez, Memphis, St. Louis, Louisville, and Nashville. In total, Lind gave more than 90 performances.

However, it was her performances in Washington, D.C., in 1851 that made the most lasting impression on the American public. Her rendition of "Home, Sweet Home" at the New National Hall before President Millard Fillmore was so moving that there was no applause at its completion. The solemn respect for Lind's ability was only overshadowed by the tears and sentiment that swept the hall. President Fillmore declared that the performance was the most exciting thing that had happened to him since entering the White House. Ironically, only a few weeks later, the New National Hall suffered the collapse of a section of its walls while it was unoccupied, sparing many of the lives that might have been lost had the collapse taken place in the packed house attending her performances.

In 1852, Lind fell out with P.T. Barnum, who threatened to sue her for more than $70,000 if she did not finish the tour. Shortly thereafter she married her music director, Otto Goldschmidt—a German American immigrant. After living briefly in the United States while giving a tour of her own, she returned to Europe to live in semiretirement and teach music at the Royal College of Music in London. Lind's grand tour of the United States created one of the first great "manias." Unfortunately, her fans sometimes seemed violent and uncontrolled with as many as 20,000 people crowding the streets around the theaters in which she appeared.

Louis Moreau Gottschalk

Although he spent so much time abroad that he was considered a foreigner by many Americans, Louis Moreau Gottschalk was actually born in America. Following a tour through France and Spain, Gottschalk made his American debut in Niblo's Garden in New York in February 1853 creating a sensation comparable only to that created by Jenny Lind. The pianist and composer might be considered America's first "matinee idol." Women literally threw themselves at him. There are reports of crowds of women rushing to his piano, grabbing his white gloves from his hands, and tearing them to bits as they fought over them. When he practiced on the second floor of a shop in New Orleans, women fought for places on the stairs where they could listen and perhaps catch a glimpse of him. He toured the country for three years before he left for the West Indies.

The Germania Society

Poverty and civil unrest in Central Europe triggered the immigration of a number of other Europeans who remained in the United States and made their mark upon American music. Perhaps the most important group that came from Europe at this time was a group of 25 musicians known as the Germania Society. They were unique in their time in that they were the first orchestra in America to make their music a full-time business and to rehearse daily. What few orchestral societies did exist in America at that time, such as the New York Philharmonic, gave only a few concerts a year. Most of the time, members of such groups were engaged in their own musical ventures.

When the Germanians arrived in New York in 1848, they brought with them music never before played in America and a style and quality of music that was uniquely theirs. The Germanians played to audiences of up to 3,000 in many large American cities. Thomas Ryan, a member of one of America's first chamber music organizations, noted that "subscription lists twenty feet long could be seen in the music stores for a series of twenty-four Saturday evenings, and the same number of public rehearsals on Wednesday afternoon."[28] The orchestra featured symphonies, overtures, and concertos by Haydn, Mozart, Beethoven, Liszt, and Wagner, with Mendelssohn's "A Midsummer Night's Dream" as a specialty. They were the first to perform Wagner's "Tannhauser" in America. The

Germanians were aware of the importance of including "crowd pleasers" in their programs. Satisfying the popular demand for descriptive fantasias, "Up Broadway" became a repertory staple. Ryan recalled the presentation of the piece.

> It was supposed to be a graphic tone-picture of sights and sounds . . . of New York's bustling life. The potpourri began with a musical picture of Castle Garden. Moving up . . . you next came to Barnum's Museum, with "Barnum's Band" of six or eight brass instruments, which . . . played all day long on a high balcony outside his Museum on Broadway. . . . It was side-splitting to hear the imitation of this brass band. . . . [A] fireman's parade with brass band came next. Naturally it was preceded by a violent ringing of fire bells, and a rushing down a side street with the machine. When that noise died away, music from the open door of a dance hall was heard; with of course all its accompaniments—the rhythm of dancing feet, and the calling out of the figures. Then . . . we passed a church whence came the sound of organ music and the chanting of a service by a number of voices. After that we heard in the distance a faint kind of Turkish patrol music; then a big crescendo and sudden fortissimo introduced us to Union Square and its life; and two brass bands in two different keys prepared our nerves for the usual collision and fight between opposing fire companies. Finally, fireworks were touched off, the Star-Spangled Banner was played, and the potpourri ended, sending every one home in smiling good humor.[29]

The Germanians disbanded in 1854, but many of their players settled in different parts of the country and continued to make contributions to American music. Carl Bergmann went on to become a conductor for the New York Philharmonic Society, where his methodology and interpretations echoed throughout the century. Carl Zerrahn remained in Boston, the Germanians' winter headquarters, and was considered to be one of the city's most influential musicians.

SLAVE MUSIC

Music was an integral part of slave life. Frederick Douglass, a former slave, writer, and abolitionist, recounted in his autobiography that there was "almost constant singing heard in the southern states." Slaves were "generally expected to sing as well as to work."[30] The singing helped overseers to know the whereabouts of the slaves, and it limited the ability of dissidents to foment unrest in the field. These work chants created rhythms for repetitious tasks, thus easing the physical burdens of labor and relieving the tedium in a manner similar to the chanteys sung by seamen. Fanny Kemble recalled the singing of the slaves as her steamboat left her husband's plantation: "As the boat pushed off, and the steersman took her into the stream, the men at the oars set up a chorus, which they continued to chant in unison with each other, and in time with their strike, till their voices were heard no more from the distance."[31]

Black slaves were ripped from Africa destitute of possessions, but they brought songs and the traditional knowledge of simple musical instruments with them. Within a generation, they had developed a number of instruments on which to play. These included several types of drums, the kalima (or thumb piano), the marimba, and the banjo. By the 19th century, their traditional tunes had been adapted to English words and their lyrics were often heavily influenced by the imagery of Bible stories taught to them by white missionaries and evangelists.

Of slave songs, plantation mistress Fanny Kemble noted, "That which I have heard these people sing is often plaintive and pretty, but almost always has some resemblance to tunes with which they must have become acquainted through the instrumentality of white men, their overseers or masters whistling Scotch or Irish airs, of which they have produced by ear . . . in one of the most popular of the so-called [N]egro melodies with which all Americans and English are familiar, is an example of this very transparent plagiarism . . . a very distinct descendent of "Coming through the Rye." The words, however, were astonishingly primitive, especially the first line, which when it bursts from their eight throats in high unison, sent me into fits of laughter: Jenny shake her toe at me, Jenny gone away.[32]

While touring a Richmond tobacco factory, William Cullen Bryant was struck by blacks singing while engaged in sedentary work. Exhibiting the typical condensation of most whites toward blacks, the factory owner commented that "their tunes are all psalm tunes and the words are from hymn books; their taste is exclusively for sacred music; they will sing nothing else. Almost all these persons are church members; we have not a dozen about the factory who are not so.[33] From these varied influences emerged the spirituals that gave America a new and distinctive music of its own.

Slave music existed in many forms including spirituals, laments, secular songs, and funeral dirges. In a way, these songs provided a certain release. The airs established a group consciousness and provided strength to withstand oppression. Slave music furnished an outlet for repressed anger, and served as a means of self-expression. Douglass described these songs as "tones loud, long and deep, breathing the prayer and complaint of souls boiling over with the bitterest anguish. Everyone was a testimony against slavery, and a prayer to God for deliverance from chains." He added that slave songs "represent[ed] the sorrows, rather than the joys of the heart; and [the slave was] relieved by them, only as an aching heart is relieved by tears."[34]

Musical accompaniment commonly came from a banjo or fiddle. Masters would sometimes let slaves borrow these for holidays and celebrations. Accomplished slave musicians were often asked to play at plantation celebrations. Some slaves were able to purchase their own instruments using extra earnings generated by gardens or crafts. Many instruments were handmade. A slave with particularly fine skills might carve his own fiddle, but it was more likely that ingenuity led to improvisation with materials at hand. Stringed instruments were made using horsehair and animal skins or bladders and gourds. Goat- and sheepskins were stretched across a variety of objects to create drums. Some Southern states prohibited the use of drums by slaves fearing that the instruments would be used to communicate between plantations to signal an uprising. Other percussion instruments drafted sheep ribs, cow jaws, tree trunks, and old kettles and pans. Animal horns provided the materials for wind instruments. If an instrument was not available, a slave might create his own unique kind of music. Northerner Lewis Paine described slaves dancing during his 1841 visit to a Georgia plantation: "Someone calls for a fiddle—but if no one is to be found, someone 'pats juber' [juba]. This is done by placing one foot a little in advance of the other, raising the ball of the foot from the ground, and striking it in regular time, while in connection, the hands are struck slightly together, and then upon the thighs. In this way they make the most curious noise, yet in such perfect order, it furnishes music to dance by."[35]

BLACK MUSICIANS

Only a few black musicians achieved professional prominence prior to the Civil War. Francis "Frank" Johnson was one of the most famous black musicians of the antebellum period. Johnson played the violin and the keyed bugle, and he published over 200 songs, dances, and other pieces. Johnson gathered other musicians who could play multiple instruments and formed a band that played as a dance orchestra and in concert. When bands switched from the Harmoniemusik to brass, Johnson and his band also made the transition. Following a trip to London, Johnson returned to the United States and began staging promenade concerts, a European format introduced in Paris in 1833. The promenade concert combined an informal mood, refreshments, and music. Aimed at a diverse audience, the music included overtures and dances, especially waltzes and quadrilles.

Elizabeth Taylor Greenfield was born a slave and was later taken to Philadelphia and given singing lessons. Her singing voice possessed such a wide range that she attracted much attention as a vocal phenomenon. She made her concert debut in 1851 and began to tour the United States as the "Black Swan." Harriet Beecher Stowe detailed the following account of one of Greenfield's concerts given in a private residence: "Miss Greenfield's turn for singing now came, and there was profound attention.

Her voice, with its keen, searching fire, its penetrating vibrant quality, its timbre as the French have it, cut its way like a Damascus blade to the heart. She sang the ballad, "Old Folks at Home," giving one verse in the soprano, and another in the tenor voice."[36]

Spirituals

The term "spirituals" is often used to reference religious songs of African American origin, but it actually has a broader evangelical meaning and aptly describes the music sung at revival and camp meetings. For many frontier areas, religious guidance came via the circuit rider, an itinerant preacher who traveled the countryside bringing the gospel to a widely scattered population. From time to time special gatherings were planned for a larger number of people drawn from a broader area. It was not unusual for preachers from several denominations to jointly arrange for such a mass meeting, and crowds ranged from 2,000 to 20,000 in size. These events came to be known as "camp meetings" because attendees often had to travel such great distances and came prepared to stay for several days. The first of these assemblages was held near the Gaspar River Church in Kentucky in July of 1800. It was an immediate success. Thereafter, the phenomenon swept the country, reaching the zenith of its popularity during the 1830s and 1840s.

Methodists quickly took the lead in early camp meetings. In his 1847 history of the Presbyterian Church, Robert Davidson attributes the Methodist success to the fact that "they succeeded in introducing their own stirring hymns . . . as books were scarce the few that were available were cut up and the leaves distributed, so that all in turn might learn them by heart."[37] These books contained the songs for the revivalist movement, but only the words of the hymns and spiritual songs and not the music. The tunes used were either those with which people were already familiar or those of such a simple and catchy nature that they were quickly learned. It was said that all that was required for a successful camp meeting hymn was "contagiousness and effectiveness."[38] No musical instruments accompanied the singing. The singing ecstasy that was achieved at these meetings relied heavily on several patterns in the songs that provided an opportunity for mass participation and shouting.

Many camp songs had a refrain, which was inserted after each line. Another practice was to insert a familiar tag line like "Roll, Jordan, roll" after each verse. Some songs had the potential of continuing on almost indefinitely merely by replacing a single word in a stanza. The word "brethren" in the line, "O brethren, will you meet me, In Canaan's happy land?" could be replaced with "brother," "sister," "sinner," or any other appropriate noun. There were also dialogue songs in which one phrase was sung by the men and another by the women. While there was no thought of musical accomplishment in these songs, they were beautiful and stirring when sung by an impassioned crowd of faithful brethren. Camp meeting and revival music drew upon many older religious songs, but it emerged as its own unique form of popular hymnody, which made its mark in America's musical culture. More than 50 songbooks of camp music were published between the beginning of the movement and the opening of the Civil War, attesting to the popularity of the format.

The antebellum period in America was a period of tremendous growth in the field of music. As the century dawned there was little in the way of native music. Outside the realm of scared singing there were few gatherings for the appreciation of musical performance. By mid-century, the nation's passion for music had become almost unquenchable. Music was found in the home, in the fields, in the camps, and in numerous public venues. The sheet music business was flourishing, permitting a widespread marketing of popular tunes, and the country was developing its own set of composers who were beginning to develop a national music consciousness.

10

Performing Arts

To the actors—less etiquette, less fustian, less buckram.
To the orchestra—new music, and more of it.
To the pit—patience, clean benches, and umbrellas.
To the boxes—less affectation, less noise, less coxcombs.
To the gallery—less grog, and better constables;—and,
To the whole house, inside and out, a total reformation.
>   —Recommendations to the theater made
>   by Washinton Irving, 1803[1]

THEATER

Prior to 1776, most Anglo-Americans considered themselves English, and
colonial New Englanders, mirroring their Puritan heritage, generally
scorned theatrical performances. Plays and theatricals of any nature were
totally banned in New England and in many of the Middle colonies as well
as in all of the British Isles during the Puritan-dominated Republican period of English history (1642–1660). Even in the early 18th century, with
Puritan political dominance waning, theater was denounced from the
pulpit for its lewdness and frequent references to biblical characters and
stories while outside the confines of a place of worship. Jeremy Collier's
formal attack, *A Short View of the Immorality and Profaneness of the English
Stage,* first published in 1698, is a classic example. It was particularly scathing, and it set the public abuzz for a considerable period thereafter. Collier
particularly decried the abuse hurled from the theatrical stage upon the
clergy in the form of ridicule, satire, and caricature. Playwrights were
persecuted, and actors and actresses were fined throughout the British

Empire. In Boston, theaters were formally prohibited by law in 1750, and the prohibition was enforced up to 1792 and not struck from the city statutes until 1796.

The response of the theatrical community to these attacks was unexpected. Rather than undertaking a sobering reformation, new plays were produced in which the laughter and mockery were turned directly upon theater's persecutors. These efforts drew in large audiences, many of which came from among those members of society considered to of low quality. In an era when American streets were considered generally unsafe, the inclusion of such riffraff led to a good deal of distrust among the socially well placed with regard to their personal security at theatrical performance. Nonetheless, the dazzling spectacle of hundreds of points of gas or candlelight, the resplendent dress of the actors and the audience, the ever-present desire for diversion, and the growing acceptance of republican sympathies ultimately eclipsed the reluctance of even the most pretentious and aristocratic members of high society, who thereafter made theater their own.

In the American South, theater enjoyed a continued and uninterrupted prestige among the planter aristocracy similar to that of their 16th-century Royalist counterparts. The popularity of theater in England during the Elizabethan and Restoration periods led to an entire genre of plays and comedies that enjoyed continued popularity into the antebellum period more than a century and a half later. While Shakespearean and other Elizabethan-era plays persisted, it was during the Restoration that the types of performances most characteristic of the American antebellum period were born. The appearance of women on stage became common for the first time, strict decorum on stage was abolished, moral outcomes at the end of plays were largely abandoned, and a new style of comedy was improvised that was considered superior to that which proceeded it.

There developed a new plain style among antebellum playwrights who attacked "earlier styles for being too much delighted with language itself, rather than the ends to which language should be directed."[2] The classical school of passionless declamation from the stage or the rostrum was coming to an end. New characters, situations, plots, and themes worked their way into theater in America. It seemed that any "cleverly contrived" diversion could impress American audiences. The modern scientist was often cast as a fraud peddling a new philosophy of nature in place of an older metaphysics; traditional heroes were often made to seem as foolish as the victims; and success was largely identified with sexual fulfillment "either in the stark performance of the act itself or in the exclusive sexual control over another." Playwrights simply bathed their audience in a sort of intellectual pleasure that was often the sole objective of their work. The source of the laughter and the connection to the audience was found in the public's own sense of superiority over the characters on stage. The value of wit as a vehicle for advancing the story line was never before held in such high regard. Witty characters undertook no actions that did not have their ultimate ends in plain sight of the audience. The essence of antebellum wit was sharp repartee among the players, and the witticisms, chiefly "egoistic and malicious," were generally directed at the fool or the fake.[3] For the first time, playwrights presented to their audiences "a world of unscrupulous persons who entertained no special prejudices, one way or the other, as touched ethical matters."[4]

On the isolated plantations of America, plays were generally given only by roving groups of professional and semiprofessional actors, many of whom came from Britain expressly for the purpose of touring the rural plantations. These roving companies formed the staple of commercial theater for both town and country, and their productions have been called "stand up and talk theater" because the sets and props were so minimal. Those who fancied more than an occasional theatrical enjoyment were often forced to resort to their own amateur productions or to reading books of plays rather than watching a live professional performance. Among the variations of legitimate theater were the *tableaux vivants,* in which actors and actresses struck attitudes from famous sculptures or paintings, viewed as if through giant picture frames. Tableaux had been a popular expedient of the diversion-starved denizens of the isolated Southern plantation houses. In the cities they were often enjoyed by the bawdier set and composed of young volunteer actresses displaying their charms—though never revealing more than the latest fashion in low-cut gowns. As the volunteers often included some of the most eligible young women from among the urban population, the practice seems to have been free of social stigma. Also popular were opportunities to attend public readings, puppet shows, fencing exhibitions, acting monkeys, dancing dogs, wrestling bears, and feats of magic, balance, dexterity, or ventriloquism.[5]

The Playhouse

Williamsburg, Virginia, was the first colonial capital in America to have a regularly established theatrical season, which began in 1716 for the company of Charles and Mary Stagg. The plays were considered a social and cultural benefit that drew the farmers and planters into the cities from their outlying holdings. This early theater was possibly held in a temporary structure or a converted warehouse for no record of the size or details of a formal playhouse have been found. Nonetheless, the *Virginia Gazette* described a refurbished playhouse for the acting company of Walter Murray and Thomas Keane in 1751.

The Company lately come from London have altered the playhouse into a regular theater fit for the reception of Ladies and Gentlemen and the execution of their own performances, and will open on the first Friday in September with a play called *The Merchant of Venice*, written by William Shakespeare. Ladies engaging seats in the boxes are advised to send their servants early in the day of the performance to hold them and prevent trouble and disappointment.[6]

As late as 1752, evidence exists that the playhouse used by the company of Lewis Hallam had to be "fitted up" in an old warehouse that stood in the woods where the actors "were wont to cater for their tables by shooting game" from the doors and windows. After several months' work, the company completed a theater with a pit, boxes, gallery, stage, scenery, and several undetermined mechanical contrivances. The layout of this playhouse remains an enigma, but it may have resembled those provincial theaters in England for which there is better evidence.

Commonly, the building used for theatrical presentation was 60 by 24 feet and could seat about 400 patrons. The stage, slightly tilted toward the audience in most English playhouses, was 20 feet in depth and 16 feet in width with four-foot wings on either side to accommodate the entrances and exits of the actors. Eight to 10 benches were placed in the pit directly before the stage. These seated 100 to 120 patrons and were the least expensive seats in the house. Behind and slightly above the pit were the boxes, providing chairs for about 160 better-healed theatergoers. Above all were the gallery or balcony seats, extending over the boxes below and supported by slender columns. The seats might be either benches or chairs depending on the sophistication of the theater clientele. One description from 1768 has the balcony rising "clean to the garret, just like a meeting-house gallery."[7]

As Southern cities grew, Alexandria, Charleston, Savannah, New Orleans, Mobile, and Richmond each established fine theaters. These early theaters could accommodate no more than a few hundred patrons. Of course, only a small number of people had the cash to support such ventures in any case. Due largely to the extremes of American weather, the theater season was modified from the English standard of summer and winter into a fall and spring season. There were three distinct theatrical circuits. New York and Boston were the principal Northern cities supporting professional performances in the antebellum period; Philadelphia, Baltimore, and Annapolis formed the center; and Charlestown and New Orleans made up the Southern circuit. It is difficult to establish which of these circuits was most profitable, but Philadelphia, the largest city in America, and Baltimore, the most active port, were enormously favored by the managers of traveling theatrical companies.

In the sociable and pleasure-seeking environment of the American South, the planter aristocracy and its government officials openly frequented plays and other forms of theatrical performance. Southern theatergoers had amazingly sophisticated tastes affected in large part by the periodic influx of upper-class English and French plantation owners from the sugar islands of the Caribbean. Charlestonians erected the New Theater in 1736, being careful to keep the price of admission just high enough to allow attendance by only the best of society. The town witnessed the first opera performed in the colonies, Colley Cibber's *Flora*. The plays of Shakespeare, Richard Sheridan, Oliver Goldsmith, and George Farquhar alike found a new popularity and attracted large audiences. In 1824, the Camp Street Theater opened as the first English-language playhouse in New Orleans. Theatergoers moved on to the Theatre d' Orleans, a grand structure costing $80,000 to erect in 1832. French and English plays were performed here, and grand opera was introduced in 1837. In 1851, the St. Charles Theater hosted a dozen performances by Swedish singer Jenny Lind.

By the 1850s, most of the major cities in the North had overcome their outdated puritanical inhibitions and sported a large number of theaters and opera houses. New York City had dozens of such establishments, including the John Street Theater of 1767, which was called the "old" theater to distinguish it from the first Park Theater built in 1798. The partly constructed Park Theater was pictured on the obverse of the New York Theater token, a large copper coin valued at a penny, struck in 1797 in response to a general shortage of coins. Few theater tokens were struck because the Federal government took over the production of coins shortly thereafter. Some of the largest theatrical establishments in New York were the Bowery Theater (2,500 seats), Christy and Woods' Theater (2,000 seats), the Broadway Theater (2,000 seats), Niblo's Garden (1,800 seats), Burton's Theater (1,700 seats), and the Academy of Music (1,500 seats). At the same time, Chicago had at least three theaters, the newest, McVicker's, costing $85,000 to build.

Washington Irving noted, "The Theater . . . begins to answer all the purposes of a coffee-house. . . . [I]t is the polite lounge, where the idle and curious resort, to pick up the news of the fashionable world, to meet their acquaintances, and to show themselves off to advantage. As to the dull souls who go for the sake of the play, why, if their attention is interrupted by the conversation of their neighbors, they must bear it with patience; it is the custom authorized by fashion. Persons who go for the purpose of chatting with friends are not to be deprived of their amusement; they have paid their dollar, and have a right to entertain themselves as well as they can. As to those who are annoyed by their talking, why they need not listen to it; let them mind their own business."[8]

Theaters were often converted warehouses or the second floors of buildings used for other purposes. Only in the second quarter of the 19th century did permanent theaters become common. These were usually financed through popular subscription. Ultimately the leisure to enjoy plays was created by money and the willingness of local patrons to support the theater. The season lasted several months with performances two or three nights a week. Maintaining a theater and company of actors could involve appreciable sums. The Beekman Street Theater in New York in 1762 grossed about 2,000. Of this about 650 was needed to fit out the playhouse, 250 to run 16 performances, 400 for scenery and clothing, and the remaining 700 for the actors. In 1818, Thomas A. Cooper, a member of an English theatrical company playing in New Orleans, received the fabulous sum of $333 per performance. After 1849, with the country bursting with cash from the gold rush in California, theater underwent a surge of popularity. Improved oceanic navigation brought many foreign plays and performers to American shores in an effort to cash in on the discovery of American gold. Moreover, an improved and proliferating railroad system allowed actors and supporting theatrical craftspersons to travel more swiftly about the nation, moving from city to city in a single season. These advances provided a wealth of entertainment unthought of a decade earlier.

Lighting and Scenery

A theatrical production required both lighting and scenery. All the lighting in early theaters was provided by candlelight. A barrel hoop chandelier or two, fitted with candles, would illuminate the auditorium, and a few dozen candles in reflective holders would be set about the walls, hung from the scenery, and ranged along the foot of the stage and on ladders in the wings. This arrangement was cheap and relatively safe, for an upset candle was less likely to cause a sudden great fire than a broken oil lamp. Not until after the Civil War did oil lamps replace candles in frontier theaters, whereas those in the cities were generally illuminated by gas. Yet "a thousand candles" were put forth as an attractive feature at a concert in New York as late as 1845.[9] The Camp Street Theater in New Orleans had gaslights in 1824, two years before any playhouse in New York City. Nonetheless, a large number of theaters suffered from fires that presumably found their start in the open flames of the lighting. The famous Park Theater in New York was rebuilt after a fire as the New Park Theater on the same site in 1821; and in 1829, the Lafayette Theater in New York burned even though it was fitted with gas illumination. The Jenny Lind Theater, burned in 1851, was replaced with amazing speed, and it burned again within two days of reopening.

The scenery was almost always of painted canvas either supported by wooden frames or hung from the ceiling. These came in four common types of flats units: wings, shutters, drops, and borders. Wings and shutters were similar pairs of tall rectangular screens painted to look like the sidewalls of interior rooms or like trees and bushes for outdoor scenes. The shutters were somewhat wider than the wings. A pair of working doors, one on either side of the stage to facilitate exits and entrances, might serve as a proscenium. Drops and borders, respectively, were large and small rolls of painted canvas combined to look like distant landscapes, room interiors, ceilings, foliage, or even the sky. Some playhouse had stages fitted with trapdoors for sudden exits and mysterious entrances. The front curtain rose at the beginning of the play and fell only at the end of an act. Scene changes within an act were made in full view of the audience by stagehands or minor players often dressed as servants. Noah Ludlow, an actor traveling with a small company from Albany, New York, to the Midwest noted how the company was equipped with "a contractable painted drop for use as a proscenium, a drop curtain, a set of three-flap wings (one flap painted for exteriors, one for fancy interiors, one for plain interiors), six roll drops (woods, street, parlor, kitchen, palace, garden), and a green baize carpet."[10]

As soon as permanent playhouses were established in America, they were fitted with the necessary machinery needed to produce the natural effects of wind, sea, and weather and the supernatural, if not realistic, portrayal of mystical appearances and celestial flights. Such devices had been invented in Italy during the 16th and 17th centuries and had spread to all of Europe. A combination of ropes, pulleys, counterweights, moving platforms, and willing hands could produce seascapes, levitations, the clouding over of the sky, thunderstorms, and quick transformations of setting with a minimum of effort.[11]

According to the *New York Mirror* of October 6, 1827, the new-built Lafayette Theater in New York sported some awe-inspiring innovations.

> The stage, with its scenery and machinery, exceeds all former attempts in this country. It is one hundred and twenty feet deep, and in some places one hundred feet wide. . . . The [gas]light is more natural, and imparts an unequalled brilliancy to the productions of the artist. It also strips the stage from the lamp ladders which prevented the wings from being opened beyond a certain width; so now the width of the stage presented to the audience may be increased at pleasure.[12]

"The Play's the Thing"

English theater companies prepared a large number of plays while crossing the Atlantic to tour America. Lewis Hallam's group in the 1750s rehearsed four of Shakespeare's plays, five of Farquhar's comedies, two late Elizabethan tragedies, a newly written sentimental comedy, and a middle-class prose tragedy during the 42-day crossing to Virginia. The large repertoire of plays was necessary as each night's performance included a main presentation and an afterpiece. The afterpiece was often a one- or two-act farce, a comic opera, a pantomime, or a burlesque. Actors worked out the dueling and physically demanding scenes on their own. Female characters were expected to flaunt their sexual proclivities and shrewdness behind a facade of witty repartee and polite formality, whereas male characters were to be played as either too calculating or too suggestive.

Each actor in the small repertory companies learned a particular line of parts for the season, while the leading performers clung to the important roles and jealously guarded them. The first traveling theatrical stars found it more profitable to move among several resident repertory companies rather than stay with one group for an entire season. Within a few decades, however, the popularity of the traveling star had weighed down and weakened the resident repertory companies that had been the core of American theater. Although the stars had their favorite roles, nearly all their favorite parts could be found in the standard repertory. According to the theater critic of the *Albion* of September 2, 1848, audiences were thoroughly acquainted with the "round of . . . well-known characters, every point and phase of which [were] familiar as 'household gods' to the masses of play goers, and on which criticism has been exhausted." Consequently, the quality of the performance and the characterization of the role by the actors often overshadowed the plot and sequence of any play in the minds of knowledgeable audiences, and the comparative worth of actors was found by comparing the quality of the stars serving in the same part.[13]

A few actors so specialized their performances that they did not play the standard roles. The first of these was the English comic, Charles Mathews, who performed a program of stories, songs, and imitations of serious leading actors. American James H. Hackett specialized as the ultimate Yankee character, and George Handel Hill became so closely associated with Hiram Dodge in *The Yankee Pedlar* (1838) that it was impossible for him to separate himself from the part. Likewise, other actors, such as Dan Marble, Joshua Silsbee, and John E. Owens, became known for their entertaining, if not realistic portrayals of "Down East" characters both in America and England. Their quaint, dry humor quickly became representative of what might be styled American comedy of the period from 1820 to 1850.

A False Start

The first play by an American playwright to be performed by professional actors was Thomas Godfrey's *The Prince of Parthia* (1767). However, English comedies, the plays of Shakespeare, and the Greek and Roman classics remained very popular for more than a century. American theater seemed to reach a level of maturity in 1773 when Goldsmith's comedy

She Stoops to Conquer was played in New York only five months after opening in London. However, the spiraling conflict between the colonies and
Britain put a temporary halt to the development of professional theater
in America for almost a decade. Nonetheless, the American Revolution
spawned a number of plays by patriots, loyalists, and even redcoat generals, but many were not intended for the stage and some had structures
that were clearly not stageable. Among the plays written during the war
were several loyalist pieces that mocked the American rebels and their
leaders: *A Dialogue Between a Southern Delegate and His Spouse on His Return from the Grand Continental Congress* (1774), *The Americans Roused in a
Cure for the Spleen* (1775), and *The Battle of Brooklyn* (1776).

Mercy Otis Warren, an American patriot, structured her anti-Tory
political comments within plays, but none were ever performed on stage
because Mercy had specifically written them for publication in the newspapers. Such writing was a common form used to express ideas to the
public. Through her plays, Mercy revealed her contempt for the Tory administration in Boston and her passion for Whig ideology. *The Adulateur*
(1773) criticized the lieutenant governor of Massachusetts and glorified
such radicals as Sam Adams and Warren's brother, James Otis. *The Defeat*
(1774) continued to mock Hutchinson, and *The Group* (1775), her most
popular play, focused on Hutchinson's family and showed Warren's disdain for Americans who maintained their loyalty to the Crown.

In 1776, British General Sir John Burgoyne, in his self-appointed role as
playwright, penned *The Blockade of Boston*, a satire that mocked the
colonials and glorified the British. Performances of this play in Boston
infuriated the patriots. Warren quickly penned a play in answer titled, *The
Blockheads; or the Affrightened Officers: A Farce* (1776), a scorching personal
attack on the British regulars and the Crown forces as a whole. In another
work, *The Motley Assembly: A Farce* (1776), she maintained a more democratic perspective, which focused on a different target: women of the upper social classes who remained absorbed in a world of fashion and luxury
rather than the cause of American liberty.

While Warren's plays could be recited, they were hardly stageable. By
contrast, several plays by American patriots could be staged, and some
became the afterpiece stock of antebellum theatrical seasons where they
were rewritten, reworked, or simply plagiarized. These included Hugh
Brackenridge's *The Battle of Bunker Hill* (1776); John Leacock's five-act
drama *The Fall of British Tryanny* (1776); and Robert Munford's comedy
The Patriots (1776).

With the outbreak of war, the professional actors had left the major cities of America. Many returned to England or fled to Jamaica and other
islands of the Caribbean. The British officers occupying the urban centers
of America amused themselves by producing plays during the long winter
months of relative inactivity. Major John Andre, who figured prominently

in the treachery of Benedict Arnold and served as adjutant to the commanding British general, designed and painted scenery for several amateur productions. Burgoyne's *The Blockade* was performed several times in Boston at Faneuil Hall; in Philadelphia an amateur company called General Howe's Thespians performed regularly at the Southark Theater; and in New York, Richard Sheridan's *The Rivals* and *The School for Scandal* made their American premieres at the Theater Royal at the hands of amateur performers in 1777 and 1782 respectively.

As soon as the war was over, the professional actors returned to America. In 1785, John Henry and Lewis Hallam joined with several other professionals from the pre-Revolutionary days to form the Old American Company, which held a virtual monopoly over theater presentations from New York to Charleston for the next decade. In New York, the first capital of the United States, President George Washington kept a box at the John Street Theater and attended frequently. When the capital switched to Philadelphia so did the chief executive's theater attendance, both at the Southark and Chesnut theaters.

Resurrection

At least 700 American plays are known to have been produced in the period between the establishment of the Constitution and the outbreak of the Civil War. Many others have escaped the keen research of historians because they were never published. The lack of any enforceable copyright protection caused the authors to limit copies of their plays to the several sheets needed by the performers to act the play. The plots for the American works were constructed based on the events and personages of the American Revolution, Jacksonian politics, disputes over the boundaries of Maine and Oregon, the gold rush, the American war with Mexico, antislavery, and temperance.

Most Northern urban areas supported American theater groups. Several of James Fenimore Cooper's novels were adapted for the Northern stage, and a number of distinctive American characters were developed such as the rural Yankee, the noble savage, or the tough-fisted Bowery Bhoy. However, some critics found the work vulgar, coarse, and in bad taste. Clearly, many stock performances were routine, tedious, or slipshod. Walt Whitman wrote that they were becoming "beyond all toleration."[14] Few Southern playwrights basked in any literary or financial success because most Southern theaters emphasized performance rather than unique writing. It was the minstrel show that was actually more important to the long-range development of Southern literature as it fixed the stereotype of plantation tradition and stimulated an interest in African American culture that would emerge in later decades. The minstrel show is thought

A newspaper illustration of the near riot among the audience at the Bowery Street Theater in New York. Theater patrons were generally unrestrained and let their feelings about the quality of the show be known during performances.

by some to actually be the earliest development of a truly indigenous American drama and the birth of American comedy.

Playwrights

Although a great many plays were written by American playwrights in the antebellum period, few were worthy of distinction. The theater simply did not attract the best writers. A playwright could expect as little as $500 for a new play and $100 for an adaptation. Since a royalty system had not yet been developed, plays were ordinarily sold for a onetime lump sum to the main actor or the director of the company of players. The author rarely saw any further income from its performance. In 1829, the actor Edwin Forrest offered a prize of $500 and half of the third night's proceeds to any author who could write a five-act tragedy in which the principal character was a Native American. John Augustus Stone rose to the occasion with *Metamora, or The Last of the Wampanoags*. The play was first presented at the Park Theater in New York, and it remained popular as an afterpiece for many years. Stone's work was so well known that it was parodied almost two decades later by John Brougham in a humorous burlesque called *Metamora, or The Last of the Pollywogs*.

John Howard Payne, a struggling American actor and poet living in England, was among the first to receive critical recognition outside the United States when in 1818 his blank verse play *Brutus, or The Fall Tarquin* was performed in London by the acclaimed actor Edmund Keane. Two years later, Payne's play *Therese, the Orphan of Geneva* opened with great success at the newly rebuilt Park Theater in New York. In 1823, he penned the libretto to a three-act opera, *Clari, or The Maid of Milan* that contained a song that would become an American classic, *Home, Sweet Home*. Opera, however, proved an abject failure in the 1830s, but experienced a popular renaissance in the 1840s and 1850s.

Richard Penn Smith of Philadelphia was a particularly prolific playwright, producing four plays in a single year (1829), but he was outdone by Robert M. Bird, who wrote a total of 54 plays. Among these was *The Gladiator* (1831), based on the life of Spartacus and very popular in the North because of its antislavery theme. Edwin Forrest played the slave revolt leader more than 1,000 times, and he took pains throughout his life to prevent the script from being published lest some other actor gain the role. Bird wrote two more successful plays for Forrest but ultimately gave up drama for other forms of writing that brought a more regular income.

Southern playwrights generally congregated in Charleston. Among them was George Washington Parke Custis who wrote *The Indian Prophecy* (1827), *The Eighth of January* (1834), and the much-celebrated *Pocahontas* (1836). Other popular plays were Robert Conrad's *Jack Cade* (1835), and George Henry Boker's *Calaynos* (1849), *Leonor de Guzman* (1853), and *Francesca Da Rimini* (1855). The last was loosely based on Dante's *Inferno* and may have been the best play of its type in the period.

Social satire was a strong theme in American drama, and reformers were well aware of its impact. Immediately after the release of Harriet Beecher Stowe's novel *Uncle Tom's Cabin* (1852), half a dozen stage adaptations appeared (one of them produced by P.T. Barnum). The play had a tremendous influence on the public. Although the South considered it a slander, huge audiences came to view it in the North. In a similar vein, *The Octoroon* (1859) by Dion Boucicault was based on Mayne Reid's successful novel *The Quadroon* (1856).

Anna Cora Ogden, the daughter of a cultivated and respectable New York family, had married the much older James Mowatt at age 15, but her husband quickly lost both his health and his money. Faced with financial embarrassment, Anna turned to her interest in theater to become the first important female playwright in America. In 1845, her comedy, *Fashion*, was produced on the New York stage at the Park Theater. She wrote in her autobiography of witnessing a particularly businesslike and solemn rehearsal of her play by the company, "The day before its representation I became anxious to witness one of these rehearsals . . . [and] I began to fancy I had made a mistake, and unconsciously written a tragedy."[15] However, Mowatt had written a good-humored satire about the society that she knew best where every change in fashion—dress, food, furniture, cosmetics, and art—was sought after by the newly rich, and everything foreign, especially if it were French, was regarded as wonderful and exciting. The comedy was quickly accepted and had a long life on the stage. Edgar Allan Poe reviewed the opening of the play noting that it was an "ingenious and really spirited . . . selection from among the usual routine of stage characters and stage maneuvers." Poe attributed the success of *Fashion* "to the very carpets, the very ottomans, the very chandeliers, and the very conservatories" of which it made sport.[16]

Thereafter, Mowatt became an important playwright but could not earn a sufficient income without making personal appearances as a public reader. Encouraged by her success before the many literary societies and clubs that employed such persons, Mowatt determined to try acting itself. She debuted as Pauline in Bulwer-Lytton's *The Lady of Lyons* in New York in 1845, and was an immediate success. Although her husband died in the interim, Mowatt survived on the stage in America and England for nine years, retiring only after her marriage to William F. Ritchie of Virginia. Thereafter, she became an admired lady in Richmond society, successfully transplanting her Northern New York ways to the Old South.

Actors and Actresses

When a group of players tried to open a theater in Lowell, Massachusetts, in 1833, they were arrested and put in jail for not "pursuing an honorable and lawful profession."[17] Yet, in most communities acting in the legitimate theater was a respectable profession. The antebellum stage was filled with excellent actors: Thomas A. Cooper, George F. Cooke, Edmund Keane, Edwin Forrest, Junius and Edwin Booth, Edward Davenport, James Wallack, and Charles Burke. Among the actresses were Fanny Kemble, Mary Ann Duff, Anna Mowatt, and Laura Keene. Below the principal professional actors were a group of paid hirelings, and below that, volunteer amateurs. Several child and teen actors graced the stage, including John Howard Payne and sisters Kate and Ellen Bateman.

Thomas A. Cooper

Thomas A. Cooper was the manager of the Park Theater in New York, and when he was not undertaking brief engagements in other cities, he was the theater's leading actor. Although Cooper frequently displayed great talent, there seems to have been an equally great inequity in the quality of his performances. His critics and admirers agreed that his Hamlet was one of his better roles, but that his great performances were given as Macbeth. Cooper's role as lead actor in a repertory company did not absolve him from hard work. His appearances as the leading actor in a series of standard repertory plays were not enough to keep a theater prosperous, and he took steps to keep the theater fresh and exciting.

Among the methods used to maintain audience interest were females acting in male dress—usually in roles traditionally reserved for male actors—the introduction of child prodigies to the stage, and the use of dwarfs, midgets and live animals. Tom Thumb, the little person made famous by P.T. Barnum, was one of these. Antebellum audiences, who were generally familiar with the plots and endings of the plays they attended, seem to have been inordinately attracted to the theater by the very thought of a woman appearing in public in male clothing. "In a day when the glimpse of a female ankle was titillating, the sight of a considerable portion of a woman's legs—though by later standards the costumes were modest—was certainly an attraction for men." When the dancer Mme. Hutin appeared on stage in New York in 1827 in a slightly abbreviated outfit, every lady in the lower boxes rushed from the theater in a fit of prudish horror.[18] After mid-century, Adah Menken would become notorious as the hero of *Mazeppa* as she was stripped naked and tied to the back of a supposedly wild horse. The adaptation of Lord Byron's poem to the stage was advertised as "A grand equestrian spectacle" with the wild horse "of true flesh and blood." In reality the horse was quite tame, and the actress was clothed in flesh-colored tights and a short tunic.[19]

One of the first of the child prodigies was the teenaged John Howard Payne, who went on to become a playwright of some note. Payne came from a poor family, but given the chance, he quickly convinced Cooper of his abilities. In eight performances at the Park in 1809–1810, the 17-year-old played six separate parts, and in another brief engagement, he was required to learn three new leading roles. He was particularly popular in the roll of Shakespeare's Romeo where his youth served as a counterpoint to the performances in the roles of many able but otherwise obviously aged actors. "Of the characters represented by this young gentlemen, those in which he has evinced [his] greatest powers are Douglas, Tancred, and Romeo . . . a performance respecting which there is but one opinion, and that highly favourable to Master Payne's reputation." Payne's appearance as Edgar in *King Lear* opposite the much older star, George Frederick Cooke as Lear, was seen as a new beginning for the American repertory theater. Unfortunately, Payne was trained in Cooper's tedious style, and while his acting career in America was brilliant, it was brief. Fearing that there was a conspiracy brewing against him, Payne removed himself to England where he acted and wrote for the theater with less-brilliant success.[20]

Cooper's acting style, which included a studied posture and precise pronunciation similar to the elocution taught to students in 19th-century grammar schools, set the standard by which many performers were judged in the early antebellum period. Modern audiences might find it affected, tedious, and even painful. The result could be dull and monotonous when used to deliver the lines of characters in common conversation, and it did not burst into a sudden glow of emotion or passion until the actor had fixed himself into some posture on the stage accompanied by great gestures of the hands and arms. According to contemporary critics, "These tedious, tardy enunciations—these laborings after grace—these rowings of the arms—twistings of the head—sawings of the air—these pauses without significance, and all the other fantastic grimaces" were seized upon and imitated by scores of less-talented actors than Cooper.[21]

George F. Cooke

Ironically, it was Cooper and his partner in the management of the Park Theater, Stephen Price, who introduced American audiences to the more natural style of the English actor, George Frederick Cooke. The English actor arrived in New York in 1810 to star in the resident company's production of *Richard III*. His portrayal was outstanding. "His style was quiet, but astonishingly impressive," noted an observer. "You felt everything he did. The face fixed your attention at once. The words that followed riveted your attention and absorbed all objects else. . . . You did not see Cooke; you only saw the character." In their production of *Othello*, Cooper and Cooke squared off against each other as Othello and Iago, respectively. While Cooper was noted for his portrayal of the impulsive Moor, Cooke's Iago had no equal. His acting power "toppl[ed] Cooper in an instant from his towering height to an oblivious position, with only the sympathies of his audience."[22]

Cooke drew in more than $20,000 in total receipts in just his first 17 performances in America. Yet his contract paid only $125 per performance plus expenses. Nonetheless, he was the first actor of note to be featured as a player from outside a resident acting company in America. The appearance of a "star" thereafter became a common feature of antebellum theater, accompanied as it was by widespread pre-appearance advertising and publicity in handbills and newspapers. Cooke's career on the American stage was brief, however. He died in 1812, and Cooper's less romantic style of acting continued to dominate stage performance for over a decade.

Edmund Keane

One of the greatest of England's visiting stars was Edmund Keane, who introduced a new romantic style of acting that paralleled similar developments in literature and music. With a childhood experience as an acrobat and carnival entertainer, it is somewhat surprising that Keane's portrayals were described as dignified, graceful, and restrained. Nonetheless, his speech and body movement on stage could suddenly erupt in bursts of emotion and violent action. He did his best work in the role of an arch villain such as Shylock, Iago, Barabas, or Richard III. An anonymous critic wrote of his performance as Richard, "He is eminently successful in situations which admit of intense fire and vivacity of action; inarticulate passion, or rapid alternations of countenance and tone. Sudden and strong vicissitudes of feeling are admirably portrayed in the movement of his features."[23]

Keane's first appearance in America was at the Anthony Street Theater in 1820, where his first critics found that he relied on the mechanics of his movements rather than the pronunciation of his oratory. "His studied play of Physiognomy borders on grimace; his animation of manner becomes incoherent bustle. . . . He obviously relies more on mechanical resources, than on his general mental preparations and powers." Nonetheless, as the audiences responded to this new romantic style of presentation, the critics found his voice "susceptible of praise" and "agreeable" in a "measured and deliberate" if not "musical" way. "There are feelings and language to which guttural notes, sepulchral sounds, even broken, harsh accents, are appropriate. [Keane] at times excels in the oratorical department of his profession." Keane electrified audiences in all the major eastern cities, and he also gave birth to a new practice in theater—the curtain call.[24]

Junius B. Booth

Contemporary with Keane's success was the arrival in America of Junius Brutus Booth from England. Although he was unsuccessful in eclipsing Keane on the American stage, Junius Booth was a formidable actor, a talented practitioner of theatrical arts, and the foundation of America's first family of theatrical performers, including the brothers Edwin and John Wilkes Booth, who would gain widely different reputations in the 1860s. Some observers considered Junius Booth to be Keane's equal as an actor, if not his superior. Their unspoken confrontation centered upon the same roles with Booth playing Richard III, Iago, and Othello. "He spoke like a man thinking aloud, not as if reciting from memory," wrote Booth admirer Thomas R. Gould. "He possessed himself of the character, and its language, and then turned it from utter inspiration and according to the emergency of the scene and the situation." In his acting, Junius swept all restraints aside and made the emotions of hate, jealousy, ambition, and anger overpoweringly real for his audiences. Booth's style embodied a series of coordinated characterizations that built into a powerful expression of emotion, whereas Keane's manner was more like "a series of disconnected brilliant effects" that burst upon the stage full-grown.[25]

Edwin Forrest

Philadelphia-born Edwin Forrest was America's first successful actor and star. Having served a theatrical apprenticeship with a touring company in the Ohio Valley and New Orleans, Forrest came to prominence in New York at the Bowery Theater in 1829. He was the leading man at the Park Theater until 1836. George Vandehoff, a visiting English actor, wrote of Forrest in 1842, "His voice surged and roared like the angry sea, lashed into fury by a storm; till, as it reached its boiling, seething climax, in which the serpent hiss of hate was heard, at intervals, amidst its louder, deeper, hoarser tones, it was like the falls of Niagara, in its tremendous down-sweeping cadence: it was a whirlwind, a tornado, a cataract of illimitable rage!"[26]

Forrest was one of the first stars to seek out new plays and new roles for his talents. Forrest's most popular roles were those of rebels: William Tell, Mark Anthony, Damon, Jack Cade, and two that were written for him, Spartacus from *The Gladiator* and Metamora from the play of the same name. He gave more than 1,000 performances of *The Gladiator*. Forrest dominated American theater, and his portrayal of Othello became the standard by which American Shakespearean actors were measured thereafter. A theater critic noted in 1848, "His Shakespearean characters are all stamped with the same intense energy of expression, and overwhelming displays of physical force. The imbecile Lear, and the melancholy Dane, are in his hands frequently like enraged Titans, both in look and manner. Macbeth is the ferocious chief of a barbarous tribe—and his Othello, with all its many beauties, becomes in his hands truly the ferocious and 'bloody Moor.' " Nonetheless, Forrest attracted some disapproval from the upper classes—and some highly valuable publicity—when, as Lear, he tore open his shirt revealing a naked chest, unclothed by the customary undershirt, to the audience.[27]

Joseph Jefferson

In 1842, Charles Dickens attended the Marshall Theater in Richmond specifically to see Joseph Jefferson, considered the greatest living actor of his day. Jefferson was well known to audiences in the nation's capital and throughout the South, especially for his portrayal of an indolent Rip Van Winkle, a role he played for 38 years. L. Clarke Davis described Jefferson in the role of Rip in the *Atlantic Monthly* in 1867: "Standing there, he is in himself the incarnation of the lazy, good-natured, dissipated, good-for-

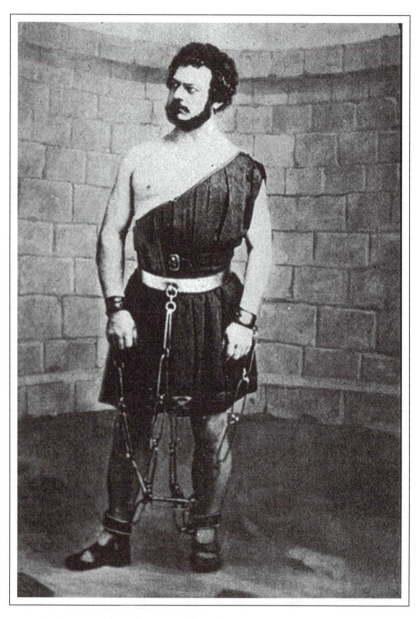

Edwin Forrest was the most famous stage actor of the antebellum period. In this period photograph, he is costumed for his signature role as Spartacus, the leader of a great slave revolt against the Roman Empire in *The Gladiator*. Audiences drew close parallels between the theme of Spartacus and the need to end Southern slavery.

nothing Dutchman that Irving drew. [A] preponderance of humor is expressed in every feature, yea, in every limb and motion of the light, supple figure." Jefferson returned to the East in 1858 and made a strong impression as the Yankee, Asa Trenchard, in Laura Keene's very successful production of *Our American Cousin*. Had Dickens visited the Marshall Theater in 1859, he might have seen a 21-year-old actor, John Wilkes Booth, who was then playing a supporting role for $20 a week in *Beauty and the Beast* and who would be forever linked with *Our American Cousin* after he assassinated President Lincoln during its performance at Ford's Theater in 1865.[28]

Fanny Kemble

In 1832, Charles Kemble, the youngest of a large and famous family of English actors, came to America with his daughter, Fanny. Charles had never gained the respect or the acclaim of audiences and critics like those of his siblings in England. Yet in America he was well received. "We think Mr. Kemble's appearance in America will do a service to the art," wrote a critic for the *New York Post*. "[I]t will raise and refine its style . . . with the grace and ease, and elegance of Kemble."[29] Nonetheless, the enthusiasm of the American audience focused largely on Kemble's young daughter, Fanny.

The impression made by this young women, and the universal applause that followed it, left audiences enthusiastic to see more of her work. "Her acting . . . is full of intellectual excellence. . . . She depicts tenderness, jealousy, hate, and despair with a truth that now melts the soul, now makes it tremble. . . . Her hate is sardonic, Keane-like, and almost intolerable; her love deeply impassioned and tender, all bashful girlishness, and full of exquisitely graceful touches—full of them." Fanny was considered by some to be strikingly beautiful and even radiant, but it was her portrayals that evinced a moral splendor beyond physical beauty. Initially, she was best known for her role as Shakespeare's Juliet, which she played with warmth and sensitivity.[30]

Ironically, Fanny's father was almost forced into playing the teenaged Romeo opposite her because the New York theaters had no young leading man capable of holding the attention of the audience. Notwithstanding the obvious mismatched ages of the actors to their roles, 19th-century audiences had not yet become accustomed to typecasting and realism, and they were perfectly willing to accept anomalies of age and costuming in their theatergoing.

Charlotte Cushman

Trained as a singer but unable to maintain a competitive voice, Charlotte Cushman played her first theatrical role in America in 1835 at the age of 19 and dominated the cadre of actresses in much the same way that Edwin

Forrest did the actors. Born in Boston, she was America's first great home-grown queen of the stage. Her debut at New York's Bowery Theater was as Lady Macbeth, and shortly thereafter she appeared in the same role in Albany and Boston to great acclaim. In 1839, she caused a considerable stir in the role of Nancy Sykes in a stage adaptation of *Oliver Twist* at the Park Theater. She was thereafter considered the leading lady of tragedy in both New York and Philadelphia. In 1844, she went to England and took the audiences there by storm. When she returned to America in 1849, she was a star of the first magnitude among all those women appearing on the English-speaking stage.

George Vandenhoff, an English actor, noted that Cushman's performances were marked by "a rude, strong, uncultivated talent," a quality that some found shocking and disturbing, yet she also brought "artistic study and finish" to her work. "The power of her scorn, and the terrible earnestness of her revenge, were immense." Her greatest part, "fearfully natural, dreadfully intense, horribly real," was as Nancy Sykes. It was almost too true to life for the reform-minded patrons of American theaters. Vandenhoff wrote, "[I]t was painful, this actual presentation of Dickens' poor abandoned, abused, murdered, outcasts [*sic*] of the streets."[31]

Cushman also aroused the popular interest of audiences by playing male roles. She portrayed Romeo in a dashing and spirited manner opposite her own sister, Susan, as Juliet. A critic was not favorably impressed, however, finding Charlotte's killing of Tybalt and Paris effective, but thinking her other characterizations neither masculine nor feminine, but rather simply asexual. Nonetheless, she played many other male roles in her career to great acclaim, including that of Hamlet and that of Cardinal Wolsey in *Henry VII*.

11

Travel

Man fell with apples, and with apples rose,
If this be true; for we must deem the mode
In which Sir Isaac Newton could disclose
Through the unpaved stars the turnpike road,
A thing to counterbalance human woes:
For ever since immortal man hath glow'd
With all kinds of mechanics, and full soon
Steam-engines will conduct him to the moon.
                    —Lord Byron, *Don Juan*, Canto the Tenth, II (1823)

IMPROVED TRANSPORTATION

The ability to move people and goods efficiently and quickly from place to place was a significant advance during this period. The Appalachian Mountains had been a barrier to communications and internal commerce between the coastal cities and the interior of America since colonial times. There were only three significant water routes through these mountains in the northeastern quadrant of the United States. Besides the Hudson River, which flowed almost directly south out of central New York State, the major rivers of the Atlantic seaboard were the Delaware and the Susquehanna. All three rivers found their headwaters in the mountains east and southeast of the Great Lakes and served as convenient routes for fur traders and explorers. However, only the Hudson was capable of carrying the heavy boat traffic that was characteristic of a growing economy. The Great Lakes themselves were an important artery of commerce and communication between the cities of the Northeast and the new states and territories of the Midwest. They were capable of hosting large sailing vessels as well as barges, flatboats, and lumber rafts. With the completion of the Erie Canal across New York, linking the lakes with the Hudson River in 1825, and with the advent of steam navigation in the first quarter of the century, the inland lake system became even more important to the economy of the nation.

The Mississippi River was the most profoundly important waterway in America. Its course formed part of the political boundaries of Kentucky, Tennessee, Missouri, Mississippi, Arkansas, and Louisiana. Its 44 major tributaries made navigable connections to other major river systems such as the Ohio, the Tennessee, the Arkansas, and the Missouri. The remaining major rivers that flowed through the South to the Atlantic tidewater included the Potomac, the Rappahannock, the James, and the York in Virginia; the Roanoke and the Cape Fear in North Carolina; the Pee Dee and the Santee in South Carolina; and the Oconee, the Ocmulgee, the Altamaha, and the Savannah in Georgia. These and their tributaries wore gaps in the ranges of small Appalachian foothills to flow to the coast. The Shenandoah River was one of the few Southern rivers that flowed to the Northeast, emptying into the Potomac at Harper's Ferry. Along the Gulf Coast, the Coosa and Alabama Rivers flowed to the port of Mobile, Alabama, and the Tombigbee reached deep into the state of Mississippi.

The rivers of the Old South served as connections to the interior and were navigable up to the division between the piedmont and the coastal plain, which was known as the Fall Line. It was along the Fall Line that the swiftly flowing mountain streams that turned the waterwheels of mills and factories became the deep, lazy, navigable rivers that flowed quietly to the coast. Here also were many important cities and Southern capitals. Richmond, Raleigh, Columbia, Augusta, and Montgomery are all situated along the Fall Line. A smooth curve connecting these cities precisely locates the Fall Line on a modern map as it crosses the Southern states. Flatboats, keelboats, and rafts used these rivers to float cargoes from the interior to the coast in the early years of the republic, and it was said that two-thirds of all the markets in the South were within five miles of some navigable steam. Few plantations lacked a river landing and such natural waterways continued to have traffic on them well into the railroad era. Modern steam vessels further complimented the transportation efficiency of the South's river system.

Internal Improvements

One of the major political questions in the early decades of the 19th century was government financing of internal improvements. The building of roads, railroads, and canals and the dredging of harbors and waterways required a good deal of private capital and investment. When money was missing or unavailable, as during the major financial panics of 1819 and 1837, there was a clamor for such projects to be undertaken at national expense in order to stimulate commerce. State money had been used to finance canals and roads in New York and Pennsylvania, and Federal money had helped to open highways into the Great Lakes region. However, sectional interests largely dictated the general attitude of the voting population toward programs like these.[1]

In the East, with population centers more closely placed than in other sections of the country, the issue of internal improvements was not a vital one. The center of the American maritime trade in New England had many convenient and efficient means of commercial transportation. The existing road networks in the Northeast were, for the most part, well engineered, numerous, and funded by private money.

For the Midwest, where a large part of the potential profits from farming were expended in transporting crops to market by wagon and where consumer goods were rare and expensive, the development of alternate means of transportation and communication was viewed as a dire necessity. The fertile but inexpensive lands of Iowa, Kansas, Nebraska, and Missouri would gain in value if connected to the eastern markets by efficient and relatively inexpensive means of transportation. Many ardent westerners pledged their votes to political candidates solely on the basis of their position on this issue, and they were rewarded with roads, canals, telegraph lines, and railroads that allowed them to ship directly to eastern markets. The Federal government also helped midwestern farmers by dredging shallow rivers and by helping to create harbors in the Great Lakes to facilitate steam shipping.

The most successful canal project in American history, the Erie Canal (1825), connected western New York and the Great Lakes to New England through a flourishing road and railway network that managed to transport raw materials and agricultural products from the Midwest to the American coast and thence to the more remote European markets. New York, New Jersey, Pennsylvania, and all the New England states had almost 3,000 miles of canals, some owned by the states and others by private companies. The Southern states by comparison had less than 500 miles of major canals, and many short canals of under three miles length that were not "of much importance."[2]

For the South, with its natural system of inland rivers that moved agricultural produce at little expense, the building of roads and artificial waterways in other parts of the country was a sore point. Southern farmers and planters had no need for extensive canals and highway systems, and they saw no reason to pay taxes to aid western farmers who were their natural competitors in the area of agriculture. The development of canals and railroads generally displaced the smaller Southern ports as points of transfer from river barges to coasting vessels for western produce floated down the Mississippi River system. The differing opinions concerning internal improvements generally weakened an otherwise natural political alliance of western and Southern farmers against the northeastern industrialists in the U.S. Congress.

MODES OF TRAVEL

Antebellum Americans utilized a wide range of methods when traveling from place to place. As the period began, horse-drawn carriages, stagecoaches, and wagons were the primary means of personal transportation, especially in the North. For short trips between neighboring farms, to go to church, or even to go to the next village or town, most simple people walked, rode astride a horse, or traveled on an oxcart. For longer trips stagecoaches, boats, and railroad trains were all used. In the course of a single trip, many combinations of transportation modes might be employed.

In 1832, Fanny Kemble, a celebrated English actress, journeyed from New York City to Utica, New York, by steamboat and stagecoach. She found the steamboat very large, commodious, and well appointed, but she

Before the development of a network of practical rail lines, travel by stagecoach was often the quickest means of getting from place to place. Enterprising individuals established inns, taverns, and transfer stations approximately every ten miles along the most frequented routes.

disliked her experience in the stagecoach. She could not conceive of a more clumsy or wretched conveyance as she was bumped, thumped, jolted, shaken, tossed, and tumbled over the wickedest roads cut through bogs and marshes and over ruts, roots, and protruding stumps with overhanging tree branches scratching at the windows. Oddly her American companions on the coach, including several young women, seemed quite unaffected by these inconveniences, incessantly laughing and talking at the very top of their voices. In order to provide high-speed travel, horses were usually changed every ten miles at conveniently placed stops such as inns, taverns, and river crossings. Each interval was considered a "stage" along the route, hence the term stagecoach.

Before the widespread development of steam railways in the Northern and middle states, horse-drawn omnibuses crossed through many major cities. The first horse-drawn railroad appeared in England in 1795. In 1826, a horse-drawn railroad paralleled the "Main Line" from Philadelphia to Columbia on the Susquehanna River, but it was quickly replaced by the more efficient Pennsylvania Canal built to compete with the Erie Canal in New York. In 1828, Quincy, Massachusetts, had the first horse-drawn line of the Old Colony System. In 1831, Rochester, New York, established a two-mile-long line that ran to Lake Ontario from the Erie Canal. The Rochester system used 16 cars and moved 800 persons a day. New York City opened a horse-drawn service in 1832 from Prince Street to 14th Street, and it was still adding to the extent of track with a line in East Harlem in 1853. Two of the more extensive systems, the Metropolitan Horse Railroad in Boston (1856) and the Baltimore City Railroad (1859), served their cities with well-appointed, horse-drawn cars and miles of interconnecting track right through the Civil War. Travel on the horse-drawn railroad was not without hazard, however. John H.B. Latrobe reported that his ride in a horse-drawn railroad car was accompanied by a thundering noise caused by the combination of iron wheels on iron rails and street stones that was almost deafening. The *New York Herald* also reported an accident that left a 70-year-old man "mangled in a most shocking manner" by a runaway horse-drawn car on May 28, 1850.

In the South and West, men were particularly fond of riding astride a horse, a mode of transportation not generally favored by those in the Northeast. Westerners, who had to cross great distances between population centers unconnected by good wagon roads or any other means of transportation, were compelled by circumstances to ride; but for Southerners, walking almost any distance was viewed with complete disdain. A contemporary observer noted that Southern males, from early childhood, rode almost everywhere and would mount their horses to go only a short distance down the street. Many men seemingly could not be made to dispense with their horses even under the most trying of economic or meteorological conditions. Moreover, they often provided their servants with four-footed transportation in order to provide care for their own mount. While these sometimes took the form of an ancient mule or jenny, it was not uncommon for a black slave to be provided with a fairly good horse so that he would not impede his master's progress.

The elderly, the females, and the disabled among then gentry (if they traveled at all) traveled mostly in some form of carriage or chaise. These took the form of high-wheeled road carts, chariots, barouches, phaetons, and other meticulously crafted conveyances. Southern roads, unlike those of the North, were composed in large part of lesser-used lanes between plantations, which proved too narrow and overhung with branches to make a large coach practicable. Stagecoach lines between the plantations and the city centers would attract too little traffic to be practical. Nonetheless, well-heeled city dwellers sometimes supported a coach as a sign of their affluence even though they never left the urban districts in it. The gentry would go into debt in order to maintain their own coach and team; and great pride was taken in being seen in a fine conveyance, pulled by matched horses and manned by properly attired drivers and footmen. Rented vehicles were considered by many among the elite as an embarrassment to those who could not afford the ownership of a carriage, and those who resorted to rentals were viewed with contempt.

Commerce had been the business of America since colonial times. Packhorse trains of 10 to 12 horses had been and remained the main carriers of trade goods along Indian trails and forest pathways. Drovers and their helpers often walked along these trails driving sheep, pigs, or cattle to market with the help of their dogs. Whereas men on horseback and small herds of livestock could make their way cross-country, the widespread use of wagons, carriages, public coaches, and other wheeled conveyances had to await the development of turnpikes and highways paved with crushed stone or surfaced with boards and pitch that avoided the persistent mud that could mire any wheeled vehicle. As the nation expanded, itinerant Americans developed a large four-wheeled farm wagon known as a "mover" for journeys over improved roads like these. Into their movers they would pack all their worldly possessions to travel from Pennsylvania to Missouri or from the Carolinas to Mississippi in search of a better homestead or richer soils. For those traveling across the seas of grass on the Great Plains, the mover came to be called a "prairie schooner."[3]

These movers should not be confused with the very large commercial freight wagons known as "Conestogas" that were developed in Pennsylvania for the movement of goods. These had a boat-shaped bed and sloping sides that gave them a swaybacked appearance along their overhanging canvas covers. Capable of carrying almost two tons of goods, these huge and lumbering wagons required six horses or oxen to pull them at even a slow pace. Hundreds of freight and express companies operated with Conestogas in the middle states and in the North at the beginning of the antebellum period. The Conestoga cargo wagon was also the principal means of transporting freight along the Santa Fe, California, and Oregon trails in the far West, but it was not generally used by immigrant trains to the West because it was just too large and heavy for their purpose. Among the earliest professional freight haulers were Alvin Adams, who by the 1850s had turned his pioneering effort into a nationwide business, and the experienced expressmen Henry Wells and John Butterfield, who began the American Express Company. William Fargo joined with Wells in 1852 to form Wells Fargo and Company to handle the freight business west of the Mississippi. They later began a prominent stagecoach line, the Overland Express, to serve the American Southwest.

ROADS

The very poor condition of Southern roads was one of the few circumstances of daily life that most Southerners wanted to change. Many of the roads in the South were very narrow. An observer described them as ditches surrounded by dense forests of second-growth pine or virgin oak that would snarl the movement of any wagons that left the beaten path. Tall stagecoaches, popular in Europe, were impeded by the low, overarching tree branches of the American South. With high humidity and abundant vegetation, the rain-soaked road surfaces of the South remained wet and were easily churned into a sticky morass that was barely passable to wheeled vehicles. Early travelers to the area complained constantly about the condition of the roads, yet few attempts were made to improve them until just before the outbreak of the Civil War. Plantation owners saw little reason to invest in roads because the rivers served well enough for transport. Many attempts to provide private turnpikes or toll roads were blocked by the politically powerful tidewater gentry.

Nonetheless, in 1796, Congress authorized the construction of Zane's Trace, a road from western Virginia to Kentucky that became a major westward route for settlers in the upper South during the antebellum period. The Great Wagon Road through the valley of the Shenandoah River followed the old Warrior's Path south through Maryland to the Carolinas and Georgia. In the 1850s, it was developed into a fine road paved with crushed stone. Known as the Valley Pike during the Civil War, it was a main artery of North-South travel through much of the Southern backcountry, and it proved a strategically important lifeline to the Confederacy. The Natchez Trace, also known as the Old Chickasaw Trail, was an Indian path that led from New Orleans, Louisiana, to Natchez, Mississippi, and thence to Nashville, Tennessee. Except in the immediate vicinity of Natchez and Nashville, it was little more than a track used by pedestrians and those on horseback. Like many of the roads "discovered" by white explorers that were actually thousands of years old, the Natchez Trace had been used by Native Americans for centuries as part of a network of well-worn trails frequented by the pre-Columbian inhabitants of the continent. In the antebellum period, the Natchez Trace was used by the bargemen who floated rafts, flatboats, and keelboats down the interior rivers to the mouth of the Mississippi River and who, lacking the propulsion of the great steamboats, were forced to walk back up the river. Runaway slaves often chose the Trace as a route to freedom in the North. The Trace offered little danger to travelers from unfriendly Indians, but unscrupulous white outlaws continually terrorized small groups of travelers. These grim criminals, lacking any shred of gallantry or romanticism, were among the most inhuman highwaymen in American history.

The generally poor condition of publicly financed roads throughout the country led to the development of privately owned turnpikes and toll roads. Toll keepers placed a large gate or pike across the road to stop traffic every few miles and collected money for passage in lieu of the time and money they invested in maintaining the road. Municipalities often let concessions to private firms on roads of this sort and required that those who lived in the vicinity or who were on public business travel free. Some of the earliest turnpikes were "corduroy" roads. Here, bundles of saplings and small tree trunks were laid across the muddiest parts of the road surface and covered with a thin layer of soil to act as a cushion. Although uneven and bumpy, this arrangement allowed wheeled vehicles pulled by teams of oxen or draught horses to pass without sinking into the mud. Corduroy, however, was very hard on foot traffic and almost impossible for single horses carrying riders who often opted to ride across the open fields rather than pay the toll. Plank roads, as the name suggests, were built with several layers of tarred wooden planking covered with dirt and angled to each side for drainage. They provided a very serviceable and long-lasting traveling surface, but the amount of planking laid in completing such an enterprise required a considerable investment in capital and labor. Such roads, which were in vogue from 1845 to 1857, proved critical to the movement of freight and produce during periods of wet weather. In winter, a stagecoach might still need up to seven hours to cover 10 miles. The road from Albany to Binghamton was a plank road of almost 100 miles that passed through the mineral springs region of upstate New York. Many plank roads survived into the automobile era of the 20th century.

A type of paved road, known as "macadam," was made popular by John Loudon McAdam, a Scottish engineer for whom it was named. It was composed of several layers of compacted, broken cubes of stone that were compressed by the passing traffic. The roadbed was crowned in the middle and ditched on the sides for drainage. The major advantage of this road surface was its ability to virtually ignore the effects of rain. The first

The macadam road was a major improvement in the area of civil engineering. Layers of broken stone were placed one upon the other with the smallest stones on top. The roadbed was crowned and graded to the sides to remove rainwater. Macadam roads eliminated the mud and mire that clogged normal traffic flow.

macadam road in American was laid on the Boonesborough Turnpike in Maryland between Hagertown and Boonesborough in 1823. This was the last section of an improved road leading from Baltimore, Maryland, to Wheeling, West Virginia, on the Ohio River. In 1830, a second macadam road was completed on the National Pike, sometimes called the Cumberland Road. The 73-mile-long stretch of macadam took five years to complete at Federal expense. The Valley Pike in Virginia and the Columbia Pike south out of Nashville, Tennessee, paved in the 1850s, were also macadams.

VACATION TRAVEL

During the antebellum period, upper-class families usually traveled for a summer vacation. Northern families tried to escape the heat of cities crowded with immigrants, and Southern families tried to absent themselves from the coastal regions during the malaria and yellow fever seasons that coincided with the worst of the intolerably hot and humid weather. Throughout the South, it was the habit of the plantation families to remove themselves inland to a seasonal cottage, a resort, or a city with a finer climate than that of the coastal tidewater. It has been estimated that the gentry of South Carolina alone spent more than a half million dollars annually outside their state on such trips.

Historic sites, mineral springs, beaches, caves, waterfalls, mountains, and other natural features became fashionable vacation destinations for antebellum families. Washington's home at Mount Vernon and Jefferson's at Monticello were popular travel destinations in Virginia by both stagecoach and by water along the Potomac River. Tours of the ruins of the French and English forts from the era of the colonial wars at Crown Point and Ticonderoga in New York were very popular. From New York City, by way of the Hudson River and the Champlain Canal, "passengers leave the Champlain boat [at Whitehall, New York] for stage coaches by which they are conveyed over a hilly but romantic road about three miles to Ticonderoga, at the head of Lake George, and thence down the lake, 36 miles, by steamboat, to the Lake House, at its southern extremity . . . and from thence to Saratoga Springs."[4]

Whereas Southerners abandoned their beaches as pestilential and unhealthy in summer, Northern beaches were considered a "delightful retreat in the summer months, for those who wish to enjoy the luxuries of sea air, bathing, fishing, fowling, etc." "The constant sea breeze and convenient sea bathing" were considered to "have a fine effect in restoring the exhausted energies of the human system."[5] Good accommodations, fine hotels, and boarding houses "of the first order" could be found at most seaside resorts, and some places provided special services for invalids and the elderly. Coney Island, "much resorted to by visitors for the sea air and bathing, as it directly faces the Atlantic" was considered a convenient destination for residents of New York City even though they had to pay a toll over the narrow channel that separated it from the mainland.[6] Rockaway Beach on New York's Long Island was 20 miles from the city, but it could be easily approached by railroad—12 miles by rail to the town of Jamaica and 8 miles by coach. The Marine Pavilion was "a splendid establishment erected in 1834 upon the beach," and a number of boarding houses offered "invigorating ocean breezes with less cost and display than at the hotels."[7] No less a personage than President Abraham Lincoln visited the seashore on vacation at Cape May, New Jersey, during the war years. This place, "situated at the mouth of Delaware Bay . . . [had] become an attractive watering-place, much frequented by the citizens of Philadelphia and other [cities]. During the summer season, a steamboat runs from the city to the cape, and affords a pleasant trip. The beach is unsurpassed as a bathing place."

Natural cataracts, like Montmorenci Falls near Quebec, Bellows Falls in Vermont, and Catawba Falls in North Carolina, were considered great natural wonders, as was St. Anthony's Falls on the far away Upper Mississippi River. "The river seems to stop for a moment [before] it encounters the fall; then, breaking through every obstacle, it plunges on, its huge billows breaking on the rocks, and throwing a shower of spray [with] great grandeur and beauty." Flowing from the Great Lakes, Niagara Falls, the outlet of one-half of all the fresh water on Earth, was "justly regarded as one of the most sublime and imposing spectacles in nature." The volume of falling water, estimated at over half a million tons per minute, the precipitous heights, and the tremendous roar were amazing. "It is the vastness of elements like these, entering into the conception of this stupendous natural phenomenon, which carries the emotions of wonder and sublimity with which it strikes the outward senses to their highest bounds."[8]

Tours of caves were considered "agreeable and instructive" with a "pleasant sensation of refreshing coolness." Nonetheless, caving could be physically difficult for some visitors. Mammoth Cave in Kentucky catered to its visitors by supplying "a large and commodious hotel . . . two or three hundred paces from the mouth of the cave . . . with lights, guides, and whatever else may be required for their expeditions." This afforded the visitors to the cave with a view of "its vast dimensions, its great heights and depths in different apartments, and of the singularity and beauty of the natural decoration they contain."[9]

Touring the Springs

Few people would spend weeks traveling along bumpy roads in coaches or on smelly railroad cars to drink spring water at its source today, but 19th-century medical science suggested that the taking of mineral waters had beneficial effects on the health of those who could afford a month at the springs. The mineral laden waters were commonly taken internally to correct real or supposed intestinal ailments, dyspepsia, or general aches and pains. "The decidedly beneficial influence upon consumptive patients, in the earlier stages of that disease, has given them an extensive reputation. Neuralgic cases, also, of the most obstinate character, have yielded to their influence. Scrofula, diseased liver, chronic diarrhea, chronic rheumatism, gravel, dropsy, and diseases of the skin are among the disorders for which these waters have been found a efficacious remedy." In an 1853 list of fashionable vacation destinations, more than a dozen mineral, sulfurous, or hot springs were identified.[10]

The United States Hotel at Saratoga Springs in New York was one of America's most popular luxury hotels and a favorite destination of many wealthy families. Also located in central New York were the mineral springs at Balston Spa and Cobleskill, and the sulfur springs at Sharon.

Antebellum Travel Destinations
Mineral Springs, Waterfalls, Caves, Beaches, and Other Fashionable Resorts
As Identified by Hayward's *Gazetteer*, 1853.

Ascutney Mountain, VT
Avon Springs, NY
Balston Spa, NY
Bellows Falls, VT
Black Mountain, SC
Blennerhasset's Island, OH
Blue Hills, MA
Blue Sulphur Springs, VA
Booth Bay, ME
Brandywine Springs, DE
Burning Springs, NY
Cape Ann, MA
Cape May, NJ
Carrolton Gardens, LA
Catawba Falls, NC
Cohasset Rocks, MA
Cohoes Falls, NY
Coney Island, NY
Crown Point, NY
Dighton Rock, MA
Drennon Springs, KY
Flushing, NY
Fort Ticonderoga, NY
Franconia Notch, NH
Gingercake Rocks, NC
Guilford Point, CT
Hampton Beach, NH
Harper's Ferry, VA
Harrodsburg Springs, VA
Hoboken, NJ
Hopkins Springs, MA
Hot Springs, AK
Hot Springs, VA
House of Nature, IL
Indian Springs, GA
Isles of Shoals, ME
Latonia Springs, KY
Long Beach, NJ
Lookout Mountain, GA

Madison's Cave, VA
Madison Springs, GA
Mammoth Cave, KY
Mitchell's Peak, NC
Monadnock Mountain, NH
Montauk Point, NY
Montmorenci Falls, Canada
Mount Everett, MA
Mount Holyoke, MA
Mount Hope, RI
Mount Vernon, VA
Nahant, MA
Nantasket Beach, MA
Natural Bridge, VA
New Lebanon Springs, NY
Newport, RI
Niagara Falls, NY
Nicojack Cave, GA
Old Man of the Mountain, NH
Old Orchard Beach, ME
Onondaga Salt Springs, NY
Passaic Falls, NJ
Phillip's Point, MA
Pine Orchard, NY
Plum Island, MA
Pleasant Mountain, ME
Plymouth Rock, MA
Red Sulphur Springs, VA
Richfield Springs, NY
Roan Mountain, NC
Rockaway Beach, NY
Rye Beach, NY
Sachem's Head, CT
Saguenay River, Canada
Salisbury Beach, MA
Salt Sulphur Springs, VA
Saratoga Springs, NY
Saybrook Point, CT
Weir's Cave, VA

Well-maintained plank roads connected Albany, New York, to all of these, and stagecoach lines served those passengers without independent means of travel until they were replaced by railroads. Nonetheless, it was at Saratoga that the richest families could be found. They included wealthy financiers and businessmen from all over the Northeast, as well as merchants from New Orleans; wealthy planters from Arkansas, Alabama, and Tennessee; and the more haughty and polished landowners from Georgia, North Carolina, South Carolina, and Virginia.

The city of Chattanooga in the hill country of Tennessee was also known for its sulfur springs, and it attracted a good deal of patronage among the Southern gentry who chose to limit their social contact with antislavery Northerners. In the 1840s and 1850s, a particularly popular and affordable trip for Southern families was the "Springs Tour" that took in a number of the various natural springs in the region of western Virginia that straddles the Alleghenies. In this region, a number of fashionable resorts were to be found, connected by well-maintained turnpikes and dependable stagecoach lines. The location was convenient to the best families of the South and within the financial means of the moderately blessed ones. From the Virginia tidewater, one traveled due west, and from Tennessee and the Carolinas one headed straight north. The seven best-known springs on the tour at the time were: the Warm, the Hot, the White Sulphur, the Red Sulphur, the Blue Sulphur, the Sweet, and the Salt—all located in a 75-mile square within a reasonable traveling distance of most coastal plantations. Adherents could cut back and forth through this area in their carriages and stay at the different resorts without logging more than 200 miles from the time they entered the region.

The hotels and cottages that served this clientele varied in their appointments and hospitality, and the warm and hot springs were commonly fitted with pools or tubs for soaking. Doctors and chemists often charted a particular itinerary for their patients that would, in their opinion, provide a proper "cure," but many happy travelers followed their own designs in the hope of stumbling upon Nature's antidote. While the women gossiped and loitered, the men talked politics, played chess, billiards, or cards, and smoked and drank prodigiously. Young unmarried men and women were expected to be polite and openly socialize, but they were warned to avoid any lasting attachments. Most travelers invested six weeks of their time in gossiping, socializing, and soaking while having consumed brandy juleps, ham, mutton, ice cream, and many gallons of mineral spring water.

CANALS

Roads and turnpikes remained the main avenue of personal transportation throughout the period, but, as time wore on, canals came into

The quiet, relaxed atmosphere that attended travel by canal belied the tremendous efficiency of the system. Waterborne transportation was the best way to move heavy cargoes of coal, lumber, grain, and ore. Unlike the scene above, canals were often filled with barges crowded stem to stern along their entire length.

fashion for transporting merchandise. Canals had a long history dating back to Roman times, and they were used successfully in Europe as supplements to navigable rivers. Many short canals had been built in America during the colonial period. A great number of Southern canals were built through swamps and marshlands, both draining the surrounding land and providing sufficient depth of water for small craft and barges. Others were built slightly higher than the nearby waterway or in a manner that incorporated a waterway, pond, or lake into part of its length. Canals took a good deal of effort and time to construct, but they were long lasting and required little maintenance once they were finished.

The techniques required to overcome differences in elevation had been developed and refined by hydraulic engineers in England in the 18th century, and Americans had developed a domestic source of water-proof (hydraulic) cement used to join stones in locks and along the route.[11] Early canals in America were often built parallel to or in close proximity to natural waterways that were otherwise unnavigable in order to tap their supply of water and take advantage of what was called "the natural water

Major Canals in the North and East Completed by 1853	
New England	
Cumberland and Oxford Canal	51 miles
Middlesex Canal	27 miles
Blackstone Canal	45 miles
Farmington Canal	78 miles
New York	
Erie Canal	364 miles
Champlain Canal	64 miles
Black River Canal	78 miles
Chenango Canal	97 miles
Oswego Canal	38 miles
Cayuga and Senaca Canal	21 miles
Chemung Canal	39 miles
Genesee Valley Canal	109 miles
Delaware and Hudson Canal	110 miles
New Jersey	
Delaware and Raritan Canal	42 miles
Morris Canal	102 miles
Pennsylvania	
Tidewater Canal	45 miles
Pennsylvania Canal—Eastern Division	45 miles
Pennsylvania Canal—Western Division	104 miles
Pennsylvania Canal—West Branch	75 miles
Pennsylvania Canal—North Branch	73 miles
Pennsylvania Canal—Delaware Branch	60 miles
Juniata Canal	128 miles
Susquehanna Canal	39 miles
Bald Eagle Canal	22 miles
Lehigh Navigation Canal	47 miles
Schuylkill Navigation Canal	108 miles
Union Canal	82 miles
Beaver and Erie Canal	136 miles
French Creek Feeder Canal	27 miles
Franklin Canal	23 miles

Source: John Hayward, *Gazetteer of the United States* (1853).

level route." Some canals suffered periodically from low water due to leakage in the rock structure and unreliable source streams, and others relied on portages by cart or along rails set on the hillsides to overcome the most obstinate topographical feature. One common technological characteris-

tic of successful canals was the lock that used the natural ability of water
to lift or lower great loads over topographical obstacles. The lock was
simple and efficient, had few moving parts, and could be operated by one
or two lockkeepers. By placing the barges in a large enclosure secured with
water gates and allowing millions of gallons of water to flow in or out in
a short period, a lock could raise or lower them several feet in one operation. A series of several locks could move barges hundreds of feet vertically with little effort and without the need to off-load and reload the
cargo.

The Erie Canal (1825) across New York State served as the prime example of the process used to provide canals. New York State raised $7
million through lotteries, a special $1 tax on all persons traveling more
than 100 miles by steamboat, and a tax on all the salt moving on the canal. Governor DeWitt Clinton personally oversaw the planning and construction phases of the 364-miles-long canal and its 82 locks. The double
set of five locks at the western end of the canal at Lockport with their 50
feet of vertical rise, were considered an engineering wonder. Called
"Clinton's Ditch," the canal was 40 feet wide and 4 feet deep. It dropped
571 feet from Buffalo to the Hudson River at Albany. Clinton initiated the
opening of the canal with a dramatic mixing of the waters of the Great
Lakes with that of the Atlantic in 1825. The *Albany Daily Advertiser* of
November 4, 1825, noted, "We had ocular demonstration that the great
work of the age is completed, and our inland seas made accessible from
the ocean." The newspaper further declared Clinton's Ditch, "the majesty
of genius, supported by a free people, that rode in triumph and commanded the admiration of men of stout heart and firm purpose."[12]

The effect of canals on antebellum life cannot be overstated. Scores of
small towns and cities along the canal route, or its system of short spurs
called "feeders," boomed with economic activity because of their proximity to the canal. Small towns, like Lockport, Rome, Syracuse, Rochester,
and Utica in New York, became places of import and attracted manufacturing and shipping concerns. However, New York City gained the greatest benefit as it pulled ahead of Philadelphia, Boston, Baltimore, New
Orleans, and Charleston in terms of the value of the trade that passed
through its port. "The central position of New York, in reference to other
parts of the Union, having New England on the N.E., the middle and
southern states on the S.W., and much of the vast interior of the Mississippi Valley brought into free communication with it by canals and railroads, in connection with the navigation of the Hudson, gives to this city
preeminent advantages for being a great commercial mart for the whole
country."[13]

A trip along the entire length of the Erie Canal took almost five days,
but it was the fastest and cheapest route for freight and passengers of its
day. The largest barges on the Erie Canal carried up to 200 tons. It took

very little effort to move heavy loads along the canal because the weight of the cargo was support by the buoyant force of the water. A pair of mules could easily move many tons of cargo along the smooth, slow-flowing water at three miles an hour when not waiting their turn in the many locks. Westbound traffic was given precedence over eastbound boats, which allowed their towlines to lay slack in the water as the opposing traffic floated over them. Thanks to the canal, the cost of shipping a ton of goods from Buffalo to New York City fell from $100 to $12, and the Midwest was opened to commercial farming. Initially designed for freight, canals quickly attracted a good deal of passenger traffic, and packets— those canal boats primarily carrying people—were given a right of way over all freight.

For people unaccustomed to traveling at no speed faster than a brisk walk, railroad and stagecoach speeds often proved disconcerting. The slow, even progress of the passenger packet proved far less stressful for most passengers than the rough roads, dust, and noise experienced when traveling by coach or rail. "A cent and a half a mile, a mile and a half an hour," was the largely accurate claim of proponents of passenger travel on the canal. Although more plush accommodations could be had, passengers generally sat out on top of the canal barge in good weather, carefully ducking when passing under a bridge, and they slept in cabins on shelflike berths at night. Snacks were available on the barge, but meals were generally taken ashore while the barges were lined up awaiting their turn in the locks.[14]

The Erie Canal in New York, which had cost millions to build, had rapidly redoubled the investment of its backers from the tolls charged for its use. An initial investment of $7 million returned $42 million. The phenomenal success of the project attracted imitation, and in the second and third decades of the century, capital placed in canals far outstripped investments in any other form of transportation. The most celebrated canal projects of the period, other than the Erie Canal, were the two-and-one-half-mile-long Louisville and Portland Canal, finished in 1831, that enabled barges to pass the Falls of the Ohio River and opened 484 miles of navigable rivers, and the Chesapeake and Ohio Canal, completed in 1850, that extended 184 miles west from Georgetown, Maryland, in the general direction of Pittsburgh. The longest canal was the Wabash and Erie Canal, passing 452 miles through Ohio and Indiana from Toledo to Terre Haute. Begun by the combined efforts of the state governments, the entire enterprise was transferred to private companies by 1853.

However, not all canals projects were financially successful, their navigation "having been mostly abandoned in favor of railroads along their banks." The Farmington Canal, begun in 1825, was planned to connect the Long Island Sound at New Haven to the Connecticut River 78 miles inland at Northampton, Massachusetts. It was dug by hand through the

Major Canals in the Midwest and South Completed by 1853	
Ohio	
Ohio Canal	307 miles
Sandy and Little Beaver Canal	76 miles
Pennsylvania and Ohio Canal	75 miles
Miami Canal and Extension	181 miles
Wabash and Erie Canal*	76 miles
Sidney Feeder Canal	13 miles
St. Mary's Feeder Canal	11 miles
Waren County Canal	19 miles
Indiana	
Wabash and Erie Canal*	376 miles
White Water Canal	76 miles
Illinois	
Illinois and Michigan Canal	113 miles
Kentucky	
Louisville and Portland Canal	3 miles
Delaware	
Chesapeake and Delaware Sloop Canal	14 miles
Maryland	
Chesapeake and Ohio Canal	184 miles
Virginia	
James River and Kanawa Canal	197 miles
Dismal Swamp Canal	34 miles

*Shared by both states.
Source: John Hayward, *Gazetteer of the United States* (1853).

rocky New England soil with nothing but picks and shovels. Parts of the canal actually passed over the Farmington River via stone aqueducts that were 36 feet wide to accommodate the barges and the towpath for their mule teams. The 10-year-long project was finished in 1835 at a cost of about $500,000. It enjoyed a short period of commercial activity with lumber, cider, maple sugar, and grain moving toward the coast and salt, oysters, rum, coal, and manufactured goods moving inland. Pleasure excursions were a specialty. The first steam-powered, screw propeller barge made its debut on this canal, but the disturbance it caused in the water proved detrimental to the structural stability of the banks. Taverns and inns sprang up along the canal way to serve the passengers and bargemen, and the whole central part of the state of Connecticut boomed for a decade. Yet by 1845, general maintenance, rising operating costs, and repairs were totaling $75,000 more than the tolls provided annually, and the project had lost a staggering $1.4 million in total. In 1847, a railroad was completed to Plainville, Connecticut parallel to the canal route, further cutting commercial traffic. With the canal investors unable or unwilling to put in more capital, the Farmington Canal died almost overnight. The taverns became residential dwellings, the banks fell in, and the water level dropped to that of a sluggish rural stream, making further navigation impossible.[15]

Pennsylvania built almost 1,300 miles of canals in the second quarter of the century. Not all of them were successful. The Union Canal in Pennsylvania (completed in 1827 as part of the Ohio Canal system) ran 82 miles from Reading to Middletown. The locks raised the barges 518 feet, and a long tunnel passed them through the highest elevation. Because each lock slowly raised the barges only 6 to 10 feet at a time, it took five days to make a one-way trip.

In 1840, the popularity of canal projects reached their peak. Thereafter, with the most feasible canal routes already under development by private syndicates, investment capital generally transferred from canals to railroads. Canals could compete with railroad freight rates because of their characteristic efficiency, but they could not match the rails for speed of transportation in terms of personal travel. Those canal construction projects initiated in the 1840s and 1850s generally continued to completion, but the railroad building mania, which swept the country and continued unabated through the war years, made the initiation of further canal projects unpopular with private investors.

The Advent of Steam

The technologies needed for efficient steam propulsion for vessels and steam engines for railroad locomotives developed separately. Simple steam systems were advanced enough to be applied to small boats, but powerful steam locomotives were not developed until improved steam technology was adopted. Thereafter, railroads began to flourish. The superiority of steam-powered vessels over flatboats and keelboats on the nation's rivers quickly demonstrated itself, especially on the upriver leg of the journey. Moreover, there were significant developments in the use of steam on the Great Lakes, in the Lake Champlain–Lake George corridor, and on the Finger Lakes in New York. It was on the lakes that American steamers proved the feasibility of operating steam vessels in the swell of open waters, but it was not until the post–Civil War years that meaningful advances were made in transoceanic steam propulsion. The Great Lakes route, when combined with the Erie Canal and Ohio Canal, caused marine traffic to grow steadily. Although it would have been possible to build a continuous canal-lake system that would have accommodated most of the steam-powered craft of the period, the cost of such a project would have been prohibitive. Nonetheless, steamboat lines sprang up to span the gaps between eastern railroads and the incomplete western lines. In 1857, with the rails finally connected, the steamboat lines began to fail under the competition from rail service. Historian K. Jack Bauer noted, "The nation stood with its back to the waterways and exalted the ribbons of steel [ignoring] both the efficiency of water transportation and its critical role in the economic health of the country."[16]

Steam engine technology often outpaced thermodynamic theory in the early parts of the period. Steam technology for propulsion was generally regarded as superior to that used for locomotion because the engines carried aboard vessels could be made larger than those used on early locomotives. Nonetheless, steam propulsion was wasteful of fuel, and river steamers could be seen steaming up to large piles of firewood stacked on the bank by local landowners expressly for this purpose. A woman visiting the Mississippi Valley from England in 1828 noted, "I never witnessed human nature reduced so low as it appeared in the woodcutters' huts on the unwholesome banks of the Mississippi." Nonetheless, the humble woodcutter played an essential role in the steamboat industry and could make a tidy annual sum by contracting with the steam lines to have the firewood available for their use. Similar arrangements were made with railroad lines, particularly in the South where wood instead of coal continued in use as a fuel before the Civil War.[17]

The publication of William Rankine's *The Steam Engine and Other Prime Movers* in Great Britain in 1848 was a major step forward for the application of steam technology to transportation. Rankine's book soon became the standard text for all steam-engineering students and practitioners. Engineers using Rankine's principles were able to make steam locomotives and steamboats much more efficient and powerful by utilizing double and triple expansion engine designs. Prior to 1825, steam boilers were made in a "box" shape by riveting iron or steel plates together. This design proved particularly prone to fatal boiler explosions because pressure stresses tended to build up in the corners of the boiler. Consequently, most applications of steam to propulsion were of a low-pressure type. The earliest boilers were based on the English designs of Bolton and Watts and had boiler pressures between 10 and 12 pounds per square inch, but with time, a high-pressure boiler, invented by Oliver Evans of Philadelphia, with 30 to 40 pounds per square inch of pressure became the standard. Boiler explosions averaged about 10 per year, killing more than 200 persons annually.

There were many dangers inherent in this form of transportation, although some disasters could be avoided with the application of some common sense. In April 1845, the steam packet *Swallow*, racing the *Express* to New York on the Hudson River at night, ran aground, broke in two, and sank in minutes. Forty persons died. Such races were common and reflected the popular notion that those vessels with the quickest times could charge the highest fares or attract the greatest passenger traffic. The *New York Herald* reported several fatal incidents in the single month of May 1850, including a steamboat collision in Jackson, Mississippi, between the *Luna* and the *Duchess*; a steamboat fire at the wharf in Memphis, Tennessee, that left several people unaccounted for; and the unexplained explosion of a new steamboat in St. Louis that caused a frightful and heartrending scene in which the total number of persons lost exceeded 30. Alarmed by the persistent problem of steamboat safety, the Federal government stepped in with the establishment of several safety regulations embodied in the Steamboat Act of 1852. Thereafter, with the widespread adoption of a cylindrical fire-tube boiler design, which made high-pressure steam safer and more efficient, the incidence of boiler explosions decreased to an average of four per year with a national death toll of less than 50. Notwithstanding the improved record of safety, the explosion of the river steamer *Princess* on the Mississippi near Baton Rouge in 1859 killed more than 200 persons, one of the greatest losses of life on a river steamer prior to the war.

Robert Fulton

In 1807, inventor and businessman Robert Fulton became the first to operate a steamboat as a commercial success on an inland waterway in America. The successful steamboat, *Clermont,* went from New York City to Albany along 150 miles of the Hudson River in about 32 hours, averaging a speed of about five miles per hour. *Gentlemen's Magazine* (December 1809) carried the following description of one of the many steamboat designs by Fulton:

> The passage boat between New York and Albany is one hundred and sixty feet long, and wide in proportion for accommodations, consisting of fifty-two berths, besides sofas, etc., for one hundred passengers; and the machinery, which moves her wheels, is equal to the power of twenty-four horses and is kept in motion by steam from a copper boiler eight or ten feet in length. Her route is a distance of one hundred and fifty miles, which she performs regularly twice a week.[18]

In 1811, Fulton designed the *New Orleans*, built in Pittsburgh, for use as a passenger and freight hauler on the lower Mississippi River. Before his death in 1815, he offered regular steamboat service between New Orleans, Louisiana, and Natchez, Mississippi, at a rate of three miles per hour upstream and eight miles per hour down. He had began a steam ferry service across the harbor from New York to Jersey City, New Jersey, and two separate steam ferries across the East River from Manhattan to Brooklyn. The last boat to be built under Fulton's direct supervision navigated the Long Island Sound from New York City to New Haven, Connecticut, passing through the dangerous current at the Hell's Gate, where for more than a mile the tides surged at five or six miles per hour and rocks and whirlpools flanked the steamer within a few yards. The Hell's Gate passage was thought to be impassable for sailing vessels except at high tide.

In response to the need for a harbor defense during the War of 1812, Fulton designed and built a large vessel capable of supporting heavy artillery that could steam at four miles per hour in New York Harbor. Congress funded the venture with $320,000. The double-hull, steam battery was 156 feet long and 56 feet wide. It displaced almost 2,500 tons and sat 20 feet deep in the water. The engine cylinder was 4 feet in diameter with a piston stroke of 5 feet. The armament consisted of 30 canons, each designed to throw a 32-pound ball that could be heated red-hot in the onboard furnaces to set fire to attacking enemy ships. The battery plied the tidal waters around New York for the duration of the War of 1812, but never saw action. Near the end of the conflict, Congress authorized the president to build an entire series of similar defensive steam-powered batteries for other U.S. ports.

Fulton patented many of the novel features of his steamboats and held a monopoly on steamboat operations and routes in and around New York through his alliances with the politically powerful Livingston family. Yet there were continued attempts by his rivals to create vessels and to design engines of all kinds, both practical and impractical, that violated his patents.

The number of steamboats on America's rivers and in its ports rapidly increased. The second successful steam vessel, *Phoenix*, built in 1807 by John Stevens of Hoboken, New Jersey, was the first to successfully venture into the open ocean. In 1816, a boat designed by Henry M. Shreve completed the river voyage from New Orleans to Louisville, Kentucky, in just 25 days. During the 1820s and 1830s, passages of the Mississippi River by steamboats increased from 20 to 1,200 trips per year. There were more than 200 western steamers in 1830 and at floodtide their traffic could block the river passage. The port of New Orleans was described in a child's geography text of the period as remarkable for the number of ships and steamboats that crowded its levee. Steamboat capacity on the Mississippi system alone had grown to more than 120,000 tons, greater than the entire steam-powered tonnage of the British Royal Navy at the time.

Steamboats transported agricultural produce and livestock in the South and all types of industrial supplies, manufactured goods, iron and copper ore, and agricultural produce in the North. Timothy Flint, an 1830s observer, noted the scene at New Madrid, Missouri:

> You can name no point from the numerous rivers of the Ohio and the Mississippi, from which some of these boats have not come. In one place there are boats loaded with planks from the pine forests of the southwest of New York. In another quarter there are Yankee notions of Ohio. From Kentucky, pork, flour, whiskey, hemp, tobacco, bagging, and bale-rope. From Tennessee there are the same articles, together with a great quantity of cotton. From Missouri and Illinois, cattle and horses. The same articles generally from Ohio together with peltry and lead from Missouri. Some boats are loaded with corn in the ear and in bulk: others with barrels of apples and potatoes. Some have loads of cider. . . . There are dried fruits, every kind of spirits manufactured in these regions and in short, the products of the ingenuity and agriculture of the whole upper country of the west. They have come from regions, thousands of miles apart. They have floated to a common point of union. The surfaces of the boats cover some acres.[19]

By 1850, the 25-day trip on the Mississippi of 1816 had dwindled to only four and half days. Multidecked, multipurpose steamers had become common, and those that carried passengers grew larger and more luxurious with the years. Riverboats were just as romantic to the antebellum traveling public as they are to us today. The 1850s proved to be the golden age of river steamers, with their cabins splendidly appointed with carved woodwork and furniture, crystal chandeliers, carpeting, and mirrors. Some boats were fitted with a steam calliope, on which popular tunes were played when approaching a city.

Sir Charles Lyell, an English scientist visiting the American South, wrote an account of his travels that included a fine description of a river steamboat of the period called the *Amaranth*. He rode the steamer up the Tombigbee River to Montgomery, Alabama.

> The principle cabins run the whole of the ship on a deck above that on which the machinery is placed, and where the cotton is piled up. This upper deck is chiefly occupied with a handsome saloon, about 200 feet long, the ladies' cabins at one end, opening into it with folding doors. Sofas, rocking chairs, tables, and a stove are placed in this room, which is lighted by windows from above. On each side of it is a row of sleeping apartments, each communicating by one door with the saloon, while the other leads out to the guard, as they call it, a long balcony or gallery, covered with a shade or a verandah [sic], which passes around the hole boat. The second class, or deck passengers, sleep where they can on the lower floor, where, besides the engine and the cotton, there are prodigious heaps of wood, which are devoured with marvelous rapidity by the furnace, and are as often restored at the different landings, a set of Negroes being purposely hired for that work.[20]

No other vehicle better symbolizes the antebellum period than the paddlewheel river steamer. Often luxurious in their passenger appointments, steamers were nonetheless efficient cargo carriers extending the range of commerce up America's many navigable rivers. Steamboat races like the one pictured above were common events.

The only limit to the use of river steamers was the availability of a navigable waterway. Nonetheless, riverboats were often seen to regularly travel seemingly impassable routes filled with snags and overgrown with hanging vegetation. River steamers were designed to draw very little water. In other words, they could float in as little as two or three feet of water if not overly loaded. Some riverboat pilots bragged that a river steamer could run on dew if need be. The pilot was housed in an elevated structure on the roof of the steamer called a pilothouse. Its position afforded an uninterrupted view of the river. The pilothouse contained a large wheel for steering the rudder and controls for operating the engine. The boilers were generally placed in the bow of the boat to balance the weight of the engines that were in the rear. It was quickly found that two engines were better than one on most vessels, and from this fact came the distinctive twin smokestack design of river steamboats. To increase firebox draft under the wood-fired boilers, very tall smokestacks were used. In 1840, their standard height was more than 50 feet above the river surface.

Two types of propulsion were developed for inland steamers: twin side wheels and the stern paddle wheel. Screw propeller technology was in its infancy and was rarely found on riverboats. The use of two separately connected direct action side-lever engines driving independent paddle wheels placed amidships had many advantages over stern paddle wheel operation. It cleared much of the machinery from the centerline of the boat and allowed the variable speeds of the engines to be used to increase the boat's maneuverability. Side-wheel steam tugboats were operated into the 20th century because of their ability to "turn on a dime." Nonetheless, it was the grandeur and glamour of the rear paddle wheel river steamers that gave steamboats their distinctive place in the antebellum environment. The major advantage of the stern paddle wheel was its ability to avoid snags and other debris floating in the water because the hull of the boat had already pushed them aside. Riverboat pilots had to take great care when backing the vessel to avoid having unseen snags foul the paddlewheel.

The first steamboat capable of navigating the very shallow waters of the Missouri River was the *Yellow Stone,* built in 1830 for the American Fur Company. On is first voyage in 1831, the *Yellow Stone* ascended the river to Fort Tecumseh (Pierre, South Dakota) and was stopped only by low water. The next year it reached the mouth of the Yellowstone River near Fort Union, about 2,000 miles from St. Louis. This feat demonstrated that steam could be used to bring trade goods into the Rocky Mountain West and to take out a fortune in furs. Moreover, it opened the region to visitors other than the hardy mountain men and fur traders, particularly minor noblemen and artists from Europe who came to view and record the life of the American Indian.

Coastal steam lines developed slowly in the first half of the 19th century due to monopolies granted by the individual states to local investors. However, in 1824, the Supreme Court overturned the state grants as invasions of the Federal power to regulate interstate commerce. A willing public advanced the cash needed to develop the coastal steamship lines, and by 1840, all the major East Coast ports were connected by steam. Several steam lines had been established from northeastern cities directly to New Orleans and Savannah prior to the Civil War, and they met with some success. Nonetheless, the steamboat trip from Boston around Cape Cod was particularly difficult, and only seasoned travelers avoided becoming seasick. In 1857, the paddle wheeler *Black Warrior* of the Livingston Line established a record of four and a half days from New York to Havana, Cuba.

In January 1840, the coasting steamboat *Lexington* was making its way up through the generally sheltered waters of Long Island Sound with a load of raw cotton bales bound from New York City to the fabric mills near Stonington, Connecticut. The 205-foot wooden steamboat had 150 bales arranged on its deck, and it carried 143 passengers and crew. Sparks from the smokestacks were blamed for starting a fire among the bales as the *Lexington* passed the town of Sands Point on the north shore of Long Island. Although only a few hundred yards from the land, all but four of the people on board were lost as the steamboat burned. Some died in the fire, but many others were lost due to exposure in the ice-cold waters of the sound. One person, David Crowley, the first mate, was found barely alive 43 hours after the disaster. He had clung atop a floating cotton bale that kept him from freezing to death in the wintry water. The *Lexington* disaster was the single greatest loss of life on a coasting steamboat prior to the Civil War.[21]

Steam was slower in replacing sailing vessels on the transoceanic routes than it was for inland transportation. In the first half of the 19th century, Americans were considered the world's best sailing-ship builders, but the wooden wind-ship design reached its practical engineering limits with the development of the clipper ships of the 1850s. The change to steam-driven, metal-hulled vessels, which helped to sustain the growth of inland navigation, was almost totally ignored by American builders of oceangoing craft. It was the British that made the greatest strides in this area sending steamers around Africa to India decades before the Americans crossed the Atlantic.

At mid-century, the engineering fundamentals of steamship construction for the oceanic trade had several common characteristics. The hulls were made of wood; the vessels were propelled by paddle wheels housed amidships; the engines were physically very large and of a single-expansion, low-pressure type, also located amidships; and the steam was exhausted into jet condensers so similar to those devised by James Watt in 1769 as to be considered identical. Low-pressure, water tube boilers, had been common since their invention in 1791. Paddle wheels—a design well suited to low-pressure operation—were slow rotating devices of large area that maximized the impulse imparted to the vessel; increased the reliability of the engines; and minimized the stress on the hull. Although economical in terms of fuel consumption, the low-pressure steam boilers retarded the introduction of the more efficient screw propeller that required high-speed rotation. Moreover, paddle wheels provided greater acceleration than the screw propeller designs of the period.[22]

The first American steamship in regular transatlantic service was the *Washington,* owned and operated by the Ocean Steam Navigation Company. This vessel made its first voyage to Bremerhaven, Germany in 1847. Nonetheless, *Washington* was equipped, like most oceangoing steamers of the period, with auxiliary sails and three masts to extend its operable range. However, vessels with this combination of motive power commonly experienced some disadvantages when under sail, as the paddle wheels produced considerable drag and were particularly noted for adversely effecting the overall sailing qualities of a vessel. When equipped with the higher pressure, fire-tube boilers, introduced in the1850s, and screw propellers, the restrictions of increased fuel consumption served to severely limit the speed that the steamer could maintain for any extended period of time. Fast American steamers were costly to build and costly to operate. Their designers often sacrificed cargo space for larger engines and more spacious fuel bunkers. Wind ships, by comparison, could cover hundreds of miles in a day; a record 400 nautical miles in 24 hours was reached in the 1850s by the American clipper ship *Challenger*. The Collins Line paddle steamer *Baltic* made the transatlantic jump in nine and a half days in 1852, but it was the last American steam vessel to hold the speed record for a century. In 1854, the sailing ship *Champion of the Seas* eclipsed its own previous one-day record, traveling 465 miles from noon to noon, a speed that many commercial vessels of the early 20th century could not attain.

Under these conditions, it seemed unlikely that steam would ever compete economically with sail, particularly on the long distance routes where fuel and fresh water for the engines became major limiting considerations. The tremendous demand for a quick passage to the California gold fields in 1849 and 1850 kept the fast-moving clipper ships profitable for a short time, but by 1856, the transoceanic passenger trade had in fact collapsed and was taken over by the more technologically advanced British steamers. Nonetheless, American wind ships continued to compete as bulk carriers into the 20th century, mostly because their operating costs remained low.[23]

RAILROADS

Although Americans were slow to revise their thinking about ocean navigation, they were quick to see the value of steam locomotion. A railroad-building mania swept the country in the 1840s. By 1860, there were more than 30,000 miles of railway and more than 400 railroad companies, but there was little coordination among competing lines to devise a national rail system. "In no direction could cars run long distances without changes and delays." Freight, as well as passengers and their luggage, often had to detrain and cross towns from one line to another either by wagon or on foot. For example, in 1841, a trip by rail from Albany to Buffalo required the use of nine separate New York railroad lines. Moreover, until 1847, there was a state ban on railway freight in central New York because of the fear of competition with the Erie Canal. In the interim, railroads could carry freight only in winter when the canal was frozen.[24]

Judge Gillis, an observer of the first train from Albany to Schenectady, New York, penned the following description of the inaugural trip:

The train was composed of coach-bodies, mostly from Thorpe & Sprague's stage-coaches, placed upon trucks. The trucks were coupled together with chains and chain-links, leaving from two to three feet of slack, and when the locomotive started it took up the slack by jerks, with a sufficient force to jerk the passengers, who sat on seats across the top of the coaches, out from under their hats, and in stopping they came together with such force as to send them flying from under their seats. They used dry pitch-pine for fuel, and, there being no smoke or spark-catcher to the chimney or smoke stack, a volume of black smoke, strongly impregnated with sparks, coals, and cinders, came pouring back the whole length of the train. Each of the outside passengers who had a umbrella raised it as a protection against the smoke and fire. They were found to be but a momentary protection, for I think in the first mile the last one went overboard, all having their covers burnt off from the frames. [T]hen a general melee took place among the deck passengers, each whipping his neighbor to put out the fire. They presented a very motley appearance on arriving at the first station.[25]

Most of the railroad construction had taken place in the Northeast above the Ohio River because investment capital was available there. In the South, with capital largely tied up in land and slaves, railways were slower to develop. Yet the abominable condition of Southern roads during the rainy season and in the winter added to the importance of its railways as a dependable means of transportation. Although the South controlled only one-third of the railway mileage in the North, Southern railways were strategically located. Virginia, in particular, was crossed by several important railways that would be used with great effect in the coming war.

Much of the Northern rail mileage was used for the distribution of manufactures in the Northeast. The most prominent railways were the Pennsylvania, the Erie, and the New York Central. The major north-south lines were the Illinois Central and the Cleveland, Columbus, and Cincinnati. The Baltimore and Ohio was a strategically important east-west line between Washington and Ohio that ran through the border states between the North and the South. In May 1861, Confederate General Thomas J. "Stonewall" Jackson was able to "steal" 300 railroad cars and 56 locomotives from the B. & O. in a single operation. Such raids along the B. & O. were a constant source of trouble to Northern commanders in the Civil War. The railways of the near West, which had been built in the 1850s far in advance of any immediate need, were very important. The line between Louisville, Kentucky, and Nashville, Tennessee, provided a vital link for the prosecution of commerce and settlement.

The Northern lines were well stocked with locomotives, cars, and support vehicles. Yet no strategic railways were built in anticipation of the looming civil conflict, and no thought was given to the development of the principles of military operations and maintenance of railways in case

Major U.S. Railroads of 100 Miles or More Completed by 1853		
Railroad	Length in Miles	Average Speed in MPH
Albany & Buffalo	328	32
Atlantic & St. Lawrence	122	30
Baltimore & Ohio	282	21
Central Georgia	191	21
Cincinnati, Cleveland, & Columbus	135	24
Cleveland & Pittsburgh	100	20
Erie	409	28
Georgia	171	17
Harlem	130	21
Housatonic	110	21
Hudson River	144	36
Macon & Western	101	20
Mad River & Lake Erie	158	17
Michigan Central	278	26
Michigan South & North Indiana	247	21
Northern Ogdensburg	118	28
Ohio & Pennsylvania	134	18
Rutland & Burlington	120	28
Sandusky, Mansfield, & Newark	117	18
South Carolina	127	25
Vermont Central	162	28
Virginia Central	104	15
Western	200	27
Western & Atlantic	140	14
Wilmington & Weldon	162	16

Source: John Hayward, *Gazetteer of the United States* (1853).

of a war. The construction of five short connections between competing lines, for a total of 140 miles, would have provided an uninterrupted railway from Washington, D.C., to the entire North. By comparison, the length of Southern railway mileage, the available tonnage of rolling stock and engines, and the number of interconnecting systems was severely limited. Nonetheless there were more than 1,000 miles of important track in Tennessee with connections passing to the Southeast. The heart of the Southern rail network lay in Corinth, Mississippi, where several lines came together. The line connecting Cairo, Illinois, with Corinth continued directly south on to New Orleans, creating a transportation artery that pumped vital supplies from the Gulf ports north to Tennessee and then east to Virginia. This was a remarkable system given the generally dilapidated state of Southern railways and the fact that cargoes had to be transferred between a number unconnected lines.

An obstacle to rail transport in all parts of the country was the different gauges, or track widths, used on different lines. In New York and New England, a gauge of 4 feet 8 1/2 inches was used between the rails. In Ohio, and to the west and south of Philadelphia, the gauge was 4 feet 10 inches. Some rails were placed as much as 6 feet apart in special cases. Many ingenious expedients were used to overcome this problem. These included third rails, wide wheels that would accommodate both narrow and wide track, and adjustable train axles. There was an attempt to adopt a standard gauge of 5 feet throughout the nation, but the required reinvestment of capital by established lines to refit their track and improve their roadbeds generally got in the way of any standardization.[26] The longest single-gauge track of the period belonged to the Atlantic and Great Western line, which connected New York with St. Louis more than 1,000 miles away.[27]

A major limitation on the more efficient use of Southern railways remained a lack of maintenance. Damaged cars and worn-out engines were often the victims of the South's limited industrial technology. A single commercial engine could be required to lug a train of freight weighing up to 120 tons. A damaged locomotive boiler might take more than a thousand man-hours to repair if the boilerplate could be found locally to do the job. Moreover, many Southern routes were laid down in a narrow gauge, some less than four feet, with soft iron rails designed for use by small "donkey" engines that carried agricultural produce only a few times a season after harvest. Track bent back and forth in violent curves around hills and rock outcroppings, and waterways and depressions that could not be filled were bridged with wooden trestles of the simplest kind. The average life expectancy of wooden ties and beams was no more than five years, a problem made worse by the hot and moist climate of the South.

Track was composed of a wide range of wrought-iron rails and many of the types that were incorporated into critical stretches of connecting routes were technically obsolete. The rails originally had enough durability to withstand a decade of light traffic and slow speeds, and were spiked directly to the ties without tie plates. Rails and the wooden ties that held them in place were simply not designed to withstand the wear and tear of increasing demands for regular passenger service and heavy industrial cargoes. Proper stations, timetables, and signaling were in their infancy. The semaphore was adapted to railways as a way of signaling in the decade of the 1840s. The station manager and track crew set the signals. Providing that the weather was clear, the position of the semaphore arm could indicate to the engineer a clear track, the need for caution, or the need to stop. The horizontal presentation of the arm indicated the need to stop. Likewise, at night white (Clear), green (Caution), or red (Danger) lights could be used. These were later changed to green, yellow, and red like modern traffic signals. In the 1850s, the telegraph was adapted to the control of railroad signals. However, it was not until 1860 that John Saxby in England produced a system by which the signals could be absolutely governed between stations.

These factors tended to keep down speeds, but the lack of efficient braking also kept trains from exceeding about 25 miles per hour. Derailments due to higher speeds were much more common than one would think. A collision with great loss of life between two trains in Rhode Island in 1853 was essentially caused by the inability of the trains to stop even though the crews were alerted to the impending collision. In 1857, a freight train crashed into its station in New York City because of inadequate brakes. Incidents like these had a chilling effect on high-speed railway operations and engendered a good deal of technological rethinking throughout the country.

The construction and maintenance of railroad roadbeds and bridges involved a small army of specialized "mechanics," few of whom were to be found in the South. Many short-route roadbeds were built on wooden pilings driven into the swampy ground across low-lying regions. Initially constructed for only light traffic, the roadbeds of even the newest lines soon began to fail under increased use. The lack of an adequate bridging technology was also an obstacle to railway construction, not only in the South, but also throughout the country. The development of north-south lines in the Atlantic coastal region was made more difficult because of the need to bridge the numerous eastward flowing rivers of New England and the Middle States.

American engineers and schools of engineering immediately attacked the problem. The first all-wood truss design capable of holding the weight of a locomotive was patented by Lt. Col. Stephen H. Long of the U.S. Engineers in 1839. In 1840, William Howe designed a wood and iron composite truss, which was adapted by Thomas and Caleb Pratt and became the standard for American railroad bridges. The "Pratt" truss is still in use today. Meanwhile, all-iron designs were developed by a number of engineers, including Squire Whipple, who took out the first all-iron patent in 1841. James Millholland built an all-iron truss for the B. & O. Railroad in 1850, and Frederich Horbach built another in the same year for the Boston and Albany line near Pittsfield, Massachusetts. On April 26, 1856, the first bridge to span the wide Mississippi River was completed from Rock Island on the Illinois side to Davenport on the Iowa side. This was a steel truss railroad bridge built by the Chicago and Rock Island line.[28]

By the late 1850s, American railroad bridge technology had reached such a state of maturity that Europeans were carefully copying American truss designs. However, not all the railroad bridge designs developed in this period were successful. In 1850, an all-iron truss designed by Nathaniel Rider for the Erie Railroad failed, which resulted in some loss of life. His design was similar to that patented by Whipple a decade earlier. When a Whipple design also failed over the Dee River in England, there was a great public outcry concerning the safety of travel by rail. Ultimately, all the Rider and Whipple types in America were inspected for defects, and they were scheduled to be taken down and replaced by iron-and-wood composite types.

Turnpike concessionaires, canal investors, teamsters, and stagecoach operators were bitter enemies of railroad development. These forces spread stories of the dangers of railways. Boilers—as anyone could see from similar disasters on steamboats—were a great danger. Noisy locomotives scared horses, purportedly dried up dairy cows, and allegedly caused hens to stop laying eggs. Railroad bridges could collapse. Moreover, the sparks from the smokestacks actually did set fire to forests and fields along the railroad right-of-way with amazing regularity. These were strong arguments against railways, and some of them were true. Railway operators took note of the genuine dangers by fitting their smokestacks with spark-suppressing screens and placing bales of hay or cotton as a protective barrier on a flat car behind the engine to separate the passenger cars from a possible boiler failure. Passenger amenities like well-appointed coaches, sleeping cars, and dining cars were not introduced until 1858. Notwithstanding its detractors, railroad building continued unabated through the Civil War years. By the1850s, Northern railroads had generally driven the turnpikes out of business. Not until the advent of the automobile in the 20th century would these toll roads reappear.

Southern railway construction was characterized by a strange, regional pattern of development. The planters of Virginia, Georgia, and the Carolinas warmly supported the development of railways, whereas those of the Gulf states who relied on easily navigable waterways to ship their produce to coastal seaports were much less supportive. Nowhere was this difference between them better evidenced than in the disparity of Southern railway mileage on the eve of the Civil War. Although the Southern states along the eastern Atlantic coast had more than 5,000 miles of interconnecting track, the much larger states of Mississippi, Alabama, and Louisiana had less than 1,800, much of it represented by stray threads of track, providing individual plantations with a connection to a river landing and going nowhere else. The minimal rail mileage in Arkansas and Texas also proved to be scattered and local. Nonetheless, the strategically placed railways of Tennessee and southwestern Kentucky, planned far in advance of any immediate need and built largely in the1850s, totaled an amazing 1,300 miles by 1860. Even half-explored Florida had more than 600 miles, mostly in the northern portion of the state.

Although there was no overall developmental plan, by the eve of the Civil War the Southern states had the outline of two major railroad systems, one complete and the other unfinished. Ironically, the construction of several short connections between competing lines, estimated at less than 200 miles of track, would have provided an uninterrupted railway system throughout the entire South. Both routes joined the Gulf states to the capital of Virginia, but Richmond, as the eastern terminus of both networks, had only a single line directly connected to Washington, D.C., and the markets and factories of the Northeast. No physical characteristic of the country serves as a better indicator of the sectionalism that was affecting the nation.

Peter Cooper's steam engine *Tom Thumb* of 1829 was more of a scientific model than a proper locomotive, conceived as a method to show American business investors that steam traction was a practical idea. *Tom Thumb* was run on the Baltimore and Ohio Horse Railway as a demonstration. The first true American locomotive was the *Best Friend of Charleston*, which hauled passengers along the South Carolina Railroad in the 1830s until its boiler burst. *Old Ironsides* pulled passengers on the Philadelphia and Germantown Railway for most of 10 years. The *DeWitt Clinton*, built by the West Point Foundry in New York in 1831, was very much like the *Best Friend*, which was made by the same manufacturer. The *DeWitt Clinton* made its first run on the Hudson and Mohawk Line from Albany to Schenectady, covering 14 miles in 46 minutes, and was still pulling cars at the Chicago World's Fair in 1893.

These early engines were very unlike the locomotives that made railroads practical in the antebellum period. These were commonly of a distinct "American" type known as the 4-4-0 with large funnel-shaped "Balloon" smokestacks. The weight of the engine was initially distributed only over the four drive wheels. The four-wheel swivel truck helped the engine to negotiate the sharp curves of American railways. Locomotives weighed between 10 and 30 tons, and with a proper arrangement of reciprocating arms and drive wheels, an appropriately heavy engine could pull a train of between 120 and 150 tons.

Invariably, behind the engine came the tender, which held as much as 1,000 gallons of fresh water and had space for firewood. A few Northern engines used coal or charcoal on local runs, but without exception every Southern locomotive burned wood as a fuel in the antebellum period. The large smokestacks on period engines were needed to divert wood smoke and produce a draft large enough to maintain a satisfactory head of steam. Cordwood was stacked at intervals along every line, and the best and cleanest-burning firewood was reserved for passenger traffic. Depending on the engine, load, and topography, an engine averaged between 50 and 60 miles per cord of wood and thus required long delays every few hours to reload the tender.

Railroad cars were differentiated into freight and passenger types and were generally unimaginative things innocent of luxury. The earliest types were simple open boxes for freight and these were fitted with roofs and wooden seats for travelers. Some passenger cars were almost indistinguishable from stagecoaches. Passenger cars were designated as first or second class, and there is some evidence of separate cars for servants. Nonetheless, by 1838, bed-carriages that were precursors to sleeping cars were making an appearance.[29] Freight cars were commonly distinguished as boxcars or flatcars. Tank cars and the caboose existed only in rudimentary form. Rolling stock had a load limit of about 8 tons with a gross weight of 10 tons. Freight trains were generally limited to 15 cars due to the need for individual braking.

12

Visual Arts

The delight which a work of art affords, seems to rise from our recognizing in it the mind that formed Nature again in active operation.

—Ralph Waldo Emerson

We certainly either by Nature, which is not very probably, or by accident, have something that appears like a decided predisposition for painting in this country.

—John Neal

NEOCLASSIC STYLE

In the earliest years of 19th century, American art was still dominated by the neoclassical doctrines of the past that prized the rendering of scenes from history, religion, and classical literature above all other subject matter. These principles of art contended that humans should be shown in their most lofty postures. Neoclassicists believed that art should deal primarily with great events, heroic actions, or momentous decisions. This form of art was known as "historical painting." The typical subject matter of these artworks was drawn from the Greek and Roman classics with figures costumed in toga-like robes of state because it was thought that contemporary attire might compromise the universality of the artist's message. If modern themes were to be invoked, they had to be cloaked as classical allegories. Historical works of this type were often commissioned by wealthy patrons who might require that their image appear in the scene.

Historic painting in the neoclassic fashion was considered, therefore, the epitome of the artist's craft as the antebellum period started. Other, less highly regarded categories of art were portraiture and landscape painting. Portraits were thought to challenge the artist's skill at rendering at exact likeness, but landscapes, because of the commonality of their subject matter, were less valued as examples of accurate renderings. A fourth category of artwork, narrative or genre paintings that focused on a specific environment and sought to tell a story, were thought to be too commonplace to tempt the talents of serious artists. European tastes dictated what was considered good art, and professional American painters often trained amid the recognized talents that frequented Paris, London, The Hague, or Düsseldorf.

Americans Benjamin West and John Singleton Copley, whose careers spanned the change in centuries, were steeped in these traditions, but they sought to push the conventions to their limits. Although American born and trained, both West and Copley spent almost all their working careers abroad in London. Nevertheless, they were sensitive to their times and managed to nudge painting away from the classical and toward the romantic by the beginning of the antebellum period.

Benjamin West rose from a rural Pennsylvania limner to become a cofounder and the second president, after Sir Joshua Reynolds, of the Royal Academy of Arts in London. Although the majority of his work was in portraiture, West's *William Penn's Treaty with the Indians* (1771) was a departure from the way neoclassical works had been done previously. The figures of the Englishmen are clothed in the costume of the period and the Indians are proudly represented as "noble savages." Curiosity about the dying native race in America would attract many European artists in the 19th century. Nonetheless, West's figures were posed in a sort of classical frieze that lacked emotion and action.

West's *Death of Wolfe* (1778) established a new mode for historic battle scenes. He painted his subjects, including Native Americans, in the costume of the French and Indian War, and he added a sense of realism and drama to the work. This was a breakthrough in style at the time that continued to be followed by American painters throughout the 19th century. In 1805, West produced a similar notable work based on 16th-century English history, *The Fatal Wounding of Sir Philip Sidney*, which possessed many of these same qualities. Sidney's horse, white and wild-eyed against a generally dark background occupied by imposing figures in armor, lent drama, theatrical flavor, and a romantic sense to this mature historical painting.

In 1783, English painter Sir Joshua Reynolds wrote that West's use of modern dress in historical painting was "mean and vulgar." However, West responded that "the same truth that guides the pen of the historian should govern the pencil of the painter."[1] He thereby set a precedent for

A detail from a historical painting by Benjamin West showing his use of authentic costume and clothing. Note the romanticized treatment of the muscular and well-formed Indians—common characteristics espoused by authors of novels during the antebellum period.

historical painting thereafter. By the beginning of the 19th century, West began to experiment with more romantic subjects. His *Death on a Pale Horse,* created as a preliminary painting in 1802 for a larger work, exposed his contemporaries to romanticism. "The movement of this brightly-colored painting was explosive, characterised by violent action and emotion." Although the 1802 painting did not quite fill a two-by-three-foot canvas, the 1817 work measured 15 by 46 feet. No American painter would again show the same control of such a huge composition until Emanuel Leutze painted *Washington Crossing the Delaware* in 1851. Yet West's importance to antebellum art is not so much in his works, but rather in the influence that he had on the American students that came to study under him. These included Charles Wilson Peale, Samuel F.B. Morse, Henry Sargent, and John Trumbull.[2]

Although he worked until 1815, John Singleton Copley is generally considered the greatest American painter of the 18th century. Best known for his portraiture in colonial times, Copley painted both the young and the old of his native Boston, but he emphasized the setting and background to convey a desired mood in a manner previously never so extensively done. In meticulous detail, Copley painted ladies posing before fine furniture and draperies and men surrounded by books, hunting dogs, and guns. When he settled in London in 1775, Copley turned to the more fashionable historical painting and specialized in multifigure compositions showing heroic action. His first important work of this kind was *Watson and the Shark* (1778), depicting the romantic notion of man's struggle against nature. Another major work, *The Death of Major Pierson* (1781), was an early landmark in contemporary historical painting.

Unlike most American painters, who chose to study in London, John Vanderlyn was the first American painter to study in Paris. Vanderlyn initially trained as a painter at the Columbian Academy and studied under the celebrated 18th-century portrait painter, Gilbert Stuart. In Paris, he turned his back on all that was American and embraced the French notions of historical composition, including the use of flat colors, precise modeling, and smooth surfaces. Upon his return to America, Vanderlyn tried to support himself by painting enormous panoramas of European scenes, but Americans cared little for his views of the Old World. Vanderlyn failed to embrace a unique American taste in his art. Yet his place as a notable American historical painter is generally based on American themes. Vanderlyn was given a commission by Robert Fulton, the inventor of the first practical steamboat, to do 10 illustrations for Joel Barlow's epic patriotic poem, "The Columbiad." One of these he turned into a full-size rendition, *The Death of Jane McCrae*, a young woman who was scalped by Indians during the American Revolution. This proved a particularly popular image at the time; it was reproduced in lithograph in many works of American history and copied by Currier and Ives in 1846. The flowing dress of the pleading victim, the native costume of her merciless attackers, and the threatening tomahawk raised above her head create a dramatic scene from the struggle to found a new nation. Vanderlyn was also chosen to do the *Landing of Columbus* for the rotunda of the United States Capitol in 1841.

AMERICAN HISTORICAL ART

In the first decades of the 19th century, a rising sense of nationalism provided inspiration for American painters to pursue historical paintings of their own, particularly those dealing with maritime subjects. Works commemorating the events of the Revolutionary War, strongly influenced by the desire to tell a story, became popular subjects for both painting and engraving. At the time, America was a major maritime trading power, and Americans were the undisputed premiere shipbuilders and mariners in the world. These facts engendered a wealth of artwork with a maritime theme. In many of these artworks, ships crashed through boiling seas, were wrecked on imposing shoals, or glided into the serene waters of foreign ports. The Barbary Wars offered subject matter for historical painting with an American theme, such as Francis Kearney's *Burning of the Frigate Philadelphia, Harbor Tripoli*, which memorialized Lieutenant Stephen Decatur's 1804 heroics. During the War of 1812, the land operations of the U.S. Army offered little that Americans wished, in good conscience, to memorialize beyond the Battle of New Orleans. However, the self-acclaimed triumphs of the nascent American Navy over Royal Navy warships, although few and insignificant to the outcome, demanded dramatic representations for a young nation building its martial traditions.

As an example, Thomas Birch, born in England but living in America, produced a series of paintings narrating the encounter between the USS *Constitution* and the HMS *Guerriere*. He divided the historic engagement into three scenes: the preparation for battle, the closing broadsides, and the surrender of the Britons. The strength of *Constitution's* sides in this battle was so great that many of the enemy's shots bounced off into the sea. This observation led to the frigate's nickname, *Old Ironsides*. Birch was trained by his father William Birch, who was a noted enamelist and miniature painter. Thomas began as a portrait painter, but he became better known for his ship portraits, seascapes, and winter scenes, both in oils and watercolors. He may have been the first to paint a view of the whaling town of Nantucket.

Michele Felice Corne, an immigrant Italian painter and decorator, brought his talents with him from Naples to New England. There, the versatile artist enjoyed great success. His American masterpiece is *The Landing of the Pilgrims at Plymouth Rock*, painted between 1803 and 1806. This work epitomized the field of American historical painting with its period costumes, maritime setting, and historical theme. Corne's landscapes were particularly accurate. A painting of Ezekiel Derby's farm outside of Salem, Massachusetts, done by Corne in 1800, was matched with a surviving photograph taken at a later date showing that his depiction was precise down to the decorative details on the buildings.

In the early decades of the antebellum period, many American painters were not interested in the frontier, the natural beauty of the land, or the newly formed customs and character of American society. These artists were consumed by art as an ideal and viewed themselves as an intellectual elite stationed above the common people. They remained bewildered and frustrated by the nation's failure to embrace the high style of art that they exalted, and they persisted in trying to foist it on the American public. Even in their own time, they were seen as failures cemented in the past and bound to European style. Notable artists like Washington Allston and Samuel F.B. Morse also failed to shake themselves free of the past in terms of technique and subject matter. Allston was a very gifted artist and an articulate workman. He read romantic literature, and his work was influenced by it. Despite a neoclassical condescension toward doing landscapes and portraits, Allston painted both, injecting personality and mood into his work. Even so, Ralph Waldo Emerson wrote, "Allston's pictures are Elysian; fair, serene, but unreal."[3]

Morse, noted for his later work in telegraphy, spent many years as an artist. Like many other painters of the period, he sought to secure Federal commissions for his paintings. This was one of the means by which painters who were without rich patrons or influential sponsors could make a livelihood. However, he failed to obtain a Federal contract for his work. Moreover, Morse's artwork, although skillfully executed, lacked imagination and never gained the popularity he expected. His lack of success left him bitter. He wrote to his friend, the novelist James Fenimore Cooper, "Painting has been a smiling mistress to many, but she has been a cruel jilt to me."[4] Morse eventually gave up painting and moved on to pursue science and invention with greater success.

Charles Wilson Peale started in career as a saddle maker in Maryland, but briefly studied painting, modeling, and mezzotint engraving in London under Copley and for more than two years under West. He returned to America in 1776 expecting to earn a living as a portrait artist, but he became involved in fighting the American Revolution. After the war, he continued his artistic career, wrote several books, and helped to start both a museum of natural history in Philadelphia and the Pennsylvania Academy of the Fine Arts. In 1808, he recorded his own scientific triumph in unearthing the bones of a great woolly mammoth near Newburgh, New York. *Exhuming the Mastodon* was a documentary of sorts recording the event from a realistic point of view. Peale's more traditional work, *Noah and His Ark*, which was completed in 1819, showed his interests both as a painter and a naturalist. Along with the allegorical harmony of the various animals, at age 78, Peale was still able to demonstrate in this painting his skill at rendering many different textures and forms.

THE HUDSON RIVER SCHOOL

The generation that grew up in the Jacksonian age was very different from that of the previous century. They saw the land and its people without the condescension of colonialism and had always known the United States as a free and independent nation. They matured in an age of nationalism, egalitarianism, and widespread social reform. A group of artists that sought to capture the nation's present and predict its future emerged from this period. Although these artists were centered mainly in New York, they shared common ideals with the transcendentalists of New England. Rallying to Ralph Waldo Emerson's plea for artists "to ignore the courtly Muses of Europe," they took a step forward both culturally and artistically, determined to show the Old World the transcendental beauty of the young nation. They captured the spirit of romance, the lofty ideals, and spiritual values intrinsic in the American self-concept. These artists saw the beauty of nature as a conduit through which people might connect to a higher truth, the awesome power of God.

In July 1833, in an article titled "The Fine Arts in America," the editors of *Knickerbocker Magazine* were the first to assert that the Hudson River artists were a distinctively American type. It is important to note that there was no Delaware River, Mississippi River, or other river schools of American artists, although most of the nation's valleys offered vistas worthy of the artist's craft. The designation reflected rather the tremendous attention and approval the Hudson River artists had garnered from the public. "To every landscape painting for which our country has such eminent advantages, we have artists competent to represent our scenes. The pictures of [Thomas] Doughty and [Thomas] Cole have a character decidedly American. The former infuses into his pictures all that is quiet and lovely, romantic and beautiful in nature."[5]

Many of the artists who embraced this romantic view of America in their work came to be included in the Hudson River school of painters, the only recognized and titled group of painters America has ever offered to the world of art. The movement seems to have begun in 1825 with Thomas Cole's retreat to New York's Catskill Mountains. The Hudson River Valley was unique in offering scenery unmatched anywhere else in the world less than 100 miles from New York City. A flood of likeminded artists followed Cole into the Hudson highlands to reproduce nature as realistically as God had wrought it. Formerly unknown artists like Asher B. Durand, John F. Kensett, Jasper Cropsey, Worthington Whittridge, Frederick Church, and a score of others produced images of the region. They were all good friends and had many memorable times together. "They tramped the wooded slopes of the Catskills looking for vistas they might literally translate [to canvas]."[6]

Each of these artists had distinct technique, training, and compositional preferences. The style of the Hudson River school emerged, not as a result of formal training or direct imitation among its members, but in reaction to the subject matter that they painted. Variety lay not in their approach, but in the natural diversity of landscapes. Nonetheless, the result was somewhat predictable—"a foreground rock or plant to show the virtuousity of the painter, then the river, misty in the middle ground, and last, the mountain rising majestically to prove the divinity of the Creator." These painters were idealists, and they shared a spirit of cooperation and a desire to reveal to the public the beauty of the nation.[7]

Images of the American landscape were particularly popular during the 1830s, even in Europe, and the Hudson River artists focused on producing them throughout the remainder of the century. Their landscapes were not simple topographical renderings, but rather interpretive and poetic views of nature. Asher B. Durand's *Kindred Spirit,* completed in 1850, is a classic of the Hudson River type. It depicts Thomas Cole showing the beauties of a steep-sided Catskill gorge to literary great William Cullen Bryant. The picture is filled with detail—overhanging ledges, intertwined trees, and a boulder-strewn stream with a cascading waterfall. The work emphasizes a connection with nature that forged a link between literature and art in the antebellum period. Cole wrote, "To walk with nature as a poet is the necessary condition of the perfect artist."[8]

Another noted author, Washington Irving, who was familiar with the folklore and history of the valley, was well aware of the Hudson River artists, and he encouraged the residents of the region to support their work. Many canvases were sold to rich patrons to adorn expensive Hudson Valley homes. Yet contemporary art critics sometimes scorned the work of the Hudson River school as overly simplistic, valuing historic painting and portraiture as better expressions of the artist's skill. Cole wrote to a friend, "It is usual to rank [the landscape] as a lower branch of art, below the historical. Why so? Is there better reason than that the vanity of man makes him delight most in his own image? . . . In landscapes there is a greater variety of subjects, textures, phenomena, to initiate. It has ex-

A detail from Durand's *Kindred Spirits*. This painting from the Hudson River school features artist Thomas Cole and literary giant William Cullen Bryant. The scene is filled with the luxuries of nature, including waterfalls, forested ravines, precipitous heights, rocky crags, and breathtaking views.

pression also, not of passion, to be sure, but of sentiment, whether it be tranquil or spirit-stirring."[9]

Hudson River artists generally preferred panoramic views with small human figures, often with the viewer placed a great distance away or observing from an elevated perspective. This juxtaposition of mighty panoramas and tiny human beings was meant to show the grandness of Nature and the insignificance of man. The majestic views also served as a peaceful escape from an increasingly industrialized society. For those who saw the hand of God in Nature, these landscapes were thought to be excellent vehicles for visual sermons.[10] Emerson noted, "The delight which a work of art affords, seems to rise from our recognizing in it the mind that formed Nature again in active operation."[11]

The pristine wilderness provided solace from the city's noise and filth. Many artists riled against continued expansion and development, which would destroy the virgin wilderness. In a way, they were America's first environmentalists. With a nationalistic view of America as the new Garden of Eden, artists like Thomas Doughty, Thomas Cole, Asher B. Durand, and their followers set out to preserve the idyllic and primitive landscape by recording it as if seen for the first time, unblemished by European sensibility or settlement.[12] Cole once confided in his journal, "Converse with the world is daily deadening the sense of the beautiful in nature which has been through all my early life such a source of delight."[13]

AMERICAN GENRE PAINTERS

A strong genre tradition that tended to overshadow other aspects historical painting emerged in the second quarter of the 19th century. William Sidney Mount is generally credited with the creation of American genre painting that emerged in the 1830s and 1840s. This form focused largely on the mundane daily activities of rural or frontier people. Unlike earlier painters who often depicted common people in a condescending manner, Mount accepted people as he found them and was deeply egalitarian in his point of view. Although he was against the abolition of slavery, Mount depicted blacks with understanding and dignity, preferring to paint them at rest or at play rather than at work. There were few black slaves on his native Long Island at the time; nonetheless, Mount was still able in later years to reflect the racial tensions of the prewar period. Though he never traveled in Europe, his lithograph pieces were widely circulated, making him the first well-known American painter on the Continent.

Mount was born in Setauket, Long Island, in New York, and began his career doing advertisements and business signs, but he soon moved on to the National Academy of Design where he was trained as a painter of historical scenes. He was a member, with Durand, Cole, and other noted contemporary painters of the Artists' Sketch Club formed in New York in 1844. Periodically, the members would compete to finish in just one hour a sketch in pencil and charcoal on a previously unannounced topic dealing with everyday life in America. Many of the resulting works were later turned into painting and engravings.

Mount maintained his livelihood by doing portraits and landscapes. However, while other American artists were trying to copy European styles and subjects, Mount focused on the people of Long Island and their daily lives, and he is best known as a painter of rural folk. A list of some of his paintings reveals his interest in the common things of antebellum life. They include *Dancing on the Barn Floor* (1831), *The Bar-room Scene* (1835), *Bargaining for a Horse* (1835), *The Power of Music* (1847), and *The Banjo Player* (1856). His subjects are seen conversing, dancing, and making music. Rather than attempting to tell a story, Mount allowed the viewer to become a silent observer of the scene. He remarked that a painting should reflect spontaneous events and reveal as little as possible the work of the human hand. His figures did not dominate the background but seemed to live in harmony with it. His work was skillfully executed, painstakingly glazed, and precise in its detail.[14]

Another American genre artist, who recorded people as he found them, was George Caleb Bingham. Incorporating the spirits of both artist and politician in one, Bingham made the political system of the antebellum period the subject of much of his artwork. In 1840, Bingham moved his art studio from his home in Missouri to the national capital at Washington where he made a living by rendering the portraits of orators and statesmen. He ran for Congress in 1846 and 1848, but only in the later year did he gain a seat. Although he was elected as a pro-Union Whig, during his single term in the House, Bingham generally sided with the South in upholding the rights of slave owners and recognizing the concept of states' rights. These positions discredited him with the abolitionists in the party, and he lost his seat in the next election. Eventually, he came to dismiss the necessity for partisan politics between the Whigs and the Democrats. "It will be a glorious time for the country when the present party organization shall be broken up entirely... when honesty and capacity, rather than party servility, will be the qualifications for office."[15]

Bingham's painting *Canvassing the Vote* captured the personal character of Missouri politics. He portrayed his central figure, a rural candidate wearing a fashionable beaver hat, in animated conversation with a group of rather skeptical local farmers. In his masterpiece, *Stump Speaking,* Bingham captured the essence of the frontier politician of the 1850s surrounded in a field by a varied group of potential voters, children, and dogs. Bingham wrote of this scene, "In my orator I have endevoured to personify a wiry politician grown gray with the pursuit of office and service of party. His influence upon the crowd is quite manifest, but I have

This detail from William Sidney Mount's *The Bar-room Scene* shows the utter simplicity of the interior of most taverns and inns. The "bar" at the far left is barely visible. Boys as young as 12 could purchase alcoholic beverages of many kinds, but most customers were mature males. Proper ladies did not frequent taverns.

placed behind him a shrewd clear-headed opponent . . . who will, when his turn comes, make sophisms fly like cobwebs before a housekeepers broom."[16]

The absence of any discernible women in Bingham's renderings of political events is remarkable but not unusual at a time when women were denied both the vote and an independent standing in most state courts. Unfortunately, restraint was also conspicuously absent from the politics of the 1850s. Elections, electioneering, and the political process in general often took on the characteristics of an avidly pursued hobby for antebellum Americans.[17] Bingham's works are filled with a riotous energy consistent with this fact—men arguing their political points in the streets and fueling their arguments from the ever-present cider barrel. Faces made grim by disappointing election results are balanced in his paintings with those sporting the wide grins of electoral success. Bingham knew from personal experience that Missouri men took their politics seriously; at one time, a statesman who was annoyed by how Bingham had depicted him in a painting challenged him to a duel. Unfortunately, proslavery Missourians abandoned the political process in the mid-1850s and invaded neighboring Kansas armed with bowie knives and revolvers to bar Free Soil men from voting slavery out of the state constitution.

Bingham did not restrict his work to politics, and he was a keen observer of many facets of antebellum life. His paintings included a number of works that helped to define the look of the period in the years before the common employment of photography. Paintings such as *Fur Traders Descending the Missouri* (1845), *Boatmen on the Missouri* (1846), *Raftsmen Playing Cards* (1847), *Daniel Boone Escorting a Band of Pioneers into the Western Country* (1851), and *The Jolly Flatboatmen* (1857) cut across many of the interests of antebellum Americans. His masterful handling of his subjects, his use of color, line, and shadow, and his excellent and meticulous recording of even small details, made prints of his works very popular.

Henry Sargent initially showed no interest in being an artist, although he was tutored by his elder brother, a professional painter, and trained by Benjamin West in London. He was much more interested in serving in the military and took a commission in the Massachusetts militia of his native Boston and served in the War of 1812. After the war, he turned to portrait

A detail of *The Jolly Flatboatmen*, a genre painting by George Caleb Bingham celebrating life on the rivers of America. In the 19th century, before the widespread building of railroads, river barges and flatboats like this one were used for almost all of the transportation of bulk cargo.

painting and showed a profound ability to render the surface texture of fabrics and objects. He is best known, however, for his genre painting, which carefully depicted the restrained upper-class society of Boston. *The Tea Party* and *The Dinner Party*, painted between 1821 and 1825, carefully recorded the details of upper-class costume and furnishings. The dates of these works make Sargent one of the earliest genre painters, but he is usually excluded from the rest of the group, who focused their work on lively rural scenes and simple unrestrained people.

In an era of light, optimism, and romanticism, it is odd to find David Gilmour Blythe, a dark, disaffected, and gloomy artist. Possibly because of his own battles with depression, alcoholism, and financial embarrassment, Blythe's genre work was somber and filled with bitterness. At age 40, he began to produce the grim artwork for which he is best known—disturbing and pitiable scenes of emaciated, spavined horses; angry, angular men; and bloated, self-absorbed women—quite the opposite of Sargent's poised and perfectly formed representations.

Apprenticed as a woodcarver at the late age of 16, before his twentieth birthday Blythe had abandoned woodworking and set himself up as a house painter in Pittsburgh. He then moved on for a time to New Orleans. Always restless, he served an enlistment in the Navy and then turned to portrait painting, a profession for which he had no formal training. By 1846, he was surviving on a small income from a studio in an upper room of a boarding house in Uniontown, Pennsylvania. Bad tempered, alcoholic, and somewhat neurotic, Blythe was able nonetheless to go into a brief, but successful partnership with two other artists in 1850. With funding from these men, he painted a giant panorama showing views of the landscape and historical events of western Pennsylvania. The 300-foot-long canvas, made of separate seven-foot-high strips of fabric sewed together, was passed from one roller to another across the front of a stage simulating a passing scene for the audience. In front of this changing panorama, Blythe's partners would make presentations, give lectures, and speak rhetorical pieces regarding the background. Such theatrical presentations were not uncommon in this period. Nonetheless, Blythe's personal behavior soon became uncontrollable, and his partners abandoned him in 1851.

Blythe, now in the depths of his personal depression, returned to portrait painting, but his work was uneven and subject to the effects of alcoholism and deep neurosis. The genre paintings he produced thereafter showed a fascination for violence and physical suffering, and he featured many of his human subjects as disheveled, grotesque, and brutalized. "It was Blythe's personal maladjustments that made him seek what was ugly in a smiling world, made him express angers, depressions, and sadisms" in his work. His canvases lacked brilliant colors, tending toward an overall yellow-brown, and in many cases his figures lacked a definite line and form.[18]

Blythe chose to record his fellow man as squat and unhealthy in order to portray the degradation and hopelessness of all of human society. His theme and his technique have been compared to that of the 18th-century engraver William Hogarth, mocking the lower classes and ridiculing the haughty rich.[19] In this manner he judged society in much the same way as many period writers such as Edgar Allan Poe or Charles Dickens. Yet, Blythe's visual appraisals of American society were more poorly wrought than the written indictments of his contemporaries largely because he liked to hide the clues to his social conscience in the dark corners of his pictures where the observer's eyes had to grope for them. He did three pictures satirizing the law and the system of American justice from 1858 to 1860. His audiences often mistook his message for humor—lampooning and mocking well-known characters and situations of the day. During the Civil War, Blythe followed the regiments onto the battlefield to record the horrors of war. More than once, military officials apprehended him because of his eccentric appearance and seeming lack of purpose among the troops. His most moving work from the period of the Civil War was of the sufferings of Union soldiers in the foul conditions of a tobacco warehouse in Richmond called "Libby Prison."

Painters of the West

In the early part of the antebellum period, the region drained by the upper Missouri River was largely an enigma thought to contain an unfamiliar and formidable geography, an undiscovered set of exotic flora and fauna, and a myriad of aboriginal tribes. Both Americans and Europeans were fascinated by the idea of recording what actually existed in the region bounded by the Great Lakes, the Rocky Mountains, and the shifting border with British America. "Even in its most primitive stage a cosmopolitan strain ran through the American borderland: it was a vastly thinned-out back yard of the world at large, where men of all nations and stations might meet and mingle in the course of their adventures."[20] Much of what we know about this region of America and its inhabitants has come down to us through the work of the naturalists, explorers, and artist/authors who visited there. These men traveled widely and lived for extended periods among the Indians often in little-known or uncharted regions, recording their impressions not only in the written word, but also in sketches, paintings, engravings, and lithographs. In the decades before the common use of the photographic camera, these artists made their images bristle with nervous energy and romantic fervor. In many cases, they captured actions and reactions on canvas that the slow-acting photographic process of the day was incapable of recording. Many of their works were so precise in depicting the details of Native American life that

Indian clothing, possessions, and homes have often been reproduced only by the careful study of the artwork created by these men.

No painter of the antebellum period is more closely associated with depicting the American Plains Indian than George Catlin. Trained as a lawyer, Catlin was a self-taught artist whose interest in Native American life may have stemmed from the fact that his mother had once been a captive in an Indian village. In 1831, he moved from his home in Wilkes Barre, Pennsylvania, to St. Louis where he became acquainted with William Clark, the explorer of the Louisiana Purchase, who was also the illustrator and mapmaker of the official journal of the 1805 Lewis and Clark expedition. It is uncertain how much Clark influenced his work, but during 1831 and 1832, Catlin ventured up the Platte River on two expeditions with Major Jean Dougherty to make sketches of the Mandan Indians. He again ascended the Missouri River by steamboat and canoe in 1833 to finish the work he had begun. Catlin probably did not know that he was helping to document the culture of a vanishing people. The Mandans were decimated by disease and shortly thereafter ceased to exist as a separate identifiable culture, having been absorbed into other related tribes.

Catlin also visited a large Comanche village in present-day Oklahoma at the foot of the Wichita Mountains in 1834, and he made many sketches among the almost 800 skin-covered lodges that housed thousands of Indians. Catlin was fond of including himself in his artwork. In one sketch, he drew himself as a hunter along with an Indian companion, both covered with wolf skins and creeping up on a great herd of buffalo. He also recorded the process by which Indian women dried the buffalo meat for winter storage and worked the skins into warm clothing, hides for their lodges, or robes for trade with the fur companies.

Catlin was not the most meticulous or most skilled of the artists that recorded the great horse cultures of the plains peoples, but he was the first to expose them to the procedure of having their likenesses formally recorded—no small accomplishment among an unsophisticated and superstitious people. Even among the friendly Mandans, artists were occasionally subjected to threats and mistreatment. His initiation of the Indians to the protocols of sitting and posing no doubt made the work of those who followed him "more productive and less dangerous than [it] might otherwise have been."[21]

In 1838, Catlin offered his paintings for sale to Congress, but they were rejected. He spent much of his life unsuccessfully trying to persuade his own government to buy his work. He moved to Europe where his work much more admired and profitable. Catlin benefited from the twin movements of romanticism and scientific inquiry, which valued recording aboriginal cultures before they were contaminated by civilization. Europeans, especially those in France and Germany, were intensely interested in America, and they consumed hundreds of journals, guides to immigrants, and novels illustrated with engravings and lithographs of the American frontier.

In the 1850s, Catlin was hired by Samuel Colt to create a series of advertising prints for his firearms. The original oil canvases were to depict Colt firearms being used in exotic places. Six of the resulting works were lithographed in color and widely distributed. Each featured Catlin, once again in the role of hunter, using a weapon from Colt's civilian line. The line of military weapons was not included. Catlin pictured himself in Texas hunting buffalo with a pistol and hunting flamingos with a revolving shotgun; in Argentina hunting ostriches with a rifle; and in Brazil hunting jaguars and peccaries. Faced with such romantic notions, "what man of action could resist buying a Colt?" Catlin's enthusiasm for the task was revealed in his own journals of his travels published in the 1860s, *Life Among the Indians* and *Rambles Amongst the Indians of the Rocky Mountains and the Andes*.[22]

Catlin's rise to prominence was not without controversy. In 1844, he wrote *Letters and Notes on the Manners, Customs, and Condition of the North American Indians*, an important documentary source for the study of the Native American people before they were completely contaminated by contact with the white man. In this work, Catlin predicted, 50 years before the event, the destruction of the great buffalo herds of the American plains. "The poor buffalo have their enemy man, besetting and besieging them at all times of the year and in all the modes that man . . . has been able to devise for their destruction. They struggle in vain to evade his deadly shafts." In words and pictures, Catlin sometimes included highly mystical and seemingly cruel elements of Native American religious life. He was even accused in 1856 of having imagined many of the ceremonies that he recorded. Because the Mandan culture had all but disappeared in the intervening years, Catlin was forced to seek out the testimony of other visitors to these Indians in order to vindicate his reputation. He published *O-Kee-Pa* (1867), a journal of his travels in the 1830s complete with testimonials to its accuracy and 13 chromolithographs. Ultimately, Joseph Henry, secretary of the Smithsonian Institution, came to the defense of Catlin's accuracy and helped to retrieve his reputation.[23]

Although Catlin is the first name that comes to mind with regard to the painting of the American West, there were many other artists that traveled there. Titian Ramsay Peale, youngest son of the accomplished portrait artist Charles Wilson Peale, accompanied an expedition to Florida in 1818 and made a record of the fauna and flora there. In the next year, as a member of Stephen Long's expedition along the South Platte River, he collected specimens and sketched birds, mammals, reptiles, fish, and insects found there. His work included more than 100 separate pieces of art, many of which became part of the collection of the American Philosophical

Society. As a member of this expedition, Peale was also one of the first official parties to climb Pikes Peak.

Peter Rindisbacher was the first of many foreign-born artists to portray the American-Canadian borderland, and his work preceded that of other eminent artists by a decade. If Rindisbacher had not died at 28 (1834), he probably would have become as famous an artist as Catlin. In 1821, the family of the teenaged Swiss artist was recruited by agents of the Hudson's Bay Fur Company to move to the struggling Red River colony south of Lake Winnipeg. In this period, the Red River region was a wilderness made worse by the armed insurrection of the mixed race, French-speaking Metis Indians. For a decade, the colony had been on the verge of collapse, but in 1820 a temporary peace had taken hold.

Rindisbacher lost no time beginning his sketches once he reached America, first in pencil and pen and then in watercolors. In just five years, he produced hundreds of drawing and paintings of the frontier region of Minnesota and Manitoba. His portraits, landscapes, and scenes of Native American and white life were accurate and graphic in their detail. Many of his works portrayed people and animals in violent action. He was the first artist to depict the interiors of the bark-covered lodges and buffalo-skin tepees of the regional Indians. His Native subjects were primarily from among the Chippewa, Cree, Assiniboine, Winnebago, Sauk, Fox, and Sioux. He also recorded the activities of the Metis and British fur traders and the home life of the Swiss and Scottish settlers of the Red River colony.

In 1826, Rindisbacher moved to St. Louis, Missouri, and produced a lithograph of one of his sketches, *A Sioux Warrior Charging*. This stirring image first appeared in Baltimore in a new periodical, the *American Turf Register and Sporting Magazine*. The print was an instant sensation. Subsequently, nine more of his works were printed. Flying high on his apparent popularity, in 1831 Rindisbacher opened an art studio, took out advertisements in the St. Louis *Times*, and planned to settle down to life as a professional portrait painter. However, his work was less accomplished and less meticulous than that of his professionally trained competitors. In the last years of his life, he turned out his finest work dealing with the Indians, much of which revisited and improved on his earlier images. In 1834 he died suddenly, perhaps from cholera.

When a minor German prince, Maximilian von Wied, traveled to the American West, he chose Charles (Carl) Bodmer, a Swiss painter, to make a pictorial record of his 1832 expedition to the upper Missouri. Almost everything that Bodmer produced was intended for reproduction as part of Maximilian's record of his observations, and more than 400 of Bodmer's sketches and drawings remained concealed in the prince's family home in the Rhineland until the middle of the 20th century. Bodmer made detailed illustrations of the life, habits, customs, and costumes of the Indians that they encountered. By 1833, the explorers had reached St. Louis where they placed themselves under the protection of John Jacob Astor's American Fur Company. They then moved up the Missouri River by steamboat, passing through parts of present-day Nebraska, South and North Dakota, Montana, and Wyoming.

The subjects of Bodmer's work were largely portraits of individual Native Americans or river scenes, some of which included Indian villages. He was observant, and his work shows a conscious attention to detail. His meticulous painting of the interior of the hut of a Mandan chief was the first of its kind to be published. Unlike many other artist of this genre, Bodmer made no attempt to romanticize his subjects. In 1834, he moved to France where he completed 81 paintings based on his sketches and watercolors. These he exhibited in a Paris art salon in 1836. He also completed a number of plates to illustrate a journal of his American trip including several likenesses favorable to his employer, the prince.

In 1846, Paul Kane, a wandering artist from Toronto, Canada, set out from Sault Sainte Marie for the farthest reaches of the Canadian West. Kane was determined to record the life of the North American Indians before the alcohol, gunpowder, and diseases of the white man changed them forever. He went all the way to the Pacific Ocean, making sketches of Native Americans, their homes, villages, possessions, and cultural activities in Wisconsin, Alberta, British Columbia, and Vancouver. Along the way, he also recorded the activities of the fur traders among the Indians in Saskatchewan and particularly at their post on the Columbia River. He drew a sketch of a minor eruption of Mount St. Helens in the Cascade Mountains of present-day Washington State, and he recorded the life of the people native to Idaho and the disputed Oregon border region. In 1847, Kane made final portraits of Reverend Marcus Whitman and his wife, Narcissa, before their death at the hands of two Indians at their mission in Oregon. Returning to his studio in Toronto in 1848, Kane began transferring his sketches to canvas, thereby leaving a precise and detailed record of the region for future historians and ethnographers.

Heinrich Mollhausen made three trips to America from Germany between 1849 and 1858, and he served as an artist/reporter and draftsman for several U.S. government expeditions. On his first trip, he joined the Rocky Mountain expedition of the German naturalist Prince Paul of Württemberg. These sketches and those he produced on his subsequent trips were later lithographed. Some were made part of the official reports of the expeditions of Lieutenant A. W. Whipple and of Lieutenant J.C. Ives, who he accompanied from Arkansas to California and along the Colorado River, respectively. Like other artists, Mollhausen shared his work with an interested European public by writing journals that he illustrated with his own engravings and lithographs. He also wrote a German-language novel about pioneer life among the Indians called *Das Mormonenmadchen*.

Alfred Jacob Miller was an American-born portrait painter of German extraction who studied painting and drawing in both France and England. Originally from Baltimore, Miller moved to New Orleans in 1837 were he was selected by Captian William D. Stewart to served as an artist on an expedition to the Rocky Mountains by wagon along what would become the Oregon Trail. He sketched Native Americans and mountain men along the way, and was the first to document the annual rendezvous of the fur traders in what is now southwestern Wyoming. Miller made 166 sketches that he turned into oil paintings upon his return to his studio in New Orleans. From 1840 to 1842, he also produced a portfolio of 83 small drawings and watercolors in his studio in Baltimore from his remaining notes.

Charles Wimar came to America at 15 and made friends with the Indians that lived on the outskirts of St. Louis. He retained a great love of the Native Americans even after he returned to Germany in 1852. In Düsseldorf, where many of the painters of this genre obtained their training, Wimar painted several studies of American Indians. Nonetheless, he did his best work after returning to America in 1856. He painted several scenes made popular by early U.S. historians and by novelist like James Fenimore Cooper. One of his most famous works was *The Abduction of Daniel Boone's Daughter.* This romanticized the chilling facts of the actual event of 1776 by changing the skulking woodland abductors into a noble mounted warrior astride a massive and well-muscled steed like that of a medieval champion. This image was reproduced in many formats in subsequent years.

There were also a number of lesser-known German author/artists who traversed the United States in this period. In 1832, Traugott Bromme published a thorough account of Native American life among the peoples of the Arctic Circle (commonly known as Eskimos) that included 18 engraved plates. Rudolph Kurz, a professional painter, filled his sketchbooks with scenes from New Orleans to St. Louis from 1846 to 1852. Karl Kohler visited America's well-settled cities and urban areas in the 1850s and recorded his impressions along with illustrations in his book, *Briefe aus Amerika.* Gustavus Sohon enlisted in the U.S. Army and served as an artist on several government survey teams. Finally, F. W. von Egloffstein, also a foreign Army enlistee, served as a topographical artist to several government teams, and during the Civil War he rose to the rank of brigadier general in the Federal Army.

Portrait Painters

Journalist John Neal opined that Americans had "a decided predisposition for painting. . . . There are . . . more [painters] than we know what to do with." Portraiture abounded in antebellum America. Important persons, and those that aspired to importance, all had their portraits painted and hung ostentatiously in their homes. Artists painted likenesses from head size to full length, but it was the head-and-shoulders format that seems to have been most favored. "You can hardly open the door of a best room anywhere, without surprising or being surprised by, the picture of somebody plastered to the wall and then staring at you with both eyes and a bunch of flowers."[24]

One of the most sought after portrait artists of the period was Thomas Sully, a Southerner who moved his studio to Philadelphia to attract a wider trade. Despite relocating, Sully never lost his Southern patronage, and he was a mentor to a number of noteworthy Southern artists. His style included rich, soft colors and a very effective use of light that greatly flattered his subjects. Sully explained, "Resemblance is essential but no fault will be found with the artist—at least not by the sitter—if he improves the appearance."[25] Some critics suggested that this philosophy short-changed Sully's artistic skills, but it made him rich and famous, nonetheless. Although he is best known for his portraits of women, Sully's subjects included many prominent men including Andrew Jackson and the Marquis de Lafayette, who he painted during his 1825 visit.

The majority of portraits done during the antebellum years were simpler, more linear, and more hard-edged in style than the romantic manner of Sully and his students. This naive form of art, which is often labeled today as "folk" or "primitive" art, flourished from the beginning of the century until well after the Civil War. This was not the result of a conscious tradition or movement, but rather a personal method of expression due to the temperament and ability of the individual artist. These artists came from very diverse backgrounds and demonstrated a wide range of sophistication. Some studied with academic painters or established studios whereas others were self-taught and had only instruction manuals and popular prints of the day as their guide. Naive art is often characterized as a simplistic, two-dimensional form presented primarily in outline. Bright colors are applied independently to each figure and used more to indicate the importance of a subject rather than its natural hue.

The price of a portrait was directly related to the amount of labor and skill that was involved in producing the work. William Matthew Prior advertised that "persons wishing for a flat picture can have a likeness without shade or shadow at one quarter price." Another artist announced that "those who wish for a likeness at a reasonable price are invited to call soon. Side views and profiles of children at reduced prices."[26]

Many naive painters were itinerant artists who traveled the countryside rendering portraits for rural inhabitants. Some would set up informal exhibitions in hotel lobbies in order to promote their work. These itinerant painters were often classified as limners. The archaic term "limner" was used in relation to those who illuminated manuscripts. By the 19th century, it was generally used to describe an artist whose skill was more dependent on line than on shadings or color. Many itinerants did post-humous paintings, sometimes from the corpse, to supplement their income. When John Wood Dodge painted *Posthumous Likeness of Felix Grundy Eakins, Aged Three Years,* he included such death imagery as wilted flowers and a broken toy with tools cast aside to symbolize the unfinished life. This characteristic of the antebellum mourning process, which seems odd to us today, was largely taken over by photographers once cameras became common.

Ammi Phillips was one of the most prolific itinerant American paint-ers of the period. Most active in the region where the borders of New York, Connecticut, and Massachusetts meet east of Albany, Phillips traveled the regional villages with easel and paints seeking commissions from the growing middle class. He developed a formula approach to portraiture that facilitated his work, yet he managed to seemingly personalize each portrait. Commenting on Phillips work, John Vanderlyn wrote to his nephew, "Were I to begin life over again, I should not hesitate to follow this path, that is, to paint portraits cheap and slight, for the mass of folks can't judge the merits of a well finished picture. . . . Moving about the country as Phillips did, and probably still does, must be an agreeable way of passing one's time." Vanderlyn also observed that the itinerant painter could "gain more money than you could by any mechanical business, which you know is far more laborious and less genteel." In his travels, Phillips would become acquainted with "the best society and if he was wise, [this] might be the means of establishing himself advantageously in the world."[27]

One of the few known black American painters prior to the Civil War was A. Joshua Johnson. He was brought to Baltimore in the 1790s as a slave for a family that was related to the portrait painter Charles Willson Peale. Within a decade, Johnson became a freeman and was listed in a Baltimore directory as a limner. The fact that he earned his living as a portrait painter working for white patrons in Maryland and Virginia in-dicates his acceptance as a skilled craftsman even in a slaveholding soci-ety. Johnson's earliest works evidence the influence of Peale, but he ultimately developed his own, less-academic style. Johnson favored bright, strong color. His treatment of facial features was highly idealized, yet the ancillary details, such as a fine lace, were treated with meticulous precision. Johnson is the earliest known African American painter with a recognized body of work in the United States.

The profession of art was not limited to males. Deborah Goldsmith worked in watercolor, pencil, and ink. She was an unusual woman for her time in that her correspondence shows that she actively sought commis-sions away from her home. It was not common for unmarried women to travel for reasons other than visiting family and friends during this period. Goldsmith worked in various towns in upstate New York for several years until her marriage to George Addison Throop, a gentleman she met through a portrait commission.

The story of Ruby Devol Finch was more common for a female painter of the period. She worked in watercolor painting mostly for friends and neighbors near her Massachusetts home. Finch personalized her portraits by paying special attention to costume details and jewelry. All of her works are accompanied by poetic verses. Some contain devout remarks or morals, whereas others make specific reference to the sitter's life. A portrait in profile of widow Susannah Tripp contained the following message in handwritten script:

Of late I've met with a great loss,
A partner and a friend.
No one is left but children dear
On whom I can depend
Many the years we had lived in peace
Although in natures path we trod
Yet previous to his death I trust
Were redeemed by Christ's own blood.[28]

MURALISTS

The antebellum period witnessed a change in terms of middle-class home decoration from the common whitewashed plaster walls of colonial times to strong and vibrant wall decorations. Although wallpaper was increasingly popular, many homeowners chose to have murals featuring floral designs and landscapes painted directly on their walls. This created an entirely unprecedented demand for muralists in America.

Rufus Porter was the most prolific itinerant muralist working during the second quarter of the 19th century. Porter was more than a mere wall decorator. He was a man of many and varied skills. He was a painter, a writer of art instruction manuals, a founder of *Scientific American* magazine, and an inventor. Porter's inventions included a turbine waterwheel, several rotary machines, unusual clocks, railway signals, churns, and an early washing machine. Porter even applied his ingenuity to his painting by developing a method for decorating walls with landscapes more cheaply and more quickly than could be done with wallpaper. He was also a self-promoting and somewhat disingenuous businessman, explaining to his prospective customers that wallpaper was "apt to get torn off and often affords behind it a resting place for insects."[29]

Porter's artistic strategies in attacking a project included a pallet of premixed colors, the use of stencils for drawing common solid forms such as houses, fences, or horsemen, and the application of carved corks to stamp in background foliage. Porter claimed that he had seen an artist paint the "entire walls of a parlor with all the several distances, and a variety of fancy scenery, palaces, villages, mills, vessels, etc. and a beautiful set of shade trees in the foreground, and finish the same complete in less than five hours." Porter would often offer to do portraits of the principal household members while he was waiting for the layers of paint on a mural to dry.[30]

Sometimes more than one muralist was required to complete a work. Both Porter and his stepson, Stephen Twombly, signed a mural at the Howe House in Westwood, Massachusetts. Porter and Moses Daton Jr. collaborated on the murals in the Joshua Eaton house in Bradford, New Hampshire. Porter's nephew, Jonathan D. Poor, apprenticed with his uncle and went on to have his own prolific career as a muralist. It is thought that another painter, with the last name of Paine, also assisted Porter.

Whether alone or with a partner, Porter was prolific. Farmhouses, taverns, inns, ballrooms, and public meetinghouses from Maine to Virginia were decorated with Porter's stylized landscapes, elegant in their innocent simplicity. Writing in the *New York Mechanic* in 1841, Porter boasted that "hundreds of rooms and entries have been painted in New England scenery."[31] Whereas some of Porter's scenes are based on European views, most were inspired by the New England landscape. However, they do not appear to replicate the actual surroundings of the locations in which they are housed.

MINIATURES

Since the founding of the nation, miniature paintings have been cherished tokens of affection exchanged by family members and lovers. The small size of the miniature allowed the portraits to be carried about and easily hidden from public view. Miniatures were often exchanged to celebrate betrothal or marriage. Portrait miniatures often contained locks of hair on the reverse and were given to spouses during periods of long separation.

Charles Fraser was a prominent miniaturist who painted many of Charleston's leading citizens. Between 1818 and 1846, Fraser's account book recorded 633 works. Fraser had developed a bold technique that modeled the popular oil paintings of the day. A study of period advertisements documents at least four popular categories of miniatures. The simplest and least expensive were silhouettes. Slightly more expensive were detailed profiles painted in watercolor on paper. Next, there were full-face portraits painted in watercolor on paper. The most costly of all were miniatures painted on ivory.[32] "Miniatures painted on Ivory—8.00 [dollars]." Of course, for the last the artist, muralist Rufus Porter offered, "Those who request it will be waited on at their respective places of residence."[33]

Miniaturists traveled the country in search of patrons. Many offered their services as instructors of dancing, drawing, or other activities of refinement in order to maximize their earning potential. This also allowed them to gain access to more cultured clients who were more likely to be interested in their painting talents. At the turn of the 19th century, the demand for miniatures flourished as a growing middle class with strong romantic sensibilities gained the financial capability to commission them.

In the prior century, thick, densely colored miniatures were popular, but 19th-century miniaturists created more luminous portraits painted against a paler background. Antebellum miniatures were also painted on larger yet thinner wafers. The larger size permitted more space on the reverse for sentimental inscriptions or allegorical scenes of friendship or love, although the antebellum trend was away from the allegorical scenes of former times. During the Jacksonian era, some miniatures were mounted in larger, rectangular frames that could be displayed on a mantel, a desk, or a table in the parlor. Nonetheless, small miniatures continued to be popular through the Civil War.

The advent of photography brought about a further evolution of the miniature. The precision and sharp contrasts of the photographic image had a great influence on miniature portraits. The converse influence of painting on photography can be seen in the poses, expressions, and props found in many early daguerreotypes. The similarity between the miniature painting and the photographic image in terms of portability and display alternatives brought the two processes into strong competition. Miniaturists had to compete with photographers to meet their client's expectations for more accurate likenesses and quicker completion. Miniatures began to fall out of style in the 1840s due in part to a weakening interest in portraiture in general, the rising popularity of landscapes, and a weakening of demand due to economic hard times. Yet some miniaturists continued to try to compete. A handwritten label on the back of a portrait of Nathaniel Todd proclaimed, "Portraits painted in this style! Done in about an hour's sitting. Price $2.95, including Frame, Glass, &c."[34]

Gradually, the daguerreotype overtook the miniature as the preferred means of capturing the human image in portable form. An article in *Gody's Lady's Book* in 1849 commented on the new phenomenon:

If our children and children's children to the third and fourth generation are not in possession of portraits of their ancestors, it will be no fault of the Daguerreotypists of the present day; for verily, they are limning faces at a rate that promises soon to make every man's house a Daguerrean Gallery. From little Bess, the baby, up to great-grandpa', all must now have their likenesses; and even the sober Friend, who heretofore rejected all the vanities of portrait-taking, is tempted to sit in the operator's chair, and quick as thought, his features are caught and fixed by a sunbeam.[35]

SILHOUETTES

Traditional portraits could cost $50 and required repeated, tedious sittings. People who would never even consider having a portrait commissioned could afford to have a silhouette of their profile done. Silhouettes flourished during the period 1760 to 1860. Some silhouettes were simply mounted on paper, but others were enhanced with watercolors. Sometimes the profile was combined with a printed body. There are examples of silhouettes with woodblock printed bodies and some with lithographed bodies, which were cut out and pasted below the head. Silhouettes without details were a fast and easy way for portrait artists to supplement their income. Their low cost and rapid completion made them extremely popular. By folding a piece of paper in half, two profiles could be cut at the same time. A handbill of the period offered "Correct Likenesses" at the following rates: "Common Profiles cut double—$.20," "Front views—3.00 [dollars]."[36] Charles Willson Peale remarked, "Profiles are seen in nearly every house in the United States, never did any invention of making the likeness of men, meet so general approbation as this has done."[37]

While the best silhouette artists worked freehand with a scissors, a variety of mechanical techniques were employed to achieve high-quality likenesses. These contrivances, characteristic of the quest for all sorts of mechanical inventions during the antebellum period, included a special chair and frame, the pantograph, and the camera obscura. The first of these aided in achieving proper proportion, but the camera obscura was an optical device that had been used by artists for centuries. It employed a mirror and a convex lens in a darkened box that could be accessed by the artist from the rear. The image of the subject was formed, rebounded and greatly reduced in size to fit on a small piece of paper where it could be traced. The camera obscura could be used in profile drawing, perspective drawing, and the projection of outdoor scenes. However, its use was considered a form of "cheating" by serious artists.

In 1802, John Isaac Hawkins patented an improved pantograph or "physiognotrace," which moved along the actual facial structure of the subject from forehead to chin. The device could be operated either by an artist or by the subject. Hawkins partnered with the artist Charles Wilson Peale to market the device to others. His device produced a different kind of image than those of the century before. The pantograph moved a steel point that traced a reduced silhouette upon a folded white paper. Once completed, the paper was carefully cut to produce four identical profiles. The interior portions of the paper, known as "blockheads," were thrown away and the outer portion was mounted against a black background.

Although the mystique of various mechanical instruments may have served to attract some clients, artist William King advertised the fact that he did not employ such devices. Describing his technique in a broadside he proclaimed, "Ladies are particularly informed that he [King] takes their profiles without their faces being scraped with the Machine, or their being under the agreeable necessity of retiring to a dark room or having the shadow varied by the flare of a candle, as he makes use of neither."[38]

One of the best silhouette artists of the period was August Edouart. He established himself in England before moving to America in 1839. Edouart insisted that a silhouette should be a plain black outline without embellishment. Some silhouette artists embellished their work with gold. He always cut full-length silhouettes, usually with the subject standing. He had a special ability to capture the essence of his subject. Although he returned to Europe in 1849, he is considered by many to be the father of the art in America.

Moses Williams has been immortalized by a silhouette of himself that identified him as a "cutter of profiles." Williams was a silhouette artist who began his career as a slave of Charles Wilson Peale. He later operated on his own as a freedman. Williams charged between 6 and 8 cents for each of his profiles. Peale's son Rembrandt recalled that Williams's business was so sizable that he had two barrels full of discarded blockheads.

Charlestonian William Henry Brown was one of the last great silhouette artists of the period. He snipped silhouettes of such distinguished personages as Andrew Jackson, Henry Clay, John C. Calhoun, and Abraham Lincoln. Brown did more comprehensive pieces that captured entire families, military and fire companies with their equipment, sporting scenes, marine views, and scenes portraying plantation life than other contemporary artists.

LITHOGRAPHY

Prints were very popular during the antebellum period. They satisfied the need of art for the masses. A growing, literate middle class read books and periodicals in greater numbers and illustrations contributed greatly to the reader's enjoyment. Improvements in engraving technology permitted inexpensive, easily duplicated prints. With the increase in interest in prints, the variety of prints increased as well. Journals contained illustrations, sketches, and cartoons. Sheet music was adorned with illustrations, which could be displayed atop the parlor organ. The demand for prints suitable for framing grew rapidly. Many painters supplemented their income by making prints from their works. Cole's allegories, Vanderlyn's *Ariadne* and Trumbull's *Declaration of Independence*, which was engraved by Durand, were widely distributed and extremely popular. Panoramic views of landscapes and cityscapes were popular. J.W. Hill was particularly skilled in this format.

Portraits of famous people were also very popular. In order to enhance the tones of these portraits, some metal engravers began to specialize in stipple engraving. Through the engraving of countless dots the artist was able to get striking tonal contrasts. James Barton Longacre was one of the most skilled practitioners of this method. His *Andrew Jackson*, which was made from the portrait painted by Thomas Sully, was an outstanding example of stipple engraving.

Lithography was invented in Bavaria in the late 18th century and began to overtake the more laborious methods of engraving as the 19th century progressed. The process produced inexpensive reproductions of unequaled richness and tonal subtlety. Many companies began to produce and distribute framable prints. The firm of Currier & Ives was the uncontested leader in this field. Nathaniel Currier started the firm in 1835 and was joined by Merritt Ives in 1857. Their catalogs offered prints for every taste, including portraits, landscapes, renderings of farm and frontier life, fires, shipwrecks, transportation, sporting events, and sentimental scenes. One of their most prolific artists was Flora (Fanny) Palmer. She exhibited tremendous technical skill and artistic sense.

SCULPTURE

At the beginning of the 19th century, most of America's sculptors were woodcarvers and stonecutters employed in the practical application of their craft. The expansion of shipbuilding at the end of the 18th century created a great demand for skilled woodworkers to provide details and ornament on ships. Although they were talented professionals, many woodcarvers thought of themselves as workmen rather than artists. Carving figureheads was a major enterprise in seaport towns. Located at the front of the ship just under the bowsprit, the figurehead was the symbol of the ship. Figureheads served no practical purpose, but it was believed that they conveyed a sense of prosperity that reflected favorably on the owners and shipbuilders. Figureheads in this period reflected the interests of the time and took the form of generals, statesmen, ladies, and Indians. Some depicted the wives and daughters of the sea captains or the ship owners. Others drew inspiration from maritime myths or symbolized the name of the ship. More traditional forms included animals, sea serpents, and dolphins. The earliest figureheads stood almost erect against the large rounded hull, but as ships became sleeker and narrower the figureheads leaned forward until they were nearly horizontal beneath the bowsprit. Figureheads could be extremely elaborate works of art. They were painted with bright colors and even gilded. Most were carved from white pine, usually in a single block of wood. Some had pieces that could be unscrewed, enabling the figurehead to be removed and stored safely away once the ship was out to sea. When the vessel neared a port, it could then be replaced in order to make a favorable entrance. Isaac Fowle carved some of the finest figureheads in

Boston during the antebellum period. His work was highly sculptural and rich with detail.

Woodcarvers were also engaged to make wooden figures that were placed at the entrance to business establishments. They helped to attract attention and enabled prospective customers to identify the business at some distance. While they came in a variety of characters and shapes, the classic examples of these figures would have to be the tobacconist's *Cigar Store Indian*. This figure became popular after 1840 with the arrival of cigar smoking. By mid-century, 200 to 300 such figures were being made annually.

During the 1830s, a phenomenon known as the "rural cemetery movement" had begun. Romanticism, with its emphasis on the boundary between life and death, demanded an idyllic place where peace and calm would reign and the family bond could remain forever unbroken. Cemeteries were transformed into parks filled with monuments and paths that meandered over landscaped hills and valleys. Monuments were three-dimensional works carved in imitation of European sculptors, creating a virtual museum of memorials. The monuments generally heralded symbols of hope, immortality, and life. The draped urn, the weeping woman, and the sleeping child were all popular images. The young child with a lamb was another recurring subject. Equally frequent were the trappings of home and family. Books, hats, dogs, chairs, even home facades were carved in loving memory of the departed. The stonecutters who created these monuments were more concerned with imagery and symbolism than artistic expression.

One man who made the transition from woodcarver to sculptor was William Rush. The son of a ship's woodcarver, Rush grew up in the craft. His works include figureheads, allegories, and portraits. Although wood was his preferred medium, he worked with other materials as well, including bronze and terra-cotta. Rush's carvings were renown. English architect Benjamin Latrobe remarked that Rush's figureheads "seemed rather to draw the ship after them than be impelled by the vessel."[39] Most of Rush's portraits were busts, but one of his most distinguished pieces was a full-figure bronze of George Washington.

John Frazee was another native-born sculptor who made the transition from artisan to artist. He apprenticed himself to a stonecutter when he was 20 and learned the craft of carving gravestones. In time, he established his own business offering a variety of decorative items including sculpture and carved stone, wood, and cast-metal ornamentation. Frazee continued to expand his skills taking every opportunity to learn. His bust of John Wells of Saint Paul's Chapel in New York was the first marble sculpture completed in the United States by a native sculptor. This accomplishment brought him a commission for seven busts for the Boston Athenaeum. It was quite an honor for him to be chosen for such a project considering his background, and his selection shows the respect in which he was held.

When Thomas Jefferson wanted to adorn the interiors of the Capitol designed by Benjamin Latrobe, he initially looked abroad for skilled artisans. Native sculptors were not sufficiently respected to be given the task. Even though Latrobe had admired the figureheads of Rush, professing that no one in Europe could equal them, Jefferson did not give Rush any commissions for the project.[40] And although a small enclave of Italian stone masons had grown in the American South since colonial times because of the need to fabricate columns and other ornaments for plantation houses, Jefferson preferred sculptors and carvers recruited directly from Italy for work on the Capitol. These immigrant Italian artists brought with them the neoclassical style, which influenced American sculpture for generations and helped to establish Italy as the mecca to which aspiring American sculptors traveled to study.

One of the few American expatriates to Italy to obtain a commission for the Capitol was Horatio Greenough. While at Harvard, he had made the design from which the Bunker Hill monument was constructed. One of his most important works was a colossal statue of George Washington. The 20-ton statue depicted Washington seated like Zeus from Olympia. The statue was surrounded by controversy and structural problems, and it was the object of many jokes. Philip Hone wrote in his diary that "it looks like a great herculean Warrior-like Venus of the bath . . . with a huge napkin lying on his lap and covering his lower extremities, and he preparing to perform his ablutions is in the act of consigning his sword to the care of the attendant. . . . Washington was too prudent, and careful of his health, to expose himself thus in a climate so uncertain as ours."[41] Greenough also executed *The Rescue*, which depicted a frontiersman defending his family from Indian attack in 1853.

Hiram Powers became one of America's best-known sculptors during the antebellum period, but his fame has been described as "excessive" and "impermanent." He was responsible for inventing new tools and techniques in finishing marble, and he devised a revolutionary method of modeling and carving plaster. Prior to this innovation, making a marble statue involved making a clay model, casting it in plaster, and then copying the original plaster in marble by a pointing process. The original clay figure created by the sculptor was destroyed in the process. Powers's new method permitted carving directly in the plaster and eliminated the need for the clay model. The original plaster was now retained as the artist's original conception.[42]

Powers spent several years in Washington modeling busts of well-known men before moving to Florence, Italy. There, in 1843, after he heard that Turks sold female prisoners in slave markets, he produced the *Greek Slave*. Powers sought to give to the expression of the Greek slave "what trust there could still be in a Divine Providence for a future state of exist-ence, with utter despair for the present, mingled somewhat of scorn for all around her." He said of the subject of his work, "It is not her person but her spirit that stands exposed." The *Greek Slave* was probably his most famous work. Miniature copies of the piece could be found in parlors from Boston to San Francisco. Author Henry James recalled that they were "so undressed, yet so refined, even so pensive, in sugar-white alabaster, ex-posed under little glass covers in such American homes as could bring themselves to think such things right."[43]

Americans had mixed emotions about sculpture as pure art. They ad-mired the beauty and understood the labor involved in the creation of a statue but were often uneasy about the exposed human form. A nude female by Joel Hart was first called *Venus*, then *Purity*, and finally *The Tri-umph of Chastity*. In Cincinnati, the Ladies' Academy of Art hired some-one to make fig leaves to impose modesty on nude statues imported from Europe. Any statue that hoped to be accepted in America at this time had to be justified as some literary or moral illustration.

The antebellum period marked a new and dynamic age in American art. Never before had so much encouragement been available to painters and sculptors. Many patrons spent freely on native work and on copies of the old masters made by American artists. Civic-minded collectors periodi-cally opened their assembled works to the public. The National Academy of Design in New York and the Pennsylvania Academy of Fine Arts held exhibitions, displayed and sold works of art, offered instruction, and set up models of good artistic taste in the form of casts of celebrated statues and copies of eminent paintings. By mid-century, art galleries began to appear around the country. In 1846, European firms selling prints and engravings began opening shops in New York in order to capitalize on the burgeoning picture market in the United States. Artists formed groups such as the Lunch Club and the Sketch Club wherein they cultivated friendships with art connoisseurs and the literati.

The Art Union was created in 1839 as a means of eliminating exorbi-tant dealers' profits from art sales. The Union was very different from some of the art institutions that had existed at the beginning of the cen-tury, such as The American Academy of Fine Arts of New York (1802) and the Pennsylvania Academy of Fine Arts in Philadelphia (1805). Unfortu-nately, these institutions did little to help to instruct aspiring artists or to exhibit native work. Run by businessmen rather than artists, these acad-emies were repositories for casts of classical sculpture and a few modern paintings. The snobbish connoisseurs who ran the institutions imagined their knowledge of the arts to be superior to that of the artists and thus disparaged many accomplished practitioners.

Each year, the Union distributed an engraving or statuette based on a work by an American master to its membership of subscribers, and original works were awarded to a small number of lottery winners. In its first year, the Union had 800 members. By its 10th year, membership had risen dramatically to almost 19,000. The managers of the Union acquired a variety of landscapes, figure paintings, and genre works. The works were exhibited at the Union's New York gallery until the end of the year when the originals were given to the fortunate ticket holders. Thomas Cole, George Caleb Bingham, and Richard Caton Woodville were among the artists whose work was selected for reproduction. The Union was disbanded in 1852 following a newspaper campaign sponsored by the *New York Herald* and a group of disgruntled artists who claimed the Union violated state lottery laws. Through the Art Union, thousands of small-town Americans were given the opportunity to become familiarized with the work of leading American artists.

In 1834, William Dunlap's *History of the Rise and Development of the Arts of Design in the United States* was the first record of artistic progress in the United States. Other works on American art history and criticism began to appear as well. Adam Badeau gathered pieces on music, drama, sculpture, and painting in *The Vagabond*. Henry T. Tuckerman's *Artist-Life* of 1847 offered mostly scholarly essays on the topic, but it made art more exciting and increased understanding of the arts in general. *The Crayon* was a 16-page weekly newspaper founded in 1855 by John Durand and William J. Silliman. It carried installments by notable artists and critics like John Ruskin and Charles Eliot Norton, and remained in publication until 1861 when it was overshadowed by the war. Asher B. Durand's *Letters on Landscape Painting*, published in *The Crayon* was "the most important formal statement on art theory produced by any artist of the Hudson River school." Art history and art criticism were not considered professions at this time; rather they were just one field among the mass of interests in American culture that marked the period. Nonetheless, the antebellum period witnessed the birth and the rise toward maturity of many American forms of art. A national artistic identity separate from Europe developed. It was the first time that Americans of moderate means were able to participate in the appreciation and ownership of works of art.[44]

Costs in the Antebellum Period

PRICES FOR COMMODITIES AND FOODSTUFFS

Approximate price per pound in 1850, unless otherwise stated.

Firewood, $10.00/cord

Lumber for building, $5.00/100 bd-ft

Milk, 10 cents/quart

Butter, 20 cents

Cheese, 22 cents

Eggs, 3 cents/dozen

Flour (in barrels of 100 pounds), 2 cents

Cornmeal (in barrels of 100 pounds), 2 cents

Bread (store bought 1 pound loaf), 5 cents

Coffee, 25 cents

Tea, 47 cents

Sugar (in 1 pound cone), 50 cents

Beef, 10 cents

Pork, 14 cents

Bacon, 18 cents

Ham, 18 cents

Lamb, 17 cents

Chicken, 16 cents

Lard, 13 cents

Potatoes (in 60 pound sacks), 2 cents

Rice, Beans, 8 cents

Onions, 8 cents

Cabbage, 5 cents

Corn (canned), 14 cents

Peas (canned), 15 cents

Tomatoes (canned), 12 cents

Beans (canned), 11 cents

PERIOD WAGES AND COST OF LIVING

Approximate—1850

Value of an 1850 dollar vs. a 2004 dollar, $1 = $22

Wages

Farmhand Pay + Upkeep (10 to 16 hours), $2.00/day

Day laborer (8 to 12 hour shift), $2.50/day
    (6 days not Sundays), $15.00/week
    (1 year or 52 weeks), $780/year

New York City Policy, $600/year

New York City Lamplighter, $125/year

Living

Costs for food and fuel for a family of five, $6.00/week

As a percent of earnings, 40 percent

Rent (if applicable—varied widely), $2–3/week

Stabling and feed for one horse, $1–2/week

Newspaper, 1 cent each

Notes

CHAPTER 1: EVERYDAY AMERICA

1. Richard H. Sewell, *A House Divided: Sectionalism and the Civil War, 1848–1865* (Baltimore, MD: Johns Hopkins University Press, 1988), xi.

2. Don E. Fehrenbacher, *The Era of Expansion, 1800–1848* (New York: John Wiley and Sons, 1969), 100.

3. Sir Walter Scott, *The Fair Maid of Perth* (New York: Harper, 1831), 9. The actual quote reads: "'Yes—respect; and who pays any respect to me?' said the haughty young lord. 'A miserable artisan and his daughter, too much honored by my slightest notice, have the insolence to tell me that my notice dishonors them.'"

4. John Tosh, "New Men? The Bourgeois Cult of Home," *History Today* (December 1996): 9–15.

5. George Fitzhugh, *Cannibals All, or Slaves without Masters*, 1857.

6. Fitzhugh, *Cannibals All*.

7. Catherine Clinton, *The Plantation Mistress: Woman's World in the Old South* (New York: Pantheon Books, 1982), 52–53.

8. See Clinton, *The Plantation Mistress*, 57–58, 233.

9. James M. McPherson, *For Cause and Comrades: Why Men Fought in the Civil War* (New York: Oxford University Press, 1997, 24.

10. McPherson, *For Cause and Comrades*, 24.

11. Bec C. Truman, *Duelling in America* (n.p., 1884).

12. See Herbert Asbury, *The French Quarter, An Informal History of New Orleans with Particular Reference to Its Colorful Iniquities* (New York: Neal Publishing, 1938).

13. John W. Blassingame, *Black New Orleans* (Chicago, IL: Chicago University Press, 1973), 77–78.

14. Paul A.W. Wallace, *Conrad Weiser: Friend of Colonist and Mohawk: 1696–1760* (Lewisburg, PA: Wennawoods Publishing, 1996), 51.

15. The Congregationalists had 658 congregations, mostly in New England. The Presbyterians were strongest in the middle states with 543. Scattered throughout the early republic were Baptists with 498, Anglicans with 480, Quakers with 295, German and Dutch Reformed with 251, and Lutherans with 151. The Methodists, with 37, were largely found in Maryland and Virginia. The Catholic churches were mostly confined to Maryland and numbered about 50; and a very small undetermined number of Jewish synagogues—composed of Sephardic Jews whose ancestry lay in the Iberian Peninsula—were found mostly in New York City. See North Callahan, *Royal Raiders: The Tories of the American Revolution* (New York: Bobbs-Merrill, 1963), 125–126.

16. Joshua Glipin, "Journey to Bethlehem," *The Pennsylvania Magazine of History and Biography*, 46 (1922): 25.

17. Henry Beston, ed., *American Memory* (New York: Farrar & Rhinehart, 1937), 299.

18. Beston, *American Memory*, 299–300.

19. Gilbert Chase, *America's Music: From the Pilgrims to the Present* (New York: McGraw-Hill, 1966), 211.

20. A form of deism, the Unitarian faith was first officially preached at King's Chapel, Boston in 1783. The deism espoused by Thomas Jefferson, Benjamin Franklin, and other founders of the United States was partly a response to the political needs of the young nation.

21. Ralph Bennett, ed., *Settlements in the Americas: Cross-Cultural Perspectives* (Newark: University of Delaware Press, 1993), 146.

22. Ibid., 149.

23. Ibid., 152, 157.

24. Ibid., 169.

25. Ibid., 152–153.

26. Wallace, *Conrad Weiser*, 56.

27. Ralph Waldo Emerson, "Uncollected Prose," *The Dial* (1840).

28. Harvey Wish, *Society and Thought in Early America: A Social and Intellectual History of the American People Through 1865* (New York: Longmans, Green and Co., 1950), 319.

29. Ibid., 319.

30. Margaret M. Coffin, *Death in Early America* (New York: Thomas Nelson, 1976), 19.

31. Thomas Manahan, "Comrades, I Am Dying" (Boston: Henry Talman, 1864). A sheet music cover.

32. Charley Hunt, "The Star Vision," *Christian Parlor Magazine* 9, no. 12 (1852): 370.

33. Charles East, ed., *Sarah Morgan: The Diary of a Southern Woman* (New York: Simon & Schuster, 1991), 11.

34. Quoted in James M. Volo and Dorothy Denneen Volo, *Daily Life in Civil War America* (Westport, CT: Greenwood Press, 1998), 286.

35. Coffin, *Death in Early America*, 183.

36. David Stannard, "Calm Dwellings," *American Heritage* (September 1979): 47.

37. Mrs. L.G. Abell, "The Dying Girl," *Christian Parlor Magazine* 9, no. 12 (1852): 274.

38. Minrose C. Gwin, *A Woman's Civil War* (Madison: University of Wisconsin Press, 1992), 72.

39. Gwin, *A Woman's Civil War,* 91.

40. George F. Root, "The Vacant Chair (or We Shall Meet But We Shall Miss Him)" (Chicago: Root & Cady, 1862). A sheet music cover.

41. Judith McGuire, *Diary of a Southern Refugee During the War by a Lady of Virginia* (Lincoln: University of Nebraska Press, 1995), 250.

42. Tim Halliman, *A Christmas Carol Christmas Book* (New York: IBM, 1984), 111.

43. Gwin, *A Woman's Civil War,* 53.

44. Martha Gandy Fales, *Jewelry in America* (London: Antique Collector's Club, 1995), 211. Quoting *Godey's Lady's Book,* Book 54 (1857).

45. C. Vann Woodward, *Mary Chesnut's Civil War* (New Haven, CT: Yale University Press, 1981), 589.

46. Arthur Martine, *Martine's Hand-Book of Etiquette, and Guide to True Politeness* (New York: Dick & Fitzgerald, 1886), 122.

47. E.A.B. Mitchell, "Bear Gently, So Gently, Roughly Made Bier" (Louisville, KY: Wm. McCaroll, 1864). A sheet music cover.

48. McGuire, *Diary of a Southern Refugee,* 143.

49. Fales, *Jewelry in America,* 215.

50. From a memorial card, in the authors' collection, for 12-year-old Maria Jane Hurd, who died in Springfield, Massachusetts, on March 12, 1848.

51. Caroll C. Calkins, ed., *The Story of America* (Pleasantville, NY: Reader's Digest Association, 1975), 280.

52. Calkins, *The Story of America,* 280.

53. One of the first targets of the Confederate Army in 1861 was the Federal arsenal at Harper's Ferry, Virginia, with its inventory of arms and its two complete sets of precision rifle-making machinery, which were captured and removed to Richmond.

54. Michael Blow, "Professor Henry and His Philosophical Toys," *American Heritage* 15, no. 1 (December 1963): 104–105.

55. Mitchell Wilson, *American Science and Invention: A Pictorial History* (New York: Simon & Schuster, 1954), 106.

56. Harold S. Wilson, *Confederate Industry, Manufactures and Quartermasters in the Civil War* (Jackson: University Press of Mississippi, 2002), ix.

CHAPTER 2: THE WORLD OF YOUTH

1. Drew Gilpin Faust, *The Creation of Confederate Nationalism: Ideology and Identity in the Civil War South* (Baton Rouge: Louisianna State University Press, 1988), 86.

2. Lydia Child, *The Mother's Book* (Boston: Applewood Books, 1831), 11.

3. Ibid., 90.

4. Charles W. Sanders, A.M., *The School Reader Third Book* (New York: Sower, Barnes & Potts, 1860), 185–186.

5. Catherine Clinton, *The Plantation Mistress: Woman's World in the Old South* (New York: Pantheon Books, 1982), 54.

6. Ibid., 47.

7. Ibid., 49.

8. James M. Volo and Dorothy Denneen Volo, *Encyclopedia of the Antebellum South* (Westport, CT: Greenwood Press, 2000), 179–180.

9. Clinton, *The Plantation Mistress*, 202.

10. Thomas H. Burrowes, *Report of the Superintendent of Common Schools of Pennsylvania* (Harrisburg, PA: A. Boyd Hamilton, 1861), 27.

11. Ibid., 14.

12. David J. Rothman, "Our Brother's Keepers," *American Heritage*, December 1972: 41.

13. Ibid., 38–42, 100–105.

14. Reprint of *Nautical Economy* (1836) found in William Robinson, *Jack Nastyface: Memoirs of a Seaman* (Annapolis: Naval Institute Press, 1973), 92.

15. Attributed to Dr. Walter Channing. As quoted in Rothman, "Our Brother's Keepers," 42.

16. These views were widely compared to the views of the 17th-century radicals of the English civil wars called Levelers.

17. Don E. Fehrenbacher, *The Era of Expansion, 1800–1848* (New York: John Wiley and Sons, 1969), 98.

18. Henry Barnard, *Military Schools and Courses of Instruction in the Science and Art of War, in France, Prussia, Austria, Russia, Sweden, Switzerland, Sardinia, England, and the United States (1872)*, The West Point Military Library Series (Westport, CT: Greenwood Press, 1969), 867.

19. Burrowes, *Report of the Superintendent*, 51.

20. Michael Blow, "Professor Henry and His Philosophical Toys," *American Heritage* 15, no. 1 (December 1963): 28.

21. Lawrence A. Cremin, *American Education, The Colonial Experience: 1607–1783* (New York: Harper & Row, 1970), 324.

22. Clinton, *The Plantation Mistress*, 138.

23. Islamic culture required that the mother and child be freed on the death of a free father.

24. Burrowes, *Report of the Superintendent*, 20–97.

25. Ibid., 80.

26. Ibid., 81, 97.

27. Ibid., 20–97.

28. Ibid., 24, 20.

29. Ibid., 4, 32.

30. Quoted from the *Janesville (WI) Gazette*, March 15, 1849, 1.

31. *The Boston Directory for the Year Ending June 30, 1860 Embracing the City Record, A General Directory of the Citizens, and a Business Directory* (Boston: Adams, Sampson, and Co., 1859), 487.

32. Burrowes, *Report of the Superintendent*, 43.

33. Ibid., 27.

34. Ibid., 83.

35. Ibid., 40.

36. Shirley Blotnick Moskow, *Emma's World: An Intimate Look at the Lives Touched by the Civil War Era* (Jersey City, NJ: New Horizon Press, 1990), 193.

37. Burrowes, *Report of the Superintendent*, 91.

38. Daniel Leach, *Leach's Complete Spelling Book* (Philadelphia: H. Cowperthwait & Co., 1859), 140.

39. Moskow, *Emma's World*, 99.

40. Burrowes, *Report of the Superintendent*, 36.

41. Anonymous, *Marmaduke Multiply's Merry Method of Making Minor Mathematicians* (1841, repr. New York: Dover Publications, 1971), 13, 65 (hereafter cited as *Marmaduke*); Burrowes, *Report of the Superintendent*, 42.

42. Moskow, *Emma's World*, 122.

43. Ibid., 139.

44. Burrowes, *Report of the Superintendent*, 21.

45. Salem Town, A.M., *The Fourth Reader or Exercises in Reading and Speaking* (Cooperstown: H. & E. Phinney, 1849), iv.

46. Burrowes, *Report of the Superintendent*, 22.

47. S. Augustus Mitchell, *An Easy Introduction to the Study of Geography* (Philadelphia: Thomas Cowperthwait & Co., 1852), 5.

48. *Marmaduke*, 41.

49. Ibid., 33.

50. Caroline Cowles Richards, *Village Life in America 1852–1872* (New York: Corner House Historical Publications, 1997), 132.

51. Carroll C. Calkins, ed., *The Story of America* (Pleasantville, NY: Reader's Digest Association, 1975), 127.

52. Cremin, *The Colonial Experience*, 330n.

53. J.P. Mayer, ed., *Alexis de Tocqueville: Journey to America*, trans. George Lawrence (New Haven, CT: Yale University Press, 1960), 78.

54. Morris Bishop, "The Lower Depths of High Education," *American Heritage* 22, no. 1 (December 1969): 59.

55. Cremin, *The Colonial Experience*, 513–514. See Michael Blow, "Professor Henry and His Philosophical Toys," 24–105.

56. Barnard, *Military Schools and Courses of Instruction*, 739.

57. Quoted in Barnard, *Military Schools and Courses of Instruction*, 840.

58. Bishop, "The Lower Depths of High Education," 58.

59. Quoted in Barnard, *Military Schools and Courses of Instruction*, 840.

60. Bishop, "The Lower Depths of High Education," 29.

61. Ibid., 30.

62. Barnard, *Military Schools and Courses of Instruction*, 865–866.

63. Ibid., 865.

64. Volo and Volo, *Encyclopedia*, 187.

65. Barnard, *Military Schools and Courses of Instruction*, 721.

66. Ibid., 740–741.

67. Gerard A. Patterson, *Rebels from West Point* (Mechanicsburg, PA: Stachpole Books, 2002), 8.

68. Volo and Volo, *Encyclopedia*, 187–188.

69. Ibid.

70. For a short history of these concepts see United States Department of Agriculture, *Early American Soil Conservationists* (Washington, D.C.: Soil Conservation Service, 1990).

CHAPTER 3: ADVERTISING

1. Organizations and communities often held lotteries to raise funds. Both Harvard and Yale sponsored lotteries to finance the construction of university buildings.

2. *Harper's Weekly*, February 18, 1859, 111. See the historical newspaper collection available at www.ancestry.com/. Accessed March 2004.

3. *The Genesee (NY) Eagle*, September, 13, 1824, 1.

4. *The Ohio Star*, January 13, 1830, 2.

5. *American Citizen*, October 4, 1842, 4.

6. *The Ohio Star*, January 13, 1830, 2.

7. Ibid., June 28, 1832, 3.

8. *American Citizen*, October 4, 1842, 4.

9. *The Ohio Star*, June 7, 1832, 3.

10. Ibid., January 6, 1830: 3.

11. Ibid.

12. *Harpers Weekly*, November 10, 1860, 720; December 1, 1860, 768; December. 8, 1860, 784.

13. *The Ohio Star*, June 7, 1832, 3.

14. *Harper's Weekly*, November 17, 1860, 735; November 24, 1860, 751; December 8, 1860, 783.

15. *The Boston Directory* (Boston: Adams Sampson, 1859), 4.

16. Ibid., 14.

17. Maurice I. Mandell, *Advertising* (Englewood Cliffs, NJ: Prentice-Hall, 1984), 33.

18. *Harper's Weekly*, December 8, 1860, 783.

19. Ibid., August 20, 1861, 255.

20. Ibid., April 13, 1861, 239.

21. Ibid., December 22, 1860, 815.

22. Mandell, *Advertising*, 32.

23. *New York Times*, June 17, 1859, 5.

24. Ibid., June 17, 1859, 5.

25. *Harper's Weekly*, April 4, 1857, 223.

26. Ibid., December 18, 1858, 815.

27. Ibid., June 27, 1857, 112.

28. Ibid., 111.

29. Letter dated February 5, 1843. Available at www.disabilitymuseum. org/lib/docs/1633card.htm. Accessed March 2004.

30. Phineas T. Barnum, *Struggles and Triumphs or the Life of P.T. Barnum* (New York: Alfred A. Knopf, 1927), 153.

31. Ibid., 252.

32. Ibid., 243.

33. Available at www.com/fame/Barnum.html. Accessed March 2004.

CHAPTER 4: ARCHITECTURE

1. Virginia Jeans Laas, ed., *Wartime Washington: Letters of Elizabeth Blair Lee* (Chicago: University of Illinois Press, 1991), 313.

2. Arthur Martine, *Martine's Hand-Book of Etiquette, and Guide to True Politeness* (New York: Dick & Fitzgerald, 1866), 113.

3. Ibid., 112–113.

4. Ibid., 116.

5. Ibid.

6. Ibid.

7. Richard Crawford, *The Civil War Songbook* (New York: Dover, 1977), v.

8. Quoted in John Trasker Howard, *Our American Music: A Comprehensive History of Music from 1620 to the Present* (New York: Thomas Y. Crowell, 1965), 199–200.

9. Patricia Anderson, "Romantic Strains of the Parlor Piano," *Victorian* 3, no. 3 (1997), 22.

10. William Walton, *A Civil War Courtship: The Letters of Edwin Weller from Antietam to Atlanta* (New York: Doubleday, 1980) 25.

11. *Carte de visite* in the authors' collection from Isaac S. Lachman, 984 North Second Street, Philadelphia, Pa.

12. Walton, *A Civil War Courtship*, 65.

13. Shirley Blotnick Moskow, *Emma's World: An Intimate Look at Lives Touched by the Civil War Era* (Far Hills, NJ: New Horizon Press, 1990), 68.

14. Laas, *Wartime Washington*, 212.

15. Catherine E. Beecher, *Miss Beecher's Domestic Receipt-Book* (New York: Harper & Brothers, 1850), 253.

16. Laas, *Wartime Washington*, 313.

17. Margaret Leech, *Reveille in Washington* (New York: Harper & Brothers, 1941), 5–6.

18. C. Vann Woodward, ed., *Mary Chesnut's Civil War* (New Haven, CT: Yale University Press, 1981), 397.

19. *Harper's Weekly* 4, no. 205 (December 1, 1860).

20. Salem Town, A.M., *Fourth Reader or Exercises in Reading and Speaking* (Cooperstown, NY: H. & E. Phinney, 1849), 218.

21. Frank Leslie, ed., "Mourners Strewing Flowers on the Graves of the Slain," *Frank Leslie's Illustrated Newspaper* 16, no. 395 (April 25, 1863): 1.

CHAPTER 5: FASHION

1. Elisabeth McClellan, *History of American Costume 1607–1870* (New York: Tudor, 1937), 406.

2. E.F. Haskell, *The Housekeeper's Encyclopedia* (Mendocino, CA: R.L. Shep, 1992), 15–23.

3. R.L. Shep, *Civil War Ladies: Fashions and Needle Arts of the Early 1860's* (Mendocino, CA: R.L. Shep, 1987), 127–129; Mrs. Merrifield, "The Use and Abuse of Colors in Dress," *Peterson's Magazine* (September 1861).

4. From a *Godey's Lady's Book* print in the authors' collection.

5. Editor, *Peterson's Magazine* (September 1856): 204.

6. Ann S. Stephens, "Demorest's Prize Medal Hoop Skirts," *Perterson's Magazine* (October 1861); Shep, *Civil War Ladies*, 184.

7. Arthur Martine, *Martine's Hand-Book of Etiquette, and Guide to True Politeness* (New York: Dick & Fitzgerald, 1866), 55.

8. Amelia Bloomer, "Female Attire," *The Lily* (February 1851): 13.

9. Amelia Bloomer, "Mrs. Kemble and Her New Costume," *The Lily* (December 1849): 94.

10. Martine, *Martine's Hand-Book of Etiquette*, 49.

11. R.L. Shep. *Civil War Ladies*, 290; Jane Weaver, "Gentlemen's Braces," *Peterson's Magazine* (May 1864).

12. Shep, *Civil War Ladies*, 326; Editor, "Editor's Table," *Peterson's Magazine* (September 1864).

13. Charles East, ed., *Sarah Morgan: The Diary of a Southern Woman* (New York: Simon & Schuster, 1991), 102.

14. Shep, *Civil War Ladies*, 326; Editor, "Editor's Table," *Peterson's Magazine*.

15. Haskell, *The Housekeeper's Encyclopedia*, 384.

16. Ibid., 383–384.

17. Ibid., 385–386.

CHAPTER 6: FOOD

1. Catherine E. Beecher, *Miss Beecher's Domestic Receipt-Book* (New York: Harper & Brothers, 1850), 30–31.

2. Ibid., 286.

3. Karin Giannitti, "Ice Houses," *The Chronicle Quarterly* (Winter 1994).

4. Waverly Root and Richard de Rouchemont, *Eating in America* (New York: William Morrow, 1976), 148.

5. William Hutchinson Rowe, *The Maritime History of Maine: Three Centuries of Shipbuilding and Seafaring* (Augusta, ME: Bond Wheelwright, n.d.), 207–220.

6. Beecher, *Miss Beecher's Domestic Receipt-Book*, 224.

7. Ibid., 153.

8. Eliza Leslie, *Miss Leslie's Directions for Cookery* (Mineola, NY: Dover, 1999), 264.

9. Ibid., 238.

10. Ibid., 405-406.

11. *New York Times*, September 14, 1857, 5.

12. R.L. Shep, ed., *Civil War Ladies, Fashions and Needles Arts of the Early 1860's* (Mendocino, CA: R.L. Shep, 1987), 155; Editor, "Editor's Table," *Peterson's Magazine* (September 1861).

13. Katie Stewart, *Cooking and Eating* (London: Hart-Davis, MacGibbon Ltd., 1975), 202.

14. James Fenimore Cooper, *The Chainbearer* (New York: AMS Press, 1970), 97. The expression "scrape the bottom of the barrel" refers to the pork barrel. When a family had to scrape the bottom of the pork barrel, they were out of an important food resource.

15. Beecher, *Miss Beecher's Domestic Receipt-Book*, 206–207.

16. George Thomas Tanselle, ed., *Herman Melville: Reburn, White Jacket, Moby Dick* (New York: Literary Classics of the United States, Inc., 1983), 214.

17. Emerson David Fite, *Social and Industrial Conditions in the North During the Civil War* (Williamstown, MA: Corner House, 1976), 26.

18. Beecher, *Miss Beecher's Domestic Receipt-Book*, 230–231.

19. Ibid., 227.

20. Ibid.

21. Ibid., 183.

22. Jack Larkin, "Dining Out in the 1830's," *Old Sturbridge Visitor* (Spring 1999): 10.

23. Ibid.

24. Baynard Rush Hall, *The New Purchase* (Princeton, NJ: Princeton University Press, 1916), 27.

25. Larkin, "Dining Out in the 1830's," 11.

CHAPTER 7: LEISURE ACTIVITIES

1. Alexander Gardner, preface to *Photographic Sketchbook of the Civil War* (1866, New York: Dover, 1959).

2. Drew Gilpin, Faust, *Mother of Invention: Women of the Slaveholding South in the American Civil War* (Charlotte: University of North Carolina Press, 1996), 153–154, 156.

3. Available at www.thevictorianscrapbook.com/riding.html.

4. Ibid.

5. Ibid.

6. Morris Bishop, "The Lower Depths of High Education," *American Heritage* 22, no. 1 (December 1969): 58.

7. Jeanmarie Andrews, "Nineteenth Century Base Ball," *Early American Life* 33, no. 4 (August 2002): 23.

8. The National Association of Base Ball Players, an organization of amateur clubs, adopted the first set of official rules at a convention in 1866.

9. Roderick Kiracofe, *The American Quilt* (New York: Clarkson Potter, 1993), 109.

10. Ibid., 119.

11. William A. Fletcher, *Rebel Private: Front and Rear* (1908, repr. New York: Meridan, 1997), 2.

12. John S. Bowman, ed., *The Civil War Almanac* (New York: Bison, 1983), 383–384.

13. Fletcher, *Rebel Private: Front and Rear,* 2.

14. Henry Beston, *American Memory* (New York: Farrar & Rhinehart, 1937), 300–301.

15. Carlton McCarthy, *Detailed Minutiae of Soldier Life in the Army of Northern Virginia, 1861–1865* (1882, repr. Lincoln: University of Nebraska Press, 1993), 3.

CHAPTER 8: LITERATURE

1. Don E. Fehrenbacher, *The Era of Expansion, 1800–1848* (New York: John Wiley and Sons, 1969), 118–119.

2. Vincent dePaul Lupiano and Ken W. Sayers, *It Was a Very Good Year: A Cultural History of the United States from 1776 to the Present* (Holbrook, MA: Bob Adams, 1994), 60.

3. Emerson David Fite, *Social and Industrial Conditions in the North During the Civil War* (Williamstown, MA: Corner House, 1976), 256n.

4. Harvey Wish, *Society and Thought in Early America: A Social and Intellectual History of the American People Through 1865* (New York: Longmans, Green and Co., 1950), 299.

5. Linda K. Kerber, *Women of the Republic, Intellect and Ideology in Revolutionary America* (Chapel Hill: University of North Carolina Press, 1980), 192–193.

6. David Kaser, *Books and Libraries in Camp and Battle: The Civil War Experience* (Westport, CT: Greenwood Press, 1984), 14.

7. Lupiano and Sayers, *It Was a Very Good Year,* 119.

8. Paige Smith, *The Nation Comes of Age: A People's History of the Antebellum Years* (New York: McGraw-Hill, 1981), 907.

9. Joel Hawes, *Lectures to Young Men on the Formation of Character* (Hartford, CT, 1835), 144–158.

10. Drew Gilpin Faust, *Mother of Invention: Women of the Slaveholding South in the American Civil War* (Charlotte: University of North Carolina Press, 1996), 154.

11. Smith, *Nation Comes of Age,* 158.

12. Arthur Pierce Middleton, *A Virginia Gentlemen's Library* (Williamsburg, VA: Colonial Williamsburg Foundation, 1952), 7.

13. Donelson F. Hoopes and Nancy Wall Moure, *American Narrative Painting* (Los Angeles: Praeger, 1972), 15.

14. V.M. Rice, *Code of Public Instruction* (Albany, NY: 1856), 325.

15. Lydia M. Child, *The Mother's Book* (Boston: Applewood Books, 1831), 93–94.

16. Stanley J. Kunitz, ed., *British Authors of the Nineteenth Century* (New York: Wilson, 1936), 105–106.

17. See E.A. Duyckinck, *Cyclopedia of American Literature* (Detroit: Gale Research, 1965).

18. Kunitz, *British Authors of the Nineteenth Century,* 511–512.

19. Ibid., 383–384.

20. A pseudonym for Mary Ann Evans, author of several works beginning in the 1850s, including *Adam Bede* (1858–1859), *Silas Marner* (1861–1862), and *Middlemarch* (1872–1873).

21. These were *Guy Mannering* (1815), *Tales of My Landlord* (1816), *Rob Roy* (1817), *The Heart of Midlothian* (1818), *The Bride of Lammermoor* (1819), *A Legend of Montrose* (1819), *Ivanhoe* (1819), *Kenilworth* (1821), *The Fortunes of Nigel* (1822), *Peveril of the Peak* (1823), *Quentin Durwood* (1823), *The Talisman* (1825), *Woodstock* (1826), *The Surgeon's Daughter* (1827), and *Anne of Geierstein* (1829).

22. Dorothy Denneen Volo and James M. Volo, *Daily Life in Civil War America* (Westport, CT: Greenwood Press, 1998), 208.

23. Alan Taylor, "Fenimore Cooper's America," *History Today* 46, no. 2 (February 1996): 21–27.

24. Allan Nevins, ed., *The Leatherstocking Saga* (New York: Pantheon Books, 1966), 2.

25. Ibid., 24.

26. Ibid., 7.

27. Ibid., 34.

28. Joel Hawes, *Lectures to Young Men on the Formation of Character* (Hartford, CT, 1835), 144–158.

29. James H. Croushore, ed., *A Volunteer's Adventure by Captain John W. DeForest* (New Haven, CT: Yale University Press, 1949), vii, 130–131; Kaser, *Civil War Experience,* 4, 5; see Duyckinck, *Cyclopedia of American Literature,* and James Morgan, "Send No Trash: Books, Libraries, and Reading During the Civil War," *Camp Chase Gazette,* July 1992, 32.

30. Croushore, *A Volunteer's Adventure,* vii. Originally appearing as a monthly series in *Harper's.*

31. Tim Halliman, *A Christmas Carol Christmas Book* (New York: IBM, 1984), 111.

32. Ibid.

33. Smith, *Nation Comes of Age,* 255, 907.

34. Ibid., 257.

35. Wish, *Society and Thought in Early America,* 500, 507.

36. Smith, *Nation Comes of Age,* 769–770.

37. Ibid., 945.

38. Wish, *Society and Thought in Early America,* 368–369.

39. Smith, *Nation Comes of Age,* 257.

40. Ibid., 258.

41. Charles A. Beard and Mary R. Beard, *The Rise of American Civilization* (New York: Macmillan, 1927), 785.

42. Smith, *Nation Comes of Age,* 974.

43. Bernard DeVoto, *The Year of Decision: 1846* (Boston: Little Brown, 1943), 31–32.

44. Ibid., 101.

45. Ibid., 32.

46. Wish, *Society and Thought in Early America,* 456.

47. Beard and Beard, *The Rise of American Civilization,* 749.

48. Smith, *Nation Comes of Age,* 985.

49. Ibid.

50. Ibid., 986. Quoting Smith.

51. Ibid.

52. Ibid., 987–988.

53. Ibid., 991. Quoting Smith.

54. Ibid., 992.

55. Ibid., 993.

56. DeVoto, *The Year of Decision,* 208–209.

57. Smith, *Nation Comes of Age,* 993.

58. Ibid.

59. Ibid., 998.

60. Ibid., 1003.

61. Ibid., 1001.

62. Beard and Beard, *The Rise of American Civilization,* 787.

63. Wish, *Society and Thought in Early America,* 452.

64. See C.E. Stowe, *Life of Harriet Beecher Stowe: Compiled from Her Journals and Letters* (1889; 1991).

65. Available at www.iath.virginia.edu. Accessed October 2002.

66. C. Vann Woodward, *Mary Chesnut's Civil War* (New Haven, CT: Yale University Press, 1981), 381, 307, 245.

67. Available at www.iath.virginia.edu. Accessed October 2002.

68. Smith, *Nation Comes of Age*, 972.

69. Ibid., 976–977.

70. Beard and Beard, *The Rise of American Civilization*, 792.

71. Smith, *Nation Comes of Age*, 977. Quoting Carl Schurz.

72. Ibid., 982.

73. Ibid., 977.

74. Van Wyck Brooks, *The World of Washington Irving* (New York: The World Publishing Company, 1944), 22.

75. Mitchel Wilson, *American Science and Invention: A Pictorial History* (New York: Simon & Schuster, 1954), 96–97.

76. John T. Cunningham, "Historian on the Double," *American Heritage* 19, no. 4 (June 1968): 78–79.

77. Brooks, *The World of Washington Irving*, 167–168n.

78. Lawrence A. Cremin, *American Education: The National Experience 1783–1876* (New York: Harper, 1980), 409.

79. Brooks, *The World of Washington Irving* 159.

80. Careful scrutiny of such prints can reveal the boundaries between the individual blocks.

81. Edwin Forbes, preface to *Civil War Etchings* (1876, repr. New York: Dover, 1994). Forbes may have been the archetype of the young reporter featured in the TV miniseries *The Blue and the Gray*. Also see John E. Stanchak, ed., *Leslie's Illustrated Civil War* (1894, repr. Jackson: University Press of Mississippi, 1992), v–xii.

82. The lack of a widespread circulation of these photographs in newspapers may have been fortunate as there was no need to additionally fuel the growing antiwar sentiment in the North.

83. Drew Gilpin Faust, *The Creation of Confederate Nationalism: Ideology and Identity in the Civil War South* (Baton Rouge: Louisiana State University Press, 1988), 17 (hereafter cited as Faust, *Nationalism*).

84. Ibid., 8.

85. Ibid., 16.

86. Thomas A. Lewis, *The Guns of Cedar Creek* (New York: Bantam, 1991), 86.

87. Wish, *Society and Thought in Early America*, 526.

88. See Frederick Douglass, *Narrative of the Life of an American Slave Written by Himself* (New York: 1845).

89. Ibid., vi.

90. See Charles East, ed., *Sarah Morgan: The Civil War Diary of a Southern Woman* (New York, NY: Touchstone, 1991); Dolly Sumner Hunt, *A Woman's Wartime Journal* (Atlanta, GA: Cherokee, 1994); C. Vann Woodward, ed., *Mary Chesnut's Civil War* (New Haven, CT: Yale University Press, 1981); and Frances Anne Kemble, *Journal of a Residence on a Georgia Plantation in 1838–1839* (New York: Alfred A. Knopf, 1961).

CHAPTER 9: MUSIC

1. Sigmund Spaeth, *A History of Popular Music in America* (New York: Random House, 1964), 69.

2. Richard Crawford, *America's Musical Life: A History* (New York: W.W. Norton, 2001), 147.

3. John Tasker Howard, *Our American Music: A Comprehensive History of Music from 1620 to the Present* (New York: Thomas Y. Crowell, 1965), 139.

4. Ibid., 148.

5. Spaeth, *History of Popular Music*, 73–74.

6. Howard, *Our American Music*, 159.

7. Ibid., 150.

8. Crawford, *America's Musical Life*, 232.

9. Ibid., 234–235.

10. Thomas Hastings, *Dissertation on Musical Taste* (New York: Mason, 1853), 122–123.

11. Ibid.

12. Van Wyck Brooks, *The World of Washington Irving* (New York: The World Publishiung Company, 1944), 153.

13. There grew a superstition among players of *Mabeth* concerning Locke's music after several persons in the cast suffered personal tragedies while doing the play to his score.

14. Jon W. Finson, *The Voices That Are Gone: Themes in Nineteenth-Century American Popular Song* (New York: Oxford University Press, 1994), 19–20.

15. Ibid., 20.

16. William Austin, *The Songs of Stephen C. Foster from His Time to Ours* (New York: Macmillan, 1975), 133.

17. Crawford, *America's Musical Life*, 238–239.

18. Howard, *Our American Music*, 174.

19. Dale Cockrell, ed., *Excelsior: Journals of the Hutchinson Family Singers 1842–1846* (Stuyvesant, NY: Pendragon Press, 1989), 149.

20. Ibid., 254.

21. Crawford, *America's Musical Life*, 272–273.

22. Anthony Baines, *Brass Instruments: Their History and Development* (New York: Dover, 1993), 212.

23. Ibid., 216.

24. Quoted in Howard, *Our American Music*, 220–221.

25. Ibid., 222–223.

26. Ibid.

27. Howard, *Our American Music*, 224.

28. Thomas Ryan, *Recollections of an Old Musician* (New York: E.P. Dutton, 1899), 62.

29. Ibid., 60–62.

30. Frederick Douglass, *Autobiographies* (New York: Library of America, 1994), 184.

31. Frances Anne Kemble, *Journal of a Residence on a Georgia Plantation in 1838–1839* (New York: Alfred A. Knopf, 1961), 128.

32. Kemble, *Journal of a Residence on a Georgia Plantation*, 128–129.

33. Gilbert Chase, *America's Music: From the Pilgrims to the Present* (New York: McGraw-Hill, 1966), 236.

34. Douglass, *Autobiographies*, 183–185.

35. Eileen Southern, ed., *Readings in Black American Music* (New York: Norton, 1983), 89–90.

36. James M. Trotter, *Music and Some Highly Musical People* (1878, repr. New York: Johnson, 1968), 82–83.

37. Chase, *America's Music,* 208.

38. Ibid.

CHAPTER 10: PERFORMING ARTS

1. Quoted in Barnard Hewitt, *Theater USA: 1668 to 1957* (New York: McGraw-Hill, 1959), 63. The authors recognize the value of this rare work as a resource filled with period commentaries, news articles, and first-person accounts concerning the theater.

2. Robert Adolph, *The Rise of Modern Prose Style* (Cambridge, MA: The M.I.T. Press, 1968), 243.

3. Ibid., 290–291.

4. James Branch Cabell as quoted by Martha Fletcher Bellinger, *A Short History of the Theater* (New York: Henry Holt, 1927), 249.

5. Harvey Wish, *Society and Thought in Early America: A Social and Intellectual History of the American People Through 1865* (New York: Longmans, Green and Co., 1950), 276–277.

6. Hewitt, *Theater USA,* 16.

7. Quoted in ibid., 29.

8. Ibid., 65.

9. Wish, *Society and Thought in Early America,* 470.

10. Quoted in Hewitt, *Theater USA,* 89.

11. Ibid., 49.

12. Ibid., 105.

13. The theater critic of the *Albion*, September 2, 1848, quoted in ibid., 108.

14. Walt Whitman in the Brooklyn *Eagle*, February 8, 1847, quoted in ibid., 144.

15. Anna Cora Ogden Mowatt quoted in ibid., 134–135.

16. Edgar Allan Poe, *Broadway Journal*, March 29, 1845, quoted in ibid., 136–137.

17. Vincent de Paul Lupiano and Ken W. Sayers, *It Was a Very Good Year: A Cultural History of the United States From 1776 to the Present* (Holbrook, MA: Bob Adams, 1994), 67.

18. Hewitt, *Theater USA,* 120.

19. The *New York Mirror*, October 12, 1833, quoted in Hewitt, *Theater USA,* 117.

20. Stephen C. Carpenter quoted in ibid., 80.

21. Ibid., 77.

22. Charles Durang quoted in ibid., 83–84.

23. Ibid., 93.

24. Ibid., 94.

25. Thomas R. Gould quoted in ibid., 99.

26. George Vandenhoff quoted in ibid., 107–108.

27. Ibid., 109.

28. L. Clarke Davis quoted in ibid., 199.

29. William Leggett quoted in ibid., 111.

30. A critic for the *New York Mirror* quoted in ibid., 114–115.

31. Ibid., 126–127.

CHAPTER 11: TRAVEL

1. Although there were minor economic downturns in the 1840s and 1850s, the Panic of 1837 remained the worst economic disaster experienced by the nation until it was displaced by a similar panic in 1873.

2. John Hayward, *Gazeteer of the United States* (Hartford, CT: Case, Tiffant and Co., 1853), 846–847.

3. George R. Stewart, "The Prairie Schooner Got Them There," *American Heritage* 13, no. 2 (February, 1962): 7–16.

4. Hayward, *Gazeteer of the United States*, 646.

5. Ibid., 655.

6. Ibid., 184.

7. Ibid., 667.

8. Ibid., 657.

9. Ibid., 650.

10. Ibid., 666.

11. A particular type of limestone found in central New York when burned with charcoal was found to make an excellent hydraulic cement.

12. Henry Beston, ed., *American Memory* (New York: Farrar and Rhinehart, 1937), 279–280.

13. Hayward, *Gazeteer of the United States*, 495.

14. Roger Butterfield, *The American Past: A History of the United States from Concord to Hiroshima, 1775–1945* (New York: Simon & Schuster, 1947), 76–77.

15. Hayward, *Gazeteer of the United States*, 846.

16. Jack K. Bauer, *A Maritime History of the United States: The Role of America's Seas and Waterways* (Columbia: University of South Carolina Press, 1989), 297.

17. Don E. Ferhenbacher, *The Era of Expansion, 1800–1848* (New York: John Wiley and Sons, 1969), 97.

18. *Gentlemen's Magazine* (December 1809).

19. Beston, *American Memory*, 278–279.

20. Charles Lyell, *A Second Visit to the United States of North America* (1849), in James M. Volo and Dorothy Denneen Volo, *Encyclopedia of the Antebellum South* (Westport, CT: Greenwood Press, 2000), 256–257.

21. The greatest loss of life in a single incident took place in 1865 when the boiler of the steamboat *Sultana* exploded in the Mississippi River with 2,500 recently released Federal prisoners of war on board. Approximately 1,500 men died.

22. Stephen R. Wise, *Lifeline of the Confederacy: Blockade Running During the Civil War* (Columbia: University of South Carolina Press, 1991), 102.

23. K.T. Rowland, *Steam at Sea: The History of Steam Navigation* (New York: Praeger, 1970), 81. Much of the technical information about steam vessels of this era has come from this source. Also useful for information on the development of steam engines is Donald L. Canney, *The Old Steam Navy: Frigates, Sloops, and Gunboats, 1815–1885*, vol. 1 (Annapolis, MD: Naval Institute Press, 1990).

24. Francis A. Lord, "The United States Military Railroad Service: Vehicle to Victory," *Civil War Times Illustrated* (October 1962): 7–8.

25. Beston, *American Memory*, 295–296.

26. Emerson David Fite, *Social and Industrial Conditions in the North During the Civil War* (Williamstown, MA: Corner House, 1976), 57.

27. Ibid., 56.

28. Peter Cozzens, *No Better Place to Die* (Urbana: University of Illinois Press, 1990), 32; David B. Sabine, "Resources Compared: North versus South," *Civil War Times Illustrated* (February 1968): 5–15.

29. Hamilton Ellis, *The Pictorial Encyclopedia of Railways* (New York: Hamlyn, 1969), 216.

CHAPTER 12: VISUAL ARTS

1. Donelson F. Hoopes and Nancy Wall Moure, *American Narrative Painting* (Los Angeles: Praeger, 1972), 32.

2. Ibid., 34.

3. Alexander Eliot, *Three Hundred Years of American Painting* (New York: Time Incorporated, 1957), 42.

4. Ibid., 47.

5. Clara Endicott Sears, *Highlights Among the Hudson River Artists* (Boston: Houghton Mifflin, 1947), 10.

6. Carl Carmer, "The Lordly Hudson," *American Heritage* 10, no. 1 (December 1958): 105.

7. Eliot, *Three Hundred Years of American Painting*, 87.

8. Ibid., 70.

9. Ibid., 73.

10. Henry T. Tuckerman, *Artist-Life* (New York: D. Appleton, 1847), 80.

11. Ralph Waldo Emerson, "Thoughts on Art," *The Dial* 3, no. 1 (January 1841): 367–378.

12. Matthew Baigell, *A History of American Painting* (New York: Praeger, 1971), 109.

13. Sears, *Highlights Among the Hudson River Artists*, 69.

14. Baigell, *History of American Painting*, 119.

15. Bruce Catton, "O-Kee-Pa," *American Hertitage* 18, no. 6 (October 1967): 31.

16. Roger Butterfield, *The American Past: A History of the United States from Concord to Hiroshima, 1775–1945* (New York: Simon & Schuster, 1947), 118.

17. See Dorothy Denneen Volo and James M. Volo, *Daily Life in Civil War America* (Westport, CT: Greenwood Press, 1998), 15–30.

18. Eliot, *Three Hundred Years of American Painting*, 87.

19. James Thomas Flexner, "The Dark World of David Gilmore Blythe," *American Heritage* 13, no. 6 (October 1962): 76–77.

20. Marshall B. Davidson, "Carl Bodmer's Unspoiled West,"*American Heritage* 14, no. 3 (April 1963): 48.

21. Ibid., 65.

22. Ellsworth S. Grant, "Gunmaker to the World," *American Heritage* 19, no. 4 (June 1968): 12.

23. Catton, "O-Kee-Pa," 31.

24. Beatrix T. Rumford, ed., *American Folk Portraits* (Boston: New York Graphic Society, 1981), 104.

25. Eliot, *Three Hundred Years of American Painting,* 49.

26. Nina Fletcher Little, *Country Art in New England 1790–1840* (Sturbridge, MA: Old Sturbridge Village, 1965), 44

27. James Thomas Flexner, *Nineteenth Century American Painting* (New York: G.P. Putnam's Sons, 1970), 119.

28. Rumford, *American Folk Portraits,* 104.

29. Linda Carter Lefko, "Pictures on Plaster: Historic Wall Murals," *Early American Life* 51–55 (December 2002): 51.

30. Lefko, "Historic Wall Murals," 51.

31. Ibid.

32. Rumford, *American Folk Portraits,* 27.

33. Ibid., 29.

34. Little, *Country Art in New England,* 44.

35. T.S. Arthur, "American Characteristics, No, V—The Daguerreotypist," *Godey's Lady's Book* (May 1849): 352.

36. Rumford, *American Folk Portraits,* 29.

37. Available at http://web.mit,edu/comm.forum/papers/belion.html.

38. Rumford, *American Folk Portraits,* 31.

39. Daniel M. Mendelowitx, *A History of American Art* (New York: Holt, Rinehart and Winston, 1970), 232.

40. Ibid., 232.

41. Oliver W. Larkin, *Art and Life in America* (New York: Holt, Rinehart and Winston, 1949), 182.

42. Don E. Fehrenbacher, *The Era of Expansion, 1800–1848* (New York: John Wiley and Sons, 1969), 116.

43. Larkin, *Art and Life in America,* 180–181.

44. Hoopes and Moure, *American Narrative Painting,* 46.

Suggested Reading

Baigell, Matthew. *A History of American Painting.* New York: Praeger, 1971.

Bauer, K. Jack. *A Maritime History of the United States: The Role of America's Seas and Waterways.* Columbia: University of South Carolina Press, 1989.

Bennett, Ralph, ed. *Settlements in the Americas: Cross-Cultural Perspectives.* Newark: University of Delaware Press, 1993.

Chase, Gilbert. *America's Music: From the Pilgrims to the Present.* New York: McGraw-Hill, 1966.

Clinton, Catherine. *The Plantation Mistress, Woman's World in the Old South.* New York: Pantheon Books, 1982.

Crawford, Richard. *America's Musical Life: A History.* New York: W.W. Norton, 2001.

Cremin, Lawrence A. *American Education: The Colonial Experience: 1607–1783.* New York: Harper & Row, 1970.

East, Charles, ed. *Sarah Morgan: The Diary of a Southern Woman.* New York: Simon & Schuster, 1991.

Ellis, Hamilton. *The Pictorial Encyclopedia of Railways.* New York: Hamlyn, 1969.

Fales, Martha Gandy. *Jewelry in America.* London: Antique Collector's Club, 1995.

Faust, Drew Gilpin. *Mother of Invention: Women of the Slaveholding South in the American Civil War.* Charlotte: University of North Carolina Press, 1996.

Fehrenbacher, Don E. *The Era of Expansion, 1800–1848.* New York: John Wiley, 1969.

Fite, Emerson David. *Social and Industrial Conditions in the North During the Civil War.* Williamstown, MA: Corner House, 1976.

Flexner, James Thomas. *Nineteenth Century American Painting.* New York: G.P. Putnam's Sons, 1970.

Gwin, Minrose C. *A Woman's Civil War.* Madison: University of Wisconsin Press, 1992.

Haskell, E.F. *The Housekeeper's Encyclopedia.* Mendocino, CA: R.L. Shep, 1992.

Hewitt, Barnard. *Theater USA, 1668 to 1957.* New York: McGraw-Hill, 1959.

Kaser, David. *Books and Libraries in Camp and Battle: The Civil War Experience.* Westport, CT: Greenwood Press, 1984.

Laas, Virginia Jeans, ed. *Wartime Washington: Letters of Elizabeth Blair Lee.* Chicago: University of Illinois Press, 1991.

Leslie, Eliza. *Miss Leslie's Directions for Cookery.* Mineola, NY: Dover, 1999.

Little, Nina Fletcher. *Country Art in New England 1790–1840.* Sturbridge, MA: Old Sturbridge Village, 1965.

Lupiano, Vincent dePaul, and Ken W. Sayers. *It Was a Very Good Year: A Cultural History of the United States from 1776 to the Present.* Holbrook, MA: Bob Adams, 1994.

Mayer, J.P., ed. *Alexis de Tocqueville: Journey to America.* Translated by George Lawrence. New Haven, CT: Yale University Press, 1960.

Moskow, Shirley Blotnick. *Emma's World: An Intimate Look at the Lives Touched by the Civil War Era.* Jersey City, NJ: New Horizon Press, 1990.

Richards, Caroline Cowles. *Village Life in America 1852–1872.* New York: Corner House Historical Publications, 1997.

Root, Waverly, and Richard de Rouchemont. *Eating in America.* New York: William Morrow, 1976.

Sewell, Richard H. *A House Divided: Sectionalism and the Civil War, 1848–1865.* Baltimore, MD: Johns Hopkins University Press, 1988.

Shep, R.L., ed. *Civil War Ladies: Fashions and Needle Arts of the Early 1860's.* Mendocino, CA: R.L. Shep, 1987.

Volo, Dorothy Denneen, and James M. Volo. *Daily Life in Civil War America.* Westport, CT: Greenwood Press, 1998.

Volo, James M., and Dorothy Denneen Volo. *Encyclopedia of the Antebellum South.* Westport, CT: Greenwood Press, 2000.

Wilson, Harold S. *Confederate Industry: Manufactures and Quartermasters in the Civil War.* Jackson: University Press of Mississippi, 2002.

Woodward, C. Vann, ed. *Mary Chesnut's Civil War.* New Haven: Yale University Press, 1981.

Index

About the Authors

JAMES M. VOLO is a teacher, historian, and living history enthusiast. He has been an active historic reenactor for more than two decades, participating in a wide range of living history events, including television and screen performance.

DOROTHY DENNEEN VOLO is a teacher and historian. She has been an active living history reenactor for 20 years and has been involved in numerous community historical education projects.